Handbook of
Research and
Quantitative Methods
in Psychology:
For Students and Professionals

Handbook of Research and Quantitative Methods in Psychology: For Students and Professionals

R. M. Yaremko
Herbert Harari
Robert C. Harrison
Elizabeth Lynn

SAN DIEGO STATE UNIVERSITY

LEA
LAWRENCE ERLBAUM ASSOCIATES, PUBLISHERS
1986   Hillsdale, New Jersey   London

225127

Lawrence Erlbaum Associates, Inc., Publishers
365 Broadway
Hillsdale, New Jersey 07642

Published in 1982 by Harper & Row, Publishers, Inc. as:
Reference Handbook of Research and Statistical Methods in Psychology

ISBN 0-89859-866-4
ISBN 0-89859-867-2 (paperback)

LC card Number 81-6556

Printed in the United States of America
10 9 8 7 6 5 4 3 2 1

Contents

Preface

Handbook of Research and Quantitative Methods in Psychology: For Students and Professionals is an alphabetically organized reference text for psychology and other behavior sciences. It includes terms and concepts from research methodology, experimental design, testing and scaling, and statistics. As instructors who have taught undergraduate and graduate courses in these areas, we became increasingly sensitive to the problems created by terms with overlapping meanings, synonyms, and pseudosynonyms. We also became increasingly appreciative of the need for an organizer — a single source in which these terms could be located. To that end, we have tried to provide a book in which the entries are defined or described as clearly, broadly, and objectively as possible and one in which comparisons and contrasts with related items could readily be made.

Rather than simply writing a glossary of terms in the field, we have concentrated on providing as complete a definition as possible of each term, with informal examples as needed, and, in the case of particularly difficult and/or deserving terms, a more thorough, formal example. Necessarily, this forced us to limit the scope of our effort in several ways: (1) Our entries are limited to research and statistical *methods* and closely related terms. We have not included behavioral phenomena or concepts from specific theories. The list of such items is virtually endless, as new topics of research are invented, old topics redefined, and theoretical viewpoints changed. Thus, any entries included here that may refer both to a process and to a procedure were defined only as a procedure. For example, you will find *transfer paradigm* entered, but not *positive transfer*. (2) We have not included evaluative comments or extensive discussions of how or why a concept or method is used in a particular area of research. Textbooks and teachers are designed to do those things. (3) We recognize that certain methods may come to be more or less uniquely associated with certain theoretical or metatheoretical positions. Thus, to avoid needless controversy, we have tried to define these methods strictly as sets of operations. (4) We have generally confined our entries to those specialties typically associated with basic (nonapplied) research (e.g., learning, information processing, experimental social psychology, perception, psychometrics, etc.). (5) With a few exceptions, we have omitted apparatus and those procedures and techniques peculiar to subspecialties (e.g., brain implant techniques). Some such items, however, when they are very widely used or having multiple uses, are included.

Originally, we wanted to provide a relatively brief "survival manual" for the undergraduate who, with great trepidation, was about to enroll in a first course in experimental methods. Gradually, seeing that some undergraduates become graduate students, some of whom then become professionals in psychology or a sibling discipline, the number of advanced and even highly advanced entries increased. In these cases we tried to define the term with certain assumptions in mind about the general level of sophistication of the person seeking such information. For example, in the entry *concurrent schedule of reinforcement,* we assumed that the reader was already somewhat familiar with the notions of reinforcement, operant conditioning, and scheduling. Of course, these terms themselves are included as entries. In sum, we have tried to provide a useful reference for readers at various levels of expertise.

We wish to acknowledge, and express our genuine gratitude for the many helpful comments and clarifications by our colleagues, especially those from Edward Alf, Jeff and Rebecca Bryson, R. H. Defran, Philip Gallo, William Graham, Fred Hornbeck, and Robert Kaplan. We are also indebted to those reviewers who provided us with feedback that improved the accuracy and clarity of a number of entries. Finally, we express our sincere thanks to Bonnie Dowd, Debbie Forster, Claudia Powell, Doris Townsend, and Marva Jo West for their clerical assistance.

R. M. YAREMKO
HERBERT HARARI
ROBERT C. HARRISON
ELIZABETH LYNN

How to Use This Book

Each entry is followed by a definition of the term or concept that the entry denotes. Less widely used synonyms are entered as cross references. Some definitions include a brief example that is preceded by the phrase "For example. . . ." Some definitions are followed by a formal example that is set off, and headed "EXAMPLE." Some definitions are followed by parenthetical remarks.

(See also . . .) Items referenced this way are also entries and are particularly relevant to the entry just defined. The reader is encouraged to inspect these for more definitive coverage of the topic.

Some entries are followed immediately by parenthetical remarks in bold-face italics:

(syn.) This indicates that the word that follows is synonymous with the entry and is listed elsewhere as a cross reference only.

(contr.) This indicates that the word that follows contrasts in one or more ways with the entry and may also be an entry.

(symb.) This indicates that the character that follows is a commonly used symbol to denote the entry.

(abbr.) This indicates a commonly used abbreviation for the entry.

Terms in bold face found within an entry have also been cross referenced. They have been defined within the definition of a superordinate entry to provide a context for understanding the term and to avoid unnecessary duplication of material.

Categorical Listing of Entries

Listings by Topic Area

The eight alphabetized lists below correspond to the following topic areas:

Cross references and abbreviations are included in the lists. Some items may be listed in more than one topic area.

General Research Procedures

ABBA Sequence
Accidental Error
Accidental Sampling
Adaptation
Adaptation Phase
Ad Lib(itum) Weight
Amplitude of Response
Anecdotal Method
Antecedent Condition
Applied Research
Area Sampling
Artifact
Assumption
Atmosphere Effect

Balanced Order
Basal Level
Baseline
Baseline Trial
Basement Effect
Basic Research
Between-Subjects Variable
Bias
Biased Sample
Blank Trial
Blind Assessment
Blind Procedure
Blind Scoring
Block of Trials

Experimental Design

A × B (A by B) Design
A × S (A by S) Design
A × Subjects (A by Subjects)
  Design
ABA Design
ABAB Design
After-Test Design
Alternating Conditions Design
Among Groups
Analytic ABAB Design
Balanced Incomplete Blocks
  Design
Before-After Test Design
Between Factor
Between-Groups Design
Between-Group Variable
Between-Subjects Design
Between-Subjects Variable
Block
Block Design
Comparison Group
Completely Between-Groups
  Design
Completely Randomized Design
Condition
Confounded Designs
Control Group
Control Group Method
Correlated-Groups Design
Correlated-Measures Design
Cross-Lagged Correlation
Cross-Lagged Panel Correlation
Crossing
Design
Disordinal Interaction
Equivalent-Groups Design
Experimental Condition
Experimental Design
Experimental Group
Experimental Plan
Experimental Treatment
Ex Post Facto Study
Factor
Factorial Design
Fixed-Effects Factor

Fixed-Effects Model
Fixed/Random-Effects Factor
Fixed/Random-Effects Model
Fractional Factorial Design
Functional Design
Functional Experiment
Graeco-Latin Square Design
Half-Plaid Square Design
Hierarchical Design
Higher Order Design
Homogeneous Grouping
Horizontal Grouping
Incomplete Blocks Design
Incomplete Design
Incomplete Latin Square Design
Independent-Groups Design
Intact-Groups Designs
Latin Square Design
Lattice Design
Level
Lindquist Designs
Matched-Groups Design
Matched-Subjects Design
Mixed Design
Mixed-Effects Model
Mixed Model
Multielement Baseline Design
Multiple Baseline Design
Multiple Control Groups
Multiple Groups Design
Nested Factor
Nesting
Nonexperimental Designs
One-Between One-Within Design
One-Between Two-Within Design
One-Group Pre–Post Test Design
One-Shot Case Study
One-Way Design
One-Within One-Between Design
Paired-Groups Design
Partial Confounding
Partially Balanced Incomplete-
  Blocks Design
Partially Hierarchical Design
Plaid Square Design

Posttest Design
Pretest/Posttest Design
Quasi-Experimental Design
Random-Effects Factor
Random-Effects Model
Random Factor
Randomized Blocks Design
Randomized-Groups Design
Randomized-Subjects Design
Repeated-Measures Design
Repeated-Measures Variable
Representative Design
Reversal Design
Single-Factor Design
Single-Group Design
Single-Subject Design
Solomon Four-Group Design

Split-Plot Design
Steady-State Design
T × S (T by S) Design
Three-Factor Design
Three-Factor Mixed Design
Time Series Design
Treatment-by-Block Design
Treatment-by-Levels Design
Treatment-by-Subjects Design
Two-Factor Design
Two-Factor Mixed Design
Two-Within, One-Between
    Design
Vertical Grouping
Within-Subjects Design
Within-Subjects Variable
Youden Square Design

Statistics and Quantitative Methods

a
A Posteriori Comparison
A Posteriori Probability
A Posteriori Test
A Priori Comparison
A Priori Probability
A Priori Test
A Test
Abscissa
Acceleration
Acceptance Region
Accuracy
AD
Additivity
Alientation, Coefficient of
Alpha
Alpha Coefficient
Alpha Error
Alpha Error Rate
Alpha Level
Alternate (Alternative)
    Hypothesis
Analysis of Covariance
Analysis of Variance
Analysis of Variance for Ranked
    Data
Analysis of Variance Summary
    Table

ANCOVA
ANOVA
Apparent Limits
Arcsin Transformation
Arithmetic Mean
Association, Coefficient of
Association, Test for
Assumption
Asymptote
Autocorrelation
Average
Average Deviation
Axis
b Coefficient
b Weight
Bar Graph
Bartlett's Test
Bayesian Statistics
Bernoulli Experiment
Best-Fit Line
Beta
Beta Coefficient
Beta Distribution
Beta Error
Beta Weight
Bias
Biased Estimator
Bimodal Distribution

Deviation IQ
Deviation Score
df
Dichotomous
Dichotomous Variable
Difference Score
Directional Test
Discrete Variable
Discriminant Analysis
Discriminant Function Analysis
Disordinal Interaction
Distribution
Distribution-Free Test
Dixon's Test for Outliers
Doolittle Method
Domain
Dummy Variable
Duncan's Multiple Range Test
Dunnett's Test
Dunn's Procedure
Efficiency
Eigenvalue
Empirical Probability
Equimax Rotation
Equivalence, Coefficient of
Error Mean Square
Error of Estimate
Error Rate
Error Term
Error Variance
Estimation
Eta Coefficient
Eta Squared
Exact Limits
Exhaustive Set
Expected Frequency
Expected Mean Square
Expected Value
Experimental Effect
Exponential Function
Extrapolation
Extreme Reactions, Test of
F Distribution
F_{max}
F Ratio
F Score
F Test

Factor Analysis
Factor Loading
Factor Rotation
Fiducial Interval
First-Order Interaction
Fisher's Exact Probability Test
Fisher's Z'
Fixed-Effects Factor
Fixed-Effects Model
Fixed/Random-Effects Factor
Fixed/Random-Effects Model
Flat Distribution
Follow-up Test
Forecasting Efficiency Index
Fourfold Point Correlation
Frequency Distribution
Frequency Polygon
Friedman's Two-Way Analysis for
    Ranked Data
Function
Functional Relation
Gamma Distribution
Gaussian Curve
Geometric Mean
Gompertz Curve
Goodness-of-Fit Test
Grand Mean
Group Mean
Group Datum
Group Interval
Group Measure
Group Score
Grouped Data
Grouping Error
Growth Curve
H
H_0
H_1
H_A
Harmonic Mean
Hartley's F_{max}
Heterogeneity
Heteroscedasticity
Higher Order Interaction
Histogram
Homogeneity of Proportions, Test
    for

xxi

Unweighted $\overline{X}$
Unweighted Means Analysis x-Axis
Validity Coefficient   x-Value
Variance y
Variance Estimate   Y
Variance Ratio   Y'
Variation, Coefficient of $\hat{y}$
Vector $\overline{Y}$
Varimax Rotation   y-Axis
Wald–Wolfowitz Runs Test   y-Value
Weight(ed)   Yates' Correction for Continuity
Wherry–Doolittle Method   Yule's Q
Wilcoxon Matched-Pairs Signed- z Distribution
  Ranks Test z Score
Wilcoxon Rank-Sum Test   Z Score
Wilcoxon Signed-Ranks Test z Statistic
Wilk's Lambda Test   z Transformation
x' z' Transformation
X Zero-Order Correlation

Psychometrics

Accuracy   Educational Quotient
Achievement Test   Embedded-Figures Test
Alternate-Forms Method   Empirical Validity
Aptitude Test   E.Q.
Attitude Scale   Equivalent Forms Method
Bogardus Scale   Error-Choice Technique
Coding Test   External Reliability
Composite Score   External Validity
Concept Formation Task   Face Validity
Concurrent Validity   Fixed-Alternative Item
Construct Validity   Forced Choice
Content Analysis   Guttman Scale
Content Validity   Halo Effect
Criterion Score   Hoyt's Formula for Reliability
Criterion Variable   IQ
Critical Score   Information Test
Culture-Fair Test   Intelligence Quotient
Culture-Free Test   Intelligence Scale
Cumulative Ratings, Method of   Intelligence Score
Cumulative Scale   Intelligence Test
Cutting Score   Interest Inventory
Deterioration Index   Internal Consistency
Deterioration Quotient   Internal Reliability
Discriminant Validity   Internal Validity
Educational Age   Interrater Reliability

Interreliability
Item Analysis
Item Reversal
Item Weighting
Known-Group Validity
KR-20
Kuder–Richardson Formula
Likert Scale
Matching Task
Matching Test
Measurement Error
Multiple-Choice Task
Multiple-Choice Test
Objective Test
Odd-Even Reliability
Omnibus Test
Open-End Item
Option Task
Parallel Tests
Power Test
Predictive Validity
Projective Technique
Projective Test
Q-Sort

Questionnaire
Rating
Reliability
Reproducibility
Response Bias
Scaled Test
Scalogram Analysis
Semantic Differential
Social Acquiescence
Social Desirability
Social Distance Scale
Sociometric Index
Sociometry
Sorting Task
Speed Test
Spiral Omnibus Test
Split-Half Reliability
Summated Ratings, Method of
Tailored Testing
Test-Retest Procedure
Thurstone Scale
True Score
Validity
Validity Coefficient

Psychophysical and Scaling Procedures

Absolute Judgment, Method of
Absolute Threshold
Adjustment, Method of
Anchor Stimulus
Ascending Series
Ascending/Descending Series
Attitude Scale
Average Error, Method of
Békésey Method
Comparison Stimulus
Confidence Rating
Confusion Matrix
Constant Stimuli, Method of
Cross-Modality Matching
Cumulative Ratings, Method of
Cumulative Scale
Descending Series
Detection Threshold
Difference Limen
Difference Threshold

Discriminal Dispersion
Discriminal Process
DL
Equal-Appearing Intervals,
    Method of
Equal Category
Equal Sense Distances, Method of
Equisection, Method of
Forced Choice
Fractionation, Method of
Forced Choice
Fractionation, Method of
Free Scaling
Guttman Scale
Halving Method
Indifference Response
Interval of Uncertainty
JNND
Just Noticeable Difference
Just Not Noticeable Difference

Likert Scale
Limen
Limits, Method of
Lower Difference Threshold
Magnitude Estimation
Magnitude Production
Multidimensional Scaling
Paired Comparisons, Method of
POE (Point of Objective Equality)
Point of Objective Equality
Point of Physical Equality
Point of Subjective Equality
Production Method
PSE
Psychological Scaling
Psychophysical Function
Psychophysical Methods
Ratio Method
Recognition Threshold
Reiz Limen

Reproduction Methods
Scaling Methods
Scalogram Analysis
Sensation Unit
Sense Ratio Method
Single Stimuli, Method of
Staircase Method
Standard Stimulus
Stimulus Threshold
Summated Ratings, Method of
Terminal Threshold
Threshold
Thurstone Scale
Time Error
Titration Method
Unidimensional Scaling
Up-and-Down Method
Variable Error
Variable Stimulus
Von Békésey Method

Conditioning and Learning Procedures

Acquisition Phase
Acquisition Trial
Active Avoidance Training
Adaptation
Adaptation Phase
Adjusting Schedule of
    Reinforcement
Ad Lib(itum) Weight
Alternative Schedule of
    Reinforcement
Amplitude of Response
Anticipation Method
Anticipatory Response
Appetitive Conditioning
Associative Matching
Autonomic Conditioning
Autoshaping
Aversion Training
Aversive Conditioning
Aversive Control
Aversive Stimulus
Avoidance Training
Backward Conditioning
Backward Learning Curve

Baseline
Baseline Trial
Blank Trial
Body Weight Schedule
Buffer Trial
CCC
Chain
Chained Schedu'e of
    Reinforcement
Change-Over Delay
Classical Conditioning
Compound Conditioning
Compound Schedule of
    Reinforcement
Concurrent Chained Schedule of
    Reinforcement
Concurrent Schedule of
    Reinforcement
Conditional Response
Conditional Stimulus
Conditioned Reinforcement
Conditioned Response
Conditioned Stimulus
Conditioned Suppression

Instrumental/Operant Response
Intentional Learning
Interitem Interval
Interlocking Schedule of
    Reinforcement
Intermittent Reinforcement
Interoceptive Conditioning
Interpolated Reinforcement
Interval Schedules of
    Reinforcement
Intradimensional Shift
Intrusion Error
Irrelevant Cue
Irrelevant Stimulus
Knowledge of Results
Learned Reinforcement
Learning Curve
Learning Set Procedure
Magazine Training
Massed Practice
Matched Dependent Paradigm
Matching-to-Sample Procedure
Mechner Diagram
Melton Learning Curve
Mix
Mixed List
Mix Mult
Mixed Multiple Schedule of
    Reinforcement
Mixed Schedule of
    Reinforcement
MOC Curve
Multiple Schedule of
    Reinforcement
Negative Stimulus
Negative Transfer
Negatively Correleated
    Reinforcement
Neutral Stimulus
Noncontingent Reinforcement
Nondifferential Reinforcement
Nondiscriminated Avoidance
    Conditioning
Nonreversal Shift
Nonsense Stimuli
Noxious Stimulus
Oddity Problem

Ommission Training
Operandum
Operant Chamber
Operant Conditioning
Operant Level
Operant Response
Overlearning
Overt Response
Overt/Covert Response
Overtraining
PA Learning
Paired-Associate Learning
Paralog
Partial Reinforcement
Passive Avoidance Training
Pavlovian Conditioning
Perceptual-Motor Learning
Periodic Reinforcement
Positive Stimulus
Positively Correlated
    Reinforcement
Practice Trial
Preconditioning
Pretraining Trial
Primary Reinforcement
Primary Stimulus
Proactive Paradigm
Probability Learning Task
Probe Stimulus
Probe Technique
Pseudoconditioning Control
Punishment Training
Punishment
Random Reinforcement
Ratio Schedule of Reinforcement
Recall Method
Recitation Method
Recognition Method
Reconstruction Method
Rehearsal
Reinforcement
Reinforcement Schedule
Reinforcer
Relative Probability
Relearning Method
Releaser
Reproducibility Coefficient

Resistance to Extinction
Respondent Behavior
Respondent Conditioning
Response Differentiation
Response Generalization
Response Induction
Response–Reinforcement Interval
Response–Response Interval
Response–Stimulus Interval
Response Topography
Retention Methods
Retroactive Paradigm
Reversal Shift
Reversal/Nonreversal Shift
Reversal Training
Reward
Reward Training
S^+
S^-
S^D
S^Δ
Savings Method
Savings Score
Schedule of Reinforcement
Secondary Reinforcement
Second-Order Conditioning
Semantic Conditioning
Semantic Generalization Test
Sensory Preconditioning
Serial Anticipation
Serial Learning
Shaping
Sidman Avoidance Conditioning
Simultaneous Conditioning
Simultaneous Discrimination
Skinner Box
Spaced Practice
Spatial Discrimination
Stimulus Generalization

Successive Approximations Method
Successive Discrimination
TAND
Tandem Schedule of Reinforcement
Tailored Yoking
Temporal Conditioning
Temporal Discrimination
Time Out
Time Schedule
Trace Conditioning
Training Trial
Transfer Paradigm
Trigram
True Yoking
Type R Conditioning
Type S Conditioning
UCS
Umweg Problem
Unconditioned Response
Unconditioned Stimulus
Uncorrelated Reinforcement
Unpaired Control
UR
US
Variable-Interval Schedule of Reinforcement
Variable-Ratio Schedule of Reinforcement
Verbal Conditioning
Verbal Learning
Verbal Reinforcement
VI
Vincent(ized) Learning Curve
Visual Discrimination
VR
Weight Schedule
Word Association Test
Yoked Control

Cognition, Perception, Motor, and Information Process Procedures

a-Reaction Time
Absolute Threshold
Adaptation
Algorithm
Ambiguous Figures

Ames' Distorted Room
Ames' Window
Anchor Stimulus
Anticipatory Response
Ascending Series

Probe Stimulus
Pulfrich Illusion
Pursuit Rotor Task
Pursuit Tracking Task
Reaction Time
Ready Signal
Recognition Threshold
Redundancy
Response Bias
Reversible Figures
ROC Curve
Rotary Pursuit Task
Sampling Bias
Sander's Illusion
Schröder's Staircase
Search Task
Sensitivity
Serial Search Task
Shadowing
Signal Detection Task
Signal Probability
Simple Reaction Time
Size–Weight Illusion
Subtraction Method
Target Stimulus
Time on Target
Tracking
Trapezoidal Window
Travel Time
True Negative
True Positive
Twisted Cord Illusion
Vigilance Task
Visual Discrimination
Visual Discrimination
Visual Search
Word Association Test
Yes–No Method
Zollner Illusion

Experimental Social Psychology and Related Procedures

Asch-Type Stimuli
Attitude Scale
Bale's Technique
Bogardus Scale
Case History
Case Study
Census Data
Conformity Procedure
Cross-Cultural Method
Cross-Sectional Method
Evaluation Research
Field Sociometry
Game Research
Horizontal Grouping
Interaction Process Analysis
Interview Technique
Longitudinal Method
Mixed Motive Game
Nomination Technique
Nonzero-Sum Game
Payoff Matrix
Prisoner's Dilemma
Profile Analysis
Social Acquiescence
Social Desirability
Social Distance Scale
Sociometric Index
Sociometry
Target Person
Vertical Grouping
Zero/Nonzero-Sum Game
Zero-Sum Game

ABA Design   Any experimental design in which some treatment, environment, task, etc., is changed and then changed back, usually only once. (*See also* Retroactive Paradigm; Reversal Design.)

ABAB Design   *See* Reversal Design.

ABBA Sequence   A counterbalancing procedure applicable when two experimental treatments, A and B, are to be presented at least twice each to a subject. The treatments are given in the order A, then B, then B again, then A. If additional repetitions are given, the ABBA sequence may be repeated or inverted (i.e., BAAB). This helps ensure that such potentially confounding carry-over effects as practice, fatigue, boredom, etc., are distributed more or less equally over performance in condition A and B.

EXAMPLE: Solution times for anagrams formed from common and from uncommon words are compared. Anagrams of four common words (Treatment A) and four uncommon words (Treatment B) are presented to each subject. To distribute order effects equally over the eight trials, the subjects receive the anagrams one at a time in the sequence ABBABAAB. To control for such things as initial experience, half of the subjects could be given the inverted sequence BAABABBA.

Abscissa   The x or horizontal axis in a graph. *(For an illustration see* Coordinates.)

Absolute Judgment, Method of (*syn.* Single Stimuli, Method of)   A psychophysical method in which a subject is presented with one stimulus at a time and is asked to make a judgment in absolute terms concerning some attribute of the stimulus. The subject is not provided with a standard stimulus or other stimuli against which to compare the stimulus being judged. For example, a subject may be asked to judge the length of a line in centimeters,

1

the weight of an object in grams, the length of a time interval in seconds, the speed of an automobile in miles per hour, etc.

Absolute Scaling   *See* Absolute Judgment.

Absolute Threshold (*syn.* Stimulus Threshold, *abbr.* RL)   The smallest physical value of a stimulus that will produce a response some percentage (often 50%) of the time. The actual value of the stimulus that will produce a response will vary from subject to subject and in the same subject from time to time, so the concept of a threshold is a statistical one. For some senses there are both a lower absolute threshold and an upper absolute threshold (**terminal threshold**), that is, the maximal physical value of a stimulus that will produce a response 50% of the time. For example, in young adults the lower and upper thresholds for pitch of moderate-intensity tones are approximately 16 Hz and 16,000 Hz, respectively. For some senses the upper absolute threshold cannot be determined because excessively intense stimuli may be too painful.

A × B (A by B) Design   *See* Factorial Design.

A × Subjects (A by Subjects) Design   *See* Repeated-Measures Design.

Acceleration   A change in the rate at which one variable, y, increases or decreases in value as a function of increase in the value of a related variable, x. In psychology the y variable is ordinarily a dependent variable and x is an independent variable. Acceleration indicates that the amount by which y changes as x changes one unit in value differs, depending on whether the increase in x occurs in the range of low values of x or in the range of higher values of x. (*See also* Negatively Accelerated Function; Positively Accelerated Function.)

Acceptance Region   *See* Nonrejection Region.

Accidental Error   *See* Random Error.

Accidental Sampling   The most rudimentary form of nonprobability sampling in which subjects are selected indiscriminately until the desired sample size is reached. No attempt is made to control for biases and confounding errors. Street corner polls by mass media are typical of accidental sampling. (*See also* Incidental Sampling.)

Accuracy   Lack of bias in a measurement. It is indexed by the mean of repeated measurements. The more accurate measurements are, the closer this mean is to the true value of the object being measured. For example, if a table is actually 1.5 m long, a single measurement might give the value 1.48 m or 1.53 m; if the measuring instrument is accurate, however, the mean of a number of observations will be equal to 1.5 m.

Achievement Test   An instrument designed to measure what a person has learned within or up to a given time. (*See also* Aptitude Test.)

Acquisition Phase   That segment of an experiment during which a response is practiced or learned (i.e., "acquired"). It is defined in terms of either a fixed time period or the period prior to the response reaching some criterion of stability. (*See also* Training Trial.)

Active Avoidance Training   *See* Avoidance Training.

Activity Box   A device designed to measure the amount of activity engaged in by a subject during a given period of time.

Activity Wheel   A circular cage that rotates when the animal inside runs. It usually is used with small animals to provide exercise or to record changes in activity as a dependent variable in an experiment.

Adaptation   *See* Adaptation Phase; Habituation.

Adaptation Phase   That phase of a research project during which procedures are employed to accustom the subject to the research environment. This is done to reduce variability in the subject's behavior that might be due to the novelty of the situation or to achieve a prescribed level of behavioral or physiological change (e.g., dark adaptation) before further operations can be initiated. (*See also* Habituation.)

Additivity   A functional relationship in which a response is determined by the sum of the effects of the independent variables. In the context of the analysis of variance, **nonadditivity** usually refers to the presence of an interaction effect, that is, the response is determined by the product of the effects of the independent variables or by some other functional relationship.

Adjusting Schedule of Reinforcement   An operant conditioning procedure in which the characteristics of a subsequent reinforcement cycle are determined by the way an organism responds in the previous cycle. (*See also* Interlocking Schedule of Reinforcement.)

EXAMPLE: An operant chamber is programmed so that a rat receives food pellets on a fixed-interval 30-sec (FI-30) schedule of reinforcement. If it exhibits a high rate of responding during the early segments of that 30-sec interval, the next reinforcement interval will be lengthened (e.g., increased to 50 sec). If a low rate of responding is shown during the early segment of the interval, the next interval will be shortened (e.g., reduced to 15 sec).

Adjustment, Method of (*syn.* Average Error, Method of) A psychophysical method used to determine absolute and difference thresholds but having other applications as well. It is characterized by the fact that the subject must physically adjust some variable stimulus, often to match a designated standard.

EXAMPLE 1: Absolute Threshold Using apparatus that permits the subject to control the value of a stimulus, a subject is given a series of trials in which the task is to set the value of the stimulus at a point where it is just barely detectable. On some trials the value is started well below threshold and the subject increases the value until the stimulus is first detected (ascending series). On other trials the value is started well above threshold and the subject decreases the value until the stimulus first fails to be detected (descending series).

EXAMPLE 2: Difference Threshold Over a series of trials a subject is asked to adjust a variable stimulus to be equal to a standard stimulus. On some trials the value of the variable stimulus is started well below that of the standard, and on some trials it is started well above that of the standard.

Ad Lib(itum) Weight A subject's stable weight when it is allowed to feed freely.

After-Test Design *See* Posttest Design.

Algorithm A procedure or rule that is certain to provide a solution to a particular type of problem. For example, the algorithm for solving anagrams is to form all possible arrangements of the letters, investigating each to see if it is a word. This is guaranteed to find a solution, but since there are 120 arrangements of five letters, 720 arrangements of six letters, etc., most people tend to use other approaches when faced with the problem. (*See also* Heuristic.)

Alienation, Coefficient of (*symb. k*) A measure of the nonassociation between two variables. It is equal to $\sqrt{1 - r^2}$, where r is the correlation coefficient. (*See also* Nondetermination, Coefficient of.)

Alpha (*symb.* α) The first letter in the Greek alphabet, having several common technical meanings (see Appendix B). It frequently refers to the significance level of a hypothesis testing procedure. The word also is used in certain contexts as a name [e.g., the alpha test (of intelligence) and alpha brain waves]. (*See also* Coefficient Alpha.)

Alpha Error *See* Type I Error.

Alpha Error Rate *See* Error Rate.

Alpha Level   *See* Significance Level.

Alternate-Forms Method   A procedure for the assessment of the reliability of a measure. A similar or parallel form of a test given earlier, using the same type of questions, is administered after a suitable interval has passed. Responses to both test forms are then correlated to assess reliability.

Alternate (Alternative) Hypothesis   *See* Null/Alternate Hypothesis.

Alternating-Conditions Design   *See* Reversal Design.

Alternative Hypothesis   *See* Null/Alternate Hypothesis.

Alternative Schedule of Reinforcement (*abbr.* Alt)   An operant conditioning procedure in which two schedules of reinforcement are in effect simultaneously and where a behavior pattern that satisfies the demands of either schedule is reinforced.

EXAMPLE: An operant chamber is programmed so that a rat presses a bar for food pellets with both fixed-interval 30-sec and fixed-ratio-10 schedules in effect. If either 30 sec elapses or nine responses are made after a reinforcement, the very next response is reinforced.

Ambiguous Figures   *See* Illusions.

Ames' Distorted Room   *See* Illusions.

Ames' Window   *See* Illusions: Trapezoidal Window.

Among Groups   *See* Between Subjects _____.

Amplitude of Response   One index of response magnitude generally associated with physiological behaviors (e.g., skin conductance changes) and some overt behaviors (e.g., a string pull or an eyeblink). It is generally the difference between the value recorded for a resting state prior to the response and the value of the largest discrepancy from the resting state after the response has begun.

Anagram Task   The task of unscrambling the rearranged letters of a word in order to form the original word. Some anagrams have a single solution (i.e., only one word can be formed from the letters), whereas other anagrams can produce two or more solution words. Examples of single-solution anagrams are TACMH and DEJGU, which can be solved to form MATCH and JUDGE, respectively. Two-solution anagrams include GINHE, which can be solved to form either HINGE or NEIGH, and EDPAR, which can produce either DRAPE or RAPED. The anagram task is often used in the study of thinking or problem solving.

Analysis of Covariance (*abbr.* ANCOVA)   A procedure for data analysis that uses statistical control to remove the effects of a variable that is correlated with the dependent variable. It most frequently is used with subject variables, such as intelligence or pretest scores, for which strict experimental control is impractical. It is an analysis of that portion of the variability of the dependent variable that is not accounted for by the extraneous (or concomitant) variable. That is, the analysis of covariance determines whether there are differences among the groups or conditions in an experiment over and above differences that could be accounted for by the differences in intelligence, pretest performance, etc., which happen to have occurred.

Analysis of Variance (*abbr.* ANOVA)   A set of procedures for testing the significance of differences among means. The total variability of the observations from an experiment is divided into those portions that are attributable to the systematic effects of the independent variable(s) and those that are attributable to chance factors or experimental error. The analysis of variance yields one estimate of variability, called a mean square, for each independent variable; one estimate for each interaction if the experiment involves two or more independent variables; and, depending on the design, one or more error terms, which are mean squares for variability attributable to random experimental error. The effect of each of the independent variables and of their interactions is tested by forming an F ratio, which is the mean square for the effect divided by the appropriate error term. Analyses of variance are generally identified in terms of the experimental design for which they are appropriate (e.g., a mixed analysis of variance, which is the analysis of variance for a mixed design). (*See also* Analysis of Covariance; Multivariate Analysis of Variance.)

Analysis of Variance for Ranked Data (*syn.* Friedman's Two-Way Analysis of Variance for Ranked Data)   A distribution-free nonparametric test for differences among levels of an independent variable presented in a randomized-block or repeated-measurements design. The scores in each block or for each subject are ranked from 1 to k (the number of levels), then the ranks are summed for each level of the independent variable. The test statistic is $\chi^2 = \{12/[nk\,(k+1)]\}\,(\Sigma T_i^2) - 3n(k+1)$, where n is the number of blocks or subjects, k is the number of levels of the independent variable, and T_i is the sum of the ranks for each level. This statistic has a chi-square distribution with $k-1$ degrees of freedom. (*See also* Rank-Sum Test.)

EXAMPLE: Subjects are shown a series of slides of geometric forms (G), abstract drawings (A), photographs of people (P), and photographs of landscapes (L). The dependent variable is the mean number of seconds a subject looks at each type of picture. The computations for the analysis are illustrated using the data from three subjects.

Subject	Mean time (sec)					Rank order for each subject			
	G	A	P	L		G	A	p	L
1	5.3	10.2	41.7	44.2		1	2	3	4
2	17.8	15.6	43.1	26.9		2	1	4	3
3	9.1	27.4	38.5	31.8		1	2	4	3
					T_i	4	5	11	10

$n = 3$, $k = 4$; degrees of freedom $= k - 1 = 3$; $\chi^2 = [12/(3)(4)(5)] \, (4^2 + 5^2 + 11^2 + 10^2) - 3(3)(5) = 7.4$.

Analysis-of-Variance Summary Table A table that summarizes the results of an analysis of variance. The sources of variability (independent variables, interactions, and error terms) are listed, together with the corresponding mean squares, degrees of freedom, F ratios, and, usually, p values. The sum of squares for each source also may be included.

Analytic ABAB Design *See* Reversal Design.

Anchor Stimulus In psychophysics and scaling, a stimulus that serves as a reference by a subject to report judgments of stimulus values. Typically, the smallest and largest stimulus values in a series of stimuli are anchor stimuli. A new anchor may be created by introducting a stimulus from outside the range of values of the series.

EXAMPLE: Subjects are given a number of weights and told to assign them to one of five categories: "very light," "light," "medium," "heavy," and "very heavy." By definition, the lightest and heaviest weights in the series are the anchor stimuli. If the series then is revised by adding a new, lighter (or heavier) weight and the subjects are asked to recategorize the stimuli, this new extreme value becomes an anchor stimulus.

ANCOVA (*syn.* ANCOV; ANCOVAR) *See* Analysis of Covariance.

Anecdotal Method A method of gaining knowledge about the behavior of organisms that relies on collecting accounts of behavior often made by untrained or amateur observers. For example, much of the early writings on intelligent behavior among lower animals made use of anecdotes reported by pet owners or of relatively casual and uncontrolled observations made by zoologists and naturalists.

ANOVA (*syn.* ANOV; ANOVAR) *See* Analysis of Variance.

Antecedent Condition An event that precedes, and therefore may produce or modify, the behavior being investigated. Broadly, the term may refer to all events in the history of the organism, but more typically it is used to refer to the specific experimental conditions necessary to produce a behavior change. For example, an increase in light impinging on the eye of a physically normal individual will produce constriction of the pupil; the increase in light and normal physical state are the antecedent conditions for the pupillary response. (*See also* Causal Relationship.)

Antedating Response   *See* Anticipatory Response.

Anticipation Method   In verbal learning, a method that combines learning and testing of an item in a single trial. The subject is asked to produce the correct response during a brief period between some cueing signal and presentation by the experimenter of the correct item. In serial anticipation, where a list of items, such as words, is to be learned in order, the items are presented one at a time so that each item both provides information about the correctness of the previous response and is the cue for the next anticipation. For paired-associate learning, where items are paired and the subject is to produce the response member of the pair when the stimulus member is shown, the stimulus is presented alone as the cue for anticipation, followed by presentation of the stimulus–response pair. For example, if the subject is to learn the pair HEN–MOP, after all of the pairs had been shown once, the stimulus term, HEN–, would be shown and the subject would try to recall the word MOP. The complete pair, HEN–MOP, may then be shown again for feedback or additional practice. (*See also* Paired-Associate Learning; Serial Learning.)

Anticipatory Response   (1) In conditioning, a response that, with learning, tends to occur before the stimulus that would ordinarily elicit it (e.g., lifting a finger just prior to receipt of an electric shock, instead of just after the shock). (2) In verbal learning and information processing, a type of error in which the subject gives a response to one member of a series of stimuli that is appropriate only to a subsequent member of the series. For example, in testing the subject's recall of an ordered sequence of paired associates: *blue–shoe, green–bean, white–light,* etc., answering *light* to the stimulus *green* would be an anticipatory response.

A Posteriori Comparison   *See* A Posteriori Test.

A Posteriori Probability   *See* Posterior Probability.

A Posteriori Test (*syn.* Post Hoc Test; Supplemental Test; *contr.* A Priori Test)   Any significance test that the experimenter decides to carry out as a result of the inspection or analysis of data. One type of a posteriori test involves devising a new independent variable or a new dependent variable, or both, after the experiment is completed. Standard statistical procedures are used for this purpose, and the results are reported as being a posteriori tests, which generally are replicated in an experiment designed for that purpose before they are considered to be reliable. Another type of a posteriori test is for differences between pairs of means selected from a larger set of means, or other contrasts. (*See also* Follow-up Test.)

EXAMPLE: In a study of problem solving, subjects are given no hint, an abstract hint, or a concrete hint, and the dependent variable is time taken to solve the problem. During the experiment, the experimenter notices that some of the subjects emphasize the problem in their verbalizations and others emphasize the goal and that the two kinds of subjects differ in the number of unsuccessful attempts before reaching the solution. An a posteriori test of this would be made by dividing the subjects into those who were problem-oriented and those who were goal-oriented and carrying out a *t* test of the difference in mean number of attempts for the two groups.

Apparent Limits *See* Class Interval.

Appetitive Conditioning (*contr.* Aversive Conditioning) A classical conditioning procedure in which the conditioned stimulus (CS) is followed by an unconditioned stimulus (US) that has positive properties (e.g., sweet liquids, pleasant odors, etc.), so that the CS itself will acquire positive properties. The term also is sometimes used as a reference to the instrumental conditioning technique of reward training.

Applied Research (*contr.* Basic Research) Research conducted with the primary intent of solving a specific practical problem.

A Priori Comparison *See* A Priori Test.

A Priori Probability *See* Prior Probability.

A Priori Test (*syn.* Planned Comparison; *contr.* A Posteriori Test) Any significance test that the experimenter plans, before the start of an experiment, to include in the analysis of the data. The phrase usually is used with reference to planned comparisons of a few of the possible pairs of means, which are of particular interest or importance. For example, in studying recognition time for words, numbers, and pictures, the experimenter might be particularly interested in comparing the two types of verbal stimuli, words and numbers. A priori tests, unlike a posteriori tests, are carried out regardless of whether or not the overall F test is significant, using standard statistical procedures. (*See also* Contrast.)

Aptitude Test An instrument designed to measure a person's potential to acquire particular skills. (*See also* Achievement Test.)

***a*-Reaction Time** *See* Reaction Time.

Arc Sine Transformation *See* Data Transformation.

Area Sampling (*syn.* Block Sampling) A form of nonprobability sampling that uses selected geographical areas to serve as representative samples. For example, a particular neighborhood may be identified as predominantly Protestant, black, and low-income and presumably reflect that type of population within a larger area. Similarly, certain election districts may be selected (usually on the basis of past performance) as typical of the entire voting population in the state.

Arithmetic Mean A measure of central tendency for a set of measurements, found by dividing the sum of the measurements by the number of measurements. It usually is called the **mean.** For example, the five numbers 6, 9, 4, 3, and 8 sum to 30. The arithmetic mean of these numbers is 30 divided by 5, which equals 6.

Artifact An artificial datum or relationship that is a product of the procedures or methodology used in the research, and not a genuine effect of the independent variable under study. (*See also* Confounding; Experimenter Bias; Instrumentation Effects.)

EXAMPLE: Changes in electrical conductivity of the skin are one indicant of emotional activity. They may be produced by a startling stimulus and measured by a pen deflection tracing. However, the stimulus may produce muscle twitches or other overt movements that also produce pen deflections, often independently of skin conductance changes. Thus, under such circumstances the pen deflections do not represent conductance changes and do not reflect emotional behavior.

Ascending/Descending Series In psychophysics, a procedure for obtaining absolute thresholds or difference thresholds by systematically increasing or decreasing the value of a comparison stimulus relative to a standard stimulus, or relative to an approximation of the subject's threshold. In an ascending series, the stimulus is set at a value well below the standard (or threshold) and is increased continuously, or in discrete steps, until it is reported as equal to the standard (or is just detected). In a descending series, the initial value of the comparison stimulus is well above the standard and is systematically decreased until judged equal to the standard, or until it is no longer detected. (*For examples of ascending and descending series see* Adjustment, Method of, and Limits, Method of.)

Ascending Series *See* Ascending/Descending Series.

Asch-Type Stimuli Sets of visual stimuli used in conformity experiments. Each set consists of a standard stimulus and, usually, three comparison stimuli differing somewhat from the standard. Subjects are asked to report which comparison stimulus most closely resembles the standard.

Association, Coefficient of (*symb. Q; syn.* Yule's *Q*) A measure of association, or relationship, for categorical data classified on two dichotomous dimensions. Schematically, the data are arranged as follows:

	B	not B	
A	a	b	$a+b$
not A	c	d	$c+d$
	$a+c$	$b+d$	n

where a, b, c, and d are the frequencies in the cells. The coefficient of association is $Q = (ad - bc)/(ad + bc)$ and ranges from -1 to $+1$, with 0 being no association and ± 1 being perfect association.

Association Test   A procedure for determining a subject's associations to various stimuli, usually verbal. The task may be simply to name a visually presented stimulus, which may be a word, letter, number, color, etc. In free association for words, the stimulus may be any word, and the response can be whatever other word first comes to mind. In *controlled association*, the response word must be one that stands in some specified relation to the stimulus word, such as a superordinate, coordinate, or subordinate, a rhyme, a synonym, or antonym, etc. *Associative reaction time* (i.e., the interval between the presentation of the stimulus and the subject's response) is often obtained.

Association, Test for   *See* Independence, Test for.

Associative Matching   A variant method for testing learning in the paired-associate paradigm. The subject is presented stimulus–response pairs in the usual manner, but at the time of testing, all the stimulus items are presented simultaneously in one group and all the response items in another group. The subject's task is to match each response item to the appropriate stimulus item.

Associative Reaction Time   *See* Association Test.

Assumption   (1) In theory construction, a basic tenet that is held to be true without proof, and from which further consequent tenets may be deduced. (2) In statistics, a condition that must be met before certain computations may be performed legitimately (e.g., assumptions of normality, homogeneity of variance, etc.).

Asymptote   A theoretical limit that a curve, such as a learning curve, approaches but can only reach at infinity. Behaviors that have grown or decayed in strength to some near maximum or minimum are said to have reached asymptote or to be asymptotic. Figure A–1 illustrates an asymptote.

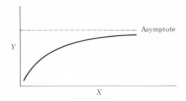

Figure A–1

A **Test (*syn.* Sandler's A Test)**   An alternative to the *t* test for correlated or paired samples, requiring the same assumptions of random sampling from a normal distributed population of differences. The test statistic is

$$A = \frac{\Sigma D^2}{(\Sigma D)^2}$$

where the *D*s are the differences between pairs of observations. The critical values of *A* are found in special tables.

Atmosphere Effect   Changes in the behavior of subjects due to the mere imposition of an experimental environment on them. For example, if experimenters enter a schoolroom and begin rewarding certain desirable scholastic behaviors, performance levels may increase (or decrease) not because of reward per se, but simply because of the presence of intruders in the room. (*See also* Demand Characteristic; Hawthorne Effect; Instrumentation Effect.)

Attitude Scale   A device for the systematic measurement of attitudes, opinions, and beliefs. The respondent is usually asked to express agreement or disagreement with a series of verbal statements concerning some issue, person, or event. The three major types— Thurstone, Likert, and Guttman Scales—involve different construction methods. (*See also* Cumulative Rating, Method of; Equal-Appearing Intervals, Method of; Summated Rating, Method of.)

Autocorrelation   The correlation between successive pairs of observations, which are measures of behavior on one subject over time. It is computed for pairs of observations that are separated by a fixed distance, called the lag. An autocorrelation with lag 1 would be found by pairing each observation with the one immediately preceding it and computing the correlation; an autocorrelation with lag 2 would be found by pairing each observation with the one two steps back, etc. Autocorrelations can be used for such things as testing the assumption of randomness in data gathered over time, or to test the goodness of fit of mathematical models, such as learning models, which predict changes in behavior over time.

EXAMPLE: An experimenter is establishing a base rate for activity of a rat in an activity cage and wishes to be sure that the level of activity is not showing systematic change because of adaptation or other causes. The number of movements in each of 20 observation periods is shown in Table A–1, and the data are shown arranged for computing autocorrelations of lag 1 and lag 2. Since neither of the correlations differs significantly from 0, the experimenter may be reasonably sure that the differences in activity are random.

Table A–1

Data		Lag 1 pairs		Lag 2 pairs	
Trial	Score	Trials	Scores	Trials	Scores
1	9	1, 2	9 13	1, 3	9 23
2	13	2, 3	13 23	2, 4	13 15
3	23	3, 4	23 15	3, 5	23 11
4	15	4, 5	15 11	4, 6	15 11
5	11	5, 6	11 11	5, 7	11 5
6	11	6, 7	11 5	6, 8	11 19
7	5	7, 8	5 19	7, 9	5 19
8	19	8, 9	19 19	8, 10	19 10
9	19	9, 10	19 10	9, 11	19 16
10	10	10, 11	10 16	10, 12	10 6
11	16	11, 12	16 6	11, 13	16 26
12	6	12, 13	6 26	12, 14	6 13
13	26	13, 14	26 13	13, 15	26 26
14	13	14, 15	13 26	14, 16	13 15
15	26	15, 16	26 15	15, 17	26 28
16	15	16, 17	15 28	16, 18	15 20
17	28	17, 18	28 20	17, 19	28 13
18	20	18, 19	20 13	18, 20	20 24
19	13	19, 20	13 24		
20	24		$r = -.16$		$r = .27$

Autokinetic Effect *See under* Illusions.

Autonomic Conditioning Conditioning of response systems that are controlled by the autonomic nervous system, such as heart rate or skin resistance.

Autoshaping A procedure for training a voluntary response to a neutral stimulus by pairing that stimulus with the occurrence of a reinforcer and making the two paired events independent of the subject's behavior. The neutral stimulus eventually elicits part or all of the response that originally was involved in obtaining the reinforcement.

EXAMPLE: A hungry pigeon is placed in an operant chamber. At intervals, a key or disk on the wall is lighted, followed by the delivery of a bit of grain. This sequence is repeated many times. Eventually the bird may peck at the lighted key in a manner similar to which it pecks at the grain.

Average   *See* Mean.

Average Deviation (*abbr.* AD)   A measure of variability for a set of measurements. It is the arithmetic mean of the absolute value (disregarding the sign) of the deviations of the measurements from their mean. It is not useful in statistical inference, but it sometimes is preferred for descriptive purposes, since it is less sensitive to large deviations than is the standard deviation, or the range. (*See also* Standard Deviation.)

EXAMPLE: The mean of the five numbers 6, 9, 4, 3, and 8 is 6. The absolute values of the deviations of these numbers from their mean are 0, 3, 2, 3, and 2. The average deviation for these numbers is the sum of the deviations, 10, divided by 5, which equals 2.

Average Error, Method of   *See* Adjustment, Method of.

Aversion Training   *See* Aversive Conditioning.

Aversive Conditioning (*contr.* Appetitive Conditioning)   A classical conditioning procedure in which the conditioned stimulus (CS) is followed by an unconditioned stimulus (US) that has negative or aversive properties (e.g., electric shock, bitter liquids, loud noises, etc.), so that the CS itself will acquire aversive properties. In certain contexts, the procedure is referred to variously as **aversion training, defense conditioning,** and **fear conditioning.**

EXAMPLE: A dog is placed in a harness, and shock and heart rate recording electrodes are attached. A pure tone (CS) is sounded for a few seconds and followed immediately by a brief electric shock (US) to one limb. The procedure is repeated at intervals for a prescribed number of trials. Changes in heart rate response to the tone (CR) are recorded.

Aversive Control   Any conditioning procedure in which the strength of a behavior is increased, maintained, or decreased through the application or removal of an aversive stimulus. (*For examples see* Aversive Conditioning, Avoidance Training, *and* Punishment Training.)

Aversive Stimulus (*syn.* Noxious Stimulus)   Any stimulus that has negative properties such that the organism would normally attempt to avoid, escape, or reduce it. Examples include electric shock, loud noises, etc. (*See also* Negative Stimulus; Punishment.)

Avoidance Training   A means of establishing a response, or of increasing its strength, by arranging to prevent the scheduled occurrence of an aversive stimulus if the response is made. (*See also* Escape Training; Punishment Training.)

EXAMPLE: A dog is placed in one compartment of a box with a wire grid floor. A buzzer is sounded and several seconds later an electric shock is delivered through the grid floor. The animal may escape the shock by jumping over a barrier into the "safe" portion of the box. When it does, the shock (and often the buzzer) is terminated. On subsequent trials the dog may escape the shock more efficiently. Eventually it responds to the buzzer by jumping prior to onset of the shock.

Axis   *See* Coordinates.

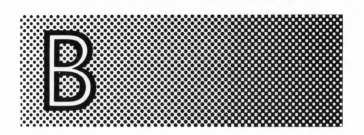

Backward Conditioning (*contr.* Forward Conditioning) In classical conditioning, a procedure in which the conditioned stimulus follows the unconditioned stimulus instead of preceding it. Sometimes it is used as a control procedure. (*See also* Simultaneous Conditioning.)

Backward Learning Curve One of a class of learning curves that permit direct comparison and averaging of data when subjects require differing numbers of trials to reach a fixed performance criterion. It is obtained by first recording performance on the criterion trial (Trial 0) for each subject, then recording performance on the trial immediately preceding the criterion trial (Trial 1), and so on, for successive trials preceding the criterion trial. It usually is graphed with zero (the criterion trial) on the right and trial numbers increasing to the left. (*See also* Melton Learning Curve; Vincent Learning Curve.)

EXAMPLE: Subjects are given the task of learning a list of 12 items in serial order to a criterion of two perfect trials. The number of correct responses on each trial for three subjects is as follows:

	Trial																
	1	2	3	4	5	6	7	8	9	10	11	12	13	14	15	16	17
Subject 1	0	2	3	4	6	6	8	8	9	10	9	11	12	11	11	12	12
Subject 2	2	2	6	4	7	8	10	10	7	11	12	12					
Subject 3	4	5	7	8	7	10	9	11	12	11	12	12					

Next the number correct is recorded for the first criterion trial and for successive trials preceding this trial, and these are averaged:

	Trial										
	0	1	2	3	4	5	6	7	8	9	10
Subject 1	12	11	11	12	11	9	10	9	8	8	6
Subject 2	12	11	7	10	10	8	7	4	6	2	2
Subject 3	12	11	12	11	9	10	7	8	7	5	4
Totals	36	33	30	33	30	27	24	21	21	15	12
Means	12	11	10	11	10	9	8	7	7	5	4

The graph of the backward learning curve is shown in Figure B–1.

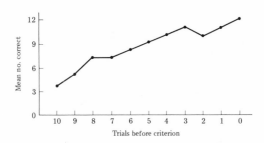

Figure B–1 Backward Learning Curve.

Backward Masking *See* Masking.

Balanced Incomplete Blocks Design *See* Incomplete Designs.

Balanced Order *See* Counterbalancing.

Bale's Technique *See* Interaction Process Analysis.

Bar Graph A format for illustrating data in which rectangular columns (bars) represent values of the x, or independent variable. The height of each bar indicates the amount of the y, or dependent variable associated with each value of x. Infrequently, levels of the independent variable are placed on the y-axis, and the bars extend horizontally. Bar graphs typically are used with nominal or ordinal data or when discrete variables are represented. (*See also* Line Graph.)

EXAMPLE: Figure B–2 is a typical bar graph showing the frequencies of different degrees of belief in extrasensory perception expressed in samples of sophomore and senior college students. The variables placed on the x-axis are (1) type of believer, in five categories from strong believer to strong disbeliever, and (2) academic status of

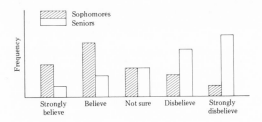

Figure B-2

the student: sophomore or senior. The y-axis shows the range of frequencies with which subjects are placed into one of the categories.

Bartlett's Test   A test for homogeneity of variances. (*For more commonly used tests see* Cochran's Test; F_{max}.)

Basal Level (*syn.* Baseline; Operant Level)   The typical or characteristic level, rate, or magnitude of some behavior. It usually is obtained prior to the introduction of some experimental treatment. The effect of that treatment in influencing the behavior is measured by comparison with the basal level. (*See also* Pretest.)

Baseline   *See* Basal Level.

Baseline Trial   A trial given prior to the introduction of an experimental treatment. Performance on this trial may be compared to performance during or after the treatment condition.

Basement Effect   *See* Ceiling/Floor Effect.

Basic Research (*syn.* Pure Research; *contr.* Applied Research)   Research conducted with the primary intent of increasing general information about a subject, without regard to immediate practical application of the information.

Bayesian Statistics (*contr.* Classical Inference Procedures)   An approach to statistical inference that is based on a subjective definition of probability rather than a relative frequency definition of probability. It explicitly incorporates prior (preexperimental) knowledge into the statistical procedures and emphasizes estimation and decision making over hypothesis testing. (*See also* Subjective Probability.)

EXAMPLE: An experimenter believes that the odds are 2 to 1 that girls score higher than boys on a general vocabulary test, that is, the experimenter's subjective probability is $\frac{2}{3}$ that the girls score higher, and the subjective probability is $\frac{1}{3}$ that sex and vocabulary score are independent. A number of children are given the vocabulary test and are classified by sex and by whether they scored high or low on the test. It is found that the girls did score higher, but the appropriate computations show that the observed frequencies are three times as likely to occur if the variables are independent. That is, the data favor independence by a factor of 3 to 1. The experimenter's prior odds of 1 to 2 in favor of the independence are multiplied by this factor of 3 to 1 to give posterior odds of 3 to 2 in favor of independence. The experimenter would now believe that the probability is $\frac{3}{5}$ that the two variables are independent and $\frac{2}{5}$ that girls score higher. The corresponding procedure in classical inference would be a chi-square test of independence, which for this case would not be significant.

b Coefficient (*syn. b* Weight) One of the coefficients of the predictor variables, expressed in raw scores, in the multiple regression equation $Y' = a + b_1X_1 + b_2X_2 + \cdots + b_kX_k$. (*See also* Beta Coefficient; Multiple Regression.)

Before–After Design *See* Pretest–Posttest Design.

Bernoulli Experiment *See* Simple Experiment.

Best-Fit Line *See* Regression Analysis.

Beta (*symb.* β) (1) The second letter of the Greek alphabet, having several common technical meanings (see Appendix B.) (2) In signal detection, the designation for a measure of response bias. For example, beta provides a numerical index of a subject's tendency to respond "Yes" rather than "No," or vice versa, on trials where there is considerable uncertainty as to whether or not a faint signal has been presented. (*See also* Signal Detection Task.)

Beta Coefficient (*syn.* Beta Weight) One of the standardized coefficients of the predictor variables in the multiple regression equation $z'_y = \beta_1z_1 + \beta_2z_2 + \cdots + \beta_kz_k$, where z'_y is the standardized predicted value and the z values on the right side of the equation are the standardized values of the k predictor variables. The beta coefficients are independent of the scales of measurement of the predictor variables and can be compared directly with each other. (*See also b* Coefficient; Multiple Regression.)

Beta Distribution A probability distribution particularly useful in Bayesian statistics, since different choices for the two parameters of the distribution can produce distributions that are U shaped, rectangular, skewed, or symmetric bell shaped.

Beta Error *See* Type II Error.

Beta Weight *See* Beta Coefficient.

Between Factor *See* Between-Subjects Variable; Mixed Design.

Between-Groups Design *See* Randomized-Groups Design.

20

Between-Groups Variable   *See* Between-Subjects Variable.

Between-Subjects Design (*syn.* Between-Groups Design; *contr.* Within-Subjects Design)   Any experimental design in which every level of each independent variable is assigned to a different group of subjects, so that each subject serves in only one treatment condition. (*For an example see* Between-Subjects Variable.)

Between-Subjects Variable (*syn.* Between-Groups Variable; *contr.* Within-Subjects Variable)   Any independent variable studied by assigning its different levels to different subjects and ensuring that a given subject serves in one and only one level. (*See also* Mixed Design.)

EXAMPLE: The effect of sleep deprivation on strength of hand grip was studied. Sleep deprivation was defined as keeping subjects awake for 12, 24, or 48 hours after their normal bedtime. Since subjects were deprived for *either* 12, *or* 24, *or* 48 hours but did not serve in more than one of these conditions, sleep deprivation is a between-subjects variable.

Bias   Systematic deviation from a true value. For example, biased sampling results in a sample that differs systematically from the target population; the subjects might tend to be older, more intelligent, stronger, etc. Biased judgments tend to be more positive, or more negative, than some reference population of judgments. A **biased estimator** is a statistic, such as a sample variance, which tends to underestimate, or to overestimate, a population parameter. (*See also* Experimenter Bias; Response Bias; Sampling Bias.)

Biased Estimator   *See* Bias.

Biased Sample   *See* Sampling Bias.

Bimodal Distribution   *See* Mode.

Binary   Describing any event having two possible values. For example, a binary sequence is a sequence of two kinds of things, such as lefts and rights; a binary choice is a choice between two options; a binary number is a number in the binary system (expressed as a series of 0s and 1s).

Binary Digit   *See* Bit.

Binomial Distribution   *See* Multinomial Distribution.

Binomial Test   Any statistical test for which the null and alternative hypotheses can be expressed in terms of the probability of occurrence of one of the two values of a dichotomous variable and for which exact probabilities are computed from the binomial formula or approximated by the normal or χ^2 distributions. The test statistics for the approximate tests are $z = (O_1 - Np)/\sqrt{Npq}$ or

$$\chi^2 = \frac{(O_1 - Np)^2}{Np} + \frac{(O_2 - Nq)^2}{Nq}$$

where O_1 is the obtained frequency of one value of the variable, p is the hypothesized probability of that value, O_2 is the obtained frequency of the other value, $q = 1 - p$, and N is the total number of observations $(O_1 + O_2)$. The χ^2 statistic has one degree of freedom. (*See also* Correction for Continuity.)

Bisection *See* Equisection, Method of.

Biserial Correlation Coefficient (*symb.* r_b, r_{bis}) An index of the degree of correlation between two continuous variables, when one has been reduced to a dichotomy. Examples of dichotomized variables include performance test scores reduced to pass versus fail or above the median versus below the median, anxiety test scores reduced to pathological versus nonpathological, etc. The statistic estimates what the correlation coefficient would be if the second variable had not been dichotomized.

EXAMPLE: A researcher is interested in the correlation between scores on an aptitude test and performance in a training course, but the only measure of performance available is whether the student passed or failed. For computing the biserial correlation, the relevant data are the following: the proportion of students who passed the course was $p = .86$, and the proportion who failed was $q = .14$; the mean aptitude score for those who passed was $\overline{X}_p = 65$, and the mean aptitude score for those who failed was $\overline{X}_q = 50$; the standard deviation of the aptitude scores for all of the students was $s = 10$. The computation also requires the y-ordinate (height of the curve) at a point that divides the normal distribution into two portions, one part equal to the proportion passing (.86) and the other equal to the proportion failing (.14). This value is found in many tables of the normal distribution; for this problem it is $y = .2227$. The biserial correlation now can be computed as follows:

$$r_b = \frac{\overline{X}_p - \overline{X}_q}{s} \times \frac{pq}{y} = \frac{65 - 50}{10} \times \frac{(.86)(.14)}{.2227} = .81$$

Bit In information theory, a unit of measurement of information and of uncertainty; the term "bit" is a contraction of "binary digit." (*For an example see* Information.)

Bivariate Distribution The joint distribution of pairs of observations on the same subject or on subjects matched in some manner (e.g., litter mates). In correlational research, it usually is assumed that the pairs of values are sampled from a *bivariate normal distri-*

bution, meaning that for any selected value of one variable, the values of the other variable are normally distributed. For example, if height and weight have a bivariate normal distribution, the weights of all people of a specified height would be normally distributed and the heights of all people of a specified weight would be normally distributed. (*See also* Scattergram.)

Bivariate Statistics Descriptive and inferential statistical procedures, such as correlation, designed for use when the analysis involves two dependent measures on each subject, or one measure on a matched pair of subjects. (*See also* Multivariate Statistics; Univariate Statistics.)

Blank Trial (1) A trial in which a subject's behavior is not recorded, or from which the data are not used. Often these serve as filler or buffer trials between critical trials. (2) A trial in which a subject is given no information that would indicate whether a response made was either correct or incorrect. (3) In psychophysics, a trial on which no stimulus is given.

Blind Assessment *See* Blind Procedure.

Blind Procedure Any procedure designed to ensure that subjects and/or experimenters are not aware of the true nature of the treatment being administered or assessed. The procedure is designed to reduce the influence of experimenter or subject bias, or placebo effects. In a **single-blind** procedure, the subjects remain uninformed about the purpose of the experiment and the particular treatment given them. In a **double-blind** procedure neither the subject nor the experimenter(s) administering the treatment or assessing its effect knows the assignment of subjects to treatments. In a double-blind drug study, for example, dosage levels and placebos would be coded and the code would be known only to those researchers not directly involved in treatment administration or data collection.

Blind Scoring *See* Blind Procedure.

Block A group or set of things that are in some way treated as a unit. A block may be defined temporally (e.g., a block of trials), spatially (e.g., an area in the field of vision), or in terms of some common property (e.g., a block of subjects).

Block Design *See* Treatment-By-Blocks Design.

Block of Trials *See* Trial Block.

Block Randomization A means by which a series of events is arranged to ensure that each event occurs with equal frequency in any segment of an experimental session. Each event occurs n times before any event may occur $n + 1$ times (using a new randomized order). Additional series or blocks may be added to provide any desired number of repetitions of the events. The method may be used to assign subjects to different experimental groups as the subjects report to an experiment, to ensure relatively equal sample sizes throughout an experiment. (*See also* Counterbalancing; Order Effect; Randomized-Blocks Design; Restricted Randomization.)

EXAMPLE: (1) Treatment conditions A, B, C, and D are to be administered to a subject five times each. The four conditions are arranged in a random order for Block 1 (e.g., CDAB). Then all four conditions are randomized again to form Block 2 (BACD). The procedure is repeated until five blocks have been formed. This entire sequence of 20 treatments then is administered to the subject.

(2) In an experiment containing three groups, subjects are scheduled to report to the laboratory at regular intervals throughout the day. Simple random assignment of the subjects to groups as they arrive allows for the unlikely possibility that one group may have a disproportionate number of subjects at any given time during the study. The possibility thus exists of confounding the treatment variable with the time of day the subjects were run. To avoid this, the first subject to arrive is randomly assigned to one of the groups, the second is randomly assigned to one of the remaining groups, and the third is assigned to the last remaining group. The procedure is repeated throughout the experiment.

Block Sampling *See* Area Sampling.

Blocked Presentation Presenting a block (series) of items of one type and then a block of a different type, intermingling items of different types. A block may include all or only part of the items from a class.

EXAMPLE: Patterns of high (H), medium (M), or low (L) complexity are to be rated on attractiveness. Twenty patterns of each type are constructed and randomly divided into four blocks of five designs each. Then the sequence of blocks is randomly determined, for example, L, H, M, H, L, H, M, M, L. A subject then would rate, one at a time, five designs of low complexity, then five designs of high complexity, etc. The blocks each could have included all 20 of the designs of each type, or there could have been two blocks of 10 designs of each type.

Blocking Variable In a block design, a subject variable or response variable used for forming blocks of subjects. For example, weight may be used as a blocking variable in an experiment concerned with the effect of body weight on food preference. Equal numbers of subjects may be chosen from the classifications "underweight," "normal," and "overweight," or the assignment of subjects to conditions may be block randomized on the basis of weight. (*See also* Randomized-Block Design.)

Body Weight Schedule   *See* Deprivation Schedule.

Bogardus Scale   *See* Social Distance Scale.

Bonferroni *t* Statistic (*syn.* Dunn's Procedure)   A procedure for a posteriori tests that divides the level of significance (α) evenly among the planned comparisons. The critical value for the tests is obtained from special tables.

Boring's Mother-in-Law   *See under* Illusions.

Boundary Condition   A limiting condition; one of the values that specifies the circumstances for which a prediction is valid, or within which a relationship is true. The values selected for controlled extraneous variables form the boundary conditions for an experiment and specify the conditions to which the results of an experiment can be validly generalized.

***b*-Reaction Time**   *See* Reaction Time.

Buffer Trial   *See* Blank Trial.

***b* Weight**   *See* b Coefficient.

Byte   In computer terminology, a unit used primarily to describe the size or capacity of memory storage. Usually, a byte is 6 to 8 bits in length and corresponds to a single character (letter, numeral, or other symbol).

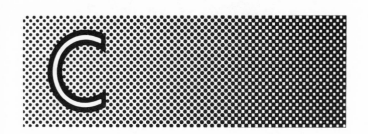

Canonical Correlation   A statistical procedure that correlates two sets of variables with each other. One set, consisting of two or more X variables, may be considered predictor variables, and the other set, consisting of two or more Y variables, may be considered criterion variables. For example, an experimenter may administer several personality tests, measure different aspects of dating behavior, and then correlate the two groups of measures. The personality tests could be considered predictor variables, and the measures of dating behavior could be considered criterion variables. Canonical correlation methods find the pairs of linear combinations of these two sets of variables that are maximally correlated; a pair consists of a linear combination of X variables and a linear combination of Y variables, correlated over subjects. Each linear combination is called a **canonical variate.**

Canonical Variate   *See* Canonical Correlation.

Carryover Effect (*syn.* Multiple Treatment Interference; Residual Effect)   Any temporary or permanent change in the subject's behavior from prior exposure to one or more experimental procedures that may contaminate or otherwise modify the subject's performance in a subsequent experimental treatment. For example, the effects of a drug administered in one session may partially carry over to a no-drug control session to influence the subject's behavior there. Other types of carryover effects include warm-up, practice, and fatigue effects.

Case History   *See* Case Study.

Case Study (*syn.* Case History)   The collection of data on a single individual or single social unit (e.g., family group), using all available evidence from records, observations, and interviews.

Causal Relationship An association between an antecedent condition (Event A) and a consequence (Event B) such that if A occurs, then B will occur.

CCC *See* Trigram.

Ceiling Effect *See* Ceiling/Floor Effect.

Ceiling/Floor Effect A restraint on the upper limit (ceiling) or lower limit (floor or basement) that the value of a dependent variable can take and that produces a skewed distribution.

EXAMPLE: A moderately difficult test of mathematical concepts is given to a group of advanced math majors and to a group of entering English majors. For the advanced math majors a ceiling effect will occur if the test is too easy, so that a large number obtain perfect scores. On the other hand, a floor effect will occur if the test is too advanced for the entering English majors, so that a large number obtain scores of zero.

Cell The portion of a data table or other matrix formed by the intersection of a level from each of two or more variables. (*For an example see* Contingency Table.)

Cell Entry The value entered in a cell of a data table. (*For an example see* Contingency Table.)

Census Data Data obtained from a survey. The most common census data are age, sex, income, residence, and the like.

Centile *See* Percentile.

Centile Rank *See* Percentile Rank.

Central Tendency, Measure of Any of several measures of average or general magnitude of the scores in a distribution; a statistic that represents a "typical" score. These measures locate the distribution on a continuum from − infinity to + infinity. The most common measures of central tendency are the arithmetic mean, the median, and the mode.

Centroid In multivariate statistics, a single value representing the average profile over a set of variables for a group, analogous to the mean. The term also is used to describe a set (vector) of means on each of the variables.

Centroid Method A method for extracting factors in factor analysis.

Chained Schedule of Reinforcement (*abbr.* Chain) An operant conditioning procedure in which the requirements of two or more component schedules of reinforcement must be met sequentially before reinforcement is delivered. A single manipulandum is used, and each schedule is accompanied by a discriminative stimulus. (*See also* Tandem Schedule of Reinforcement.)

EXAMPLE: An operant chamber is programmed to deliver reinforcement to a pigeon pecking a lighted key on a chained fixed-interval 1-min; fixed-ratio-10 schedule. The animal must first make at least one response after 1 min has elapsed. This will initiate the fixed-ratio component schedule and change the color of the key. After 10 additional responses, reinforcement will be delivered.

Chance   *See* Probability.

Chance _____   *See* Random _____.

Chance Result   *See* Nonsignificant Results.

Chance Variation   *See* Random Error.

Change-Over Delay   In operant conditioning, a period of time during which reinforcement is not available. It is imposed when the subject changes from responding to one schedule of reinforcement or one manipulandum to responding to another schedule of reinforcement, or another manipulandum.

Change Score   *See* Difference Score.

Chi-Square Statistic (*symb.* χ^2)   Any of several test statistics that have a chi-square distribution:

1. The square of a unit normal *(z)* variable has a chi-square distribution with one degree of freedom; $z^2 = \chi^2(1)$.
2. For testing a hypothesis about the variance (σ^2) of a normally distributed population, the test statistic $s^2(n-1)/\sigma_0^2$ has a chi-square distribution with $n-1$ degrees of freedom. (s^2 is the variance estimate for a sample of n observations and σ_0^2 is the hypothesized value of σ^2.)
3. For categorized data, a chi-square statistic is obtained by summing the squared differences between observed and expected frequencies, each squared difference being divided by the expected frequency:

$$\chi^2 = \Sigma \frac{(O-E)^2}{E}.$$

This statistic has an approximate chi-square distribution, with degrees of freedom that depend on the particular test. (*See also* Goodness-of-Fit Test; Independence, Test for.)

Choice Experiment   Any experiment situation in which the subject's task is to select from among two or more alternative stimuli or responses. (*See also* Decision.)

Choice Reaction Time   *See* Reaction Time.

Classical Conditioning (*syn*. Pavlovian Conditioning; Respondent Conditioning; Type S Conditioning; *contr*. Instrumental Conditioning)   The repeated pairing of one stimulus (conditioned stimulus or CS) with a second stimulus that reliably elicits a response (the unconditioned response or UR). Classical conditioning occurs when the first stimulus elicits a response (the conditioned response or CR) similar to the UR. Typically, the CS precedes the second stimulus (unconditioned stimulus or US) by a brief period of time.

EXAMPLE: Apparatus is arranged so that a brief puff of air (US) can be delivered to a subject's eye, producing an eye blink (UR). The apparatus also sounds a tone (CS) briefly. A number of trials are given in which the tone precedes the puff by 1 sec. A conditioned response (CR) is said to occur when the subject shows a partial or complete closure of the eyelid any time after the tone comes on but before the puff is given (an anticipatory response). Alternatively, a test trial may be given in which the tone is sounded but not followed by the puff. A partial or complete eye blink during the interval when the puff would have been given also is considered a CR.

Class Interval (*symb. i*)   The width of interval used when making a frequency distribution for grouped data. For example, a distribution of IQ scores might use intervals of . . . 80–89, 90–99, 100–109, . . . etc. The upper and lower numerical values of a class interval (e.g., 90 and 99) are termed the **class limits, apparent limits,** or **stated limits.** It is generally assumed, however, that each interval actually extends a half unit below the lower apparent limit and a half unit above the upper apparent limit, so that the **real limits,** or **exact limits,** of the interval would be 89.5–99.5. The width of the interval, i, is the difference between the upper and lower real limits of the interval, in this case, $99.5 - 89.5 = 10$ points.

Cloze Procedure   A procedure for measuring the comprehensibility of verbal material, or the redundancy (predictability) of the material. Every nth (e.g., every fifth) word is omitted from a passage, and the subject attempts to fill in the missing words.

Cluster Analysis   A multivariate statistical procedure similar to factor analysis, in which the principal interest is in identifying groups of subjects who perform in the same way on the tests, rather than in identifying groups of tests that measure the same factor. That is, cluster analysis determines profiles of scores on the various factors for different clusters of subjects (subjects who score similarly on the set of tests), rather than assuming that a single profile exists for all subjects.

Cochran's Test (*syn.* Cochran's *C*)   A test for homogeneity (equality) of variance that is especially sensitive when the variance of scores in one of the experimental treatments is notably larger than the variances of scores in the other experimental treatments. The test involves computing a value:

$$C = \frac{\text{largest } S_i^2}{\Sigma S_i^2}$$

where S_i^2 is the variance of the ith experimental treatment in a set of k treatments. The level of significance of the obtained value of C can be determined by comparing it with critical values shown in a special table. (*See also* Bartlett's Test; $F_{\max}$.)

Cochran's *Q* Test   A nonparametric test for differences among a set of items or tasks when each subject gets a score of 1 or 0 (pass–fail, yes–no) on each item. That is, it is used for a single-factor repeated-measures design with a dichotomous dependent variable.

Coding   (1) In statistics, the transformation of scores from a distribution into other values by such procedures as adding a constant to or subtracting a constant from each score, multiplying or dividing each score by a constant, etc. For example, z-scores are a coded form of the original values of X in a distribution, involving subtracting the mean of the distribution from each score and dividing the result by the standard deviation of the distribution. For any given distribution, the mean and standard deviation are constants. (2) In other contexts (e.g., information processing), the conversion of information from one form to another as it is passed along communication channels. For example, light reflected from the word "dance" is converted into neural impulses in the visual system, then perhaps coded again into an image related to dancing, perhaps into an auditory form of the sound of the word, and again into a verbal form if the word is read aloud. (*See also* Dummy Variable.)

Coding Test   A test of the ability to make symbolic transformation. For example, a person may be given two sets of symbols, numbers (1, 2, 3, etc.), and letters (A, B, C, etc.). After being informed about a systematic relationship between the two sets (e.g., 1 = A, 2 = B, 3 = C, etc.), the person is asked to perform various transformation tasks (e.g., translate CAB into numbers, spell out 321, etc.).

Coefficient Alpha   A measure of reliability based on internal consistency for tests in which the items are not scored dichotomously, such as rating scales. The formula is identical to the Kuder–Richardson Formula 20, except that the sum of the individual item variances, $\Sigma \sigma_i^2$, is used in place of Σpq.

Coefficient of _____ These entries are listed under their first significant word. (*For example, see* Coefficient of Alienation *as* Alienation, Coefficient of.)

Combination A group or subset selected from n different objects. The number of different combinations of r objects that can be formed is given by the formula $n!/r!(n - r)!$. The term $n!$ (n factorial) is defined as $n(n - 1)(n - 2) \ldots (2)(1)$.

EXAMPLE: Given a set of five colored stimuli—red, green, yellow, blue, and orange—there are $5!/2!3! = (5 \times 4 \times 3 \times 2 \times 1)/(2 \times 1)(3 \times 2 \times 1) = 10$ different pairs, that is, combinations of two colors, that can be formed: RG, RY, RB, RO GY, GB, GO YB, YO, and BO. The order of listing the objects in a combination is irrelevant; for example, red and blue is the same combination as blue and red. (*See also* Permutation.)

Common-Factor Variance In factor analysis, the variance in the scores on one of the variables (e.g., a test) that is due to factors that the variable has in common with other variables (e.g., other tests). (*See also* Communality; Specific Variance.)

Common Variance *See* Communality.

Communality In factor analysis, the proportion of variance in the scores on one of the variables (e.g., a test) that is common-factor variance, i.e., that is due to factors that the variable has in common with other variables (e.g., other tests). (*See also* Uniqueness.)

Comparison *See* Contrast.

Comparison Group *See* Control Group.

Comparison Stimulus (*syn.* Variable Stimulus) In psychophysics, the stimulus that is manipulated in order to match or otherwise be compared to the standard stimulus.

Compensatory Tracking Task (*contr.* Pursuit Tracking Task) A psychomotor task in which the subject attempts to keep a target in a fixed position; when the target deviates from this position, the subject operates a control to return it. For example, the subject may be asked to use a lever to keep a needle centered on a gauge. If the needle moves to the left, it can be returned to center by pushing the lever forward, and if it moves to the right, by pulling the lever back.

Complete Counterbalancing *See* Counterbalancing.

Completely Between-Groups Design *See* Randomized-Groups Design.

Completely Randomized Design *See* Randomized-Groups Design.

Complex Schedule of Reinforcement   Any operant conditioning procedure in which two or more basic schedules of reinforcement are in effect simultaneously, or successively. Complex schedules include compound schedules as well as schedules involving more than one manipulandum.

Composite Score   A test score that is the sum of the scores on the subtests that are components of the total test [*See also* Weight (ed).]

Compound Conditioning   A classical conditioning procedure in which the conditioned simulus (CS) is composed of two or more distinct elements.

EXAMPLE: The onset of a pure tone is accompanied by an increase in room light intensity. This *CS compound* is followed by the unconditioned stimulus. After a number of such trials, each element of the compound (tone or light) is presented alone to assess the ability of each to evoke conditioned responses. (*See also* Sensory Preconditioning.)

Compound Schedule of Reinforcement   Any operant conditioning procedure in which a response on a single manipulandum is reinforced according to the requirements of two or more different schedules of reinforcement. Examples include mixed and multiple schedules of reinforcement.

Comprehension Test   A type of test that measures aptitude or achievement. As an aptitude test, it measures the appropriateness of reactions to given situations (e.g., What should you do if you are about to cross the street and suddenly hear a siren?). As an achievement test, it features selected questions about a printed passage to assess the degree of the reader's comprehension of that passage.

Concept Formation Task   A task in which the subject is presented a number of stimuli that may be classified on any of several dimensions. The subject may be given all of the stimuli and asked to find some basis for sorting them into categories; the stimuli may be arranged in categories and the subject asked to identify the basis; or the subject may be given examples of a category and asked to say if new stimuli belong to the same category. For example, if subjects were given the words "fork," "stone," "pen," "putty," "knife," and "butter," they might choose to categorize them in terms of number of letters, words that contain the letter *n* and those that do not, or things that go on the dinner table and things that do not. Alternatively, the subjects might be told that *fork, pen,* and *knife* are in one category, and *stone, putty,* and *butter* are in another, in which case *sharp* and *dull* might be identified as the basis for classification. If subjects are told that *fork, pen,* and *knife* are examples of a category, they would say that *stone* belongs to the same category if they were using the concept *hard things,* and they would say that stone does not belong if they were using the concept *sharp things.*

Concomitant Variable (*syn.* Covariate) Any variable that covaries (is correlated) with the dependent variable of interest to the experimenter. In the analysis of covariance, it is the variable whose effect on the dependent variable is controlled statistically rather than experimentally. For example, in a study of extinction under different conditions, amount of learning at the start of extinction is an important concomitant variable.

Concordance, Coefficient of *(symb. W)* A measure of the agreement between several different rankings of a number of objects, which ranges from 0 (no agreement) to 1 (perfect agreement). For example, subjects (judges) may be asked to rank a set of photographs in order of attractiveness. A high value of W would indicate that the judges tend to agree on the ranking of attractiveness. The coefficient of concordance is computed by the formula

$$W = \frac{12 \Sigma T^2}{m^2 N (N^2 - 1)} - \frac{3(N+1)}{N-1}$$

where m is the number of judges, N is the number of objects being ranked, and the Ts are the sums of the ranks for each of the objects.

Concurrent Chained Schedule of Reinforcement (*abbr.* CONC Chain) An operant conditioning procedure in which the requirements of two different chained schedules of reinforcement are in force simultaneously, each one on a different manipulandum. Responding on one manipulandum does not affect the requirements of the schedule associated with the other manipulandum until the requirements of one chained schedule are completed. Then the other manipulandum becomes inoperative.

EXAMPLE: An operant chamber is programmed so that a chained variable-interval 1-min–variable-ratio-25 schedule of reinforcement is in effect on the left lever. A rat, therefore, must make one bar press after an average of 1 min, followed by an average of 25 responses on this lever to obtain reinforcement. Concurrently, a chained variable-interval 1-min–fixed-ratio-25 schedule is in effect on the right bar. Reinforcement will be given on this bar for making one response after an average of 1 min, followed by 25 additional responses. When all the requirements are satisfied for one bar, the other bar will become inoperative, and the cue light associated with it will be extinguished.

Concurrent Schedule of Reinforcement (*abbr.* CONC) An operant conditioning procedure in which the requirements of two different schedules of reinforcement are in force at the same time, each on a different manipulandum. A response pattern that satisfies the requirements of either schedule will produce a reinforcement.

EXAMPLE: An operant chamber is programmed so that fixed-ratio-10 schedule of reinforcement is in force on the left lever and a variable-ratio-8 schedule is in effect on the right lever. If a rat presses the left lever 10 times or the right lever an average of 8 times, a food pellet will be delivered.

Concurrent Validity   The extent to which a test correlates highly with an accepted measure of the construct under study. For example, a new short-form test for intelligence has concurrent validity when it yields scores that are similar (not necessarily identical) to those of a more established and comprehensive measure (e.g., the Stanford-Binet intelligence test).

Condition (*syn.* Experimental Condition)   In an experiment with two or more factors (independent variables), a combination of one level or value of each of the factors with any one level or value of another factor (*For an example see* Factorial Design.) The term may also refer to a value or level of the independent variable in a single factor design. (*See also* Treatment.)

Conditional Probability   The probability that an event will occur given the prior or simultaneous occurrence of another event. Given two events, A and B, the conditional probability of B with respect to A is expressed $P(B|A)$ and is read as the probability of B occurring given that A has occurred, or more simply as the probability of B given A. It is defined as $P(B|A) = P(A$ and $B/P(A)$, where $P(A$ and $B)$ is the joint probability of the occurrence of both A and B, and $P(A)$ is the unconditional probability of the occurrence of A. Similarly, the conditional probability of the occurrence of A with respect to B is $P(A|B) = P(A$ and $B/P(B)$. (*See also* Independence; Joint Probability.)

Conditional Response   *See* Conditioned Response.

Conditional Stimulus   *See* Conditioned Stimulus.

Conditioned Reinforcement (*syn.* Learned Reinforcement; Secondary Reinforcement; *contr.* Primary Reinforcement)   Presentation of a stimulus event whose reinforcing capability has been acquired through learning, that is, by its association with another reinforcer. Examples include the sounds associated with delivery of food to a hungry organism, a tone that signals the termination of electric shock, the receipt of money or praise, etc.

Conditioned Response (*abbr.* CR; *syn.* Conditional Response)   As a general term, any learned response. In classical conditioning, the learned response evoked by the conditioned stimulus.

Conditioned Stimulus (*abbr.* CS; *syn.* Conditional Stimulus) In classical conditioning, a stimulus that is paired with, or precedes, the unconditioned stimulus. It initially is neutral with respect to the response to be conditioned.

Conditioned Suppression/Facilitation A procedure in which a respondent behavior (e.g., a classically conditioned response) is inferred from the degree to which its stimulus modifies the rate of a steadily performed operant response.

EXAMPLE: To demonstrate suppression, a rat is given a series of classical conditioning trials in which a tone is followed by an electric shock to the feet. Separately, the animal also is trained to press a bar for food reinforcement on a very high ratio schedule of reinforcement (e.g., a VR 40 schedule) until a very steady pattern of bar pressing is established. If classical conditioning has occurred, presentation of the tone CS while the rat is bar pressing will result in some degree of disruption (suppression) of bar pressing. The amount of disruption is used as a measure of the aversiveness of the tone.

Conditioning A general term that refers to classical conditioning or to instrumental (operant) conditioning.

Confidence Interval A range of numerical values that, with some specified probability, contains the true value of a population parameter, such as a mean, a standard deviation, a proportion, etc. The confidence interval is determined from data obtained from a sample taken from the population. The numerical values of the upper and lower boundaries of the confidence interval are referred to as **confidence limits.** The 95% and 99% confidence intervals are commonly determined, meaning that the probability is .95 and .99, respectively, that the interval contains the true value of the parameter.

EXAMPLE: In a state poll, a random sample of 1200 voters shows that .54 (54%) favor a certain issue. Appropriate computations show that the 99% confidence interval derived from these data is .503–.577. Thus, the probability is .99 that this interval contains the true proportion of all voters in the state who favor the issue. Since the lower limit exceeds .50 (50%), officials can be quite confident that a majority of voters in the state favor the issue.

Confidence Limits *See* Confidence Interval.

Confidence Rating In a signal detection task, a subject's indication of the degree of confidence in reaching a decision that a weak signal was or was not presented on a given trial.

EXAMPLE: Using the "Yes–No" procedure, on each trial a subject must respond "Yes," the signal was present, or "No," the signal was not present. Since the signal is weak relative to the background level of noise, there is uncertainty on many trials. On each trial the subject must not only decide "Yes" or "No" but give a numerical index of confidence in either decision on a scale of 0–2, where 0 indicates very low confidence, 1 indicates moderate confidence, and 2 indicates a high degree of confidence.

Configural Conditioning *See* Compound Conditioning.

Conformity Procedure An experimental procedure in which subjects are first presented with prearranged responses from other actual or fictional subjects to a set of stimuli and then measured for their responses to the same stimuli. (*For an example of such stimuli see* Asch-Type Stimuli.)

Confounded Designs A general term for experimental designs in which one or more combinations of the levels of the independent variables is omitted, so that one or more main effect and/or interaction is uninterpretable. Usually the term is reserved for complex designs involving deliberate confounding to limit the size of the experiment. In this case, the main effects and interactions of interest to the experimenter can be obtained from the analysis, while the confounded effects appear as pooled or residual effects. General procedures for confounding have been developed, and specific plans for experiments of various sizes (depending on the number of factors and number of levels of each) have been drawn up. In addition to the Latin and Graeco-Latin square designs, the most common classes of confounded designs include **quasi-Latin square, plaid square,** and **half-plaid square** designs; **fractional factorial designs;** and **balanced** and **partially balanced incomplete blocks designs,** including **lattice designs** and **Youden square** and other **incomplete Latin square designs.**

Confounding The presence of one or more extraneous variables that vary *systematically* with the independent variable(s) under investigation. Confounding variables destroy the internal validity of an experiment and render it such that cause–effect relationships between independent and dependent variables are difficult or impossible to infer. (*See also* Internal Validity)

EXAMPLE: An experimenter administers a standard achievement test to a group of high school juniors at the beginning of the school year, introduces a new method of teaching, and then tests the group again at the end of the year. If there is a statistically significant difference between the pre- and posttest measures, it is attributed to the manipulation of the independent variable (new teaching method). However, several other events could have varied systematically in the interim to affect the internal validity of the study. Among them are:

1. Historical events inside or outside of the school environment, such as a labor dispute or a flu epidemic, could have critically affected the students' progress during the school year.

2. Maturational changes may have occurred affecting subsequent performance of the students under study.
3. A practice effect derived from the pretest measure may carry over to the posttest measure and thus confound the results.
4. The experimenter(s) themselves, or the instruments that they use, may have undergone changes in the interim.
5. Some students are lost for posttest measurements because they have dropped out of school.

Confusion Matrix A table showing the frequencies with which each of a set of stimuli is responded to appropriately and the frequencies with which each stimulus is responded to inappropriately.

EXAMPLE: Table C–1 presents a confusion matrix for 60 subjects. Each subject was given a set of five letters, exposed individually for brief periods of time, and asked to identify the letter. The matrix shows, for example, that A was always identified correctly (60/60), whereas X elicited a number of incorrect responses and frequently was confused with Y.

Table C–1

		Response given					
		V	A	X	Y	N	Total
	V	53	0	2	1	4	60
	A	0	60	0	0	0	60
Stimulus	X	3	1	44	12	0	60
presented	Y	0	0	8	51	1	60
	N	0	1	0	1	58	60
	Total	56	62	54	65	63	300

Conjoint Schedule of Reinforcement (*abbr.* Conjt) An operant conditioning procedure in which two or more different schedules of reinforcement are in effect simultaneously for the same response. The organism receives reinforcement whenever the requirements of either schedule are met. Meeting the requirements of one schedule does not modify the status of the other schedule.

EXAMPLE: An operant chamber is programmed to deliver food pellets to a rat pressing a bar on a conjoint fixed-ratio 10, fixed-interval 30-sec (CONJT FR–10, FI–30) schedule of reinforcement. Thus, a food pellet will be delivered after every 10th response and after the first response made 30 sec or more following a previous reinforcement.

Conjunctive Concept A concept that is defined by the joint presence of two properties. (*See also* Disjunctive Concept.)

EXAMPLE: The concept *pen* is a conjunctive concept, since an object must both be a writing implement and use ink in order to be called a pen. If it is a writing implement but does not use ink it may be a pencil, engraver, etc.; if it uses ink but is not a writing implement, it may be a rubber stamp, mimeograph machine, etc.

Conjunctive Schedule of Reinforcement (abbr. Conj)   An operant conditioning procedure in which the requirements of two or more different schedules of reinforcement, in force simultaneously, must be met in order to receive reinforcement. A response, or sequence of responses, may partially satisfy the requirements of either one or both schedules.

EXAMPLE: An operant chamber is programmed so that a fixed-ratio 50, fixed-interval 3-min schedule of reinforcement is in effect. In order to obtain a food pellet, a rat must press a bar 50 times, with at least one of the 50 responses occurring 3 min or more after the previous reinforcement.

Constant   A numerical value that remains the same, at least within the context of a given problem. For example, in the formula for a z score $z = (X - \overline{X})/s$, $\overline{X}$ and s represent the mean and standard deviation of a sample and are constant only for that particular sample. There are also absolute constants whose values remain the same regardless of the context in which they appear. For example, pi (π) has the same value in any formula in which it is used. (*See also* Data Transformation.)

Constant Error (*contr.* Random Error)   A consistent overestimation or underestimation in judging a stimulus. Illusions provide good examples in that nearly all observers are subject to them. For example, when adjusting a horizontal line to appear equal in length to an adjacent vertical line, nearly all observers will set it to be longer than the vertical line, although the magnitude of this constant error may differ for different observers.

Constant Stimuli, Method of   A psychophysical method used to determine absolute and difference thresholds. It is characterized by the fact that the subject deals with a fixed set of stimuli varying in graduated steps over a particular range of stimulus values presented in random order. (*See also* Limits, Method of.)

EXAMPLE 1: Absolute Threshold   A series of stimuli is presented in random sequence to a subject one at a time, and the subject is asked to report whether or not the stimulus is present. Stimuli in the series range in intensity from well below to well above the intensity needed to be detected. The proportion of times that each stimulus elicits a "Yes" response, meaning that the subject has detected its presence, is determined. By suitable graphic or statistical procedures, the magnitude of the stimulus that would elicit a "Yes" response 50% of the time can be determined, and this magnitude defines the absolute threshold for that subject.

EXAMPLE 2: Difference Threshold   The subject compares a standard stimulus of given intensity a number of times with each of several comparison stimuli whose intensities range in graduated steps from well below to well above that of the standard. On each trial the subject is given the standard stimulus and a randomly selected comparison stimulus and is asked to judge which is the greater. The proportion of times that each of the comparison stimuli is judged greater than the standard is determined. By suitable graphic or statistical procedures, the magnitudes of the stimuli that the subject judges reliably to be greater than the standard and less than the standard can be determined, and the difference between these intensities and that of the standard constitute the upper and lower difference thresholds, respectively. The difference threshold typically is reported as the average of the upper and lower difference thresholds.

Construct Validity   The extent to which scores are consistent with theoretical expectations. For example, if one wishes to validate a new test for political conservatism, it is possible to correlate scores from that test with scores from a well-established test for authoritarianism. On the theoretical assumption that authoritarian people also are politically conservative, scores on the authoritarian test should correlate highly with scores on the test of conservatism.

Contamination   (1) The introduction of bias and/or random error into a set of data such that the relationships among various treatment means are either distorted or obscured. (2) Confounding.

Content Analysis   The systematic assessment of the manifest content of communications. The assessment involves standardized procedures for the analysis of written, oral, musical, or gestural communications. Content analyses are useful for research if for some reason it is impossible to obtain opportunities for direct observations.

EXAMPLE: An investigator wishes to study the cultural patterns (attitudes, interests, and values) that are typical of a country inaccessible because of political and/or economic reasons. The country's mass-media content is assessed by counting the number of newspaper pages or column inches, length of footage, minutes of radio and TV time dedicated to various issues. Statistical analyses are conducted in order to establish which issues are predominant in the country's cultural pattern.

Content Validity (*contr.* Empirical Validity)   The extent to which test items cover the content area the test purports to measure. In achievement tests, for example, content validity is of critical importance. A math test for junior high school students containing advanced calculus items, overloaded with simple multiplication tables, or containing long and complex questions (which may be affected by reading ability) would appear to have poor content validity. (*See also* Construct Validity; Face Validity.)

Contingency Coefficient *(symb. C)* A measure of association between two variables that is sometimes used in conjunction with a test of independence for a two-way contingency table:

$$C = \sqrt{\frac{\chi^2}{N + \chi^2}}$$

where N is the total number of observations and χ^2 is the computed value of the χ^2 statistic. The statistic C varies from 0 (no association) to a maximum value that depends on the number of categories for the two variables but that cannot exceed 1. (*See also* Cramer's Statistic; Phi Coefficient.)

Contingency Table A data table that shows the number, or frequency, of observations in each of the cells formed by the intersection of different levels of two or more classification variables.

EXAMPLE: Table C–2 shows the frequency of men and women college students who classed their attitude toward extrasensory perception (ESP) into one of three levels—"More Disbelieve than Believe," "Completely Neutral," or "More Believe than Disbelieve." Since there are two levels of sex and three levels of attitude, the table consists of $2 \times 3 = 6$ cells. The six *cell entries* of 18, 23, . . . , 121, show the frequencies of students of each sex expressing each of the attitudes.

Table C–2 Attitude Toward ESP

	More Disbelieve	Neutral	More Believe	Total
Male	18	23	75	116
Female	17	40	121	178
Total	35	63	196	294

Contingent Reinforcement (*contr.* Noncontingent Reinforcement) Reinforcement that is delivered only after a specified response is made. For example, to reinforce a pigeon for pecking a green key, the reinforcement is delivered only when a green key is pecked and never after any other response.

Continuous Reinforcement (*contr.* Partial Reinforcement) (1) (abbr. CRF) In instrumental (operant) conditioning, a procedure in which every correct response is reinforced. (2) In classical conditioning, a procedure in which the conditioned stimulus is always followed by the unconditioned stimulus. (*See also* Reinforcement Schedules.)

Continuous Variable (*contr.* Discrete Variable) A variable that may take on any of an infinite number of values. For example, intensity of a tone may be of any value in the decibel scale.

Contrast (*syn.* Comparison) In the analysis of variance, a technique for comparing differences among means, used for either a priori or a posteriori tests. A contrast is a weighted sum of treatment means in which the sum of the weights is zero. For example, in an experiment with four treatment groups, $\overline{X}_1 - \overline{X}_2$ is a contrast with weights of $+1$, -1, 0, and 0, which compares the means of the first two groups. The contrast

$$\frac{(\overline{X}_1 + \overline{X}_2)}{2} - \frac{(\overline{X}_3 + \overline{X}_4)}{2}$$

has weights of $+\frac{1}{2}$, $+\frac{1}{2}$, $-\frac{1}{2}$, and $-\frac{1}{2}$ and compares the average level of the first two groups with the average of the last two groups. A distinction sometimes is made between a comparison of two group means and a contrast among more than two group means. (*See also* Multiple-Comparison Test; Orthogonal Contrast; Pairwise-Comparisons Test.)

Control Group A group of subjects selected in a way that makes them comparable to subjects in the experimental group(s), except that, unlike the latter, they are not exposed to the experimental treatment(s).

Control Group Method Any experimental procedure that employs one or more control groups.

Control Variable In research design, any variable other than the independent variable that is in any way controlled by the experimenter, by being eliminated, minimized, held constant, or explicitly randomized, or by using statistical control.

EXAMPLE: In an experiment on problem solving, extraneous noise can be eliminated by testing subjects in a soundproof room, minimized by testing in a quiet area, or held constant by providing white noise in the testing room. The effects of practice can be eliminated by giving all subjects a single problem to solve, held constant by giving the subjects the same number of problems in the same order, explicitly randomized by randomly determining the order of the problems for each subject, or controlled statistically by counterbalancing the order of problems and isolating the effects of order as a source in an analysis of variance.

Controlled Association *See* Association Test.

Conversion of Scores *See* Data Transformation.

Coordinates The ordered pair of x and y values that locate a point on the plane formed by a set of rectangular, or Cartesian, axes, or the ordered set of values that locate a point in space formed by three or more axes, where each axis is perpendicular to the others. Coordinates always are expressed by showing first the value of x, then y, then z if three dimensions are involved, with the values separated by commas and enclosed in parentheses.

EXAMPLE: Figure C–1 shows a set of Cartesian axes in which are located the points (3,2), (−2,3), and (−3,−2). The point (3,2) is located by moving along the x-axis three units to the right of the origin at 0, then going two units parallel to the y-axis, and thus perpendicularly away from the x-axis at $x = 3$. The point (3,2) is thus located at the point of intersection of imaginary perpendiculars located in the xy-plane and passing through $x = 3$ and $y = 2$. Points (−2,3) and (−3, −2) are located in a similar manner.

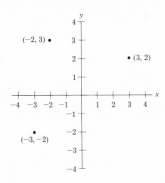

Figure C–1

Correct Rejection   *See* Decision.

Correction for Continuity (*syn.* Yates' Correction for Continuity)   A modification of the computed test statistic when the data are frequencies. It may be used when either the normal *(z)* distribution or a χ^2 distribution with one degree of freedom is used to approximate the binomial distribution (e.g., for a binomial test or test for independence), especially when one or more expected frequency is small. The correction consists in subtracting .5 from the absolute value of each difference between observed and expected frequencies.

Correction Term   In the analysis of variance, the grand total of all the observations in the analysis, squared and divided by the total number of observations. It appears in the computation of every main effect and interaction sum of squares.

Correlated-Groups Design   *See* Correlated-Measures Design; Matched-Groups Design.

Correlated-Measures Design   A general term that may refer to either a randomized-blocks design or a repeated-measures design.

Correlated-Proportions Test (*syn.* McNemar Test; Test for Significance of Changes)   A significance test for paired samples classified on the same dichotomous variable. For example, the same subjects may be classified before and after some experimental treatment as to whether their attitudes on a particular topic are positive or negative; or husbands and wives may be classified as to whether they are above or below the median on some measure, such as a personality scale. The pairs of data usually are displayed in a two-by-two contingency table. The test, however, only considers the cases in which there is a change or disagreement, and in most applications it is identical to the sign test. A binomial test is used to test the null hypothesis that the probability of a change or difference in either direction is equal to .5. Computational formulas are usually given as

$$\chi^2 = \frac{(a-d)^2}{(a+d)} \quad \text{or} \quad \chi_c^2 = \frac{(|a-d|-1)^2}{(a+d)}$$

where a and d are the obtained frequencies in the two categories of change or difference. The statistic χ_c^2 includes the correction for continuity.

Correlated Reinforcement   An instrumental conditioning procedure in which reinforcement is delivered in amounts that are directly or inversely related to a measure of response strength. Positively correlated reinforcement occurs when strong or intense responses are followed by large rewards and weak responses are followed by small rewards. **Negatively correlated reinforcement** is the opposite of this. (*See also* Differential Reinforcement of Rates.)

EXAMPLE: A rat runs down a straight alley for pellets of food reward. For each 0.5 sec of travel time an additional pellet becomes available. Thus reinforcement is negatively correlated with running speed; longer delays (slower speeds) incur larger rewards.

Correlation   A general term describing the relationship between two variables that are associated or covary. If the relationship is positive (**positive correlation**), large values of one variable tend to be associated with larger values of the other and small values with small; if the relationship is negative (**negative correlation**), large values of one variable tend to be associated with small values of the other. There are a number of statistics that provide a measure of the degree of correlation or association, designed for different types of data and experimental procedures. (*See also* Correlation Coefficient; Multiple Correlation.)

EXAMPLE: Factory workers are measured on a number of variables. Examination of the data shows that workers who are rated high by their co-workers on popularity tend also to be rated high by their supervisors on job skill and to have few on-the-job accidents. Workers who are rated lower on popularity tend to be rated lower on job skill and to have more accidents. Thus, there is a positive correlation between popularity and job skill and a negative correlation between popularity and accident proneness.

Correlation Coefficient (*symb.* ρ, r) In general, any index of the degree of relationship between two variables. Specifically, the correlation coefficient refers to the **Pearson product-moment correlation,** an index of the degree of linear relationship between two variables that are measured on an interval or ratio scale. Usually, the correlation is computed for a bivariate sample, that is, where the data consist of randomly sampled pairs of scores so that both variables are random. The Pearson correlation coefficient ranges from -1 (perfect negative linear relationship) through 0 (no linear relationship) to $+1$ (perfect positive linear relationship). It is defined as the covariance of the variables divided by the product of the standard deviations of the variables. Thus, for a bivariate population the true correlation is

$$\rho = \frac{\sigma_{xy}}{\sigma_x \sigma_y}$$

For samples the correlation coefficient is defined similarly, or in deviation form as

$$r_{xy} = \sqrt{\frac{\Sigma(X - \bar{X})(Y - \bar{Y})}{\Sigma(X - \bar{X})^2 \Sigma(Y - \bar{Y})^2}}$$

where X and Y are the observations on the two variables and $\bar{X}$ and $\bar{Y}$ are their respective means. (*See also* Biserial Correlation; Correlation Ratio; Point Biserial Correlation; Rank-Order Correlation; Scattergram; Tetrachloric Correlation.)

Correlation Matrix *See* Intercorrelation.

Correlation Ratio (*symb.* η) A measure of the degree of relationship between two variables. It reflects both linear and nonlinear relationships and cannot be less than the correlation coefficient r for the same data. However, its primary use is as a measure of **curvilinear (nonlinear) correlation,** when a graph of the means for the dependent variable or a scatter gram of the data suggest such a relationship. In a single-factor design, η is computed as the square root of the ratio of the between-groups sum of squares

45

to the total sum of squares. (The term **correlation ratio** sometimes is used for the statistic **eta squared.**)

Correlational Research (*contr.* Manipulative Research) Any research strategy that is designed to establish the degree of relationship between two or more variables, that is, the degree to which they covary, without actively manipulating the variables. For example, one might establish the extent to which subjects' scores on a general intelligence test are related to their scores on a test of abstract reasoning or the degree to which average daily low temperature and average rainfall are related to the frequency of common colds. (*See also* Nonmanipulative Research.)

Counterbalancing Any systematic (nonrandom) technique used to distribute various carryover effects so that they will not be confounded with the different experimental treatments. Complete counterbalancing can be achieved by presenting the treatments in all possible orders, thus assuring that each treatment occurs equally often at each position in the sequence (e.g., first, second, third, etc.), and also that each treatment precedes and follows all other treatments an equal number of times. (*See also* ABBA Sequence; Incomplete Counterbalancing; Latin Square Design.)

EXAMPLE: In a study of alcohol absorption rate, subjects must consume drinks with alcohol concentrations of 30, 60, or 90 proof. The subjects consume each drink in three sessions that are separated by 24 hours. To counterbalance any effects of residual alcohol, all possible orders of presentation of the three concentrations are used. There are $3! = 3 \times 2 \times 1 = 6$ possible orders, as shown in Table C–3. An equal number of subjects is assigned to each of the six possible orders.

Table C–3

Order	Sessions		
	1	2	3
1	30	60	90
2	30	90	60
3	60	30	90
4	60	90	30
5	90	30	60
6	90	60	30

Counterconditioning The extinction of one response and the reinforcement of a new, incompatible response as a substitute behavior.

Covariance (*symb.* σ_{xy}; S_{xy}) A measure of relationship between two variables. It is defined as the average (for a sample) or expected value (for a bivariate population) of the products of deviations of paired scores from their respective means. Symbolically, the population covariance is

$$\sigma_{xy} = E(X - \mu_x)(Y - \mu_y)$$

and the sample covariance is

$$S_{xy} = \frac{\Sigma (X - \overline{X})(Y - \overline{Y})}{N}$$

where X and Y are paired observations on the two variables, $\overline{X}$ and $\overline{Y}$ are their respective means, and N is the number of paired observations.

Covariance Analysis   *See* Analysis of Covariance.

Covariate   *See* Concomitant Variable.

Covert Response   *See* Overt/Covert Response.

CR   *See* Conditioned Response.

Cramer's Statistic *(symb.* ϕ', *C)* A measure of association for a two-way (rows by columns) contingency table, sometimes used in conjunction with a chi-square test of independence. The statistic ranges in value from 0 (no association) to 1 (complete association). It is defined as

$$\phi' = \sqrt{\frac{\chi^2}{N(S-1)}}$$

where χ^2 is the computed chi-square statistic for the test of independence, N is the total number of observations, and S is the smaller of the two values R, the number of rows in the table, and C, the number of columns in the table. (*See also* Contingency Coefficient; Phi Coefficient.)

CRF   *See under* Continuous Reinforcement.

Criterion Score   A score on the criterion variable, to be predicted from scores on other variables. (*See also* Criterion Variable.)

Criterion Variable   (1) In testing, the measure taken as the standard against which other measures (e.g., a new test) of the construct are validated. (2) A measure to be predicted from one or a combination of several predictor variables. (3) In experimental design, the dependent variable.

Critical Ratio   An infrequently used term for a z statistic.

Critical Region   *See* Rejection/Nonrejection Region.

Critical Score   *See* Cutting Score.

Critical Value   *See* Rejection/Nonrejection Region.

Cross-Cultural Method The systematic observation of social practices, values, environmental conditions, etc., in various cultures. For example, a common cross-cultural comparison involves the study of child-rearing practices in various cultures and their effects on individual behavior.

Cross-Lagged Correlation *See* Cross-Lagged Panel Correlation.

Cross-Lagged Panel Correlation A correlational technique that assumes that if certain coefficients of correlation of two variables are available at more than one time, one might infer some causal influence from one variable to another.

EXAMPLE: Figure C–2 shows a cross-lagged correlation panel. A group of high school sophomores was tested for mental ability and for social skills, and the scores are correlated (r_{12}). The same measures are obtained for the students when they are high school seniors (r_{34}). The vertical panel correlations r_{12} and r_{34} are *unlagged,* that is, there is no meaningful time lag between the administration of the two measures. On the other hand, r_{13} and r_{24} are *lagged* because of the time between sophomore and senior status. Both r_{13} and r_{23} are cross-lagged correlations; since r_{14} is significantly larger than r_{23}, it may be assumed that intelligence affects social skills. If r_{23} were larger than r_{14}, it might be assumed that social skills affect intelligence.

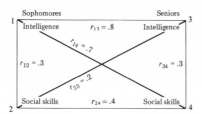

Figure C–2

Cross-Modality Matching Matching sensations from one sense with sensations from another sense. For example, subjects might be asked to adjust the brightness of a light until it is judged to be equivalent to the loudness of a tone, or to draw a line that is equal in length to the intensity of a shock.

Cross-Sectional Method (*contr.* Longitudinal Method) In developmental psychology, a research strategy in which selected characteristics of a wide variety of subjects from different populations are studied at a particular time.

Cross Tabulation   The tabulation of the number of cases that occur jointly in two or more categories, as in contingency tables.

Cross Validation   Evaluation of a prediction equation, discriminant function, etc., in a different sample than the one used for deriving the equation. A single sample may be randomly divided into two groups, with each group serving as the cross-validation sample for the other, or a new independent sample obtained for the purpose.

Crossing (*contr.* Nesting)   An arrangement of two variables in which each level of one variable is paired with every level of the other. In a factorial design, each independent variable is crossed with every other independent variable.

Crude Score   *See* Raw Score.

CS   *See* Conditioned Stimulus.

Cued Recall   A variant of free recall in which, during the test of retention, the subject is provided information that may help in reproducing verbal material that had been presented earlier. For example, a subject may be presented a list of words composed of members from different categories such as animals, vegetables, professions, etc. At the time of recall, the subject is provided the names of the categories as cues that may help in recall of the original words.

Culture-Fair Test   A test designed to minimize selective biases that could favor one culture, class, or group over another.

Culture-Free Test   An idealized version of a culture-fair test, in which, theoretically, all selective biases that could favor one culture, class, or group over another have been removed.

Cumulative Distribution   A distribution of scores showing the total frequency and/or the proportion falling at or below the successive scores in the distribution. The cumulative values for the frequencies or proportions are obtained by summing the frequencies or proportions, starting with the lowest score and moving up through each successive score to the highest score in the distribution.

EXAMPLE: Table C–4 shows scores *(X)* and the frequency *(f)* with which each score occurs. Each frequency is also expressed as a relative frequency or proportion *(p),* for example, the proportion of values of $X = 10$ is $4/50 = .08$. The *cumulative frequency* (cf) column shows the accumulated frequencies falling at and below each score, starting with the lowest score, and the *cumulative proportion* (cp) column shows the accumulated proportion of scores falling at and below each successive score.

Table C–4

X	f	cf	p	cp
10	4	50	.08	1.00
9	12	46	.24	.92
8	21	34	.42	.68
7	8	13	.16	.26
6	5	5	.10	.10
Total	50		1.00	

Cumulative Frequency   *See* Cumulative Distribution.

Cumulative Frequency Curve   A graphic representation of a cumulative distribution. (*For an example see* Cumulative Record.)

Cumulative Proportion   *See* Cumulative Distribution.

Cumulative Ratings, Method of   A test construction method in which items are arranged so that test takers who respond affirmatively to a given item will be likely to do so to all items of lower-rank order. (*See also* Reproducibility, Coefficient of.)

EXAMPLE: An investigation of attitudes toward socialized medicine may involve the following statements:

1. The socialization of medicine clearly is in the best interest of this country.
2. It probably is a good idea for this country to begin a program of socialized medicine.
3. Socialized medicine might in the long run prove beneficial to this country.

In this three-point cumulative scale, those who respond in the affirmative to item 1 are also likely to do so for items 2 and 3; and those who respond in the affirmative to item 2 are likely to do so for item 3. Affirmative responses in the opposite direction, however, are not likely to occur.

Cumulative Record   In operant conditioning, a graphic record of the total number of responses made by a subject at any point during an experimental session. Figure C–3 illustrates such a record. Each vertical displacement of the line represents one response. The horizontal segments indicate periods of inactivity. Thus, rate of responding can be measured by the slope of the record.

Cumulative Scale   *See* Cumulative Ratings, Method of.

Curve Fitting   *See* Regression Analysis.

Curvilinear Correlation   *See* Correlation Ratio.

Curvilinear Regression   *See* Nonlinear Regression.

Curvilinear Relationship   *See* Linear/Nonlinear Relationship.

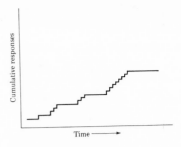

Figure C–3

Cutting Score   A single score that serves as a critical point for dividing an array of scores into two groups with reference to some criterion. For example, a university decides that the minimum requirement (cutting score) for admission (the criterion) is a combined Graduate Record Examination score of 1000, and a grade point average of 3.0. (*See also* Decision; Discriminant Analysis.)

CVC   *See* Trigram.

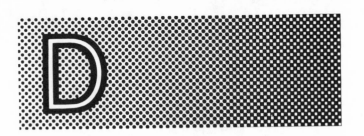

d' In signal detection, a measure of a subject's sensitivity to or skill at detecting the presence of a weak stimulus (signal) imposed on a background of interfering stimuli (noise). It is the difference between the mean of the signal distribution and the mean of the noise distribution divided by the standard deviation of the noise distribution and may vary between zero and infinity. (*See also* Signal Detection Task.)

Data (1) The collection of scores obtained when a subject's behavior is measured, (2) or the summary information on a topic.

Data Analysis The computational procedures of hypothesis testing and estimation; the step that follows data reduction and precedes interpretation.

Data Point A datum. The term is used primarily when referring to data that are plotted on a graph.

Data Protocol The record of a single individual's performance, as obtained in the data-gathering phase of research.

Data Reduction The process of obtaining raw scores from the raw data of the data protocol through consolidation, and of organizing, tabulating, and computing the descriptive statistics of these data.

Data Table An array of raw scores, usually arranged in a manner compatible with the analyses to be performed on the data.

Data Transformation Any procedure that changes all the values in a sample or a population by the same function. Data transformations are used primarily for one of three purposes:

1. To simplify computations. Linear transformations are used for this purpose. For example, data in grouped frequency distributions may be coded; a constant may be added to each score to eliminate negative values, a constant may be subtracted

to obtain smaller numbers, or the scores may be multiplied by a constant to eliminate decimals or fractions.

2. To obtain scores having a standardized distribution, that is, to obtain *standard scores*. Standard scores may be obtained in either of two ways.

   a. A linear transformation of the form $a + bY$ may be used to obtain scores having a specified mean and standard deviation. Commonly used transformations give a mean of 0 and a standard deviation of 1 (**z scores**), a mean of 50 and a standard deviation of 10 (**Z scores** or **T scores**), or a mean of 500 and a standard deviation of 100. **Deviation IQs** are standardized IQ scores with a mean of 100 and a standard deviation of approximately 15.

   b. A nonlinear normalizing transformation, based on percentiles of the normal distribution, may be used to obtain scores having a normal distribution in addition to specified mean and standard deviation. The most common of these are **T scores,** with a mean of 50 and a standard deviation of 10, and **stanine scores** (from *sta*ndard *nine*), consisting of appropriate percentages of the digits 1 through 9 to give a mean of 5 and a standard deviation of approximately 2.

3. To obtain a dependent variable that meets the assumptions required for statistical testing, or to obtain additivity of treatment effects in factorial experiments. Nonlinear transformations are used for this purpose. The following are the most frequently used transformations of the dependent variable Y. The modifications to be used when some of the Y values are very small are shown in parentheses.

   a. **arcsine** (*abbr.* arcsin) **transformation,** for example, for negatively skewed data or proportions: $\arcsin \sqrt{Y}$ ($\arcsin \sqrt{Y + 1/2n}$)

   b. **logarithmic** (*abbr.* log) **transformation,** for example, for positively skewed data: $\log Y$ [$\log (Y + 1)$]

   c. **reciprocal transformation,** for example, for time data: $X = \dfrac{1}{Y} \left(\dfrac{1}{Y + 1} \right)$

   d. **square root transformation,** for data such as frequency counts that have a Poisson distribution: $\sqrt{Y}$ ($\sqrt{Y + .5}$)

Datum A single observation, score, or statistic; the singular form of *data.* (*See also* Group Datum; Individual Datum.)

Debriefing A postexperimental conference between the subject and the experimenter in which the purpose of the experiment is explained. The subjects are sometimes asked to provide additional formal or informal information about their experiences during the experiment.

Decile One of the nine score points that divide a distribution into tenths. The deciles are labeled D_1 through D_9. The third decile, D_3, for example, is the point below which 30% of the scores in a distribution lie; it is therefore equal to the 30th percentile, P_{30}. Similarly, D_5 is equal to the median, P_{50}.

Decision (1) A general term for the response of a subject whose task is to select from among several alternatives. (2) The report of an observer, or outcome of applying a rule, as to the presence or absence of some characteristic; for example, a report of the presence or absence of a signal or stimulus complex in the evironment at a given time, a diagnosis of the presence or absence of neurosis in an individual, a prediction that an individual will or will not belong to the class of trainees who succeed, etc. Decisions often are divided into four categories: (a) **true positive,** a decision that correctly reports a characteristic when it is present (also called a *hit*); (b) **false positive,** a decision that incorrectly reports a characteristic when it is absent (also called a **false alarm**); (c) **true negative,** a decision that correctly reports the absence of a characteristic (also called a **correct rejection**); and (d) **false negative,** a decision that incorrectly reports the absence of a characteristic when the characteristic is present (also known as a **miss**). (*See also* Cutting Score; Signal Detection Task.)

Decision Rule A rule that specifies the conditions for deciding in favor of one decision from among a set of two or more decisions.

EXAMPLE: In hypothesis testing a decision must be made as to whether or not to reject a null hypothesis. Customarily, the null hypothesis is rejected only if a test of significance (e.g., t test, F test, etc.) determines that the probability is .05 or less that rejection of the null hypothesis could be a Type I error.

Deductive Inference The process of logically deriving a specific prediction from a set of general principles or axioms of a theory.

EXAMPLE: From the general principles (1) magnitude of response is directly related to drive strength and (2) strength of the hunger drive is directly related to length of time since last eating, one can arrive deductively at the conclusion that a rat that has not eaten for 8 hours will jump farther to obtain food than will a rat that has not eaten for 4 hours.

Defense Conditioning *See* Aversive Conditioning.

Degrees of Freedom (*symb.* df, ν) A statistical concept associated with many tests of significance (e.g., t, F, χ^2) and with estimates of variability (e.g., the sample estimate of the variance of a population). In general, it is the number of observations on which a statistic is based, minus the number of restrictions placed on the freedom of those observations to vary. For variance estimates, this usually is the number of observations whose deviations are being squared and summed, minus the number of sample means from which the deviations are computed. For categorized data, the degrees of freedom depend on the number of categories; with one variable of classification the degrees of freedom are one less than the number of categories, and with two variables of classification (i.e., data arranged in a contingency table) the degrees of freedom are the product of one less than the number of rows and one less than the number of columns.

EXAMPLE 1: With two samples, the pooled variance estimate is obtained from the observations' squared deviations from their own sample means. If there are seven observations in one sample and nine observations in the other sample, the degrees of freedom are $7 + 9 - 2 = 14$.

EXAMPLE 2: Undergraduate students are classified on the variables class standing (freshman, sophomore, junior, senior) and attitude toward ESP (disbelieve, neutral, believe). The degrees of freedom for the 4×3 contingency table are $(4 - 1)(3 - 1) = (3)(2) = 6$.

Delay Interval (1) As a general term, the interval between the occurrence of one stimulus or response and a subsequent stimulus or response. (2) In delayed classical conditioning it is the interval from onset of the conditioned stimulus (CS) to onset of the unconditioned stimulus (US). (3) In instrumental conditioning it is the delay of reinforcement (response-reinforcement) interval. (4) In the delayed-reaction method it is the interval between termination of a stimulus and removal of restraints on the subject to respond to that stimulus.

Delay of Reinforcement Interval (*syn.* Response-Reinforcement Interval) The interval between completion of a response and onset of the event designed to reinforce that response.

Delayed Conditioning A classical conditioning procedure in which the conditioned stimulus (CS) begins prior to onset of the unconditioned stimulus (US) and remains on at least until onset of the US, that is, the two stimuli touch or overlap temporally. The interstimulus interval (CS onset to US onset) may be of any duration, but sometimes is specifically limited to intervals between 5 sec and 1 min. (*See also* Simultaneous Conditioning; Trace Conditioning.)

Delayed-Reaction Method Any task in which the subject is not permitted to respond to a stimulus until some time after the stimulus has been removed from the subject's presence. Performance under a number of different delay intervals ordinarily is measured.

EXAMPLE: A chimpanzee observes an experimenter putting a grape under one of three identical inverted cups. A screen then is lowered between the chimp and the cups, hiding them from view. After a delay period ranging from a few seconds to several minutes, the screen is raised and it is observed whether the chimp goes directly to the correct cup.

Delboeuf Illusion *See* Illusions.

Demand Characteristic Any aspect of the experimental environment or procedure that leads the subject to make some interpretation of the purpose of the experiment. Should the subject behave in accordance with the perceived purpose, the demand characteristic can be a source of experimental bias.

EXAMPLE: A subject participates in an experiment on memorization. Not only is the subject told that this is the purpose of the experiment, but other cues such as the presentation of verbal material and the presence of memory drums and similar paraphernalia are likely to induce demand characteristics in accordance with the purpose of the test. If, however, the subject interprets the presence of such cues as a test of personality characteristics, responses to the verbal material may be biased by excessive attention to potentially threatening words or themes, such as those pertaining to family constellations, sexual matters, political opinions, etc.

Demonstration A procedure in which performance is observed under one treatment, as opposed to an experiment in which that performance is observed under at least two treatments. For example, memory for a list of words measured 1 hour after learning the list demonstrates only that retention may have occurred, and is not an investigation of the factors influencing memory.

Dependent Variable The particular measure of behavior used by the experimenter to reflect the effects of the independent variable(s). The behaviors measured may range from covert physiological behavior to motor and verbal behavior. For example, in measuring the effects of various levels of stress from loud noises, one could record changes in blood adrenaline, heart rate, motor-skill performance in tracking a revolving target, pencil and paper ratings of how anxious or annoyed the subject felt, etc. (*See also* Response Variable.)

Deprivation Schedule The particular manner in which an experimental subject's access to some normally available substance (food, water, visual stimulation, etc.) is restricted so as to define the subject as "deprived." One procedure is a **time schedule** in which the subject is partially or totally deprived of the substance for a prescribed time period prior to administration of some experimental treatment. **Body weight schedules** are used to reduce the animal to some percentage of its normal (ad lib) body weight prior to the treatment.

EXAMPLE: In a maze learning study with food as reinforcer, a rat might be totally deprived of food for 24 hours or placed on a schedule of 10 grams of food per day for 3 days before starting the maze-learning procedure. Alternatively, the rat may be totally or partially food deprived until it reaches 90% of its normal (ad lib) weight, after which food is rationed to keep it at that weight until the treatment sessions are over.

Descending Series *See* Ascending/Descending Series.

Descriptive Research Gathering information from surveys, polling, or public records. Examples include finding how many schoolchildren suffer from vitamin deficiencies, how many hours per week are spent watching TV by college students, and which sports events draw the rowdiest crowds. The research does not attempt to establish cause-and-effect relationships.

Descriptive Statistics The area of statistics concerned with describing characteristics of a sample of data; also, the measures used for describing these characteristics. Descriptive statistics include measures of central tendency, variability, relationship, skewness, and kurtosis and various transformations such as standard scores. The term also includes tables and graphs used to display these characteristics. (*See also* Inferential Statistics.)

Design *See* Experimental Design.

Detection Threshold *See* Absolute Threshold; Recognition Threshold.

Deterioration Index (*syn.* Deterioration Quotient; *abbr.* DI) An index derived from the Wechsler–Bellevue intelligence tests for the purpose of ascertaining loss of mental abilities with age. It is made up of two types of intelligence subtests: "hold" portions, which as a rule show relatively little decline with age (subtests of information, vocabulary, picture completion, and object assembly); and "don't hold" portions, which tend to show more decline with age (subtests for digit span, arithmetic, block design, and digit symbol). The index is expressed by the formula

$$DI = \frac{(hold - don't\ hold) \times 100}{hold}$$

Deterioration Quotient *See* Deterioration Index.

Determination, Coefficient of (*symb.* r^2) The square of the correlation coefficient; the proportion of variance in one variable associated with, or accounted for by, the variability in a second variable. (*See also* Nondetermination Coefficient.)

Deterministic Model (*contr.* Stochastic Model) A mathematical model or theory that specifically predicts which one response from two or more responses will occur. For example, a deterministic choice model may predict which of several objects will be chosen on a given occasion.

Detour Task (*syn.* Umweg Problem) A task in which the subject's use of a particular, usually direct, path to a goal is blocked and its ability to use an alternative path is measured.

EXAMPLE: Figure D–1 shows a diamond maze with a start box at corner *S* and food located at corner *A*. A dog is placed at *S*. After the animal has learned to take path *S-A* to obtain food, that path is blocked. The new correct response is *S-B-C-A* and further starts on path *S-A* are scored as errors.

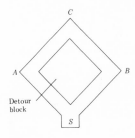

Figure D–1

Deviation IQ *See* Data Transformation (2).

Deviation Score The difference between a raw score and the mean, sometimes used in definitional formulas for z scores and statistics such as the variance and correlation coefficient. When an upper-case letter is used as the symbol for a raw score, the lower case is used for the deviation score, for example, $x = X - \overline{X}$.

df *See* Degrees of Freedom.

Dichotic Listening A procedure in which a subject is given different auditory stimuli simultaneously in each ear. In typical experiments the stimuli are delivered via a stereophonic headset; the subject must attend to the material delivered to one ear, and is then tested to determine how much can be recalled of the material delivered to the unattended ear. (*See also* Shadowing.)

Dichotomous Describing a set of stimuli, events, etc., that are divided or classified into two mutually exclusive categories. For example, responses may be classified as strong and weak, and people may be classified as males and females.

Dichotomous Variable   A variable that exists or is measured only as two mutually exclusive categories (e.g., drug—no drug, males—females, etc.).

Difference Limen (*abbr.* DL)   *See* Difference Threshold.

Difference Score (*syn.* Change Score)   The difference between two scores for a subject (e.g., pretest and posttest scores) or between scores for matched subjects.

Difference Threshold (*syn.* Difference Limen, *abbr.* DL; *syn.* Just Noticeable Difference, *abbr.* JND)   In psychophysics, the minimum change in the value of a stimulus that can be detected 50% of the time. (*See also* Absolute Threshold.)

Differential Classical Conditioning   A procedure in which a discrimination is developed by successively presenting two conditioned stimuli (CSs). One stimulus (CS+) always is followed by an unconditioned stimulus (US) and the other stimulus (CS−) never is followed by a US.

EXAMPLE: A conditioned eyeblink response is established by delivering a 500-Hz tone (CS+) followed immediately by a puff of air to the cornea. This is repeated a number of times. Randomly interspersed are trials in which a 1500-Hz tone (CS−) is delivered and not followed by an air puff. Successful discrimination is shown when the subject responds more to the CS+ than to the CS−.

Differential Instrumental Conditioning   A discrete-trials discrimination training procedure in which a response to one stimulus (S+) is rewarded and a response to another stimulus (S−) is not rewarded. The presentation of stimuli may be successive, with their order varying randomly, or simultaneous, with their position varying randomly. A distinction between differential instrumental conditioning and differential operant conditioning is made sometimes, with the latter referring to situations in which the response is emitted more or less continuously.

EXAMPLE 1: Simultaneous Discrimination   A child is seated at a video console and told that two different geometric forms (e.g., square and circle) will appear on the screen. If the button under the correct stimulus (S+) for that trial is pressed, a candy will be given. If the wrong stimulus (S−) is chosen, no reward will be given. For a **visual discrimination,** the circle is the S+ regardless of position. For a **spatial discrimination,** the stimulus on the right is the S+ regardless of shape.

EXAMPLE 2: Successive Discrimination   The child is told that two shapes will be presented, one after the other. If the button is pressed while the correct shape is in view, a reward will be given, otherwise not. Usually this correct stimulus occurs first on half of the trials and occurs second on the remaining trials in random fashion if a visual discrimination is being studied. If a temporal discrimination is being studied, the correct stimulus is always the one presented first (or second), regardless of shape.

Differential Operant Conditioning A discrimination learning procedure in which a freely emitted response is reinforced only during certain intervals; on other occasions a different response is reinforced or no reinforcement is given. A discriminative stimulus (S^D) is present during the intervals when the response is reinforced, and a negative stimulus (S^Δ) is present during intervals when reinforcement is not forthcoming. (*See also* Differential Classical Conditioning; Differential Instrumental Conditioning.)

EXAMPLE: A thirsty rat first is trained to press a bar for water. An illuminated red bulb (the discriminative stimulus or S^D) is located just above the bar. After a performance criterion is reached, the bulb is turned off periodically (the negative stimulus or S^Δ), during which time no water is given for bar pressing. Alternatively, a different bulb may be lighted and accompanied by a different schedule of reinforcement, or reinforcement of a different response.

Differential Reinforcement Any situation in which the consequences of responding to one stimulus, or in one manner, are different from the consequences of responding to another stimulus, or in another manner. For example, the subject is rewarded for touching the stimulus on the left and not rewarded for touching the stimulus on the right, or is punished for touching with the left hand and not punished for touching with the right hand.

Differential Reinforcement of Rates Operant conditioning procedures in which the subject is reinforced only when responses are emitted at some particular rate or level. The most commonly used varieties are

1. **Differential Reinforcement of High Rates (*abbr.* DRH)** The subject is reinforced only when the rate of responding meets or exceeds a criterion rate.
2. **Differential Reinforcement of Low Rates (*abbr.* DRL)** The subject is reinforced only when the rate of responding is equal to or less than a criterion rate.
3. **Differential Reinforcement of Paced Responding (*abbr.* DRP)** The subject is reinforced only when responding falls within a certain range of rates. (*See also* Correlated Reinforcement.)

EXAMPLE: An apparatus is programmed to monitor the specific interresponse times (IRTs) of a rat pressing a bar. If a DRH procedure

61

is in effect, reinforcement is given, for example, only if the IRT equals or is faster than 5 sec. Similarly, for a DRL schedule, reinforcement is given only when the IRT equals or is slower than 10 sec. In a DRP schedule, reinforcement is delivered, for example, only when the *average* IRT is 5–10 sec.

Differential Reinforcement of Other Behavior (*abbr.* DRO)   *See* Omission Training.

Differential Threshold   *See* Difference Threshold.

Differential Transfer Paradigm   An experimental design that permits comparison of the transfer effects of each of two tasks (e.g., difficult and easy discriminations) or of two training procedures (e.g., active recitation and silent reading). Each subject is tested on both tasks, with half of the subjects getting the tasks in the order AB and half getting the order BA. A significant order by task interaction would show differential transfer. As in the simple transfer paradigm, warm-up control groups, given a neutral first task, may be included in the design. (*See also* Transfer Paradigm.)

Differentiation   *See* Discrimination Learning; Response Differentiation.

Digit-Span Test   *See* Span of Apprehension.

Digram   A pair of symbols, usually letters. Digrams used as stimuli in verbal learning or perception research are generally formed by nonsystematic pairings of letters. (*See also* Paralog; Trigram.)

Directional Test   *See* One-Tail/Two-Tail Test.

Discrete Search Task (*contr.* Serial Search Task)   A task in which the subject searches through a number of stimuli until finding a specific, designated stimulus. Examples include looking for a particular word in a passage or the face of a particular individual in a picture of a crowd. Typically, but not necessarily, the search is directional, that is, the subject is instructed to begin the search at the top of a column, or the beginning of a passage, and to search in one direction only.

Discrete-Trials Procedure (*contr.* Free Operant Procedure)   Any instrumental training procedure that is structured in such a way that the response of interest can occur only in one time period. Examples of these procedures include a single run through a maze, a single problem-solving trial, or a single mirror-image tracing.

Discrete Variable (*contr.* Continuous Variable)   A variable that only takes on certain fixed values. For example, the values of the variable "number of children" can only be integers (e.g., 1, 4, 12, etc.).

Discriminal Dispersion   In scaling, the standard deviation of the theoretical distribution of discriminal processes. Since it cannot be measured directly, it usually is inferred from failures to discriminate among similar stimuli, that is, from some measure of nondiscrimination such as confusion, reversal, or judged equality of different stimuli.

Discriminal Process   In scaling, the hypothesized subjective effect of a stimulus on a particular presentation. For example, it may be assumed that the apparent loudness of a particular tone varies slightly from one presentation to another. Discriminal processes usually are assumed to be normally distributed around the true subjective effect, and the discriminal process (e.g., loudness on a particular trial) is randomly selected from this distribution.

Discriminant Analysis   A multivariate statistical procedure for describing the classification of individuals into two groups (the dependent or criterion variable) on the basis of several independent or predictor variables. **Multiple discriminant analysis** is used for classification into three or more groups. The analysis yields one or more equations (**discriminant functions**), similar to regression equations. For example, people classified as successful or unsuccessful managers might be measured on such variables as age, intelligence, education, personal traits, etc. The discriminant function would be a weighted combination of these measures that maximizes the difference in scores for people in the two groups. In **stepwise discriminant analysis,** one or more predictor variables are added or omitted at each step to determine which combination of variables provides the best discrimination among the groups.

Discriminant Function   *See* Discriminant Analysis.

Discriminant Validity (*contr.* Convergent Validity)   Validation of a measure of a construct by comparison with the measures of other constructs. If two measures are uncorrelated, the two tests are shown to be measuring different things. Thus, if the test to be validated shows little or no correlation with other tests, it has discriminant validity. For example, if a self-esteem test is to be validated, measures on this test might be correlated with tests of cognitive ability and ego strength. If the correlations are low, it would be concluded that the self-esteem test is measuring a different construct.

Discriminated Avoidance Conditioning (*contr.* Nondiscriminated Avoidance Conditioning)   Any discrete-trials avoidance conditioning procedure in which a warning signal precedes presentation of the stimulus to be avoided.

Discrimination Learning   A variety of procedures in which the subject is trained to make somewhat different responses to different stimuli. (*See also* Differential Classical Conditioning; Differential Instrumental Conditioning; Differential Operant Conditioning; Response Generalization; Stimulus Generalization.)

Discriminative Reaction Time   *See* Reaction Time.

Discriminative Stimulus (*symb.* S^D; *contr.* Negative Stimulus)   In differential operant conditioning, a stimulus whose presence signals that reinforcement is given for performance of the appropriate response. (*For an example see* Differential Operant Conditioning.)

Dishabituation   *See* Habituation.

Disjunctive Concept   A concept that is defined by the presence of one or the other of two properties. An inclusive disjunctive concept is defined by the presence of one or the other, or both, of the properties; an exclusive disjunctive concept is defined by the presence of one or the other, but not both, of the properties. (*See also* Conjunctive Concept.)

EXAMPLE: An object consisting of printed pages may be called a book if it has a hard cover, many pages, or both. If it has neither, that is, if it has a paper cover and few pages, it would be called a pamphlet. "Book," therefore, would be an inclusive disjunctive concept with regard to these properties.

Disjunctive Reaction Time   *See* Reaction Time.

Disordinal Interaction (*contr.* Ordinal Interaction)   An interaction in which rank order of the levels of one independent variable change across levels of a second independent variable.

EXAMPLE: Figure D–2 shows data from an experiment on the effects of three degrees of enriched diet (Factor A), and of being raised

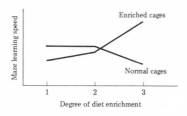

Figure D–2

with sensory enriched or normal cage surroundings (Factor B), on later maze performance of rats. Rats in normal cages showed superior maze performance with the first two degrees of diet enrichment, but with further enrichment the difference was reversed.

Display   *See* Stimulus Display.

Distance *(symb. d)*   In profile analysis, a measure of the similarity between two individuals, or for one individual and corresponding average test scores for a group.

Distorted Room   *See* Illusions: Ames' Distorted Room.

Distractor   Any stimulus or task whose function is to divert attention, to prevent the occurrence of some undesired response, or to provide interference with some performance. For example, in the study of recognition memory, new words are mixed with old words. In the study of short-term memory, a counting task may be given between learning and recall phases to prevent rehearsal.

Distribution of Practice   Manipulation of the relative duration of rest periods, which may be measured in seconds, hours, or days. For example, one group may have a 15-sec intertrial interval (ITI) and be called the **massed practice** group if a second group has a 5-min ITI or be called the **distributed** or **spaced practice** group if the second group has a 3-sec ITI.

Distribution   *See* Cumulative Distribution; Frequency Distribution; Probability Distribution.

Distribution-Free Test   Any significance test that involves no assumptions about either the shape (e.g., normal) or parameters (e.g., equal variances) of the distribution in the population from which the observations were drawn. Common distribution-free tests include the Mann–Whitney test, sign and signed rank tests, and the test for significance of the rank-order correlation coefficient. In common usage, no distinction is made between distribution-free tests and nonparametric tests, all of which are called nonparametric procedures.

Dixon's Test for Outliers   *See* Outlier Test.

DL   *See* Difference Threshold.

Doolittle Method   *See* Wherry–Doolittle Method.

Double Alternation Problem   A procedure in which the subject is required to make alternately two consecutive responses of one kind, followed by two consecutive responses of another kind, and so on, to solve the problem or earn a reward.

DRH   *See* Differential Reinforcement of Rates.

DRL   *See* Differential Reinforcement of Rates.

DRP   *See* Differential Reinforcement of Rates.

Domain   For functions, the possible values of the independent variable, X. For example, if grades are measured on a five-point scale ($F = 0$, $A = 4$), the domain of the function relating success in graduate school *(Y)* to undergraduate GPA *(X)* is the rational numbers from 0.0 to 4.0. [*See also* Range (2).]

Double Blind   *See* Blind Procedures.

Dummy Variable   In multiple regression, a coding procedure by which a dichotomous variable is given a numerical value, such as 1 for males and 0 for females or 1 for Treatment A and 0 for any other treatment.

Duncan's Multiple-Range Test   A multiple comparison procedure for testing the significance of differences for all possible pairs of treatment means. The test is similar to the Neuman–Keuls test in using ranked means, except that the critical value of the test statistic is found from special tables.

Dunn's Procedure   *See* Bonferroni *t* Statistic.

Dunnett's Test   A multiple-comparison procedure for comparing all treatment means with a single control group, but not with each other.

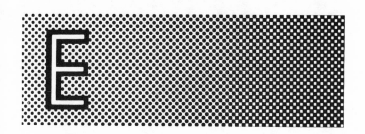

Ebbinghaus Illusion   *See under* Illusions.

Educational Age   *See* Educational Quotient.

Educational Quotient (*abbr.* EQ)   An index of relative educational achievement that compares a subject's chronological age and educational age. It is derived by dividing the educational age by the chronological age multiplied by 100. For example, a student may be 10 years old (chronological age) but displays an average performance on school subjects like a 9-year-old (educational age). Thus, $EQ = 9/10 \times 100 = 90$.

Efficiency   A property on which estimators for parameters of a distribution (e.g., sample means, medians, etc.) may be evaluated. An efficient estimator is one with a small standard error. Two estimators of a parameter can be compared in terms of relative efficiency, which is the ratio of their variances. For example, the sample mean is more efficient than the sample median as an estimator of the population mean μ, since its standard error is smaller. The relative efficiency of the sample mean is greater than 1.0, since the variance of the median divided by the variance of the mean is greater than 1.0.

Eigenvalue   In multivariate statistics, a statistic that may indicate the relative importance of a factor, variable, or function in contributing to variation in the data. As a measure of the proportion of variance accounted for, the eigenvalue depends on the number of variables present.

Einstellung   *See* Set.

Elicited/Emitted Response   In learning research, a distinction that may be made between a response to a specifiable stimulus and a response that occurs in the absence of a specifiable stimulus. An elicited response is one whose occurrence can be attributed to a specifically definable stimulus (e.g., movement toward a food object or salivation to the sight of food by a food-deprived organism). An emitted response is one whose occurrence cannot be attributed to a specifically identifiable stimulus (e.g., movement in an open field or "spontaneous" salivation). In one usage, the term *elicited* refers exclusively to reflexive or involuntary behaviors, whereas the term *emitted* refers only to behaviors under voluntary control. (*See also* Instrumental/Operant Response; Respondent Behavior.)

Eliciting Stimulus   A stimulus that is capable of evoking or does in fact reliably evoke some specified response. For example, an electric shock of moderate intensity will reliably elicit heart rate acceleration. (*See also* Conditioned Stimulus; Unconditioned Stimulus.)

Embedded-Figures Test   Any perceptual judgment test that requires test-takers to identify a visual stimulus (usually in the form of a geometric pattern) set in a large, complex field.

Emitted Response   *See* Elicited/Emitted Response.

Empirical Probability   A probability based on observations of the actual relative frequency of an event. For example, study of birth records for the United States shows the empirical probability of a new-born being male is .51.

Empirical Validity   A general term for any validation procedure that compares scores from a sample with an independent set of scores (criterion scores) derived from the same sample. For example, a teacher's grading procedure may be validated by correlating the assigned grades with the student's overall grade point average. (*See also* Concurrent Validity; Predictive Validity.)

Environmental Variable   *See* Independent Variable.

EQ   *See* Educational Quotient.

Equal-Appearing Intervals, Method of   A scaling procedure in which a subject is presented with a number of stimuli that differ in magnitude along some dimension and is asked to sort them into a specified number of piles (usually from 7 to 11) in such a way that the differences between neighboring piles represent subjectively equal increments in stimulus magnitude. The method is used with discrete stimuli that can be physically manipulated by the subject; the stimuli may have a related physical continuum, as in a set of weights to be sorted into piles that seem equally spaced in terms of heaviness, or may not, as in a set of pictures of people to be sorted into piles that seem equally spaced in terms of attractiveness. (*See also* Equisection, Method of.)

EXAMPLE: As a first step in measuring attitude toward the church, an investigator gathers a large number of statements considered to be relevant to this attitude that are as different from each other as possible (e.g., "I feel that the church gives me inspiration to live up to my best," "I believe that the church has been responsible for retarding the growth and development of emerging societies," "I think that the church as a place for religious instruction is essential in every community"). These statements are typed on separate cards, and each of a number of judges is requested to sort the statements into 11 piles that appear to be equally separated on a continuum ranging from favorable (the first pile) through neutral (middle pile) to unfavorable (the last pile). All the statements in a pile are assigned the same number from 1 (least favorable) to 11 (most favorable), and the scale value for any statement is its mean or median value. To assist in selection of items for the attitude measurement scale, the investigator also computes the dispersion of ratings, either the standard deviation or semi-interquartile range.

Equal Category In psychophysics, a category in which a subject places comparison stimuli that are judged to be equal in magnitude to a standard stimulus. (*See also* Forced Choice; Indifference Response.)

Equal-Sense Distances, Method of *See* Equisection, Method of.

Equimax Rotation *See* Factor Rotation.

Equisection, Method of (*syn.* Equal-Sense Distances, Method of) A scaling procedure in which a subject is required to divide a given interval along some psychological continuum into *n* equal intervals, or steps. Ordinarily the experimenter presents two stimuli, A and B, that represent the lower and upper limits of the interval, and the subject has an unlimited, or at least very large, number of other stimuli that vary along the continuum from which to select the ones that will divide the interval into the number of equal steps specified in the instructions. Typically, the procedure involves **bisection,** finding a stimulus that seems subjectively to lie midway between the extremes, then further bisect each half of the interval, and continue the bisection procedure until the original interval is divided into as many subjectively equal steps as were originally specified. The method can be applied to stimuli that can be varied continuously (e.g., brightness of lights, pitch of tones, or areas of circles) or to discrete stimuli such as a series of weights, provided there are a sufficient number of them that vary in sufficiently small steps so that the subject can find weights that seem subjectively midway between any two given values.

Equivalence, Coefficient of An index of the degree of equivalence of two or more parallel forms of a test. It is the reliability coefficient obtained by the alternate-forms procedure.

Equivalent-Forms Method *See* Alternate-Forms Method.

69

Equivalent Groups   Groups that were selected from some population by means of identical sampling methods. The groups themselves are, in fact, unlikely to be identical.

Equivalent-Groups Design   *See* Matched-Groups Design.

Error-Choice Technique   A test construction method in which the subject is forced to choose between wrong items as an indicator of attitudinal bias. For example, in a test for work attitudes, the choice may be between the following items: During the past year, wildcat strikes caused the loss of (1) 20,000 work-hours or (2) 200,000 work-hours. Loss of work due to wildcat strikes is socially undesirable, but the two choices offered are both extreme and wrong. The assumption is that test takers who consistently choose items such as (1) are strongly pro-labor, whereas those who consistently choose items such as (2) are strongly pro-management.

Error of _____   The entries are listed under their first significant word. See, for example, *error of measurement* as Measurement, Error of.

Error of Estimate   *See* Standard Error of Estimate.

Error Mean Square (*symb.* MS_e; *syn.* Error Term)   In the analysis of variance, an estimate of error variance. (See also F ratio.)

Error Rate (*syn.* Alpha Error Rate)   In statistics, the rate of erroneous findings of significance (i.e., the occurrence of Type I errors, in a set of related significance tests such as multiple comparisons among the means from a single experiment). Commonly considered error rates are (1) error rate per comparison: the probability that a single comparison will be falsely declared significant; (2) error rate per experiment: the expected number of Type I errors per experiment; and (3) error rate experimentwise: the probability that at least one Type I error will be made in the analysis of an experiment. (*See also* Multiple-Comparison Test; Protection Level.)

Error Reduction   *See* Control.

Error Term   In analysis of variance, the denominator of an *F* ratio.

Error Variance (*contr.* Systematic Variance)   The random variability in measurements that is due to uncontrolled extraneous variables, and measurement error.

Errorless Discrimination Learning   A discrimination learning procedure structured so that, ideally, the organism never responds to the negative stimulus, and thus never experiences nonreinforcement.

EXAMPLE: A pigeon is trained to peck at an illuminated blue key but not at an illuminated yellow key. The animal undergoes the usual shaping procedures to train a pecking response to the blue key. The yellow key also is introduced early in this phase of training but is usually only dimly lit and briefly exposed. As training progresses, the illumination intensity and exposure duration of the yellow key gradually are increased until they equal the duration and intensity of the blue key.

Escape Training An instrumental conditioning procedure in which an organism is placed in an aversive circumstance and in which a response must be learned to reduce or terminate the aversive stimulus.

   EXAMPLE: A dog is placed in one side of a box with a grid floor. Without warning the grid is electrified and the animal must jump a barrier to the safe side of the box. Learning is defined as increased efficiency in jumping the barrier and is measured by increased speed of escaping to the safe side. (*See also* Avoidance Training; Punishment Training.)

Estimation The branch of statistical inference that is concerned with procedures for finding point estimates (single values) or interval estimates for parameters, such as the mean of a population or the true effect of an independent variable, and with describing such properties of estimators as unbiasedness and efficiency. (*See also* Hypothesis Testing; Interval Estimation; Point Estimation.)

Eta Coefficient *See* Correlation Ratio.

Eta Squared (*sym.* η^2) One of several measures of the magnitude of a treatment effect. For a single-factor design, it is computed as the ratio of the between groups sum of squares to the total sum of squares. The term *correlation ratio* sometimes is used for this statistic. (*See also* Magnitude of Effect.)

Evaluation Research The assessment of social and/or industrial programs by means of scientific testing procedures that focus on the outcome of ongoing programs rather than on the need to establish new ones.

Evoked Response *See* Elicited/Emitted Response.

Exact Limits *See* Class Interval.

Exclusive Disjunction *See* Disjunctive Concept.

Exhaustive Set A set of events or categories that exhaust the possibilities for observations, so that every observation must be included in at least one of the categories. For example, in classifying people, "under 21," "21 or older," and "elderly" are an exhaustive set. The categories "under 21" and "over 21" are not exhaustive, since people who are 21 would not be included in either category. (*See also* Mutually Exclusive Events.)

Expected Frequency (*syn.* Theoretical Frequency; *contr.* Observed Frequency) The number of observations of a particular kind that is expected to occur according to some theoretical or empirical basis. For example, in 1000 births of children, the expected frequencies of boys and girls are both 500 on the theoretical grounds that births of boys and girls are equally likely to occur. However, an empirical study of birth records reveals that the probability that a newborn infant will be a boy is approximately .51 rather than .50, so in 1000 births the expected frequencies of boys and girls would be 510 and 490, respectively. (*See* Chi Square *for an example of the procedure for computing the value of an expected frequency for a cell in a contingency table.*)

Expected Mean Square [*symb.* E(MS), EMS] The expected value of a mean square, used in the analysis of variance to select the appropriate error term for an *F* ratio and to determine the procedure for estimating a treatment effect or component of variance.

Expected Value [*symb.* E( )] The average value in a probability distribution (population of values), or the long-run average in an extended series of observations of a random variable, such as a measurement or a statistic. For example, the expected value of the sample mean, $E(\overline{X})$, is equal to the expected value of a single observation, $E(X)$ or μ_X; that is, the mean of the sampling distribution of $\overline{X}$ is equal to the mean of the parent population from which the sample is drawn. The expected value of a discrete random variable is defined as $\Sigma X p(X)$, the sum of each possible value of the variable multiplied by its probability; for continuous random variables $E(X) = \int_{-\infty}^{\infty} X f(X) \, dX$.

Experiment A procedure for obtaining data in which one or more independent variables are manipulated to observe their effects on one or more dependent variables. In probability theory an experiment refers to a single observation or trial.

Experimental Control (*contr.* Statistical Control) The active manipulation of extraneous variables in an experiment in order to clarify relationships between variables of interest or to reduce error variance. Experimental control may be achieved by directly eliminating extraneous variables, by holding them constant, or by randomizing or counterbalancing them.

Experimental Design The general plan of an experiment, including the number and arrangement of independent variables, the number of levels of each independent variable and the way the levels are selected, and the way subjects are selected and assigned to conditions. The experimental design may also include plans for controlling possible confounding variables such as order effects, as in a Latin square design. Experimental designs classified in terms of number and arrangement of independent variables include one-way, factorial, and nested designs. Designs classified in terms of selection and assignment of subjects include randomized-groups, repeated-measures, and mixed designs for randomly selected subjects and randomized-blocks design for subjects selected on the basis of a concomitant variable. In some contexts the term *experimental design* may include the statistical analysis associated with a particular plan.

Experimental Effect *See* Treatment Effect.

Experimental Error *See* Random Error.

Experimental Group (*contr.* Control Group) The group(s) assigned to receive some value of the independent variable(s) as a treatment. The effect of the independent variable is assessed by comparison among experimental groups or between experimental and control groups. For example, in an experiment studying the effects of prior training on performance of a tracking task, groups receiving 2 or 4 hours of prior training are experimental groups, and a group receiving no training would be a control group.

Experimental Hypothesis *See* Research Hypothesis.

Experimental Method (*contr.* Correlation Research; Naturalistic Observation) A form of scientific investigation characterized by active manipulation of independent variables, control of extraneous variables, and observation of resulting changes in dependent variables.

Experimental Plan *See* Experimental Design.

Experimental Unit The unit to which a treatment is applied in a single trial of an experiment (e.g., a college student given a list of words to learn, a cage of rats being raised in a crowded environment, or a three-person group given a topic to discuss).

Experimenter Attribute *See* Experimenter Effect.

Experimenter Bias A type of experimenter effect in which the experimenter's expectancies or desires inadvertently cue the subject to behave in certain ways or to produce bias in the recording of data. For example, if the experimenter thinks brain-lesioned rats will perform more poorly than controls, the lesioned animals might be handled carelessly, thus impairing performance. Similarly, in situations that call for judgments of whether or not a given behavior occurred, the experimenter may unintentionally favor the control animals.

Experimenter Effect Any change in the subject's behavior that stems from the experimenter's attributes (e.g., age, sex, etc.) or expectations and that subvert the validity of the experiment. For example, an experimenter who wears casual clothing and behaves informally may induce a relaxed or even noncompliant attitude in the subject, whereas a lab coat and formal posture may elicit more cooperation, or raise the subject's level of apprehension. (*See also* Atmosphere Effect; Experimenter Bias.)

Explicit Response   *See* Overt/Covert Response.

Explicit Unpairing   *See* Unpaired Control.

Exploratory Study   Any preliminary investigation to verify the existence of a phenomenon or to identify potential independent variables for further study. Often correlational or naturalistic observation methods are used. If the experimental method is used, rigid control techniques are sometimes relaxed or foregone. (*See also* Pilot Study.)

Exponential Function   A relationship between two variables, x and y, such that a graph of the relationship can be represented by a curve whose equation is of the general form $y = ae^{bx} + c$. In the equation, e is the base of the natural logarithms and a, b, and c are constants. If b is positive, the curve will be positively accelerated; if a is also positive, y will be an increasing function of x, whereas if a is negative, y will be a decreasing function of x. If b is negative, the curve will be negatively accelerated; now if a is also negative, y will be an increasing function of x, and if a is positive, y will be a decreasing function of x. The y intercept of the curve will be equal to $a + c$, and it is characteristic of exponential functions that y always approaches some asymptotic value. Learning curves can sometimes be fitted by exponential equations. In some theories, for example, the strength of the association between a stimulus and a response is conceived to be an exponential growth function of the number of times the response has occurred in the presence of the stimulus and been followed by a reinforcement.

A variety of processes tend to follow an exponential formula (e.g., the rate of increase of the number of bacteria in a culture, the variation in the pressure of the atmosphere with height, the rate of decomposition of radium, and the growth of a sum of money invested at compound interest).

Ex Post Facto Study   Any research in which subjects are classified on the basis of whether or not, or to what degree, they were exposed to some naturally occurring event, rather than an event controlled by the experimenter. For example, to study the effect of severe trauma on various tests of personality, one might administer the tests to inhabitants of an earthquake-stricken island and also to those of an unaffected island with roughly the same racial/ethnic make-up, level of urbanization, etc.

Exposure Interval   The time period during which a stimulus is displayed.

External Reliability   The degree to which an experimental outcome can be replicated, either within a research facility by the same researchers or in a different facility and by different researchers. (*See also* Internal Reliability.)

External Validity   The generalizability of experimental results. External validity is a function of the degree to which the subjects, settings, and procedures of an experiment simulate the circumstances of some naturally occurring or "real-life" phenomenon. (*See also* Internal Validity.)

Exteroceptive Conditioning (*contr.* Interoceptive Conditioning)   Any classical conditioning procedure in which the stimuli used originate outside of the subject's body.

Extinction (*contr.* Acquisition)   Any procedure in which the event(s) that elicit or maintain a behavior are omitted in an effort to reduce or eliminate that behavior. In classical conditioning, it is the omission of the unconditioned stimulus following the conditioned stimulus. In instrumental conditioning, it is the withdrawal of the reinforcement that follows the correct response.

Extradimensional Shift   *See* Reversal/Nonreversal Shift.

Extraneous Variable   A variable that is of no immediate interest to the experimenter but that is a potential source of confounding and/or error variance and must be controlled. (*For examples of extraneous variables see* Confounding.)

Extrapolation   The process of estimating the value of a variable beyond the range of data on hand, for example predicting the height that a child will reach as an adult on the basis of data on the child's rate of growth during the first few years. In psychology extrapolation frequently involves estimating the values of dependent variables for levels of an independent variable that were not included in a given study and is often performed simply by extending the curve formed by connecting the original data points.

Extreme Reactions, Test of (*syn.* Moses Test of Extreme Reactions)   A distribution-free nonparametric test of the difference between two independent groups, when the research hypothesis is that one group of subjects (the experimental group) will have scores that are more extreme, both higher and lower, than the other group (the control group). For example, a researcher may hypothesize that when people are shown a particular type of advertising, some will have a favorable reaction, so that they become more favorable toward the product, but others will have a negative reaction, so that they become less favorable toward the product. Ratings of the product by these people would be compared to ratings by a control group that did not see the advertising. The data from the combined samples are arranged in order of magnitude and ranked. The test statistic is the span (range) of the ranks assigned to the control group, for example, the highest rank for the control group minus the lowest rank for the control group plus 1, or, more commonly, the next-to-highest rank minus the next-to-lowest rank plus 1.

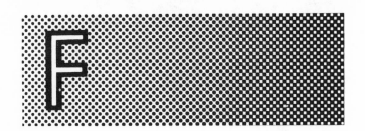

Face Validity The test-taker's impression that a test measures what it is supposed to measure. For example, a perceptual-motor skill test that consists mainly of eye–hand coordination problems would have high face validity. If, however, mathematical problems are added or the instructions are altered to convince the test taker that the test really is a measure of intelligence, face validity will suffer, and changes in subjects' performance may occur.

Factor (1) In experimental design, an independent variable. (2) In general research methodology, any event in the conduct of an experiment that is potentially capable of influencing the outcome of the experiment. In factor analysis, it is one of the components or dimensions into which the subjects' responses on a test may be categorized.

Factor Analysis Multivariate statistical methods for describing the relationships among a large number of variables in a correlation matrix by reducing them to a few relatively independent but conceptually meaningful composite variables called factors. The steps involved are (1) the preparation of a correlation matrix; (2) the extraction of initial factors; and sometimes (3) various rotation procedures aimed at obtaining the simplest and most interpretable factors. For example, a study of the factors involved in crime rate may focus first on a large number of potentially relevant variables such as crime rate in various geographical areas, the criminals' age and sex, amount of TV viewing, money spent on movies, etc. Factor analysis might then show "socioeconomic status of the criminal" as the major interpretable factor in crime rate. (*See also* Centroid Method; Factor Loading; Factor Rotation; Principal-Components Analysis.)

Factor Loading In factor analysis with orthogonal factors, an entry in the factor matrix that describes the correlation between one of the variables (tests) and a particular factor.

Factor Rotation (*syn.* Principal-Components Rotation)   In factor or principal-components analysis, rotation of the factor axes (dimensions) identified in the initial extraction of factors, in order to obtain simple and interpretable factors. In orthogonal rotation, axes are rotated to preserve the independence (i.e., lack of correlation) of the factors. Orthogonal procedures include **Varimax,** aimed at simplifying the factors themselves; **Quartimax,** aimed at simplifying the variables used in the factor analysis; and **Equimax,** a compromise aimed at simplifying both factors and variables. **Oblique rotation** is a nonorthogonal procedure, involving the rotation of one or more axes, so that the resulting factors will be correlated with each other.

Factorial Design   Any experimental design in which two or more independent variables are arranged orthogonally, that is, where the experimental conditions consist of all possible combinations of the levels of the independent variables. The design permits evaluation of the effect of each independent variable and the interaction of the variables.

EXAMPLE: To study the effects of near, medium, and far viewing distances (Factor B) and low and high levels of room illumination (Factor A) on the perceived size of a visual illusion, the two variables are arranged as shown in Figure F–1. The six cells thus formed (e.g., low-near, low-medium, etc.) represent all possible treatment combinations of light intensity and distance from the stimulus.

Figure F–1

False Alarm   *See* Decision; Signal Detection Task.

False Alarm Rate   *See* Signal Detection Task.

False Negative   *See* Decision.

False Positive   *See* Decision.

Fan Illusion   *See under* Illusions; Hering Illusion.

Fatigue Effect   *See* Order Effect.

***F* Distribution**   A probability distribution used in statistical inference, defined as the distribution of the ratio of two chi-square (χ^2) variables each divided by its degrees of freedom, or the ratio of two estimates of population variances (s^2) each divided by the true population variance (σ^2). (*See also* F Ratio.)

Fear Conditioning   *See* Aversive Conditioning.

Feedback   In experimentation, information concerning the response that has been or is being made. Positive feedback indicates that the response is correct and should be maintained. Negative feedback indicates the response is incorrect and should be modified. (*See also* Knowledge of Results.)

FI   *See* Fixed-Interval Schedule of Reinforcement.

Fiducial Interval   An interval estimate for a parameter, such as the population mean, based on Fisherian statistical theory. The interpretation of a fiducial interval is closer to that of the credible interval in Bayesian inference than to the interpretation of a confidence interval, but fiducial and confidence intervals are computed similarly, and *fiducial* and *confidence* are sometimes, though incorrectly, used interchangeably.

Field Research   A general term for data collection under natural or relatively uncontrolled environmental conditions, as opposed to such designated settings as the laboratory, clinic, or library. The most commonly used varieties are:

1. **Field Study (*syn.* Naturalistic Observation; Observational Research)**   Observations are carried out in natural settings without attempts to manipulate any variables. For example, the observer poses as a patient in a doctor's office while observing anxiety among patients expecting to undergo routine physical examinations.

2. **Natural Experiment**   A field study in which nature and/or circumstances provide the occurrence of a critical event. The investigator, knowing that some critical event is to take place, executes field studies to coincide with the critical event. For example, the investigator may study workers' attitudes before and after an already scheduled change in which some workers are to be promoted to foreman and others to union steward. If there are significant changes in attitude, the critical event (change in job status) allows for some interpretations of causal relationship.

3. **Field Experiment**   The investigator enters natural settings and manipulates certain independent variables in order to study their effect on the behavior under observation. For example, an investigator studying interpersonal attraction may pose as a summer camp director and assign the children to various housing conditions and then observe the ensuing friendship patterns.

Field Sociometry   The broad application of sociometric measures in natural settings.

Field Study   *See under* Field Research.

Figural Aftereffects   *See under* Illusions.

Figure–Ground Illusion   *See under* Illusions.

Findley Diagram   In operant conditioning, a system that employs the notation and graphics of electrical circuit diagramming in order to describe complex sequences of behavior.

First-Order Conditioning (*contr.* Higher Order Conditioning)   A classical conditioning procedure in which the reinforcing stimulus is an unconditioned stimulus (US), that is, a stimulus that elicits a response without prior training. Examples include a puff of air to the cornea to elicit an eyeblink, an electric shock to increase heart rate, etc.

First-Order Interaction   An interaction between two independent variables. (*See also* Higher Order Interaction.)

Fisher's Exact Probability Test   A test of independence for frequency data arranged in a 2 x 2 contingency table (i.e., classified on two dichotomous variables). The test is used for small samples, where the chi-square test of independence cannot be used. The exact probability associated with the observed distribution of frequencies can be computed using the hypergeometric distribution. Tables giving critical values for various sample sizes are also available.

Fisher's Z'   *See* Z' Transformation.

Fixed-Alternative Item (*contr.* Open-End Item)   A form of test or survey item in which the respondent is provided fixed alternatives. For example, rather than asking a person whether he or she intends to vote for candidate A, the person is asked to make a choice among candidates A, B, C, etc.

Fixed-Effects Factor   *See* Fixed/Random-Effects Factor.

Fixed-Effects Model   *See* Fixed/Random-Effects Model.

Fixed-Interval Schedule of Reinforcement (*abbr.* FI)   An operant conditioning procedure in which a constant period of time must elapse before the reference response is reinforced. The first response made after the interval expires is reinforced. For example, a fixed-interval 30-sec (FI–30) schedule is one in which the first response after 30 sec is reinforced, beginning a new interval. Thereafter, no response is reinforced until an additional 30 sec has elapsed. (*See also* Variable-Interval Schedule of Reinforcement.)

Fixed/Random-Effects Factor Terms that refer to the way in which levels of an independent variable are selected by the experimenter. A fixed-effects factor is one whose levels are selected arbitrarily. A random-effects factor is one whose levels are selected randomly from a population of possible levels. (Results of an experiment may be generalized only to the specific levels used for a fixed-effects factor but may be generalized to the population of levels for a random-effects factor.) Manipulated independent variables usually are considered to be fixed-effects factors in pyschological research. Common random-effects factors are subjects (in a repeated-measures design), a blocking variable (in a randomized-blocks design), and groups (in a nested design). For example, if rats are pretested for running speed and the four fastest assigned to one block, the next four to the next block, etc., the average running speed for each block is considered to be a random selection from all possible running speeds; if subjects are randomly assigned to groups of three for an experiment on decision making, the groups are considered to be a random sample from all possible three-person groups.

Fixed/Random-Effects Model The mathematical model for an experimental design whose independent variables all are of the same type, all fixed-effects factors or all random-effects factors. A mixed-effects model refers to a design that includes at least one of each type.

Fixed-Ratio Schedule of Reinforcement (*abbr.* FR) An operant conditioning procedure in which a constant number of responses must be made before a reinforcement is given. For example, a fixed-ratio-5 (FR-5) schedule of reinforcement is one in which only every fifth response is reinforced.

Fixed-Trials Criterion The designation of a specified number of trials to be conducted during one segment of an experiment. (*See also* Performance Criterion.)

Flat Distribution *See* Rectangular Distribution.

F_{max} (*syn.* Hartley's F_{max}) The ratio of the largest of several independent variance estimates to the smallest. One of several procedures for testing the hypothesis of homogeneity of variance. The critical values are found in special tables.

Floor Effect *See* Ceiling/Floor Effect.

Follow-Up Study Any study designed to determine residual or long-range effects of some earlier research activity.

Follow-Up Test Any statistical procedure used to determine the characteristics or sources of a significant main effect or interaction found in an analysis of variance or similar general analysis. (*See* *also* A Priori Test; A Posteriori Test; Contrast; Multiple-Comparison Test; Pairwise-Comparisons Test; Simple Effects.)

F_1 Generation The first generation of any hybrid mating.

Forced Choice A choice made under circumstances where the subject must choose one of two or more alternatives and does not have the option of choosing none of the alternatives. For example, a subject may be forced to specify which of two stimuli is the more intense, and judgments of "equal" or "uncertain" are not permitted. (*See also* Signal Detection Task.)

Forecasting Efficiency Index (*symb. E*) The percentage of reduction of error in predicting the value of a variable, Y, by taking into account knowledge of the value of a correlated variable, X, as opposed to ignoring the value of X. By formula, the index is $E = 100(1 - \sqrt{1 - r^2})$, where r is the coefficient of correlation between X and Y.

Foreperiod In the measurement of reaction time, the interval between the presentation of the ready signal and the presentation of the stimulus to which reaction time is being measured.

Forward Conditioning (*contr.* Backward Conditioning) In classical conditioning, any arrangement in which onset of the conditioned stimulus (CS) precedes onset of the unconditioned stimulus (US), as in delayed and trace conditioning. The term is sometimes used to describe arrangements in which onset of the CS and US are virtually simultaneous.

Forward Masking *See* Masking.

Fourfold Point Correlation *See* Phi Coefficient.

FR *See* Fixed-Ratio Schedule of Reinforcement.

***F* Ratio** The ratio of two sample variance estimates (or mean squares). With two independent samples, the F ratio is the test statistic for the hypothesis that the samples came from populations with equal variances. In the analysis of variance, the mean square in the numerator includes variability due to the effect of an independent variable (or interaction), whereas the mean square in the denominator (the error term) does not. This F ratio is the test statistic for the null hypothesis of no treatment (or interaction) effect.

Fractional Factorial *See* Confounded Designs.

Fractionation, Method Of In psychophysics and scaling, a procedure in which the subject is to report the magnitude of the ratio of two subjective magnitudes. Two general methods are employed. In the direct-estimate method, the subject is presented with two stimuli and is asked to report the ratio of the first to the second (e.g., that they stand in the ratio of $1/2$, $3/1$ etc.). In the prescribed-ratio method, the subject is presented a standard stimulus, and a second variable stimulus is manipulated until the subject reports that it stands at some prescribed ratio to the standard (e.g., $1/4$, $1/3$, etc.). When a subject is asked to set a variable stimulus to one-half of the standard, the procedure is frequently referred to as **halving.** (*See also* Equisection, Method of.)

Free Association A procedure in which a subject is presented with a stimulus item (e.g., a word, picture, nonsense form, etc.) and is asked to report whatever meanings or associations the stimulus item elicits. The associations are "free" to the extent that they are not guided or directed by the instructions or by probes that limit the type of response allowed. The procedure has a variety of uses (e.g., to establish meaningfulness norms for words and as a clinical diagnostic tool). (*See also* Association Task.)

Free Learning In verbal learning and information processing, a procedure in which a collection of items is presented to the subject either all at once or one at a time and the subject is instructed to learn the items without regard to their order of presentation. The subject may recall them orally or in writing. (*See also* Paired-Associate Learning; Serial Learning.)

EXAMPLE: A subject is asked to learn 20 five-letter words presented on individual cards. Each card is exposed for 3 sec, and the subject then is asked to write down as many items as can be remembered. The pile of cards is shuffled and presented again to the subject. This procedure may continue for any number of trials.

Free Operant Avoidance Conditioning *See* Nondiscriminated Avoidance Conditioning.

Free Operant Procedure (*contr.* Discrete Trials Procedure) Any instrumental training procedure that is structured such that the response to be modified can be freely emitted by the organism. Rate of response is the typical dependent variable. For example, key pecking and bar pressing are continuously emittable responses, whereas an alley run and shuttle responses are only periodically allowed by the experimental procedure and apparatus.

Free Operant Response *See* Emitted Response.

Free Recall In verbal learning and information processing, a paradigm in which typically a subject is presented, on a single trial, a list of items, then is given a recall test in which the items may be recalled in any order. The items may be presented all at once or one at a time, and the subject may recall them orally or in writing. If the recall test follows immediately after the presentation, rather than following a delay interval, the method also is called **free learning.** (*See also* Paired-Associate Learning; Serial Learning.)

Free Response, Method of   A variant of a signal detection task in which there are no delimited time intervals known to the subject during which a decision must be made as to whether or not a faint stimulus has been presented. In the free-response method the subject is given a long observation period during which a brief, faint signal is presented at random intervals and then is asked to make a response each time the signal is judged to be present. The experimenter may later divide the total observation period into signal intervals and noise intervals and tally separately the latencies of the first response following each type of interval. The experimenter then can establish some arbitrary criterion latency and use this to find the frequencies of responses that would be classified as hits, misses, false alarms, and correct rejections.

Free Scaling   In magnitude estimation, the procedure of allowing subjects to assign whatever values are desired to represent the perceived magnitude of the stimuli in a series, with the provision that the numerical values assigned be proportional to the perceived magnitude. This method is in contrast one in which the experimenter provides an anchor value in which one of the stimuli in the series is declared to have a specified value, usually 10 or 100. (*See also* Magnitude Estimation.)

Frequency Distribution   A set of scores arranged in numerical order with numbers showing the frequency with which each score occurs. Typically the scores are in a column headed *X*, or *Scores*, with high values at the top and low values at the bottom and the frequency for each score is shown alongside in a column headed *f*. If the scores are spread over a considerable range, they generally are grouped into class intervals of a size that will result in from 10 to 20 intervals.

EXAMPLE: Table F–1 shows a distribution of $n = 134$ scores, which are grouped into 10 class intervals of size $i = 5$.

Frequency Polygon   A graphic method for depicting a frequency distribution. In the graph, the scores, which may be grouped into class intervals, are spaced evenly along the x-axis, and frequencies, percentages, or proportions, are shown on the y-axis. The plotted frequencies for all scores are connected by straight lines.

EXAMPLE: Frequency distributions of height to the nearest inch are shown in Table F–2 for samples of men and women, and Figure F–2 shows frequency polygons for these data. In this example the height scores are grouped into intervals of $i = 2$ inches, and the frequencies are expressed as percentages.

84

Table F–1

Scores	f
75–79	1
70–74	8
65–69	14
60–64	38
55–59	29
50–54	17
45–49	11
40–44	9
35–39	5
30–34	2
	134

Table F–2

Heights	f Men	f Women
78–79	1	
76–77	1	
74–75	2	1
72–73	6	0
70–71	12	2
68–69	10	3
66–67	11	10
64–65	6	11
62–63	1	12
60–61		9
58–59		2

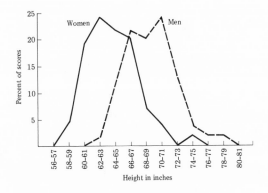

Figure F–2 Frequency Polygons Depicting Height to the Nearest Inch for Samples of Men and Women

Friedman's Two-Way Analysis of Variance for Ranked Data *See* Analysis of Variance for Ranked Data.

***F* Test** *See F* Ratio.

Function (*symb. Y* = *f(X); syn.* Functional Relation) A rule that associates one or more values of the dependent variable (variable Y) to each value of the independent variable (X), or to each combination of values for several independent variables.

EXAMPLE: The function $Y = X^2$ is a single-valued function; there is only one value of Y for any X in the number system (e.g., if X is 4, then Y is 16). The function $Y = \sqrt{X}$ is two-valued (e.g., if X is 4, then Y is $+2$ or -2). In a polygamous society, the relation *spouse of* defines a multiple-valued function; for any X who is an unmarried person, Y is *nobody* (or 0), but for any X who is a person with more than one spouse, Y is the list of spouses.

Functional Design (1) The experimental design used in parametric research. (2) In operant conditioning, experimentation characterized by the use of a small number of subjects or a single subject, and where control is demonstrated by constant and reliable changes in the subject's behavior as treatment sessions alternate between experimental and control conditions. (*For specific examples see individual listings under* Single-Subject Designs.)

Functional Experiment *See* Functional Design.

Functional Relation *See* Function.

Game Research   Simulation procedures that use games for the study of decision making, conflict, and strategy planning. (*See also* Zero/ Nonzero-Sum Game.)

Gamma   *See* Appendix B.

Gamma Distribution   A probability distribution particularly useful in Bayesian statistics because of its relationship to the Poisson and chi-squared distributions.

Gaussian Distribution   *See* Normal Distribution.

Gellerman Series   A randomized sequence of binary events (e.g., left- and right-side presentation of stimuli) designed to control for a subject's tendency to favor a given position, to alternate choices, or to control the predictability of the sequence. The sequence may include any desired restrictions on randomization, such as a maximum of three or a maximum of four consecutive events of the same type.

Generalizability of Research   *See* External Validity.

Generalization Test   *See* Response Generalization; Stimulus Generalization.

Geometric Illusions   *See* Illusions, individual listings.

Geometric Mean   A measure of central tendency consisting of the nth root of the product of the n values in a distribution of scores.

EXAMPLE: Given the two values of $X = 4$ and 9, the geometric mean is $\sqrt{(4)(9)} = 6$. Also, given the five scores of 2, 2, 4, 8, and 8, the geometric mean is $\sqrt[5]{(2)(2)(4)(8)(8)} = \sqrt[5]{1024} = 4$.

Gompertz Curve   An exponential-type growth curve in which the dependent variable is a double exponential function of the independent variable: $Y = ab^{c^x}$, where a, b, and c are three separate

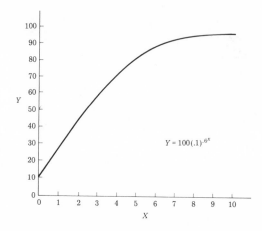

$$Y = 100(.1)^{.6^x}$$

Figure G–1 Gompertz Curve.

parameters. The Gompertz curve (Figure G–1) is more complex than the exponential curve and may show an S shape—an initial period of positive acceleration before the typical exponential form.

Goodness-of-Fit Test A chi-square test used for testing whether a particular theoretical model or set of a priori probabilities fits a set of data. For example, the frequency with which each wrong alternative is selected on a multiple-choice question may be used to test the hypothesis that all choices are equally likely to be selected. Similarly, a grouped frequency distribution may be used to test the hypothesis that the data came from a normal distribution, by comparing obtained frequencies within expected frequencies derived from a table of the normal distribution.

Graeco-Latin Square Design A balanced arrangement of four variables, each having the same number of levels. It is derived from the combination of two orthogonal Latin squares, so that each level of the two variables within the square occurs once in each row and each column, and each pairing of the levels of these two variables occurs once. Like the Latin square, the Graeco-Latin square provides a balanced fractional replication of a complete factorial design. In psychology, it is most commonly used to balance temporal effects in a within-subject design in which two independent variables are manipulated.

EXAMPLE: In a study of message format *(A)* and authorship *(B)* on attitude change, each subject is tested with three different messages

Subject	Order		
	I	II	III
1	A_1B_1	A_2B_2	A_3B_3
2	A_2B_3	A_3B_1	A_1B_2
3	A_3B_2	A_1B_3	A_2B_1

Figure G–2   Graeco-Latin Square Design.

differing in format and attribution of authorship. The order and type of message for three subjects is given by the Graeco-Latin square in Figure G–2. The sequence for another three subjects would be determined by randomly rearranging both rows and columns of this square.

Grand Mean   In the analysis of variance, the mean of all the observations from which the total sum of squares is computed. It is the grand total of all the observations divided by the total number of observations.

Group Datum (*contr.* Individual Datum)   A single score for a group of subjects. The score may be an aggregate for individuals in a group (e.g., mean, standard deviation) or a unitary score based on the group as a whole (e.g., time to reach a group solution to a problem).

Group Experiment   (1) An experiment in which data are collected from an assemblage of subjects, as opposed to gathering data from subjects one at a time. (2) An experiment in which groups are the experimental unit so that the dependent variable is a group score, as, for example, a comparison of the total output of three-person groups versus that of five-person groups.

Group Interval   *See* Class Interval.

Group Measure   *See* Group Datum.

Group Score   *See* Group Datum.

Grouped Data   A frequency distribution in which the scores have been grouped into class intervals. (*For an example see* Frequency Distribution.)

Grouping Error   Error introduced into the computation of descriptive statistics (e.g., the mean, standard deviation, centiles, etc.) using scores grouped into class intervals. (*See also* Sheppard's Correction.)

Growth Curve   Any curve, especially one that is theoretical or fitted to data, that shows the growth of some dependent variable. Growth curves generally are exponential in form. Common examples of growth curves in psychology are learning and developmental curves.

Guttman Scale   Any scale that uses the method of cumulative ratings. (*For an example, see* Cumulative Ratings, Method of.)

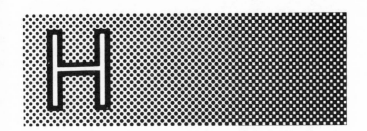

Habituation A procedure designed to reduce the novelty of a stimulus, and thus the subject's tendency to respond to it reflexively. The stimulus is presented in a relatively invariant fashion at relatively regular intervals for a set number of trials, or until the subject reaches a criterion of diminished responding. **Dishabituation** is a procedure by which one or more novel stimuli are interpolated in the habituation series in order to disrupt habituation.

Halo Effect A source of experimental bias in rating, in which the rater attributes specific characteristics to subjects on the basis of a general impression. For example, subjects whose performance is rated as neat and orderly may, as a result, be rated as highly motivated (positive halo effect). Conversely, sloppy performance may lead to a rating of poor motivation (negative halo effect).

Halving Method *See* Fractionation, Methods of.

Harmonic Mean A measure of central tendency defined as the reciprocal of the arithmetic mean of the reciprocals of the scores.

EXAMPLE: The reciprocals of the numbers 2, 3, and 4 are $\frac{1}{2}$, $\frac{1}{3}$, and $\frac{1}{4}$, and the arithmetic mean of these is .3611. The harmonic mean of the numbers 2, 3, and 4 is $1/.3611 = 2.769$.

Hartley's F_{max} *See* F_{max}.

Hawthorne Effect The effect on subjects' performance of their knowledge, or assumption, that they are participants in an experiment. In the original study at the Western Electric Hawthorne Plant in Chicago, a group of workers was studied for the effects of working hours, lighting, methods of pay, rest periods, etc., on productivity. Regardless of variations in working conditions, productivity and morale rose steadily, presumably as a function of the workers' knowledge of being participants in a special study. (*See also* Atmosphere Effect; Demand Characteristic; Instrumentation Effect.)

Hering Illusion   *See under* Illusions.

Heterogeneity   *See* Homogeneity/Heterogeneity.

Heteroscedasticity   *See* Homoscedasticity/Heteroscedasticity.

Heuristic   Describing or indicating a strategy or rule of thumb that frequently is helpful in achieving a goal, but is not guaranteed to be successful. For example, in solving anagrams, one heuristic is to try likely letter combinations, such as *gh* rather than *hg*. (*See also* Algorithm.)

Hierarchical Design   An experimental design in which there are two or more nested factors. A common hierarchical design is one in which several groups of people are assigned to each of several different conditions, so that subjects are nested within groups and groups are nested within conditions. (*For an example with three levels of nesting see* Partially Hierarchical Design.)

EXAMPLE: Students are tested for attitude toward the death penalty, and then are randomly assigned to groups to discuss the topic. There are 12 groups, each consisting of three experimental subjects and one student who is a confederate of the experimenter. In one-third of the groups the confederate uses a legalistic argument, in one-third an economic argument, and in one-third an emotional argument. Following the discussion, all students are retested on the attitude scale. In this experiment, subjects are nested in groups, and groups are nested in type of argument, and each of these, type of argument, groups within argument, and subjects within groups, is an identifiable source of variability in the analysis. The design is summarized, with G for group and S for subject:

Legalistic					Economic				Emotional		
G_1	G_2	G_3	G_4	G_5	G_6	G_7	G_8	G_9	G_{10}	G_{11}	G_{12}
S_1	S_4	S	S	S	S	S	S	S	S	S	S_{34}
S_2	S_5	S	S	S	S	S	S	S	S	S	S_{35}
S_3	S_6	S	S	S	S	S	S	S	S	S	S_{36}

Higher Order Conditioning (*contr.* First-Order Conditioning)   Any classical conditioning procedure in which a previously conditioned stimulus (CS) functions as a reinforcing stimulus, in subsequent training, to establish a response to a new CS.

EXAMPLE: A dog's heart rate acceleration response is first conditioned by presenting a buzzer (CS_1) followed by electric shock (US). This pairing is repeated until response strength reaches a prescribed criterion. A tone (the new CS_2) then precedes the buzzer, and a new series of training trials is started. The shock may remain in the series or it may be discontinued. Strength of the conditioned response (CR_2) to the tone (the second-order CR) is now measured. A third-order conditioning procedure could use a series of trials in which, for example, a click (CS_3) preceded the tone, with strength of the CR_3 to the click being measured.

Higher Order Design Any experimental design with three or more independent variables. (*See also* Higher Order Interaction.)

Higher Order Interaction A statistical interaction among three or more independent variables. Interactions between pairs of factors (e.g., AB, AC, BC) are all **first-order interactions.** All other interactions (e.g., ACD, BCD) are higher order interactions. Interactions among any three variables are called **second-order interactions,** those between any four variables are **third-order interactions,** etc.

Higher Order Schedule of Reinforcement Any complex reinforcement schedule in which one simple (first-order) schedule of reinforcement is nested within another (higher order) schedule of reinforcement. Satisfaction of the demands of the first-order schedule constitutes one step toward completion of the demands of the higher order schedule.

EXAMPLE: In a higher order schedule comprised of a fixed-interval 1-min schedule and a fixed-ratio-10 schedule [*abbr.* (FI-1, FR-10)] the ratio schedule is the first-order schedule and the interval schedule is the second-order schedule, so that every 10th response counts as one response under the fixed interval schedule. Thus, the first ratio of 10 responses to be performed after the passage of 1 min produces reinforcement.

Histogram A type of bar graph used to depict the frequency distribution for a continuous dependent variable. The variable may be grouped into class intervals.

Historical Method A procedure for obtaining data by tracing the events in life histories. For example, a clinical psychologist may uncover peoples' early traumas in order to account for fears; or a developmental psychologist may study peoples' maturation patterns in order to understand the present level of motor development.

Hit *See* Decision.

Hit Rate *See* Signal Detection Task.

Homogeneity/Heterogeneity of Variance Terms that refer to whether scores obtained under the various conditions of an experiment come from populations with equal variances (homogeneity of variance) or from populations with unequal variances (heterogeneity of variance). (*See also* Bartlett's Test; Cochran's Test; F_{max} Test.)

Homogeneity of Proportions, Test for A significance test for independent random samples from two or more populations, when the observations in each sample are classified into two or more categories. The data are arranged in a contingency table, with the rows representing the populations and the columns representing the categories. A chi-square statistic is used to test the hypothesis that the proportions in the various categories are the same for each population. Computationally, the test is identical to the test for independence.

EXAMPLE: An experimenter obtains independent random samples of male and female college students. Each sample then is classified by major. If, for example, 30% of the students (male and female combined) are engineering majors, homogeneity of proportions would require that 30% of each sex be engineering majors. If, instead, 10% of the females and 50% of the males are engineering majors, the proportions would not be homogeneous.

Homogeneous Grouping Grouping of subjects on the basis of some dominant common property or characteristic such as gender (e.g., all-male group), education (e.g., all college graduates), intelligence (e.g., only scorers above an IQ of 120), etc.

Homoscedasticity/Heteroscedasticity In correlational analysis, terms that refer to whether the data come from a population in which the variances of the distributions of Y scores are the same for all values of X (homoscedasticity) or differ for different

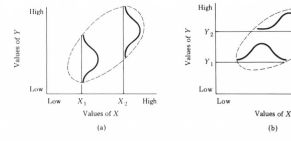

Figure H–1 An Illustration of Homoscedasticity.

94

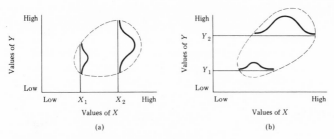

Figure H–2 An Illustration of Heteroscedasticity.

values of X (heteroscedasticity). Similar considerations hold for the distributions of X scores for all values of Y. (*See also* Homogeneity/Heterogeneity of Variance.)

EXAMPLE: Figure H-1 depicts the general shape of a scattergram showing positive correlation between values of X and Y when homoscedasticity prevails. The variability in scores is greater for X than for Y, but the variability in Y scores is the same for all values of X (e.g., X_1 and X_2) and the variability in X scores is the same for all values of Y (e.g., Y_1 and Y_2). Figure H-2, in which heteroscedasticity prevails, shows that variability in Y scores is not the same for all values of X (e.g., X_1 and X_2) nor is variability in X scores the same for all values of Y (e.g., Y_1 and Y_2).

Honestly Significant Difference Procedure   *See* Tukey's Test.

Horizontal Grouping (*contr.* Vertical Grouping)   A form of homogeneous grouping, usually within the same socioeconomic and/or organizational level. For example, an industrial task group that comprises only certain levels of management, such as all middle management or all top management, is horizontally grouped since all members are of about the same status.

Horizontal/Vertical Illusion   *See under* Illusions.

Hotelling's T^2 Test   A multivariate significance test for comparing two mean vectors representing scores on multiple dependent variables for two groups. The test may be used as an alternative to the analysis of variance for repeated-measures designs.

Hoyt's Formula for Reliability   A computational formula, equivalent to the Kuder–Richardson Formula for test reliability based on internal consistency, but using an analysis of variance format. The data are arranged in a table with test takers as rows and test items as columns, and with 1 entered for a correct response and 0 for an incorrect response. The mean squares for test takers, test items, and residual are obtained, and the reliability coefficient is computed by the formula

$$r_{11} = \frac{V_e - V_r}{V_e}$$

where V_e and V_r are the mean squares (variances) for test takers (examinees) and residual, respectively.

HSD Procedure *See* Tukey's Test.

H Test *See* Kruskall–Wallis *H* Test.

H/V Illusion *See under* Illusions: Horizontal/Vertical Illusion.

Hypothesis A statement about the relationships among events. (*See also* Null/Alternate Hypothesis: Research Hypothesis.)

Hypothesis Testing (*syn.* Significance Testing) The branch of statistical inference concerned with deciding between two (or sometimes more) hypotheses about some aspect of a distribution, such as the mean, median, variance, shape, etc., for the population(s) of interest to the experimenter. (*See also* Estimation; Null/Alternate Hypothesis; One-Tail/Two-Tail Test; Power; Rejection/Nonrejection Region; Significance Level; Type I Error; Type II Error.)

Hypothesis Testing Experiment (*contr.* Parametric Experiment) An experiment designed to determine the presence or absence of a difference, relationship, treatment effect, etc., that is, an experiment for which hypothesis testing is the appropriate form of data analysis.

Hypothetical Construct (*syn.* Theoretical Construct) An unobserved or unobservable entity or process used to explain the relationship between independent and dependent variables. For example, the term *learning* is used to explain those relatively permanent changes in behavior that occur as a result of practice. The conditions of practice and the changes in behavior are all observable, but learning is not observable and must be inferred from various stimulus-response relationships. (*For a distinction between this and a closely related concept, see* Intervening Variable.)

IQ *See* Intelligence Score.

Ideal Observer In psychophysics and detection theory, a mathematical abstraction referring to the maximum performance of the best possible system having certain properties. Performance of the ideal observer may be compared to the actual performance of observers, and the ways in which the human exceeds or falls short of the ideal observer may suggest improvements in the theory about the performance.

EXAMPLE: Subjects are told that the heights of adult males are normally distributed, with a mean of 69 in., and the heights of adult females are normally distributed with a mean of 64 in. Both distributions have a standard deviation of 3 in. A subject is given the height of a person and asked to decide whether that person is male or female. The curves are shown in Figure I–1. The curves cross at 66.5 in., which is equally likely to occur in the two distributions. Any height less than 66.5 in. is more likely to occur in the distribution for females, and any height greater than 66.5 in. is more likely to occur in the distribution for males. In signal detection theory, if there is no differential reward for correctly identifying males and females, the ideal observer should decide *female* for any person whose height is less than 66.5 and *male* for any person whose height is greater than 66.5. Actual people may or may not do this. They could, for example, be influenced by their own height and sex; they might use subjective height distribu-

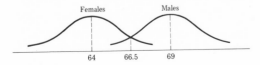

Females   Males

64   66.5   69

Figure I–1

tions that are different from the one described by the experimenter or develop a set to respond more often with their own sex, or with the opposite sex.

Idiographic Approach (*contr.* Nomothetic Approach) Pertaining to an individual case, or event. In psychology, any system for the assessment of behavior derived from a particular individual, and with an emphasis on individual differences as opposed to focusing on the average of many individuals' performance.

Illusions and Related Phenomena Note: Perceptual illusions are more properly classified as psychological *phenomena* than methods or techniques. Historically, however, the study of illusions and related topics has been a central focus of experimental psychology. Many of the methods and techniques developed in the study of sensation and perception have since been adopted in other areas of research psychology, and the illusions themselves continue to be used as research tools. The following is a compilation of the more popular and commonly researched ambiguous figures, illusions, reversible forms, and aftereffects. Letters in parentheses refer to the illusions illustrated in Figure I–2.

Ambiguous Figures Displays, including reversible forms, which are not true illusions, but are structured such that more than one veridical perception is possible. (For examples see *Boring's Mother-in-Law, Mach's Figure, Necker Cubes, Reversible Figures, Schröder's Staircase.*)

Ames' Distorted Room A room in which the apparent size of an occupant is altered because the height and depth cues provided by the walls, floor, ceiling, and windows are distorted.

Ames' Window *See* Illusions: *Trapezoidal Window.*

Autokinetic Effect The apparent movement of a tiny, stationary spot of light when viewed continuously in a completely darkened room. Also, the apparent drift in location of a stationary sound in a soundproof room.

Boring's Mother-in-Law (a) This ambiguous figure alternately is seen as a young girl looking away and an old woman in partial profile.

Delboeuf Illusion (b) The inner circle at left appears larger than the right circle although they are equal in size.

Ebbinghaus Illusion (c) The center circle on the left appears larger than its counterpart on the right, which is surrounded by larger circles.

Figural Aftereffects A temporary modification of the visual perception of some stimulus as a result of prior visual inspection of another stimulus.

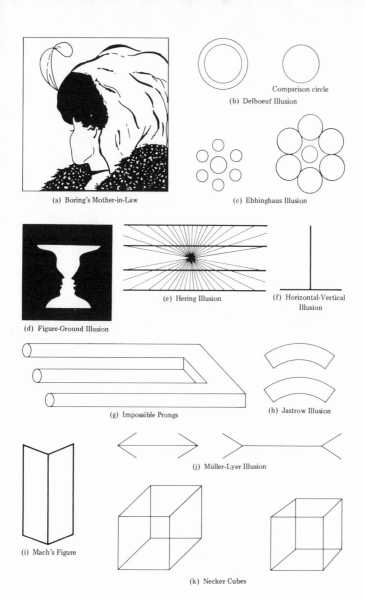

(a) Boring's Mother-in-Law

(b) Delboeuf Illusion

Comparison circle

(c) Ebbinghaus Illusion

(d) Figure-Ground Illusion

(e) Hering Illusion

(f) Horizontal-Vertical Illusion

(g) Impossible Prongs

(h) Jastrow Illusion

(i) Mach's Figure

(j) Müller-Lyer Illusion

(k) Necker Cubes

Figure I–2 Illusions.

99

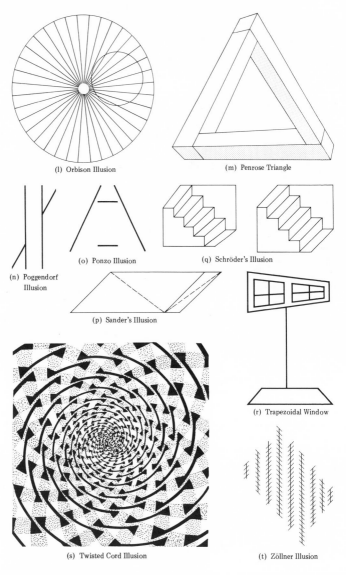

(l) Orbison Illusion

(m) Penrose Triangle

(n) Poggendorf Illusion

(o) Ponzo Illusion

(q) Schröder's Illusion

(p) Sander's Illusion

(r) Trapezoidal Window

(s) Twisted Cord Illusion

(t) Zöllner Illusion

Figure I-2 *(Continued)*

EXAMPLE: A straight line will appear curved to the left if seen after gazing at a line curved slightly to the right.

Figure-Ground Illusions (d)   Reversible forms that contain a distinctive foreground figure against a contrasting background. When the stimulus reverses, the background becomes figure, the old figure becomes ground and a different stimulus is seen. In this illustration, the white segment normally is seen first as a vase (figure) against a black background. When the stimulus reverses, two facial profiles are seen against a white ground.

Hering Illusion (e)   The horizontal lines appear to be curved but really are parallel.

Horizontal/Vertical Illusion (f)   The horizontal line appears to be shorter than the vertical line, but they really are the same length.

Impossible Prongs (g)   The inability to define discrete surfaces and spaces between the prongs presents a perceptual paradox.

Jastrow Illusion (h)   The two arcs are the same size although the top one appears smaller.

Kinesthetic Aftereffects   A temporary modification of tactual or kinesthetic sensations by prior contact with a contrasting stimulus.

EXAMPLE: An object of a given thickness will be felt as thicker than it is when prior contact is made with a thin object, and it will be felt as thinner than it is when prior contact is with a thick object.

Mach's Figure (i)   A reversible form in which the center line is seen as either foreground or background.

Moon Illusion   The horizon moon is seen as distinctly larger than the zenith moon.

Movement Aftereffects   A temporary modification of a visual perception of movement by prior observation of a moving stimulus. For example, if one gazes at a fixed object after watching a waterfall, the object will appear to move upward.

Müller–Lyer Illusion (j)   The horizontal lines are equal although the left line appears shorter than the right line.

Necker Cube (k)   The front and back surfaces of the reversible form change place in perspective.

Orbison Illusion (l)   The inner figure appears slightly asymmetrical but really is a circle.

Part–Whole Illusion   The tendency to overestimate the amount of total space of a figure that is occupied by a smaller, inner figure. For example, given a pair of concentric circles, the

101

inner circle will be seen as occupying a greater proportion of the space within the outer circle than it really does.

Penrose Triangle (m)   A perceptual paradox where it is impossible to identify more than two surfaces on the triangle that lie in the same plane.

Phi Phenomenon   The apparent motion created when adjacent members of an array of lights are lighted (and extinguished) in succession. It is the principle behind animated cartoons and the like. For example, lighting the far left member of a row of lights, followed by lighting the next members in rapid succession will produce the illusion of a streak of light moving from left to right.

Poggendorf Illusion (n)   The diagonal lines appear unable to join when in fact they can.

Ponzo Illusion (o)   The two horizontal lines are equal in length although the top line appears longer.

Pulfrich Illusion   An illusion of depth created by observing a moving object binocularly when one eye views through a filtered lens.

EXAMPLE: If a swinging pendulum is viewed with one eye covered by a sunglass lens, and one uncovered, the pendulum will appear to swing stereoscopically in an elliptical path. With the left eye filtered, the pendulum will appear to swing closer to the observer as it travels from right to left, and swing farther away as it travels from left to right.

Reversible Figures   A type of ambiguous figure in which the elements exchange or reverse form to produce, alternately, one of two different forms. (For examples, see *Boring's Mother-in-Law, Mach's Figure, Necker Cubes, Schröder's Staircase*.)

Sander's Illusion (p)   The two diagonals within the parallelogram are of equal length although the left diagonal appears longer.

Schröder's Staircase (q)   The staircase can be seen as normal or inverted.

Size–Weight Illusion   If two objects are of equal weight and different size, the larger one will be seen as heavier but felt as lighter.

Trapezoidal Window (syn. Ames' Window) (r)   A trapezoidal, windowlike object mounted vertically on a shaft connected to a motor. When rotated, the object appears to be a rectangular window that is oscillating instead of rotating.

Twisted Cord Illusion (s)   The spiral actually is a series of black and white striped concentric circles.

Zöllner Illusion (t)   The vertical lines really are parallel, not tilted.

102

Implicit Response   *See* Overt/Covert Response.

Impossible Paradox   *See under* Illusions.

Imprinting Procedure   A procedure for establishing the attractiveness of certain types of stimuli to an organism. The stimuli used often are artificial models that may bear any degree of resemblance to the animal under study. Sometimes live models are also used. Typically, the subjects are very young and are tested at different ages within a restricted range of ages. The subject commonly is placed in close proximity to the moving model for a fixed period of time, or until the subject approaches or follows the model. At a later time the subject is tested by placing it near the model and measuring the strength of its approach response, or by observing whether the subject chooses to approach the model or an alternative stimulus.

EXAMPLE: A young bird is placed in an apparatus where a model of an adult of the same species is moving slowly in a circle. The subject is left in the apparatus for a specified time period, or until it pursues the model, and then removed. At a later time the subject is placed in the center of a runway with the original model at one end and a model of another species at the other end. The subject then may be scored on the basis of which model it orients toward, how quickly this choice is made, and the speed with which it moves toward the chosen model.

Incidental Learning (*contr.* Intentional Learning)   Procedures for assessing the extent to which subjects learn in the absence of specific instructions to learn or under conditions where the information or stimulus conditions may be irrelevant to the motivational state operating at the time of learning.

EXAMPLE 1:   Subjects are given a list of forty words and told they will later be asked to recall the words. In a factorial design, half the words are typed in upper case and half in lower case; half the words are typed in red and half in black. A control group of subjects is instructed explicitly that at the time of recall they will be asked not only to indicate the words, but also to specify the color in which they appeared and whether they were typed in upper or lower case. The experimental group is led to believe that the test of recall will require only the recall of words, but not information about the case or color of the words. A comparison of the performance of the two groups indicates the extent to which the experimental group acquires incidental knowledge about the case and color of the word when not explicitly instructed to attend to these characteristics.

EXAMPLE 2:   Thirsty rats that are satiated for food receive training trials over a period of days in which they find water in one arm of a Y maze and food in the other arm. During the training trials, forced runs are used in order to assure that the rats receive an equal number of experiences with each goal box. On training trials where the rats go to the water side, they drink the water, but on the trials where they go to the food side, they do not eat the food. After these initial training trials, a test is made of whether or not the rats show incidental learning of the location of the irrelevant food reward. The rats are made hungry but satiated for water, and tested to see if they will now go immediately to the side of the maze in which they had previously found food.

Incidental Sampling   Sampling from subjects who happen to be conveniently at hand, but for which it would be difficult to specify the population represented by the sample. For example, human subjects are often first- or second-year students enrolled in a first course in psychology at the university where the research is conducted. It often is difficult to establish that the subjects are even representative of the population of first- and second-year students at that university, let alone a broader population of humans. Similarly, animal research often involves rats, dogs, monkeys, etc., that happen to be available in the animal laboratories maintained by a university, and that are not necessarily representative of the species. (*See also* Accidental Sampling.)

Inclusive Disjunction   *See* Disjunctive Concept.

Incomplete Block Design   A block design in which the number of matched subjects that form each block is less than the number of treatments, so that a randomized-blocks design cannot be used. For example, identical triplets form highly homogeneous blocks of three subjects each. If four treatment levels are to be tested, it would be necessary to use an incomplete block design with each block, or trio, given three of the treatments, making sure that each treatment was tested the same number of times. Specific plans for different block sizes and number of treatments may be found in many advanced experimental design textbooks. (*See also* Randomized-Block Design.)

Incomplete Counterbalancing (*syn.* Partial Counterbalancing)   A procedure for selecting sequences of experimental conditions, A, B, C, etc., in such a way as to distribute the effects of such extraneous variables as practice and fatigue more or less uniformly over the different conditions when complete counterbalancing is not feasible. For example, with five conditions there are $5! = 120$ possible sequences in which the conditions can be presented, e.g., DECAB. To use complete counterbalancing and assure that each condition is preceded and followed by every other condition would require using all 120 sequences, and thus would require a minimum of 120 subjects. Incomplete counterbalancing would involve using only some of the 120 sequences, usually selected in such a way that each condition occurs equally often at the first, second, third, fourth, and fifth position in the sequence. (*See also* Counterbalancing.)

Incomplete Designs   Experimental designs in which some of the combinations of treatment levels are not tested. One case in which such a design may be useful is when the number of combinations is large. For example, in a 2 x 3 x 3 x 4 design there are 72 combinations of levels. If a repeated-measures design cannot be used, a complete design would require 72 independent groups of subjects. Another case in which an incomplete design might be useful is when the number of homogeneous subjects is small. This may occur in testing special populations, such as autistic children, or with a block design, if it is not possible to obtain as many closely matched subjects as there are treatment combinations. Usually incomplete designs employ some sort of balancing, in such a way that higher order interactions are confounded and cannot be evaluated. Main effects and, sometimes, first-order interactions can be evaluated. The most common incomplete designs are Latin square, nested, and incomplete block designs. (*See also* Confounded Design; Graeco-Latin Square Design.)

Incomplete Factorial Design   *See* Incomplete Designs.

Incremental Threshold Design   A procedure used in signal detection research, similar to the ascending series of the method of limits for determining the absolute threshold in psychophysics. The signal (stimulus) to be detected is gradually increased against a background of noise (irrelevant stimuli), whereas in classical psychophysics, background stimuli are held to a minimum or eliminated. For example, a white light may be projected on a screen. In one spot, a particular wavelength is gradually increased in intensity until the subject detects the spot and/or identifies the hue.

Independence   An absence of association between two or more events or variables. Two events are independent if knowing that one event has occurred gives no information about the probability of the occurrence of the other event. Similarly, two variables are independent if knowing the value of one variable gives no information about possible values of the other variable. Conversely, if knowledge about one variable does give information about another, then the two are not independent. Mutually exclusive events are not independent, since knowing that one has occurred gives the information that the other did not occur. (*See also* Mutually Exclusive Events.)

EXAMPLE 1: In a standard deck of 52 cards, the probability of drawing a club is $13/52$ or .25. If you are told that a 4 has been drawn, the probability that the card is a club is still $1/4$ or .25, so the events "club" and "4" are independent, and by extension the variables "suit" and "value" are independent. However, if you are told that the card is black (clubs and spades), the probability that the card is a club is increased to $13/26$ or .5, so the events "black" and "club" and, by extension, the variables "color" and "suit" are not independent.

EXAMPLE 2: In general, sex and occupation are not independent. For example, a person who is a secretary may be a male but is more likely to be a female, whereas a heavy equipment operator may be a female but is more likely to be a male.

Independence, Test for (*syn.* Association, Test for) A significance test for a random sample of observations classified on two or more variables in a frequency (contingency) table. The research hypothesis is that the variables are related (i.e., not independent). A chi-square statistic is used to test the null hypothesis that the variables are independent, that is, that each cell probability is equal to the product of the corresponding marginal probabilities (symbolically, $p_{ij} = p_i p_j$). (*See also* Homogeneity of Proportions, Test for.)

EXAMPLE: A sample of college students are classified on the basis of sex and major. If 60% of the students in the college are male, and if sex and major are independent, then we would expect approximately 60% of the students in each major to be male. The test for independence would determine whether or not the actual percentages, or proportions, of males and females in the various majors differ significantly from this expectation. We would probably find that the two variables are not independent, and that, for example, more than 60% of the engineering majors are males and that less than 60% of the home economics majors are males.

Independent-Groups Design *See* Randomized-Groups Design.

Independent Variable The variable (factor) whose levels are selected by the experimenter in order to determine the effect of that variable on a dependent variable. In general, whenever a question is of the form "What is the effect of X on Y?" then X is the independent variable and Y is the dependent variable. In psychology, the independent variable can be an **environmental (situational) variable,** a **stimulus variable,** or a **subject variable.** Environmental variables are such things as climate, ambient noise and light levels, etc. Stimulus variables refer to experimenter induced conditions such as clarity of a picture, drug dosage level, etc. Subject variables (often called **organismic variables**) refer to existing characteristics of the subjects such as age, intelligence, handedness, etc. (*See also* Manipulated Variable; Nonmanipulated Variable.)

Indifference Response   A response indicating that the subject is unable or unwilling to make the required choice, such as "they're equal," "neither," or "I can't tell." Such responses often are difficult to handle in data analysis, and frequently are avoided by use of a forced-choice technique in which the subject is instructed to guess if uncertain. For example, a Likert scale consists of a number of items to which the responses are strongly agree or disagree, agree or disagree, or uncertain; using the method of constant stimuli for judging weights, the subject says if each of a series of objects feels heavier or lighter than the standard or if they feel the same. The responses "uncertain" or "the same" may reflect a true neutrality, or they may reflect such characteristics as caution or unwillingness to make difficult decisions. (*See also* Forced-Choice Technique; Interval of Uncertainty.)

Individual Datum (*contr.* Group Datum)   A single score for one subject. The score may be an aggregate of several observations (e.g., mean response rate for successive time periods) or unitary (e.g., the latency of a single response).

Individual Differences   *See* Subject Variable.

Inferential Statistics   The area of statistics concerned with making general statements (inferences) about a population on the basis of the information in a sample from that population. The two classes of inferential procedures are estimation and hypothesis testing. Frequently used inferential statistics are chi-square, t statistic, and F ratio. (*See also* Descriptive Statistics.)

Inflection Point   A point in the graph of a continuous function where the curve changes from concave upward to concave downward or vice versa. Figure I–3 illustrates an inflection point.

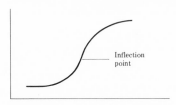

Inflection point

Figure I–3

Information   In information theory research, the information content of a stimulus is related to its probability of occurrence and is

107

proportional to the reduction in uncertainty on the part of a receiver in attempting to predict what stimulus might occur. The information content of a stimulus is measured in **bits** (a contraction of binary digit) and is defined as $\log_2 1/p$, where p is the a priori probability of occurrence of the stimulus. Thus, the more probable the stimulus, the less information it conveys. If a stimulus is certain to occur (i.e., has probability 1.00), then the information it contains is $\log_2 1/p = \log_2 1/1.00 = \log_2 1.00 = 0$ bits. ($\log_2$ of a number is the exponent to which the base number 2 must be raised in order to equal the given number, so $\log_2 1.00 = 0$ because $1 = 2^0$.) If the stimulus has probability $1/8$, the information content is $\log_2 1/p = \log_2 1/(1/8) = \log_2 8 = 3$ bits since $8 = 2^3$. Similarly, the amount of information in stimuli having probabilities $1/16$, $1/64$, and $1/1024$ are 4, 6, and 10 bits, respectively.

EXAMPLE: A subject's task in an experiment is to name a stimulus as quickly as possible. Verbal reaction time (RT), obtained with a voice key, measures the time between the onset of a light that illuminates the stimulus and the first sound of the subject's voice in naming it aloud. The stimuli consist of the nine digits, 1 to 9, the 26 letters, A to Z, 16 geometrical forms ($\square$, $\triangle$, $\star$, etc.), and the names of the 16 forms typed in capitals (SQUARE, TRIANGLE, STAR, etc.). On each trial the subject is told from which category the next stimulus to be shown is selected (i.e., whether it will be a number, letter, form, or word), but on these trials all members of the specified category are equally likely to be presented. The probabilities associated with number, letters, words, and forms are $1/9$, $1/26$, $1/16$, and $1/16$, respectively, with respective information contents (stimulus uncertainties) of 3.17, 4.70, 4.00, and 4.00 bits.

Information Processing Task   A general term for a variety of tasks in which verbal or perceptual stimuli are presented, and the subject's recognition, short-term retention, reaction time, etc., are measured. (*For examples of such tasks, see* Free Recall; Masking; Reaction Time; Search Task; Signal Detection Task.)

Information Test   A test that measures factual knowledge in a variety of areas such as politics, sports, music, current events, and the like. Information tests constitute subtests of many intelligence tests.

Insight Problems   Problems designed to study the process of insight (sudden solution in the absence of overt trial and error) in problem solving. They frequently involve some familiar object that must be used in an unusual way to achieve the solution.

Instructed Conditioning   A procedure that follows a classical conditioning paradigm in which the subject is instructed to make a response to a particular signal (the **unconditioned stimulus,** or US). Another stimulus (the **conditioned stimulus,** or CS) is introduced just before the US, and a number of such conditioning trials is given. The **conditioned response** (CR) is defined as any part of the instructed response that is elicited by the CS, (i.e., a response that anticipates the US).

EXAMPLE: A subject is instructed to lift the right index finger whenever a signal light goes on. This response may then be practiced for several trials. On subsequent trials, the light is preceded by a tone. A CR would be defined as any partial or complete finger lift made in response to the tone.

Instructional Variable The use of different sets of instructions as the levels of an independent variable. For example, rate of learning may be studied under conditions in which subjects are instructed to remember words from a given list or to think of synonyms for them. (*See also* Task Variable.)

Instrumental/Operant Conditioning (*contr.* Classical Conditioning) A conditioning procedure in which the subject's behavior determines the type of stimulus event to follow it (i.e., whether the behavior will be followed by reward, punishment, or nothing at all). A distinction sometimes is made between instrumental conditioning (*syn.* Instrumental Learning) and operant conditioning in terms of the laboratory restrictions placed on making a response. In instrumental conditioning, the response is controlled and discrete (e.g., a left or right turn at a choice point), whereas in operant conditioning responses can occur more or less "freely," e.g., pecking a target. (*For examples see* Punishment Training *and* Reward Training; *see also* Schedules of Reinforcement.)

Instrumental/Operant Response In the most general meaning, any response that in some way acts on the subject's environment or on the subject's relationship to its environment. The term also may refer to any response that is under voluntary control and/ or any response that is emitted rather than elicited by a specific stimulus. A distinction sometimes is made between instrumental and operant responses in terms of the laboratory restrictions placed on them. Within the apparatus or experimental environment, operant responses occur freely and continuously (e.g., pressing a bar, pecking a key, or scratching one's ear), whereas instrumental responses are controlled and discrete (e.g., one run through a maze or a choice made on a given trial). (*See also* Elicited/Emitted Response; Respondent Behavior.)

Instrumentation Effects Any of a variety of effects arising from the interaction between the experimental subject and the measuring instrument or stimulus instrument. These difficulties may range from minor imprecision to outright confounding with a resulting loss of validity. Instrumentation effects include categories of problems:

1. *Physical Environment* Modification of behavior as a result of the subject's proximity to, or physical coupling with the apparatus. For example, to monitor a subject's physiological functioning properly during a relaxation treatment program, it is necessary to isolate the person from distracting noises. A small, soundproof isolation chamber, however, might be too confining and increase the subject's arousal level with concomitant increases in physiological activity that might distort the effect of the treatment.

2. *Social Environment* Reactive measuring instruments may distort subjects' behavior simply because they create a nonnatural social environment for the subject. The measurement operations may create response sets or increased sensitivity to the instrument, and the resulting change(s) in behavior may be mistakenly attributed to some experimental treatment. For example, an intelligence pretest might sensitize a child to some intellectually enriching treatment such as selected television programming, and thereby increase (or reduce) its impact on an intelligence posttest relative to a subject who had not received the pretest. Also, the very nature of the task might imply to the subject some particular "right" way to respond.

3. *Measurement Error* Imprecise measuring instruments may obscure the real effects of independent variables by increasing error variance. Additionally, there may occur systematic changes in the accuracy and/or precision of the instrument and/or operator over time. For example, some older electronic instruments measure differently after "warming up," and differently again if overused. Also, an experimenter's ability to operate or read an instrument may increase or decrease with continued practice.

(*See also* Atmosphere Effect; Demand Characteristic; Experimenter Effect; Measurement Error.)

Intact Groups Design Any research design in which the values or levels of independent variables are defined by existing groups of subjects. For example, if socioeconomic status (SES) of elementary school children was selected as an independent variable of interest, test scores of students attending schools located in low-, middle-, and high-income neighborhoods could be obtained and the SES variable defined by the school attended.

Intelligence Quotient (*abbr.* IQ) *See* Intelligence Score.

Intelligence Scale *See* Intelligence Test.

110

Intelligence Score Any index of relative intelligence derived from standardized intelligence tests. Because these tests tend to differ somewhat in intent and content, it is important to mention the name of the test in conjuction with the derived intelligence score. The most commonly employed index is the intelligence quotient, a standardized score with a mean of 100.

Intelligence Test (*syn.* Intelligence Scale) A measure comprising a series of standardized tasks to assess intellectual functioning in problem solving, perceiving, thinking, reasoning, imagination, and in some cases even adaptation or adjustment. (*See also* Intelligence Score.)

Intentional Learning (*contr.* Incidental Learning) A procedure used with human subjects in which the subjects are given explicit instructions to learn the material involved, and so are presumably studying with intent to learn.

Interaction In experiments with two or more independent variables, the condition that exists when the effect of one independent variable differs at different levels of the other independent variable(s). (*See also* Higher Order Interaction; Main Effect.)

EXAMPLE 1: Figure I–4 shows data from an experiment that examined the effects of hunger level (low, medium, or high) and amount of threat of physical pain (mild to strong shock) on the subjects' speed of solving simple mathematics problems. Under low levels of threat, increasing levels of hunger produced small increases in solution speed. Under moderate levels of threat, the relationship changes to show a very positive effect of hunger on solution time. Under high levels of threat, the relationship again changes to show a negative effect on performance when both variables are present in large amounts.

EXAMPLE 2: Figure I–5 shows the outcome of a study of the effects of (1) type of teaching method (A or B) and (2) socioeconomic status (SES) of the schools' locations (low or high). Note that *overall* Methods A and B are equally effective. Similarly, achievement scores

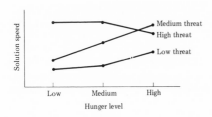

Figure I–4

111

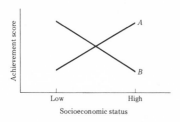

Figure I–5

from low and high SES status schools do not differ overall. The presence of an interaction, however, shows that teaching by Method A was more effective when SES was high, whereas Method B was more successful when SES was low.

Interaction Process Analysis (*syn.* Bale's Technique) A system for coding direct observations of social behavior. Trained observers classify behavior (in terms of its presumed significance for the observed person) along 12 discrete categories that are subsumed under four broad categories: active task behavior, passive task behavior, positive emotional behavior, and negative emotional behavior. Observations are converted into quantitative measures by computing the frequencies of acts in each category, which then yield individual or group profiles.

Intercorrelation With three or more variables, computation of the correlations between all possible pairs of variables. The results usually are presented in an **intercorrelation matrix,** with the names of the variables used as headings for both the rows and the columns of the table, and the correlations entered in the corresponding cells.

EXAMPLE: Table I–1 shows the intercorrelations among the magnitude of reflex eyelid response to an air puff on the cornea and several measures of the conditioned eyelid response. These data show that there is a moderate correlation between the magnitude of the unconditioned response and the frequency, magnitude, and amplitude of the conditioned response (.40, .30, and .43, respectively), but essen-

Table I–1

	Freq	Mag	Amp	Lat
Response to air puff	.40	.30	.43	−.09
Frequency of CR		.71	.47	−.48
Magnitude of CR			.89	−.25
Amplitude of CR				−.15

tially no correlation between magnitude of the unconditioned response and latency of the conditioned response (−.09). The correlations between magnitude of conditioned response and the frequency and amplitude of response are relatively high (.71 and .89) whereas latency is negatively correlated with the other three measures of the conditioned response.

Intercorrelation Matrix   *See* Intercorrelation.

Interest Inventory   A measure of an individual's interests, likes, and preferences. Standardized inventories sometimes are used for clinical diagnoses or personnel selection, but their primary usage is in the area of vocational guidance.

Interitem Interval   In verbal learning, the interval measured from the offset of one stimulus item to the onset of a subsequent item. In serial anticipation learning, this usually is the interval during which a subject is required to anticipate orally the upcoming item.

Interlocking Schedule of Reinforcement   An operant conditioning procedure in which two schedules of reinforcement are in effect simultaneously. Performance relative to one schedule modifies the requirements of the other schedule. It is usually the case that the number of responses needed to produce reinforcement decreases with the passage of some defined time interval. Thus, initial high rates of responding are not reinforced.

EXAMPLE: In the initial portion of a 2 min interval, a rat working under an interlocking fixed-interval 2-min—fixed-ratio-30 (FI-2, FR-30) schedule of reinforcement would be reinforced according to the requirement of one pellet for each 30 bar presses. During the 2-min interval, this ratio requirement gradually is reduced, so that near the end of the interval the animal may be reinforced with one pellet for every four responses, and after 2 min has expired, a single response will obtain reinforcement. Thus, the number of responses needed to produce reinforcement decreases according to some function of time.

Intermittent Reinforcement   *See* Partial Reinforcement.

Internal Consistency   The degree to which individual items in a test, or groups of items such as first and second halves or subtests, correlate with each other or with the total score on the test. Several measures of internal consistency have been devised, which are used in evaluating the reliability of tests.

Internal Reliability   The degree of consistency among measurements, either from trial to trial in a given subject or from subject to subject within a given experiment. Statistically, a low degree of internal reliability appears as a high degree of random variability (error variance). (*See also* External Reliability.)

Internal Validity   (1) In testing, the degree to which a test measures what it intends to measure. (2) In experimentation, the degree to which one can infer a cause–effect relationship between an independent variable and changes in a dependent variable in an experiment. Stated differently, it is the degree to which an experiment is free from confounding variables. (*See also* Confounding; External Validity.)

International System of Units (*abbr.* SI)   An extension and refinement of the traditional metric system, recommended for use in the United States and adopted by the American Psychological Association (APA) in 1969 for use in all APA journals. Measurements for these and for many other journals in the field of psychology must be given in SI units or in nonmetric units with SI equivalents.

Interoceptive Conditioning (*contr.* Exteroceptive Conditioning)   Any classical conditioning procedure in which the stimuli used and/or the responses measured are internal. For example, introduction of a liquid directly into the stomach could serve as an interoceptive conditioned stimulus (CS) followed by an electric shock to the foot as an unconditioned stimulus (US). A conditioned response (CR) would be defined as a limb flexion to the liquid CS. Alternatively, the liquid could serve as an US, preceded by a visual CS, with stomach contractions to the visual stimulus as the CR.

Interpolated Event   A technique used in a large variety of learning and performance studies in which a stimulus or task is presented in the interval between two other stimuli or tasks. It usually is done to observe facilitative or disruptive effects of the event on behaviors or to prevent subjects from engaging in undesired behaviors during some empty interval.

Interpolated Reinforcement   The brief substitution of one reinforcement schedule for an ongoing schedule of reinforcement. For example, fixed interval reinforcement may be reintroduced briefly and periodically in place of a fixed-ratio schedule. The term is sometimes also used to mean a brief change in the type or amount of reinforcement given or the introduction of a change in the temporal locus of reinforcement, e.g., a change in the response–reinforcement-delay interval.

Interpolated Stimulus   *See* Interpolated Event.

Interpolated Task   *See* Interpolated Event.

Interquartile Range   *See* Semi-Interquartile Range.

Interrater Reliability   *See* Interreliability.

114

Interreliability (*syn.* Interrater Reliability)   The extent to which two or more observers agree on the characteristics of an observation. A common measure of interreliability is the phi coefficient.

Interresponse Time (*abbr.* IRT)   The time between responses, usually measured either from the onset of the first response to the onset of the second response, or from offset of the first response to onset of the second response.

Interstimulus Interval (*abbr.* ISI)   The time between two stimuli within a given trial. It is measured from onset of one stimulus to onset of a second stimulus, or from offset of one stimulus to onset of the second stimulus.

Intertrial Interval (*abbr.* ITI)   The interval between repetitions of an event or set of events. In maze learning, for example, one trial would consist of one traversal of the maze, or an elapsed period of time during which such a response was allowed to occur. In verbal learning, one trial consists of one exposure to the entire set of items.

Interval Data   The data obtained when an interval scale of measurement is used.

Interval Estimation   Use of a sample from a population in order to establish a range of numerical values that will, with some specified probability, contain the true value of a population parameter such as a mean, a standard deviation, a proportion, etc.

EXAMPLE: A sample of eligible voters shows that 57% or .57 are in favor of an issue, and the sample value of .57 is the best available estimate of the exact value of the proportion in the total population who favor the issue. However, due to sampling error, it is likely that the sample value will be in error to some degree as an estimate of the population proportion. The agency making the survey may prefer to express the result in terms of an interval estimate, saying that the proportion in the population who favor the issue is some value in the interval marked by the sample proportion plus or minus some margin of error. Thus the agency may report that the population proportion is $.57 \pm .03$, or some value in the interval $.54 - .60$. If certain statistical assumptions are met, the agency would be able to specify the probability that the interval does contain the true value of the population proportion, e.g., to say that this probability is .95 or .99. (*See also* Confidence Interval; Confidence Limits; Point Estimation.)

Interval of Delay   *See* Delay Interval.

Interval of Uncertainty   In psychophysics, the range of those stimuli which are not discriminably different from the standard stimulus. Formally, it is defined as the difference between the upper and lower difference thresholds (usually the stimulus values that are judged, respectively, greater than and less than the test stimulus 50% of the time). (*See also* Difference Threshold.)

Interval Scale   A scale of measurement in which the units are equal (constant) throughout, but which lacks an absolute zero point. For example, the Celsius scale has a "0" point that is arbitrarily set at the freezing point of water, not the complete absence of heat. It has, however, equal units.

Interval Schedules of Reinforcement   Delivery of reinforcements for responding in accordance with certain temporal intervals. For example, rewarding the first response that occurs after 2 min has elapsed is a Fixed-Interval 2-min schedule of reinforcement. (*See also* Fixed-Interval Schedule of Reinforcement; Variable-Interval Schedule of Reinforcement.)

Intervening Variable   An unobservable or unobserved process or entity that is hypothesized in order to explain relationships between antecedent conditions and consequent events. In this respect, the term is synonymous with the term **hypothetical construct.** In a somewhat different usage, the term is reserved for those concepts that only summarize or define a set of relationships between antecedent conditions and consequent events. In this respect there is no implication that the concept has, or may possibly have, an independent existence.

Interview Technique   A procedure for obtaining data from observations of a person's report of his/her own behavior. Interviews may be unstructured (open-ended questions such as "What do you think of the United Nations?") or structured (specific questions that narrow the range of response, such as "Do you like the United Nations?"), or may include both types of questions.

Intradimensional Shift   *See* Reversal/Nonreversal Shift.

Intrinsic Validity   That aspect of test validity which varies according to the nature of the test-taker's preparation for the test. (*See also* External Validity; Face Validity.)

EXAMPLE: A college entrance exam should test academic skills. If the test taker prepares for it by studying extra composition and spelling, the intrinsic validity of the test increases since the advantages gained by test takers are generalizable (the test takers turn into better students). On the other hand, if preparation for the test focuses on maze solving, the test's intrinsic validity is reduced, since such knowledge is unlikely to be generalized to other aspects of being a good student.

Introspection   Historically, a formal method for obtaining psychological data through the objective, analytical description of the content of one's own conscious experience. These observations were considered to be the primary data on psychological processes. In contemporary usage, there are fewer restraints on what the observer may report, and the data generally are considered to be useful primarily as sources of testable hypotheses about psychological processes. (*See also* Subjective Report.)

Intrusion Error   In verbal learning, any incorrect response other than a grammatical change (such as singular to plural, or change of verb tense) of the correct word. Intrusion errors may be classified as *intralist,* when an item from a list of items is given in the wrong sequence; *interlist,* when the incorrect item was included in a previously learned list; and *extralist,* when the incorrect item has not been used in the stimulus materials for the experiment.

Invariance   A term that describes any property that is unchanged by certain specified transformations. The transformations that leave a property invariant are called **permissible transformations.** For example, the shape of a coffee mug is invariant over rotation and translation (i.e, as it is rotated and moved from one place to another), whereas the shape of a bouquet of flowers may be invariant over translation but not rotation. In particular, measurement scales commonly are described in terms of the permissible transformations that leave the scale invariant. For example, nominal scales, which simply classify objects, are invariant under a one-to-one transformation, relabeling the categories. Ordinal scales are invariant under any increasing monotonic transformation, preserving the order of the measurements; interval scales under any linear transformation, changing the zero point and unit of measurement; ratio scales under any multiplicative transformation, changing the unit of measurement.

Inverse Relationship   *See* Positive/Negative Relationship.

Irrelevant Cue   Any stimulus or stimulus property other than those which are defined as relevant to the correct response. Usually the term is used when the cue is of direct interest to the experimenter; otherwise it is known as an extraneous or **irrelevant stimulus.** Irrelevant cues may be completely correlated with the relevant cue(s), partially correlated, or uncorrelated.

EXAMPLE: A child is to sort a set of cards, putting circles in one pile and squares in another pile. Color is completely correlated if all the circles are red and all the squares are green; the effect of the irrelevant cue may be assessed by introducing a green circle. Color is partially correlated if most of the circles are red and most of the squares are green. The experimenter may be interested in the effect of the degree of correlation (i.e., the ratio of red circles to green circles). Color is uncorrelated if equal numbers of circles and squares are red and green. The experimenter may be interested in the effect of varying the number of irrelevant cues.

Irrelevant Reward   *See* Incidental Learning.

Irrelevant Stimulus   *See* Irrelevant Cue.

IRT   *See* Interresponse Time.

ISI   *See* Interstimulus Interval.

Isosensitivity Curve   *See* ROC Curve.

Item Analysis   In general, a term that refers to the determination of test item characteristics, such as difficulty level, clarity level, time limit, and other aspects of item selection. More specifically, the term refers to the determination of item discriminability. Since a test as a whole is expected to discriminate between various degrees of the attribute it measures, the items that comprise it should do the same. Items that are too ambiguous, too easy, or too difficult usually are discarded. For example, an achievement test item that is answered with the same ease, or encountered with the same difficulty, by both kindergarten children and high school graduates is unsuitable.

Item Reversal   In test construction, the inclusion of items aimed at breaking the test taker's cognitive set. Positively worded items on an attitude scale are balanced by some items that are negatively worded (reversed items), or vice versa. For example, in a religious attitude test, "The church has a good influence in any community" and "The church is the primary educator of proper morals" must be balanced by an item such as "The church is not a primary source of inspiration." If this is not done, the test taker may form a set that every positively worded statement is pro-church and answer accordingly, which in turn may affect the validity of the test. Item reversal also is an effective technique to counteract problems of test validity due to social acquiescence. (*See also* Social Acquiescence.)

Item Weighting   The assignment of a numerical score to a test item that reflects the proportion to which passing or failing the item contributes to the total test score. In practice, this means that test items are not of equal importance to what is measured. Most tests employ unweighted items because item weighting is a laborious process. Some forms of tests, however (e.g., Thurstone-type tests), employ weighted items successfully to make fine discriminations in the mid-range of attitudes. (*See also* Equal-Appearing Intervals, Method of.)

ITI   *See* Intertrial Interval.

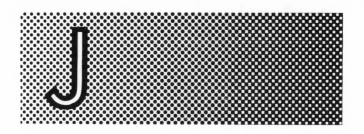

Jastrow's Illusion   *See under* Illusions.

J-Curve   A graphic presentation of an extremely skewed unimodal distribution with the mode at one end. It is characteristic of data with marked floor or ceiling effect.

   EXAMPLE: The curve in Figure J–1 illustrates workers' conformity to the institutionalized norm of on-time arrival at work. Most of the workers adhere to the norm (0-min deviation). Greater deviations via early or late arrival at work occur with decreasing frequency until a J-curve emerges.

JND   *See* Difference Threshold.

JNND   *See* Just Not Noticeable Difference.

Joint Event   The occurrence in a single observation of two or more events. For example, if students are classifed by age, class, and major, then being 20 years old, a sophmore, and a psychology major is a joint event; if a coin is tossed twice, then heads on the first toss followed by tails on the second toss is a joint event.

Joint Probability   The probability of a joint event. If two events, *A* and *B*, are independent, the probability of the joint event is the

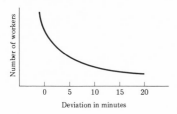

Figure J–1

product of their separate probabilities; symbolically, $P(A$ and $B)$ $= P(A)P(B)$. If the events are not independent, the probability of the joint event is the probability of one event times the conditional probability of the other: $P(A$ and $B) = P(A)P(B|A)$. (*See also* Conditional Probability; Independence.)

Just Noticeable Difference (*abbr.* JND) *See* Difference Threshold.

Just Not Noticeable Difference (*abbr.* JNND) The largest change in a stimulus that a subject fails to detect (i.e., the difference just smaller than the difference threshold).

Kendall's Coefficient of Concordance   *See* Concordance, Coefficient of.

Kendall's Rank-Correlation Coefficient (symb. t syn. Kendall's Tau; Tau Coefficient)   A measure of agreement between two separate rankings based on the number of inversions. (An inversion is an instance in which the two rankings of a pair of items disagree.) The tau coefficient is computed by taking 1 minus the proportion of inversions.

EXAMPLE: Two judges rated the friendliness of five persons from their photographs. For one judge, the rank order was B, A, C, D, E; for the other judge, the order was E, A, C, B, D. In the 10 possible pairs, six show inversion: AB, AE, BC, BE, CE, and DE. For example, B was rated higher than A by the first judge, but lower than A by the second judge. The tau coefficient for these data is 1 − 6/10 = .4.

Kendall's Tau   *See* Kendall's Rank-Correlation Coefficient.

Kinesthetic Aftereffects   *See under* Illusions.

Knowledge of Results   Information provided to the subject by the experimenter regarding the adequacy of the subject's performance. (*See also* Feedback.)

EXAMPLE: Blindfolded subjects are asked to draw a horizontal line that is 10 cm long. Any line shorter than 9.5 cm is considered "short," any line longer than 10.5 cm is considered "long," and any line between 9.5 and 10.5 cm is considered "right." The subjects in one group are told immediately after drawing each line whether it was short, long, or right. Subjects in the control group are given no information concerning the accuracy of their lines. The number of "right" responses for the two groups can be compared over a series of trials.

Known-Group Validity   In testing, a method of establishing construct validity that uses intact groups clearly known to be representative of the range and class of behavior that the construct defines. For example, if the construct is "conservationism" (i.e., a concern for the protection of wildlands and wildlife), the measure of conservationism may be validated by administering it to members of the Sierra Club and to individuals associated with land development and the building industry, with the former expected to score high and the latter to score low.

Kolmogorov–Smirnov Tests   Two nonparametric significance tests for comparing frequency distributions.

1. *Single-Sample Test*   A measure of goodness of fit between frequencies observed in a sample and the frequencies specified by some theoretical distribution. The test involves determining a statistic D that is the maximum difference between the values of the cumulative frequencies for the sample and those specified by the model.

2. *Two-Sample Test*   A test of the significance of the difference between two sample distributions. The maximum difference between the cumulative frequencies for corresponding locations in the two sample distributions is determined.

KR-20   *See* Kuder–Richardson Formula.

Kruskall–Wallis *H* Test   A nonparametric test of differences in location for two or more independent samples with a total of N observations. It is an alternative to a single-factor analysis of variance or a k-sample median test. The scores in the combined samples are ranked, and the sum of the ranks, T_i^2, is found for each sample. The test static is

$$H = \frac{12}{N(N-1)} \sum_{i=1}^{k} \frac{T_i^2}{n_i} - 3(N+1)$$

where N is the total number of observations in the combined samples, the T_i are the sums of the ranks for each sample, and the n_i are the corresponding sample sizes. If the sample sizes are sufficiently large (usually all n_i greater than 5) the statistic H has approximately a χ^2 distribution with degrees of freedom equal to one less than the number of samples; otherwise a special table of critical values is needed. (*See also* Analysis of Variance for Ranked Data.)

EXAMPLE: An experimenter tests four orangutans, six rhesus monkeys, and five squirrel monkeys, for a total of 15 subjects. Their scores (number of errors on a problem-solving task) are shown in order of magnitude and ranked and identified by species (O, R, or S):

Species:	O	O	R	R	O	R	S	O	R	R	S	S	R	S	S
Score	37	37	38	40	43	44	45	47	48	51	57	61	62	64	75
Rank	1	2	3	4	5	6	7	8	9	10	11	12	13	14	15

For the orangutans, $T = 1 + 2 + 5 + 8 = 16$ and $n = 4$; similarly, for the rhesus monkeys $T = 45$ and $n = 6$; for the squirrel monkeys $T = 59$ and $n = 5$. To test for differences among the species on this task,

$$H = \frac{12}{(15)(16)} \left[\frac{16^2}{4} + \frac{45^2}{6} + \frac{59^2}{5} \right] - 3(16) = 6.885.$$

If the sample sizes had been slightly larger this value would be compared to the critical value for a χ^2 distribution with two degrees of freedom.

Kuder–Richardson Formula Any of several formulas for estimating the reliability of a test from a single administration, based on internal consistency. The most commonly used is KR-20,

$$r_{11} = \frac{k}{k-1} \left(1 - \frac{\Sigma pq}{\sigma_x^2} \right)$$

where k is the number of items on the test, σ_x^2 is the variance of the total scores on the test, p is the proportion of persons who pass an item, $q = 1 - p$, and the summation is over the k items.

Kurtosis (*syn.* Peakedness) A term that describes the manner in which probability distributions differ from the normal probability curve (**mesokurtosis**) by being more peaked (**leptokurtosis**) or more flat (**platykurtosis**). (See Figure K-1.)

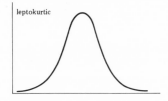
leptokurtic

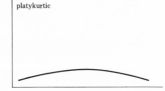
platykurtic

Figure K–1

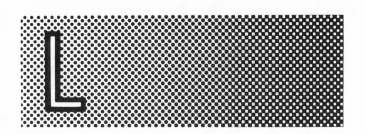

Lag   *See* Autocorrelation; Cross-Lagged Panel Correlation.

Lagged Measure   *See* Autocorrelation; Cross-Lagged Panel Correlation.

Latency of Response   The interval between the onset of a stimulus and the onset of a response to that stimulus. It is sometimes used as a measure of response strength. (*See also* Response Time.)

Latin Square Design   An experimental design with a balanced arrangement of three variables, each having the same number of levels, in an incomplete factorial design. The levels of one variable form the rows of the square, and the levels of a second variable form the columns. The levels of the third variable are placed in the square so that each level occurs once in each row and once in each column. The design permits evaluation of variability due to each of the variables, but does not permit evaluation of any interactions. It may be used to reduce the number of treatment groups in an experiment or, more commonly, to control for the effects of order of treatments in a repeated measurements design. A Latin square can also be used to determine the order of presentation of stimuli, for example by having each row represent a block of trials, with the columns representing trials within the block. In a complex Latin square design, levels of a fourth variable are assigned to different Latin square arrangements of the other three. (*See also* Graeco-Latin Square Design.)

EXAMPLE 1:   To study the effect of (A) teaching method and (B) students' ethnicity on learning, 15 students are sampled from each of three schools. Five black, five white, and five chicano students are sampled from each of the three schools. These are given different teaching methods as shown in Table L–1.

Table L–1

	Method 1	Method 2	Method 3
School 1	(5) Black students	(5) White students	(5) Chicano students
School 2	(5) White students	(5) Chicano students	(5) Black students
School 3	(5) Chicano students	(5) Black students	(5) White students

EXAMPLE 2:   To study the effects of type of print on the learning of a given material, a random sample of students is divided into four random subsamples (Groups 1 through 4). Each student is tested with material in four different types of print (A through D) as shown in Table L–2.

Table L–2

	1st test	2nd test	3rd test	4th test
Group 1	Print C	Print A	Print B	Print D
Group 2	Print B	Print C	Print D	Print A
Group 3	Print D	Print B	Print A	Print C
Group 4	Print A	Print D	Print C	Print B

EXAMPLE 3:   The simple Latin square described in Example 2 can be extended into a complex design by adding another dimension. Table L–3 shows the scores of high and low CPA students who were presented with the material in four different types of prints.

Table L–3

		1st test	2nd test	3rd test	4th test
High	Group 1	Print C	Print A	Print B	Print D
GPA	Group 2	Print B	Print C	Print D	Print A
students	Group 3	Print D	Print B	Print A	Print C
	Group 4	Print A	Print D	Print C	Print B
Low	Group 5	Print C	Print A	Print D	Print B
GPA	Group 6	Print A	Print D	Print B	Print C
students	Group 7	Print D	Print B	Print C	Print A
	Group 8	Print B	Print C	Print A	Print D

Lattice Designs.   *See* Incomplete Designs.

Learned Reinforcement   *See* Conditioned Reinforcement.

Learning Curve   Any graphic presentation which shows change in the strength of some response as a function of training trials or sessions. (*See also* Backward Learning Curve; Melton Learning Curve; Running Average; Vincent Curve.)

Learning Set Procedure   An extended transfer paradigm in which a subject is given a series of two-choice discrimination learning

126

problems. Each problem consists of a pair of stimuli (e.g., a circle and an oval), with one of the two designated as the positive stimulus. Usually, a small, fixed number of trials is given on each problem. Learning set development is measured by the speed with which each consecutive discrimination problem is mastered.

Least Squares, Method of One of several mathematical procedures for obtaining estimates of the parameters of a mathematical model, e.g., fitting a regression line. Least squares estimators are those which minimize the sum of squared deviations from the model. (*See also* Linear Regression.)

Leptokurtosis *See* Kurtosis.

Level In experimental design, one of the values of the factor (independent variable) selected for study. For example, in a study of the effects of different intertrial intervals on speed of learning a motor skill task, four levels of the intertrial interval might be 15, 30, 60 and 90 seconds. Likewise, in a study of differences in ethnic group attitudes toward religion, three levels of that variable might be French, Germans, and Swedes.

Level of Confidence *See* Confidence Interval.

Level of Significance *See* Significance Level.

Likelihood Ratio A ratio of the likelihoods or probabilities of a given observation or sample under two alternative hypotheses. Likelihood ratios can be used to choose between two simple hypotheses, and in Bayesian statistics are used in computing posterior odds and probabilities.

EXAMPLE: One theory of choice behavior predicts that, on a five-point scale, a person will use the middle category 40% of the time, and another theory predicts 20% of the time. Under the guise of an ESP experiment, a subject rates 10 unseen objects, and uses the middle category three times. The likelihood of this event if the first theory is correct (i.e., the probability of 3 successes if $p = .4$) is .2150, and the likelihood of this event if the second theory is correct is .2013. The likelihood ratio, .2150/.2013, is 1.07. Since this ratio is greater than 1, the data support the first theory. If the odds in favor of the first theory prior to the experiment were 2 to 1, the posterior odds in favor of the first theory are the prior odds times the likelihood ratio, or 2.14 to 1.

Likert Scale Any scale constructed by the method of summated ratings. (*For an example, see* Summated Ratings, Method of.)

Limen *See* Threshold.

Limits, Method of A psychophysical method used to determine absolute and difference thresholds. The subject is presented with a series of stimulus values in ascending or descending order, and for each value the subject reports whether or not the stimulus was detected, or whether the stimulus value differed from the value of a standard stimulus. (*See also* Constant Stimuli, Method of).

EXAMPLE 1—Absolute Thresholds: The subject is given a series of trials in which a small disc is illuminated, and is asked to report "yes" if the light is detected. Light intensity for the first trial is a value clearly above the subject's threshold. For each succeeding trial, the light intensity is reduced by some specified amount (descending series). This is continued until the subject reaches a criterion for failure to detect the stimulus, such as the first "no" trial. The threshold for that series is defined as the stimulus value midway between that for the last "yes" trial and that for the first "no" trial. The next series might begin with a stimulus value well below the subject's threshold, with values for each succeeding trial increased by a specified amount (ascending series). The series is continued until the subject reaches a criterion for detection of the stimulus, and another threshold is computed. After a run of ascending and descending series, the subject's mean threshold is computed.

EXAMPLE 2—Difference Thresholds: The subject is presented with a disc of light set at a constant intensity (the standard stimulus), and a comparison stimulus disc which varies in intensity. The subject reports whether the comparison is brighter, equal, or less bright than the standard. The series is started with a comparison stimulus value clearly above the standard. On each succeeding trial the intensity is decreased by some specified amount until the comparison stimulus clearly is below the intensity of the standard. An upper threshold is computed for the point at which the judgments change from "brighter" to "equal" in the same way as an absolute threshold is computed, and a lower threshold is computed for the point at which judgments change from "equal" to "less bright." The next series is started with the comparison stimulus clearly below the standard with brightness increasing to a value clearly above the standard (ascending series). After a run of ascending and descending series, the subject's mean upper and mean lower thresholds are computed The **upper difference threshold** is the difference between the upper threshold and stimulus judged equal to the standard (PSE); the **lower difference threshold** is the difference between stimulus judged equal to the standard and the lower threshold. The difference threshold is one half of the difference between the upper and lower thresholds (i.e., one half of the interval of uncertainty).

Lindquist Designs A set of labels for certain complex experimental designs as follows:

Type I   *See* Two Factor Mixed Design.
Type II   *See* Latin Square Design (Simple).
Type III   *See* Three Factor Mixed Design.
Type IV   *See* Latin Square Design (Complex).
Type V   *See* Graeco-Latin Square Design.
Type VI   *See* Three Factor Mixed Design.
Type VII   *See* Incomplete Design.

Line Graph   A format for illustrating data in which values of the X, or independent variable, are placed along the horizontal axis (abscissa), and values of the Y, or dependent variable, are placed along the vertical axis (ordinate). The values of the dependent variable are plotted and connected by straight lines. (*See also* Bar Graph.)

EXAMPLE: Figure L–1 shows free viewing times for subjects who were given sets of real pictures or sets of random geometric forms to view. In each case, the stimuli were of three different levels of complexity.

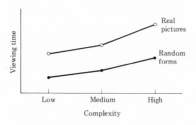

Figure L–1

Line of Best Fit   *See* Linear Regression.

Linear Correlation   *See* Correlation Coefficient.

Linear Multiple Correlation   *See* Multiple Correlation.

Linear/Nonlinear Relationship   Terms which describe the general form of the relationship between two variables, X and Y. If the value of Y changes by a constant amount each time the value of X increases one unit, the relationship is linear, and a plot of paired X and Y values will lie on a straight line. If, as X increases one unit, the amount of change in the value of Y differs depending on the value of X, the relationship is nonlinear (curvilinear), and a plot of paired values of X and Y will reveal a departure from linearity. For illustrations of linear relationships see Linear Regression; Monotonic Function (right panel). For illustrations of nonlinear relationships, see Monotonic Function (left panel); Negatively Accelerated Function; Nonmonotonic Function; Positively Accelerated Function.

Linear Regression A relationship between two variables, X and Y, such that in the population, mean values of Y for fixed values of X are linearly related to the values of X. If X also is a random variable, the mean values of X for fixed values of Y are linearly related to the values of Y. In psychological research, interest is generally in the relationship between a dependent variable, Y, and in independent variable, X. Linear regression refers to a situation in which the trend of treatment means, $\overline{Y}$, over the several levels of the independent variable, X, can be described by a **regression equation:** $Y' = a + bX$ where a is the **y-intercept**, i.e., the value of Y where the line crosses the y-axis, at $X = 0$, and b is the **slope** of the line, showing the amount of change in the value of Y as X increases one unit in value. If the values of Y increase

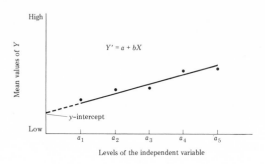

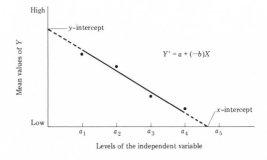

Figure L–2

as X increases in value, the relationship is positive, and b will be positive in sign. If the values of Y decrease as X increases in value, the relationship is negative, and b will be negative in sign. The **regression line,** obtained from the regression equation, is the **line of best fit,** in that the sum of the squared deviations of the treatment means from the regression line is at a minimum, i.e., $\Sigma(\bar{Y} - Y')^2$ is at a minimum. Figure L–2 illustrates trends with a positive slope (a), and a negative slope (b). (*See also* Prediction Equation.)

Linear Transformation   *See* Data Transformation.

Linear Trend Component   *See* Trend Analysis.

Lloyd Morgan's Canon   *See* Parsimony, Principle of.

Loading   *See* Factor Loading.

Logarithmic Transformation   *See* Data Transformation.

Logistic Curve   A class of growth curves of the form $Y = a/(1 + be^{-cx})$. In a logistic curve, the rate of change in Y is proportional to its reciprocal, $1/Y$. The general form of this curve is negatively accelerating.

Longitudinal Method (*contr.* Cross-Sectional Method)   A procedure used in developmental psychology in which changes in an individual or group over a period of time are noted. (*See also* Historical Method.)

Lower Difference Threshold   *See* Limits, Method of.

Mach's Figure *See under* Illusions.

Magazine Training In operant conditioning, a procedure in which the subject is repeatedly exposed to an apparatus that delivers reinforcement to a specified location, such as a food cup. The procedure is designed to allow the subject to learn the location of the reinforcement and to become accustomed to any disturbing noises or movements associated with its delivery. Training is continued until the organism uses these stimuli as cues to approach and consume the reinforcement.

Magnitude Estimation A psychophysical procedure for establishing a scale with subjectively equal units, in which the subject is asked to assign numerical values to quantitative aspects of stimuli such as loudness, brightness, area, etc. If the stimulus series involves a familiar unit of measurement such as length, the subject may be asked to estimate in inches the lengths of a series of lines. If the stimulus series involves an unfamiliar unit of measurement, such as the brightness of lights, or if the stimulus has no physical unit of measurement, as when subjects rate the palatability of a series of foods, the instructions to the subjects may simply ask that they assign a number to each stimulus in the series using any numbers they please, but in such a way that the numbers are proportional to the perceived magnitude of the stimuli. Another procedure provides the subject with an anchor by presenting a stimulus near the middle of the range of magnitudes and assigning it a value. Subjects then assign numerical values to other stimuli in the series that reflect the proportion of their perceived magnitudes relative to the anchor stimulus. (*See also* Magnitude Production.)

EXAMPLE: The subject is presented with a tone and is told that it represents a degree of loudness that will be called 100. This is the

133

anchor stimulus. A randomly ordered series of other tones of varying loudness are presented, and as each tone is sounded, the subject assigns it a number that reflects its perceived loudness relative to the anchor stimulus (e.g., assigning a value of 50 to a tone that seems to the subject to be half as loud as the anchor, a value of 150 to a tone that seems to the subject to be half again as loud as the anchor, etc.). The anchor stimulus may be presented periodically to reacquaint the subject with the tone having the loudness called 100.

Magnitude of Effect   A general term for the degree to which a dependent variable is affected by an independent variable. The simplest measures are based on changes in the mean score: (a) the difference between the mean for an experimental condition and the mean for a control condition or (b) the difference between the mean for a particular condition and the mean for all conditions combined (grand mean). Other measures are based on some form of correlation between the independent and dependent variables or on the proportion of the variability in the scores that may be attributed to the effects of the independent variable. These are called measures of **strength of association.** (*See also* Eta Squared; Omega Squared.)

Magnitude of Response   A measure of either the absolute or relative size of a response. For overt behaviors, magnitude might be measured by the length of a string pull or the diameter of a pupil dilation. For psychophysiological measures, it may be the displacement of a pen tracing, representing electrodermal activity. (*See also* Amplitude of Response; Latency of Response; Recovery Time; Recruitment Time.)

Magnitude Production   A psychophysical procedure in which a subject is presented with a stimulus that is to serve as an anchor, with the magnitude of the anchor stimulus assigned a numerical value. On each of a series of trials the subject is asked to produce stimuli having intensities of designated values above and below the value assigned to the anchor stimulus. The procedure commonly utilizes an apparatus with controls that are easily operated by the subject to produce stimuli of varying magnitudes, such as tones of varying loudness or lights of varying brightness. (*See also* Magnitude Estimation.)

Main Effect   The overall influence of an independent variable. In an experiment with two or more independent variables, it is the effect (differences between means for different levels) of one of the independent variables, averaged over the levels of all other independent variables. A test of the main effect of a variable compares the marginal means, each of which is the mean for all of the scores for a particular level of the variable. (*For an example, see* Interaction).

Mahalanobis' *D* Square Test (*symb. D²*) *See* Multivariate Tests of Significance.

MANCOVA *See* Multivariate Analysis of Covariance.

Manipulandum (*syn.* Operandum) That part of an experimental environment that a subject is required to touch, push, or otherwise operate (e.g., a key the subject is required to depress in response to a buzzer and release in response to a light).

Manipulated Variable (*syn.* Treatment Variable; *contr.* Nonmanipulated Variable) Any independent variable with levels or values determined directly by the researcher. For example, in a study of the effect of length of a persuasive message on attitude change, the experimenter can select or construct messages of any desired length.

Manipulative Research (*contr.* Nonmanipulative Research) Research in which the experimenter actively determines the values of the independent variables under study. (*See also* Experiment; Manipulated Variable.)

Mann–Whitney *U* Test *See U* Test.

MANOVA *See* Multivariate Analysis of Variance.

Marginal Frequency The sum of the frequencies in a row or column of a contingency table.

Marginal Significance A term referring to the results of a statistical test that fails to be statistically significant by a small amount. With a .05 level of significance, the term sometimes is used if the test gives a p value between .10 and .05.

Marginal Total The sum of the values in a row or column of a two-dimensional data table.

Markoff Model *See* Markov Model.

Markov Model A probabilistic model for sequences of events, such as responses over a series of trials, where either successive events are independent or the probability of an event depends only on the immediately preceding event.

EXAMPLE: A rat is put in a T maze with food in both goals, so that it receives a reward for either choice. Over many trials, the rat may show a preference for one side, for example, going to the left more often than to the right. The rat also may show a tendency to alternate, so that if it goes to the left on one trial, it is more likely to go right than left on the next trial. For example, in the sequence L R L L L R L R L R, 60 percent of the choices are L and only 40 percent are R; but of the trials following L, only 33 percent are L, whereas 67 percent are R. If a longer sequence showed these same proportions of L and R following two successive L's as following just one L, then the rat's behavior could be said to conform to a Markov model, or a Markov model could be used to describe the rat's behavior.

Masking   In information processing, a procedure in which interference in the perception of a target stimulus is brought about as a result of the presentation of a masking stimulus (usually in the same sense modality) close in time to the presentation of the target. If the masking stimulus follows the presentation of the target, the procedure is called **backward masking.** If the masking stimulus precedes the target, the procedure is called **forward masking.** (*See also* Masking Task.)

EXAMPLE: Target stimuli consisting of letters are flashed sufficiently rapidly that, with no interference, accuracy of identification is in the range of 80–90 percent. A masking stimulus consisting of a grid pattern is flashed for the same duration, intensity, and location as the target, but with an interstimulus interval varying on different trials from -150, -100, and -50 msec for forward masking, and 50, 100, and 150 msec for backward masking.

Masking Task   A general term applied to tasks whose purpose is to prevent subjects from discovering something that the experimenter wants to keep hidden (i.e., to provide a "cover" for the experimenter's true purpose) or to keep the subject from performing a response that the experimenter wants to prevent. For example, a subject may be given insoluble puzzles and told they are tests of intelligence, when the experimenter's true purpose is to observe responses to frustration, or the subject may be given problems requiring mental arithmetic in order to prevent the rehearsal of verbal material that is being memorized. (*See also* Distractor; Masking.)

Massed Practice   *See* Distribution of Practice.

Matched Dependent Paradigm   *See* Matching-to-Sample Procedure.

Matched-Groups Design   A procedure in which groups of subjects are formed in such a way as to have approximately equal means and standard deviations on some pretest. Each group then is given a different level of the independent variable. For example, the groups could be equated on a test of verbal comprehension, and then tested on memory for sentences of different length and complexity. The results of an experiment using this design are usually analyzed as though the groups were independent, but the proper interpretation of the results of such an analysis is not clear. The term *matched groups* is sometimes used synonymously, but erroneously, with **matched-subjects** design. (*See also* Randomized-Groups Design.)

Matched-Pairs Signed-Ranks Test   *See* Signed-Ranks Test.

Matched-Subjects Design   *See* Randomized-Blocks Design.

Matching Task   *See* Matching Test.

Matching Test   A test in which the subject performs a matching task, such as choosing an item from one list of items and matching it with an appropriate item from another list. The criterion for proper matching can be prescribed by the experimenter or developed by the subject.

EXAMPLE:

List A	List B
1 Child	1 Pencil
2 Doctor	2 Gray
3 Blue	3 Accountant
4 Book	4 Adult

If the subject is told to match the items of both lists, thus setting his/her own criterion, the expected correct responses would be matching 1 and 4, 2 and 3, 3 and 2, or 4 and 1. If the subject is told to match items that are objects, the criterion is prescribed, and the only correct response matches 4 and 1.

Matching-to-Sample Procedure   (1) A discrimination learning procedure in which a correct response is defined as a response to one stimulus, from a display of two or more stimuli, which matches some model or sample stimulus. (2) Any procedure in which a model behavior is provided for imitation by the subject.

EXAMPLE 1:   As one of a sequence of training trials, a child is presented with a display containing a blue block (sample stimulus) with red and blue blocks (choices) below it. Picking up the blue block is defined as a correct response and rewarded, since the blue block matches the sample stimulus.

EXAMPLE 2:   A child learning to produce the letter L is presented with a correctly completed model L and a stimulus comprised of components of the letter, such as segments of its vertical and horizontal members. The correct behavior is defined as connecting these members to form a good copy of the model stimulus.

Maximum Likelihood Estimate   The value of a population parameter that makes the observed sample data most likely (probable). For example, a sample with a mean of 16 is more likely to be drawn from a population whose mean is 16 than from any other population; therefore, 16 is the maximum likelihood estimate of the population mean.

McNemar Test   *See* Correlated Proportions Test.

Mean (*symb.* μ, M, $\bar{X}$)   Any of several measures of central tendency, for a distribution of scores. Usually, "the mean" refers to the arithmetic mean. (*See also* Arithmetic Mean; Geometric Mean; Harmonic Mean; Weighted Mean.)

Mean Deviation   *See* Average Deviation.

Mean Square (*abbr.* MS; *syn.* Variance Estimate)   A sum of squares divided by its degrees of freedom. Usually used only in the context of analysis of variance.

Mean Square Contingency, Index of (*symb.* ϕ^2)   A measure of association for a two-way (rows by columns) contingency table, sometimes used in conjunction with a chi-square test of independence. The statistic ranges in value from 0 (no association) to an upper limit that depends on the number of rows and columns of the table, but cannot exceed 1. It is defined as

$$\phi^2 = \frac{\chi^2}{N}$$

where χ^2 is the computed chi-square statistic for the test of independence and N is the total number of observations. (*See also* Contingency Coefficient; Cramer's Statistic; Phi Coefficient.)

Mean Vector   A set of means arranged in a row or a column. For example, in multiple regression, a mean vector would list the means for each of the predictor variables.

Measurement Error   The difference between an obtained value and the theoretically true value. One type of measurement error occurs in measuring a continuous variable such as time, which may be measured to the nearest year, day, second, or millisecond, but cannot be measured exactly (i.e., to an infinite number of decimal places). Another type of measurement error is due to uncontrolled factors that may affect the object being measured, the measuring instrument, or the reading of the measuring instrument. For example, the measurement of a person's reaction time may differ from that person's "true" reaction time if the electrical timer is subject to power fluctuations, if the person's attention is diverted from the stimulus, or if the timer is not correctly read. This second type of measurement error is also called **experimental error.** Measurement error usually is assumed to be normally distributed. (*See also* Random Error.)

Mechner Diagram   In operant conditioning, a notation that explicitly illustrates the relationships between the stimulus and response events occurring in various behavioral phenomena and reinforcement schedules.

Median The middle value of a set of numbers arranged in order of magnitude (i.e., the 50th percentile). For small samples, the median usually is taken as the middle value of an odd number of scores, and halfway between the two middle values of an even number of scores.

EXAMPLE: The numbers 9, 2, 1, 8, and 4 are, in order, 1, 2, 4, 8, and 9, and the median is 4. The numbers 9, 2, 1, 8, 4, and 3 are, in order, 1, 2, 3, 4, 8, and 9, and the median is 3.5.

Median Test A procedure for testing a hypothesis about the value of the median of one population or differences among the medians of two or more populations. For one sample, a binomial test is used with observations dichotomized as being above or below the hypothesized median. For two or more independent samples, a test for independence is used. The median of the combined samples is found, and the observations classified in a contingency table with samples as one variable and frequencies of observations above or below the combined median as the other variable.

Mediating Variable *See* Intervening Variable.

Melton Learning Curve One of a class of learning curves that permit direct comparison and averaging of data when subjects require different numbers of trials to reach a performance criterion of learning. The number of trials to reach successive criteria [e.g., 20%, 40%, 60%, 80%, and 100% (successive fifths) of a list] is found separately for each subject and then averaged across subjects. (*See also* Backward Learning Curve; Vincent(ized) Learning Curve.)

EXAMPLE: Subjects are given a list of 12 items in serial order to a criterion of two perfect trials. The number of correct responses on each trial is shown for one of the subjects.

Trial Number	1	2	3	4	5	6	7	8	9	10	11	12
correct	2	2	6	4	7	8	10	10	7	11	12	12

To construct a Melton curve using successive fourths of the list of 12 items, the criteria are 3, 6, 9, and 12 items. The first trial on which this subject got three items correct was Trial 3, and the subject also first got six correct on that trial. The criterion of 9 correct was first met on Trial 7, and 12 correct was first met on Trial 11. These criterion trial numbers of 3, 3, 7, and 11 would be averaged with the comparable trial numbers for the other subjects, and the learning curve would show the average number of trials to reach each successive criterion.

Mesokurtosis   *See* Kurtosis.

Method of ____   Techniques so prefaced (e.g., METHOD OF ADJUST-
MENT) are entered under their first significant word (e.g., as Adjustment, Method of, or Equal Appearing Intervals, Method of). (*See individual listings.*)

Midrange   The midpoint of a distribution, that is, the mean of the
highest and the lowest scores. The midrange is a crude measure
of central tendency.

EXAMPLE: 2, 5, 1, 4, 9, 12, 6 is a distribution of scores that
range from 1 to 12, with a midrange of $6.5 = (1 + 12)/2$.

Mirror Drawing Task   A perceptual motor task in which the subject
reproduces a pattern, such as a geometric form, under conditions
of mirror image feedback. The apparatus is arranged so that both
the form to be copied and the subject's hand are visible only
from a mirror. Thus, all visual information is in mirror image
form.

Miss   *See* Decision.

Mixed Analysis of Variance   The analysis of variance appropriate for
a mixed design.

Mixed Design (*syn.* Split Plot Design)   An experimental design with
two or more factors (independent variables), including at least
one between-subject variable and at least one within-subject variable. That is, subjects are assigned randomly to be tested under
different levels or combinations of levels of one or more factors,
but all subjects are tested with every level or combination of
levels of one or more other factor(s). A mixed design is described
like a factorial design in terms of number of factors and number
of levels of each, with the between-subject factors usually listed
before the within-subject factors. For example, a 2×3 mixed
design has two levels of the between-subject factor and three
levels of the within-subject factor, whereas a 3×2 mixed design
has three levels of the between-subject factor and two levels of
the within-subject factor.

EXAMPLE: In a study of legibility, subjects are randomly assigned to one of two groups. Subjects in one group are shown black
stimuli on a white background, and subjects in the other group are
shown white stimuli on a black background. All subjects are tested
for speed and accuracy of recognition of two-, three-, and four-letter
stimuli, under four different levels of illumination. This design would
be described as a $2 \times 3 \times 4$ mixed design with one between-subject
factor *A* (stimulus–background relationship) and two within-subject factors *B* and *C* (number of letters and level of illumination). This arrangement of variables is illustrated schematically in Figure M–1.

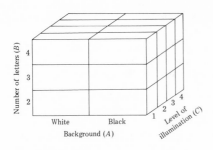

Figure M–1

Mixed-Effects Model The mathematical model for an experiment in which there are two or more factors (independent variables), of which at least one factor is a fixed effects factor whose levels are determined arbitrarily, and at least one factor is a random effects factor, whose levels are randomly selected from a population of levels. Different combinations of these two types of variables determine the choices of error terms for F tests. The most commonly used designs in psychology for which this model is appropriate are the repeated measures and randomized blocks designs (matched designs), in which subjects or blocks, respectively, are considered to be randomly selected, and levels of all other factors are arbitrary. (*See also* Fixed/Random-Effects Model.)

Mixed List A list of verbal items in which different levels of an independent variable are represented by items in the list. For example, to study the effects of item concreteness on speed of learning, a list would be constructed containing items with differing concreteness ratings.

Mixed Model *See* Mixed-Effects Model.

Mixed Motive Game *See* Zero-Sum/Nonzero-Sum Game.

Mixed Multiple Schedule of Reinforcement (*abbr.* Mix Mult) An operant conditioning procedure in which a **mixed schedule** and **multiple schedule of reinforcement** are presented repeatedly in either a random or systematic order. When the multiple schedule is in force, a change from one component schedule to another is accompanied by a change in an external discriminative stimulus. When the mixed schedule is in force, no such stimuli are present.

Mixed Schedule of Reinforcement (*abbr.* Mix) An operant conditioning procedure in which two or more component schedules of reinforcement are presented repeatedly in random or systematic

141

order. The change from one schedule to another is never associated with a change in an external discriminative stimulus. (*See also* Multiple Schedule of Reinforcement.)

EXAMPLE: An operant chamber is programmed to deliver food pellets on a mixed fixed-ratio-10, fixed-interval 30-sec (MIX FR-10, FI-30) schedule of reinforcement. During the first 15 min of a session, a rat will receive reinforcement after every 10th bar press. At the end of this interval, the schedule changes without warning, and the animal now receives a pellet for the first bar press made 30 sec or more after the previous reinforcement. At the end of this 15 min interval, the reinforcement schedule may, again without warning, return to the FR requirements.

MOC Curve   The memory operating characteristic curve, analogous to a receiver operating characteristic (ROC) curve, obtained in the application of the theory of signal detection to a recognition memory task. In this application, the "old" items that composed the original study list are considered to be analogous to signal, and the "new" items that make up the distractors are considered to be analogous to noise. The procedures for generating an MOC curve are then exactly the same as those described for generating an ROC curve. (*See also* Signal Detection Task.)

Modal Value   *See* Mode.

Mode (*syn.* Modal Value)   The score or category that has the greatest frequency of occurrence in a distribution. A **unimodal** distribution has only one mode, which is sometimes used as a measure of central tendency. A **bimodal** distribution has two modes, and a **multimodal** distribution has three or more modes. The greatest frequency may be defined relative to the surrounding scores, so that a distribution may be described as bimodal even though the two scores do not have the same frequency. In this case, the mode with the greater frequency is called the **major mode,** and the mode with the smaller frequency is called the **minor mode.**

EXAMPLE 1: The following is the frequency distribution for 52 people classified by hair color. The modal hair color is blond.

Hair color	Blond	Brown	Black	Red	Gray
Frequency	22	13	6	9	2

EXAMPLE 2: Figure M–2 shows a bimodal distribution with a major mode at 24 and a minor mode at 28; 24 and 28 are the modes or modal scores.

Moderator Variable   In correlation research, a variable that, when statistically analyzed, reveals more completely the relationships

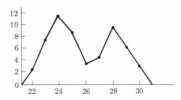

Figure M-2

between various values of a predictor variable and value of a criterion variable. (*See also* Interaction; Suppressor Variable.)

EXAMPLE: A pencil-and-paper test of sales ability (the predictor variable) is administered to a group of job applicants who are then given a probationary period of actual selling experience. The number of sales during this period (the criterion variable) is then correlated with test scores and a weak positive correlation of $r = .20$ is obtained. Subsequently, a test of situational anxiety (a possible moderator variable) is administered to the applicants, and they are divided into high-medium-, and low-anxiety subgroups. It it then found that the correlations between sales ability test score and actual sales are $r = .02$ for high-anxiety applicants, $r = .21$ for medium-anxiety applicants, and $r = .48$ for low-anxiety applicants. Thus, in part at least, anxiety moderates the relationship between sales test scores and actual sales.

Monitoring Task   *See* Vigilance Task.

Monotonic Function (*contr.* Nonmonotonic Function)   A relationship between two variables such that as the independent variable *(X)* increases in value, the dependent variable *(Y)* either increases or decreases in value without reversal, although it may approach an asymptote. Figure M-3 illustrates two monotonic functions.

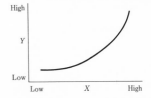
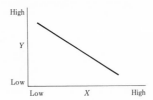

Figure M-3

Moon Illusion   *See under* Illusions.

Morgan's Canon   *See* Parsimony, Principle of.

Moses' Test of Extreme Reactions *See* Extreme Reactions, Test of.

Motor Skill Task *See* Perceptual Motor Task.

Movement Aftereffects *See under* Illusions.

Movement Time *See* Response Time.

MS *See* Mean Square.

Müller–Lyer Illusion *See under* Illusions.

Multidimensional Scaling Procedures for measuring complex stimuli that vary simultaneously on a number of psychological dimensions. The scaling procedure is used to determine (1) the number of psychological dimensions needed to describe an individual's judgments of similarity of the stimuli, (2) the positions (scale values) of the stimuli on these dimensions, and (3) the nature of the psychological dimensions. The stimuli may vary on known physical dimensions, such as geometric figures that vary in size, color, texture, etc., in which case the interest would be in how people use these dimensions to arrive at their judgments. The stimuli also may be such things as photographs of people or attitude statements, in which case the major interest would be in identifying the psychological dimensions people use in making judgments about the stimuli.

EXAMPLE: Subjects are given all possible pairs of a set of adjectives describing personality traits, such as friendly, bold, intolerant. To measure the similarity of the traits, the subjects rate each pair in terms of the likelihood that a person would have both traits. Scaling analysis shows that the trait adjectives are grouped along a small number of dimensions, which can be described as sociability, activity, intelligence, a moral/ethical dimension, etc.

Multielement Baseline Design A single-subject design in which two or more treatment conditions are administered repeatedly, usually in counterbalanced or block randomized fashion. The design often includes a number of pretreatment baseline conditions. (*See also* Multiple Baseline Design; Reversal Design.)

EXAMPLE: An experimenter wishes to evaluate the relative effectiveness of three different fresh fruits as alternatives to lab chow pellets to maintain a monkey's bar-pressing behavior. Since the subject currently is being rewarded with lab chow pellets, this condition is designated as the baseline condition (A). The fruits—apple, banana, and orange—are designated as treatment conditions B_1, B_2, and B_3, respectively. A sequence of baseline and treatment conditions extending over many sessions might then be arranged as follows:

A A A $B_2 B_1 B_3$ $B_1 B_3 B_2$ $B_3 B_2 B_1$. . . .

Multilevel Experiment *See* Parametric Research.

144

Multimodal Distribution   *See* Mode.

Multinomial Distribution   The probability distribution that describes the outcomes of a series of observations, where each observation is placed into one of several categories. In a **binomial distribution,** each observation is placed in one of two categories. The multinomial distribution can be used for an exact test for goodness of fit, in place of the chi-square approximation.

EXAMPLE: If a sample of drug users were classified into two categories (marijuana users or hard drug users) the distribution would be binomial. If the persons were classified into several categories, marijuana, opiates, barbiturates, and others, the distribution would be multinomial.

Multiple Baseline Design   A single-subject design that enables measurement of the effect of an experimental treatment on two or more behaviors, or on one behavior in two or more different environmental settings. The behaviors are monitored over several sessions to establish baselines. A treatment procedure is then introduced for only one of the behaviors, subsequently for a second behavior, and so forth. Effectiveness of the treatment is determined by the amount of change in treated behaviors relative to untreated behaviors. (*See also* Reversal Design; Multielement Baseline Design.)

EXAMPLE: To assess the effect of mild praise on "desirable" classroom behavior in third-grade children, three such behaviors—asking questions, attending to the teacher, and reading—are monitored for one week to establish base rates. During the second week, questions are followed by praise from the teacher, whereas attending and reading are not. During the third week, questioning and attending receive praise, but not reading. In the fourth week, all three behaviors receive praise. As an option, this sequence may then be reversed until praise has been removed partially or completely.

Multiple-Choice Task (*syn.* Option Task)   A task in which the subject chooses one item from several alternatives. In general, the prescribed criterion for the subject is to make the "best" choice from two or more alternatives.

Multiple-Choice Test   *See* Multiple Choice Task.

Multiple-Comparison Test   Any test of the significance of the differences between some or all pairs of means in an experiment involving more than two treatment conditions. The tests also may examine contrasts among more than two means. (*For an example, see* Pairwise-Comparison Test, *see also* Duncan's Multiple-Range Test; Dunnett's Test; Newman–Keuls Test; Scheffé's Test; Tukey's Test.)

Multiple Control Groups An arrangement in which two or more groups of subjects do not receive an experimental treatment, but serve to control for different components of the experimental treatment. For example, in a test of a drug in which rats are used as the experimental subjects, one control group might receive an injection of normal saline instead of the drug, and a second control group would receive the same type and degree of handling but no injection. Differences between the last two groups would demonstrate any effect of the injection apart from the effect of the drug.

Multiple Correlation (*symb. R*) A correlation coefficient describing the degrees of linear relationship between a dependent (criterion) variable and several independent (predictor) variables. Specifically, it is the product-moment correlation between the criterion variable and the best linear combination of the predictor variables. Like the correlation between two variables *(r)*, the multiple correlation gives the degree to which the criterion variable can be predicted by a linear function of the predictor variables, and the square of the correlation coefficient, r^2 or R^2, gives the proportion of the variability in the criterion that can be accounted for by variability in the predictors. (*See also* Multiple Regression.)

Multiple Discriminant Analysis *See* Discriminant Analysis.

Multiple-Group Factor Analysis A factor analytic technique that yields oblique factors, rather than orthogonal factors, as an initial solution. (*See also* Factor Rotation.)

Multiple-Groups Design As a general term, any design involving more than two groups of subjects. More specifically, any quasi-experimental design in which intact groups are subjected to repeated measurements before and after the experimental treatment(s). (*See also* Time Series Design.)

EXAMPLE 1: In one variation, a researcher who wants to study the effect of a smoking control technique on athletic performance in different sports observes a group of tennis players, gives them a post-hypnotic suggestion to stop smoking, and observes them again. The same procedure is repeated with baseball players and basketball players and the three groups are then compared. Similarly, three basketball teams may each undergo a different treatment (e.g., hypnosis, behavior modification, and conventional therapy), and then be compared to one another.

EXAMPLE 2: A researcher who wants to study the effects of two or more variations of a disciplinary method on convicts in prison may find it too costly or impractical to apply the two treatments at once. Thus, a group of convicts in one prison is observed, followed by the introduction of one variation of the disciplinary method, fol-

146

lowed by more observations. The procedure is repeated with a group of convicts from another prison undergoing another variation of the disciplinary method.

Multiple Prediction   *See* Multiple Regression.

Multiple-Range Test   *See* Duncan's Multiple Range Test.

Multiple Regression   The relationship between a dependent variable *(Y)* and a linear combination of two or more independent variables $(X_1, X_2, \ldots)$. The relationship is described by a multiple regression equation of the form $Y = b_0 + b_1 X_1 + b_2 X_2 \cdots$. The weights *(b)* given to the independent variables are the multiple regression coefficients. When the regression equation is used to predict future performance, the equation is called a **multiple prediction** equation; the *Y* variable is called the criterion variable and the *X* variables are called predictor variables. For example, an experimenter might be interested in studying the factors that influence an employer's judgment of an applicant's probable job success. The judgment of success would be the dependent variable, and such things as the applicant's age, marital status, employment history, appearance, aptitude test score, etc., might be used as independent variables. After validation, the same equation might be used for predicting the employer's judgments. *(For another example see* Prediction Equation, *see also b* Coefficient; Beta Coefficient; Multiple Correlation; Stepwise Regression.)

Multiple Schedule of Reinforcement (*abbr.* Mult)   An operant conditioning procedure in which two or more component schedules of reinforcement are presented repeatedly in either a random or a systematic order. The change from one schedule to another is always accompanied by a change in an external discriminative stimulus. *(See also* Mixed Schedule of Reinformcement.)

EXAMPLE: An operant chamber is programmed to deliver food pellets on a multiple fixed-ratio-10, fixed-interval 30-sec (MULT FR-10, FI-30) schedule of reinforcement. During the first 15 min of the session, a rat receives reinforcement after every 10th bar press, and a small light above the bar remains lighted. At the end of this interval, the light is extinguished and the schedule changes so that the animal receives a pellet for the first bar press made 30 or more seconds after the previous reinforcement. At the end of this 15-min interval, the schedule may return to the FR requirements, and the light be relighted.

Multiple-Treatment Interference   *See* Carryover Effect.

Multiplicative Function   A relationship in which one variable is a function of the product of two or more other variables. For example, instead of increasing everyone's score by the same amount (**addi-**

tive function), the effect of a drug might be proportional to the subject's score without the drug. That is, instead of the new score being the old score plus a value that depends on the drug dosage, the new score would be the old score multiplied by a value that depends on the drug dosage.

Multistage Experiment   Any experiment that has two or more distinct phases. Experimental manipulations are conducted during one or more of the phases, and behaviors comprising the dependent measures are monitored during some subsequent phase(s).

EXAMPLE: In an experiment designed to study the effect of interpolated material on recall, one group is given a list of words, List A, to learn, followed by List B, and finally a recall test on List A. A control group would receive the same three stages except that Stage 2 would involve a control task in place of learning List B.

Multistage Research   A general term for research projects in which the outcome of one study determines the designs and purposes of subsequent studies.

Multivariate Analysis of Covariance (*abbr.* MANCOVA)   A procedure for data analysis that uses statistical control sometimes as an alternative to experimental control of one or more extraneous variables correlated with the dependent variable. MANCOVA involves the same principle as analysis of covariance (ANCOVA), except that two or more dependent variables are analyzed. The relationship of MANCOVA to MANOVA (multivariate analysis of variance) is similar to that of ANCOVA to ANOVA (univariate analysis of variance).

Multivariate Analysis of Variance (*abbr.* MANOVA)   A set of procedures for testing the significance of differences among means as in the univariate analysis of variance (ANOVA), except that the MANOVA observes the effect of the independent variable(s) on two or more dependent variables. Since the MANOVA maintains an alpha level unaffected by the number of dependent variables, it avoids artificially inflated group differences due to intercorrelation among the dependent variables. The MANOVA yield significance tests, most commonly using Hotelling's T^2 or Wilk's Lambda, for main effects and interaction effects of the independent variables, or for other combinations of these, on a combination of the dependent variables. A **stepdown-F procedure** (*syn.* **stepdown MANOVA**) can be used in conjunction with the MANOVA to test the residual effect of one or more independent variables on one or more dependent variables, with the effects of other independent and/or dependent variables removed.

EXAMPLE: A multivariate analysis of variance shows that men and women differ significantly on a combination of three measures of cognitive skills: verbal comprehension, arithmetic reasoning, and perceptual speed. Univariate F tests may be done separately for each of the dependent variables, showing that the sexes differ significantly on each of the three measures. Since these measures are correlated with each other, a stepdown-F procedure would not necessarily show the same results. The first step might show that the sexes differ significantly on verbal comprehension. The second step might show that after removal of variation that verbal comprehension and arithmetic reasoning have in common, the sexes still differ significantly in arithmetic reasoning. The third step, however, might show that after the removal of variation shared with the preceding measures, perceptual speed no longer is a measure on which the sexes differ significantly.

Multivariate Statistics Descriptive and inferential statistical procedures designed for use when the analysis involves measures on two or more dependent variables for each subject. Multiple regression and multiple correlation, involving one dependent variable and several independent variables, frequently are considered multivariate techniques. Analysis of variance with one dependent variable and analysis of covariance with two dependent variables generally are not so classified. (*See also* Bivariate Statistics; Univariate Statistics.)

Multivariate *t* Test Any of several procedures for testing the differences between linear combination of means for each of two groups. It is analogous to the usual (univariate) t test, except that in multivariate t tests the systematic effect of the independent variable is observed on two or more dependent variables. Possible intercorrelations among the dependent variables are taken into account to avoid bias in estimating experimental effects. (*For examples of possible biases, see* Multivariate Analysis of Variance.)

Multivariate Test of Significance Any of a number of tests of the hypothesis of equal mean vectors. The principal tests, most of which can be used also for post hoc comparisons, are **Wilk's Lambda, Mahalanobis' D^2, Rao's V, Roy's GCR, Pillai's Criterion, Hotelling's T^2,** and **Hotelling's Trace Criterion.** Most of these test statistics can be converted into approximate F or chi-square statistics.

Mutually Exclusive Events Two or more events or possible observations that cannot occur simultaneously (i.e., on a single trial). For example, a person cannot be both under 21 and elderly; the events "under 21" and "elderly" are mutually exclusive. However, it is possible for an individual to be both under 21 and retired. The latter two events are not mutually exclusive. (*See also* Independence.)

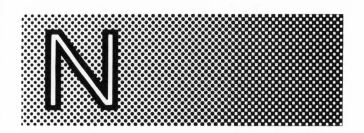

Naive Subject A subject lacking experience with the research in which they are to participate. The term may imply that the subject has never served in psychological research, has never participated in the particular type of research (e.g., naive with respect to concept learning tasks), or simply is unaware of the true nature and purpose of the particular experiment.

Natural Experiment *See under* Field Research.

Naturalistic Observation *See under* Field Research: *Field Study.*

Necker Cube *See under* Illusions.

Negative _____ In most cases, terms with the modifiers **negative** or **positive** are entered in the unmodified form; for example, *negative* correlation and *positive* correlation are defined in the entry Correlation.

Negative Relationship *See* Positive/Negative Relationship.

Negative Results *See* Nonsignificant Results.

Negative Stimulus (*contr.* Positive Stimulus) A general term for any aversive stimulus or stimulus associated with either an aversive event or the absence of reinforcement. (1) In operant conditioning, the stimulus event present when no behaviors are to be reinforced (**symb.** $S^\triangle$). (2) In differential instrumental conditioning, the stimulus a response to which is not reinforced (**symb.** $S-$). (3) In differential classical conditioning, that conditioned stimulus that is not followed by an unconditioned stimulus (**symb.** $CS-$). (*For examples, see* Differential Classical Conditioning; Differential Instrumental Conditioning; Differential Operant Conditioning.)

Negative Transfer *See* Transfer Paradigm.

Negatively Accelerated Function (*contr.* Positively Accelerated Function) A relationship between two variables such that the rate of change in the value of the dependent variable *(Y)* decreases with an increase in the value of the independent variable *(X)*. The curve connecting the values of *Y* begins to level off and become more nearly parallel to the *x*-axis. *Y* may be either an increasing or a decreasing function of *X*. Figure N–1 shows (a) a negatively accelerated growth curve and (b) a negatively accelerated decay curve.

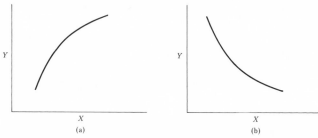

Figure N–1

Negatively Correlated Reinforcement *See* Correlated Reinforcement.

Nested Factor *See* Nesting.

Nesting (*contr.* Crossing) An arrangement of two independent variables in which different levels of one variable (the **nested factor**) are paired with each level of the other variable. For example, in a between-subjects design, subjects are nested in conditions, since different subjects are tested with each condition. If subjects are tested in groups, with different subjects in each group, and several different groups in each condition, then subjects and groups are both nested factors. (*For an example, see* Hierarchical Design.)

Neutral Stimulus A stimulus that does not elicit any response other than an orienting reaction, or one that is unrelated to reinforcement contingencies.

Newman–Keuls Test A multiple-comparison procedure for testing the significance of differences for all possible pairs of treatment means. The size of the critical difference required for significance is based on the Studentized range statistic q but varies depending on the degree of separation between the ranked means.

Noise A general term for distracting stimuli of any modality that interfere with perception of another stimulus in the same modality. For example, noise would be a visual background or overlay that interferes with the detection of a visual stimulus. (*See also* Masking; Signal Detection Task.)

Nominal Data   Data obtained from using a nominal scale of measurement.

Nominal Scale   A classification system that places items, objects, characteristics, or individuals into mutually exclusive categories (i.e., that establishes that one thing is different from another, but not more or less so). Examples include stimulus materials categorized as letters, numbers, forms, etc., or classes of responses such as aggressive, sexual, or food related. It differentiates by name only.

Nomination Technique   A sociometric technique in which an individual in a group is selected by group members or outside observers on some criterion, usually in the form of "most" or "least," such as "most able," "least cooperative," "most likeable," etc.

Nomothetic Approach (*contr.* Idiographic Approach)   Pertaining to general principles and laws. In psychology, any system for the assessment of behavior on the basis of the average of many individuals' performance.

Nonadditivity   *See* Additivity.

Noncentral Distribution   Any of several distributions (e.g., noncentral t distribution, noncentral F distribution) that are used most commonly to describe the distribution of a test statistic for a specific alternate hypothesis. The appropriate noncentral distribution can be used to compute the power of the test of the null hypothesis.

Noncontingent Reinforcement (*syn.* Random Reinforcement; Uncorrelated Reinforcement; *contr.* Contingent Reinforcement)   In conditioning, a procedure used either to assess the effects of delivering reinforcement per se or to produce extinction of a response. Reinforcement is delivered to the subject in the same amount and frequency as in the acquisition phase of conditioning, but it is not contingent on the performance of any particular response (i.e., reinforcement occurs on a random basis). (*For an example, see* Yoked Control Procedure.) (*See also* Nondifferential Reinforcement; Unpaired Control.)

Nondetermination, Coefficient of (*symb.* k^2)   The proportion of variance in a variable that is not explained, or accounted for, by its correlation with a second variable; that is, the proportion of variance that is not predictable from variability in the second variable. It is equal to the square of the coefficient of alienation k or to $1 - r^2$ where r is the product-moment correlation coefficient.

Nondifferential Reinforcement Reinforcement that is delivered equally to any instance of a class of behaviors and/or under any stimulus conditions. For example, in training a dog to lift a leg, reinforcement would follow lifting any one of its four limbs, under any stimulus conditions. (*See also* Noncontingent Reinforcement.)

Nondirectional Test *See* One-Tail/Two-Tail Test.

Nondiscriminated Avoidance Conditioning (*syn.* Free Operant Avoidance Conditioning; Sidman Avoidance Conditioning) An operant avoidance learning procedure in which no external (explicit) warning signal is used. Instead, the organism must perform a response that will delay the onset of an aversive stimulus for a (usually) fixed time interval. If no response is made and time expires, the aversive stimulus is delivered repeatedly.

EXAMPLE: A rat is placed in a Skinner box with an electrifiable grid floor. Every 5 sec (the shock–shock interval) the grid is electrified briefly, and a variety of behaviors (possibly including bar pressing) is evoked. A bar press will delay the onset of the next shock for 20 sec (the response–shock interval). Training is usually continued until the animal can respond reliably near the end of the response–shock interval, thus delaying shock indefinitely, or nearly so.

Nonexperimental Designs *See* Nonmanipulative Research; Quasi-Experimental Design.

Nonlinear Regression (*syn.* Curvilinear Regression) A relationship between two variables, X and Y, such that in the population the mean values of Y for fixed values of X are functionally related to the values of X, but the function that relates the two is not linear. If X is also a random variable, the mean values of X also are nonlinearly related to the corresponding values of Y. In experimental research in psychology, interest is generally in the relationship between a dependent variable, Y, and an independent variable, X. For example, in psychophysics, the psychological value (Y) of a stimulus frequently is assumed to be a random variable whose mean is related to the physical value (X) of the stimulus by a logarithmic, exponential, or other nonlinear function. Various procedures exist for fitting a function or curve of a particular type, or trend analysis may be used to derive a polynomial equation to approximate the true function. (*See also* Linear Regression.)

Nonlinear Relationship *See* Linear/Nonlinear Relationship.

Nonmanipulated Variable Any independent variable with levels or values not determined directly by the investigator, but selected from those that exist naturally, such as intact group and subject variables. Examples include traumatized inhabitants of an earthquake stricken island versus control subjects from a similar socio-geographical locale, or high versus low IQ subjects. (*See also* Quasi-Experimental Design.)

Nonmanipulative Research A general term for a variety of data collection procedures that do not involve the active manipulation of an independent variable. These may range from purely descriptive research such as natural observation, case studies, etc., to complex correlational and quasi-experimental research that employs hypothesis-testing strategies. (*See also* Experiment.)

Nonmonotonic Function A relationship between two variables such that as the independent variable *(X)* increases in value, the dependent variable *(Y)* first increases and then decreases in value, or first decreases and then increases in value. More than one change in direction may occur. Figure N–2 shows two nonmonotonic relationships.

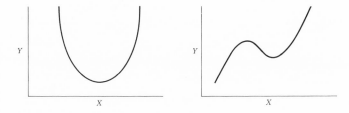

Figure N–2

Nonparametric Test (*contr.* Parametric Test) A significance test for any null hypothesis that is not a statement about a parameter of a distribution, or about randomness or trend. Common nonparametric tests include the chi-square test for goodness-of-fit and the runs test. In common usage, the term also includes distribution-free tests.

Nonprobability Sampling *See* Probability Sampling.

Nonreactive Measure (*syn.* Unobtrusive Measure) A measure of behaviors that minimizes the subjects' awareness of being studied and, thus, their tendency to react in ways that produce artifacts or other distortions of the data. For example, to study drinking behavior and socioeconomic status, one may question persons door-to-door regarding alcohol use, but there is reason to doubt the honesty of their responses. An alternative would be to record the number and kinds of alcoholic beverage containers in refuse pickups from different neighborhoods. Similarly, viewer interest in various films may be indexed by questionnaire and rating techniques. However, to avoid direct experimenter-subject confrontation, one can tally the number of viewers who visit the refreshment stand, the bathrooms, or who leave the theater during the film. (*See also* Instrumentation Effects.)

Nonrejection Region   *See* Rejection/Nonrejection Region.

Nonreversal Shift   *See* Reversal/Nonreversal Shifts.

Nonsense Stimuli   Stimuli of low meaningfulness. The most frequently used nonsense stimuli are trigrams, paralogs, and nonsense forms and patterns.

Nonsignificant Results (*syn.* Negative Results)   Data that do not permit rejection of the null hypothesis, that is, data in which the differences between conditions are not large enough to show a significant treatment effect, significant heterogeneity of variance, etc.

Nonzero-Sum Game   *See* Zero-Sum/Nonzero-Sum Game.

Norm Line   A smoothed curve representing mean or median scores of successive age or grade groups.

Normal Curve   *See* Normal Distribution.

Normal Distribution (*symb. N (*μ, σ*); syn. Gaussian Distribution)   A symmetric, unimodal, bell-shaped probability distribution, used

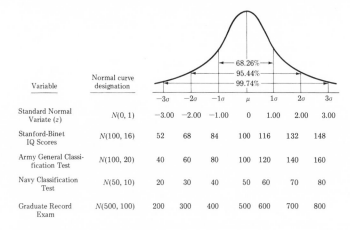

Variable	Normal curve designation	-3σ	-2σ	-1σ	μ	1σ	2σ	3σ
Standard Normal Variate (z)	$N(0, 1)$	-3.00	-2.00	-1.00	0	1.00	2.00	3.00
Stanford-Binet IQ Scores	$N(100, 16)$	52	68	84	100	116	132	148
Army General Classification Test	$N(100, 20)$	40	60	80	100	120	140	160
Navy Classification Test	$N(50, 10)$	20	30	40	50	60	70	80
Graduate Record Exam	$N(500, 100)$	200	300	400	500	600	700	800

Figure N–3   Distributions of Normally Distributed Variables.

156

as the theoretical model for the distribution of a large number of physical and psychological variables. Not all bell-shaped distributions are normal distributions. For example, t distributions are quite similar in appearance to normal distributions. Normal distributions form a family of curves, each specified by two parameters, μ, the mean of the distribution, and σ, the standard deviation of the distribution. For example, N (50, 10) symbolizes a normal distribution with a mean of 50 and a standard deviation of 10. Figure N–3 shows the percentage of the total area under the curve, and by extension the percentage of scores in a distribution that is approximately normal, that lies between plus and minus one, two, and three standard deviations on each side of the mean. These percentages are independent of the specific values of μ and σ.

Normalization   *See* Data Transformation.

Normalized Vector   In multivariate statistics, the vector of weights (*b* coefficients) associated with the independent or predictor variables when these are expressed in their natural units. For direct comparisons, normalized vectors can be transformed into *scaled vectors,* which contain weights (beta coefficients) associated with the variables measured in standard *(z)* units.

Noxious Stimulus   *See* Aversive Stimulus.

Nuisance Variable   *See* Extraneous Variable.

Null Hypothesis   *See* Null/Alternate Hypothesis.

Null/Alternate Hypothesis (*symb. H_0/H_1 or H_0/H_a*)   In hypothesis testing, the formal statistical statements of the possible outcomes of a test. Usually, the hypotheses are about means (μ), correlation coefficients (ρ), etc. The null hypothesis *(H_0)* normally is a statement of no relationship between two variables, so that its rejection provides support for the research or working hypothesis. The alternate hypothesis (H_1 or H_a) normally is that a relationship exists between two variables. For example, if the research is to examine whether performance levels differ under two different conditions, the null hypothesis would be that the means for the two conditions do not differ (symbolically, H_0: $\mu_1 = \mu_2$), and the alternate hypothesis would be that they do differ (symbolically, H_a: $\mu_1 \neq \mu_2$). Sometimes directional hypotheses are stated, if they can be justified. Thus, for example, if the researcher is only interested in whether performance is better in Condition 1 than in Condition 2, the null hypothesis would be that the mean of Condition 1 is equal to or less than Condition 2 (symbolically, H_0: $\mu_1 \leq \mu_2$), and the alternate hypothesis would be that the mean of Condition 1 is greater than the mean of Condition 2 (symbolically, H_0: $\mu_1 > \mu_2$).

Objective Test (*contr.* Subjective Test)   Any test structured in a way that minimizes bias or judgment of the particular scorer. Test-takers' scores are derived from clearly defined scoring procedures, mostly in the form of scoring keys. The results provide a highly uniform means of evaluating the functions being measured, since they are comparable when obtained from various scorers. (*See also* Multiple-Choice Task.)

Oblique (*contr.* Orthogonal)   A set of axes that do not form right angles or dimensions that are not independent. A change in the value on one dimension is necessarily accompanied by a change in the other. For example, pitch (subjective auditory frequency) and loudness (subjective intensity) are obliquely related to intensity: A change in physical intensity of a tone not only changes its loudness but also changes its pitch.

Oblique Rotation   *See* Factor Rotation.

Observation   *See* Datum; Field Research.

Observational Research   *See under* Field Research: *Field Study.*

Observed Frequency (*syn.* Obtained Frequency; *contr.* Expected Frequency)   The number of observations of a particular kind that are obtained in a sample of observations. For example, in tossing a coin 100 times, the observed frequency of tails might be 58, or a sample of 1000 students at a particular university might show observed frequencies of 312 freshmen, 248 sophomores, 186 juniors, 143 seniors, and 111 graduate students.

Observer Effect   *See* Instrumentation Effect.

Obtained Frequency   *See* Observed Frequency.

Occam's Razor   A statement of parsimony saying that new or complex explanations of some event or relationship should not be introduced unless and until the old or simpler one is inadequate.

159

Odd–Even Reliability   *See* Split-Half Reliability.

Oddity Problem   A complex discrimination task in which, on each trial, the subject is shown three stimuli of which two are identical and one is different. Selection of the odd stimulus is rewarded. There may be only two pairs of stimuli, A and B, so that on each trial the subject is shown either two As and a B or two Bs and an A, or there may be a large number of pairs of different stimuli, so that the particular stimuli vary randomly from trial to trial.

EXAMPLE: To test monkeys on the oddity problem, an experimenter used blocks painted red or blue. Which color was to be correct (odd), which was to be incorrect, and the position of the correct stimulus were randomly determined for each trial. The blocks were placed over depressions in a tray, and a peanut was placed under the correct block. The monkey was permitted to move only one block on each trial, and if the correct block was chosen, the monkey got the peanut. Otherwise no reward was received on that trial. Table O–1 shows the arrangement of the stimuli for the first five trials with the correct choice underlined.

Table O–1

Trial	Left	Center	Right
		A	
1	Red	Blue	Red
2	Blue	<u>Red</u>	Blue
3	Red	<u>Blue</u>	Blue
4	<u>Red</u>	Red	Blue
5	Blue	Blue	<u>Red</u>

Odds   The ratio of the probability that an event will occur to the probability that it will not occur. For example, if the probability of correctly guessing the answer to a multiple-choice question is $1/4$ and the probability of an incorrect guess is $3/4$, then the odds in favor of a correct guess are $1/4$ divided by $3/4$, expressed as 1 to 3. The odds against a correct guess (i.e., the odds in favor of an incorrect guess) are 3 to 1. (*See also* Bayesian Statistics; Subjective Probability.)

Ogive   A sigmoid (S-shaped) curve that is the cumulative form of a unimodal distribution. The ogive resulting from cumulating the frequencies or proportions of a normal distribution (Figure O–1) is called a normal ogive. For any symmetric distribution the ogive is symmetric around the inflection point in the S. If the distribution is positively skewed, the upper portion of the S is elongated; if it is negatively skewed, the lower portion of the S is elongated.

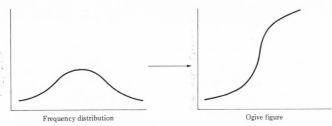

Frequency distribution   Ogive figure

Figure O–1

Omega Squared (*symb.* ω^2) One of several measures of the relative magnitude of a treatment effect. Omega squared is interpreted as the proportion of total variance accounted for by the independent variable. Several formulas have been developed for estimating the parameter for various designs. For a completely randomized one-factor design, with k levels of the independent variable, omega squared for a population can be estimated by the formula:

$$\text{est. } \omega^2 = \frac{SS_b - (k - 1)MS_w}{SS_t + MS_w}$$

where SS_b is the between-groups sum of squares, SS_t is the total sum of squares, and MS_w is the within-groups mean square. (*See also* Magnitude of Effect.)

Omission Training (*syn.* Differential Reinforcement of Other Behavior) An instrumental conditioning procedure designed to reduce the occurrence of a behavior by providing positive reinforcement when the behavior fails to occur or when it occurs below some specified minimum strength. (*See also* Differential Reinforcement of Rates; Time Out.)

EXAMPLE: A rat has been trained to press a bar for a food pellet reward. To train the animal to *not* press the bar, the arrangement is altered so that bar pressing is not rewarded and food is delivered at the end of each 10-sec interval during which the animal does not press the bar. This interval is then increased gradually until some criterion is reached.

Omnibus Test A test that contains different types of items measuring different abilities, such as vocabulary, spatial aptitude, arithmetic, etc. Ordinarily, the items are arranged in separately timed subtests, with the items of each type grouped and increasing in difficulty from easy to hard. In a *spiral-omnibus test,* the different types of items are intermixed in a single timed test, with easy items of each type given first, then each type of item from the next difficulty level, etc.

One-Between/One-Within Design *See* Two-Factor Mixed Design.

One-Between/Two-Within Design *See* Three-Factor Mixed Design.

One-Group Pre/Posttest Design A procedure in which a single group is tested, subjected to some treatment, and then retested. Differences in test performance sometimes are attributed to the event of interest that occurred between tests, but any number of extraneous variables, identified or not, may be responsible. (*For an example, see* Confounding.)

One-Shot Case Study A study in which subjects are exposed to some treatment and then observed or measured for its effect. Since it provides for no comparison measures, the one-shot case study is a demonstration rather than an experimental study.

EXAMPLE: To measure the effects of group encounter experience, subjects undergo a specified number of sensitivity training sessions, and subsequently are asked to indicate how they feel on a rating scale. Since the researcher does not know how the subjects felt before the encounter experience, and in the absence of a comparable group that did not take sensitivity training, the results are difficult to evaluate.

One-Sided Test *See* One-Tail/Two-Tail Test.

One-Tail/Two-Tail Test (*syn.* Directional/Nondirectional Test; One-Sided/Two-Sided Test) In hypothesis testing, referring to the location of the critical region for the test statistic. In a one-tailed test, the critical values of the test statistic (t, F, etc.) are located in only one tail of the distribution, so that the null hypothesis is rejected only if the test statistic is greater than the critical value that cuts off the most extreme values in the upper tail, or only if the test statistic is less than the critical value that cuts off the most extreme values in the lower tail. In a two-tailed test, the critical values of the test statistic are located in both tails, usually in such a way that the areas over the critical regions (corresponding to α, the level of significance) are equal in the two tails. The null hypothesis is rejected if the test statistic is either less than the lower critical value or greater than the upper critical value. Usually, a one-tailed test is appropriate only when a directional alternate hypothesis can be justified. Some tests, though, such as the F test in the analysis of variance and χ^2 tests for frequency data, are by their nature one-tailed tests for nondirectional hypotheses; to use such a test for a directional hypothesis, it is necessary both to inspect the data for a difference in the hypothesized direction and to adjust the size of the critical region.

One-Way Design *See* Single-Factor Design.

162

One-Within/One-Between Design *See* Two-Factor Mixed Design.

One-Within/Two-Between Design *See* Three-Factor Mixed Design.

One-Zero Sampling A measure of behavior in which the occurrence of some response during a brief time period is noted. A number of consecutive intervals are sampled, and the number of intervals in which the behavior occurred is recorded.

EXAMPLE: To score a monkey's grooming behaviors, a 60-min observation session is divided into twelve 5-min intervals. If a grooming activity begins in the second 5-min interval and continues through to the seventh interval, a score of 6 is recorded. However, if a grooming response occurs three times in the fifth and three times in the sixth interval, and not in any other interval, a score of 2 is assigned.

Open-End Item (*contr.* Fixed-Alternative Item) A form of test or survey item in which the test taker is asked to respond without the benefit of provided alternatives. For example, the respondent is asked, "For whom do you intend to vote?" rather than "Do you intend to vote for A, B, or C?"

Operandum *See* Manipulandum.

Operant Chamber (*syn.* Skinner Box) An enclosure in which an organism may manipulate a mechanism (e.g., press a bar or peck a key) in order to obtain a reward or prevent punishment. (*See also* Instrumental Conditioning.)

Operant Conditioning *See* Instrumental Conditioning.

Operant Level *See* Basal Level.

Operant Response *See* Instrumental/Operant Response.

Operating Characteristic Curve (*contr.* Power Function) A graph showing the probability of a test not rejecting the null hypothesis, as a function of alternative values for the hypothesis, that is, with β, the probability of a Type II error, on the ordinate and alternatives to the null hypothesis on the abscissa.

EXAMPLE: Figure O–2 shows the operating characteristic curve for a two-tail test of H_0: $\mu_1 - \mu_2 = 0$ at the .05 level of significance, using a z test for independent groups so the standard error of the difference between means is

$$\sigma_d = \sqrt{\frac{\sigma_1^2}{n_1} + \frac{\sigma_2^2}{n_2}}$$

The alternative values are expressed in standard error units.

Operational Definition A definition of a concept, process, or other event exclusively in terms of the operations and procedures used to produce or measure it. For example, the term *fear* generally

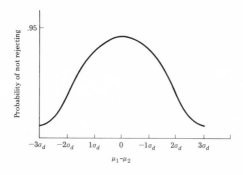

Figure O–2 Operating Characteristic Curve.

refers to an inferred internal emotional state with certain external behavioral correlates such as freezing, shaking, etc. Thus, fear may be measured by, and operationally defined as, the amount by which an ongoing behavior (e.g., pressing a bar) is interrupted by a given fear-inducing operation. (*See also* Hypothetical Construct; Intervening Variable.)

Option Task *See* Multiple-Choice Task.

Orbison Illusion *See under* Illusions.

Order Effect An experimental outcome that is determined by the order in which a series of treatment conditions is administered. For example, if the relative effectiveness of three treatments, A, B, and C, depends on the sequence in which they are given (e.g., ABC versus BCA versus CAB, etc.), then an order effect has been demonstrated. (*See also* Carryover Effect.)

Ordinal Data Data measured on an ordinal scale.

Ordinal Interaction (*contr.* Disordinal Interaction) An interaction in which the rank order of the levels of one independent variable does not change across levels of a second independent variable.

EXAMPLE: Figure O–3 shows data from an experiment that studied the effects of three degrees of enriched diet (Factor A) and whether or not the subjects (rats) were raised with sensory-enriched or normal cage surroundings (Factor B) on later maze learning performance. Normally caged rats show consistently inferior performance under all levels of diet enrichment, even though the differences become larger for levels 2 and 3 of diet enrichment.

Ordinal Scale A scale of measurement that lacks an absolute zero point and has unequal distances between scale values. Only tran-

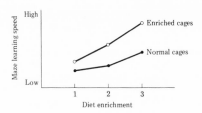

Figure O–3

sitive relationships may be established using this scale. For example, in ranking the severity of crimes, subjects may rank arson
above robbery and robbery above shoplifting. Although transitiv-
ity can be demonstrated—arson is more severe than shoplifting—
the degrees of difference in severity between the crimes are not
measured.

Ordinate   The y, or vertical, axis in a graph or figure.

Organismic Variable   *See* Subject Variable.

Orthogonal (*contr.* Oblique)   Independent, uncorrelated, perpendicular. (1) A set of axes or dimensions, such as cartesian coordinates, that meet or cross at right angles. They are independent
since a change in the value on one dimension is not necessarily
accompanied by a change on the other axis. (*See also* Factor Analysis.) (2) In experimental design, an arrangement of independent
variables in a factorial design, that is, where each level of every
variable is combined with each level of all other variables and
all combinations have an equal number of subjects.

Orthogonal Comparisons   *See* Orthogonal Contrasts.

Orthogonal Contrasts (*syn.* Orthogonal Comparisons)   Independent
contrasts among treatment means, used as a priori (planned) tests
or follow-up tests for the analysis of variance. Two contrasts
(weighted sums of the treatment means) are orthogonal if the
products of corresponding weights sum to zero. If there are k
means, no more than $k - 1$ orthogonal contrasts can be formed,
and any $k - 1$ orthogonal contrasts form an orthogonal set of
contrasts. Orthogonal trend components are a specific orthogonal
set used for trend analysis.

Orthogonal Set   *See* Orthogonal Contrasts.

Orthogonal Trend Component   *See* Orthogonal Contrasts.

Outlier Test (*syn.* Dixon's Test for Outliers)   A statistical test to determine whether an extreme score in a distribution of scores differs

165

sufficiently from the main body of scores to justify the conclusion that it comes from a different population. The test statistic consists of a ratio formed by the difference between the outlier and the main body of scores divided by an approximation of the range of the entire distribution. The particular scores chosen to compute the ratio differ with the size of the distribution. Critical values of the ratio for various significance levels are available in special tables.

Overlearning (*syn.* Overtraining) A procedure in which training trials are continued after the subject reaches some criterion of performance stability.

Overt/Covert Response (*syn.* Explicit/Implicit Response) Terms referring to responses that are directly observable (overt or explicit) versus those that are detectable only with special instrumentation (covert or implicit). For example, overt responses to the verbal command "attention" might include turning one's head or blinking one's eyes, whereas covert responses might include changes in brain wave patterning or increases in adrenal gland secretion.

Overtraining *See* Overlearning.

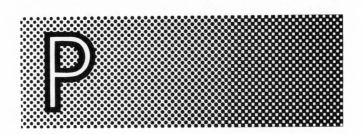

PA Learning   *See* Paired-Associate Learning.

Paired-Associate Learning (*abbr.* PA Learning)   A procedure for studying the formation of associations between the first and second members of a number of pairs of items, so that when the first member of the pair (stimulus item) is presented, the second member (response item) can be given. (*See also* Anticipation Method; Serial Learning.)

EXAMPLE: A subject is given a series of 12 pairs of nonsense syllables (e.g., JAL—RIQ, BEJ—MOS, . . . , DUR—QOC. During each trial (i.e., one presentation of all 12 pairs), the stimulus item is presented alone for 2 sec, and then the stimulus–response pair is presented. During the 2 sec that the stimulus item is presented alone, the subject attempts to recall the correct response item. The procedure is continued for a prescribed number of trials or until a performance criterion is reached.

Paired Comparisons   A scaling method in which pairs formed from members of a set of stimuli are presented to a subject one pair at a time. The subject is required to make a comparative judgment for each pair (e.g., which one is larger, better, brighter, etc.). The stimuli may be ranked, or scale values computed for the stimuli, from the proportion of times each was chosen.

EXAMPLE: A poll is taken to determine preference for one party's nominee for President from among the five leading candidates. There are 10 pairings of these candidates, and for each pair the respondent is asked to indicate which candidate is preferred. Each of the 10 pairs would be given more than once if scale values were to be obtained, or if possible order effects were to be controlled. Table P–1 shows the pairs as presented to one of the respondents, with the preferred candidate in each pair italicized. For this person, the ranking of candidates in order of the proportion of times each was preferred is Candidate B (4/4), C (3/4), E (2/4), A (1/4), and D (0/4).

Table P–1

A—C	B—C	E—A
E—D	B—E	D—A
D—B	C—D	A—B
E—C		

Paired-Groups Design   *See* Matched-Groups Design.

Pairwise Comparisons Test   Any follow-up test for the significance of the differences between all possible pairs of means. With two or more independent variables, the pairwise comparisons are among means for the levels of any one of the variables, either at a specific level of a second variable or averaged over levels of all other variables. The most common of these tests are Duncan's Multiple-Range and the Neuman–Keuls tests. The various tests differ primarily in the type of critical value used (e.g., Studentized range statistic, special tabled values) and in whether the critical value is the same for all tests or varies as a function of the distance between ranked means for the pair being tested. (*See also* A Priori Test; Multiple-Comparison Test.)

EXAMPLE: An experimenter tests information processing capacity using five different types of stimuli and three different rates of presentation. The means of the conditions could be displayed in a 3×5 table as shown:

	Rate	A	B	Stimulus C	D	E	Marginal means (rate)
	1						$\overline{X}_1$
	2						$\overline{X}_2$
	3						$\overline{X}_3$
Marginal means		$\overline{X}_A$	$\overline{X}_B$	$\overline{X}_C$	$\overline{X}_D$	$\overline{X}_E$	

If the interaction is not significant, but the main effect of stimulus type is, the experimenter might do pairwise comparisons on the marginal means to determine which ones differ. If the interaction is significant, the pairwise comparisons could be done for the five means at each rate or for the three means for each stimulus type, but not among all 15 cell means.

Paradigm   A model or characteristic arrangement of stimulus and response events that defines an experimental procedure, observed phenomenon, or theoretical process. For example, the general paradigm for instrumental reward training is

correct response   → reinforcement
incorrect response → no reinforcement
no response   → no reinforcement

Parallel Tests   Alternate forms of the same test comprised of items randomly selected from one pool. The distributions of scores yielded thus have comparable means, standard deviations, and correlations with criterion measures. (*See also* Alternate-Forms Method.)

Paralog   In verbal learning and information processing, any pronounceable five-letter verbal item.

Parameter   (1) (*contr.* **Statistic**)   In statistics, any descriptive characteristic of a population (e.g., the mean, standard deviation, etc.). (2) In experimentation, any variable that influences an empirical relationship. For example, the delay interval between a response and a reinforcing event determines, in part, the effectiveness of the reinforcement. The delay interval is, then, one parameter of reinforcement. (*See also* Parametric Research.)

Parameter Estimating Experiment   *See* Parametric Research.

Parameter Estimation   *See* Estimation.

Parametric Research (*contr.* Hypothesis-Testing Research)   An experiment designed to establish a functional relationship between one or more quantitative independent variables and a dependent variable by testing at several levels of each independent variable. This research is predicated on an already established causal relationship between the independent and dependent variables under study. For example, once it was established that a particular drug increased the general activity levels of rats, a study might be conducted using four or five different dosages to determine if the relationship between the amount of drug and activity level was linear, curvilinear, or nonmonotonic, or to determine the parameters of the equation relating the two variables.

Parametric Test (*contr.* Nonparametric Test)   Any significance test in which the null hypothesis is a statement about the parameter(s) (e.g., mean, median, correlation) of the population(s) from which observations are drawn. In common usage, the term does not include distribution-free tests and refers primarily to tests based on assumed sampling from binomially or normally distributed populations.

Parsimony, Principle of (*syn.* Lloyd Morgan's Canon)   A decision rule for choosing among otherwise equally satisfactory theoretical explanations of a phenomenon. The dictum states that the least-involved or complicated explanation, or the one involving the fewest assumptions, is to be preferred.

Part Correlation (symb. $r_{1(2\cdot3\ldots m)}$; syn. Semipartial Correlation) The correlation between two variables, with the effect of one or more other variables removed from only one of them. For example, in studying the relationship between physical health and academic performance, one might correlate amount of time spent in physical activities and college GPA, with the effect of intelligence removed from or held constant for GPA. (*See also* Partial Correlation.)

Partial Blind Any attempt to keep an experimenter ignorant of the assignment of subjects to conditions in situations where it is impossible to implement blind procedures fully.

Partial Confounding *See* Incomplete Designs.

Partial Correlation (symb. $r_{12\cdot3\ldots m}$) A measure of the relationship between two variables while mathematically holding constant the effect of one or more other variables with which both are correlated. For example, among children height and weight both are correlated with age, and the partial correlation between height and weight could be determined when the effect of age has been partialled out. (*See also* Part Correlation.)

Partial Counterbalancing *See* Incomplete Counterbalancing.

Partial Reinforcement (syn. Intermittent Reinforcement; Periodic Reinforcement; contr. Continuous Reinforcement) (1) In instrumental (operant) conditioning, the scheduling of reinforcements on an intermittent basis, that is, such that not every correct response performed is reinforced. (2) In classical conditioning, the omission of the unconditioned stimulus on some of the training trials, usually in some nonsystematic fashion. For example, in a 75% schedule of reinforcement, the conditioned stimulus would appear alone on one of every four trials on the average. (*For examples see* Reinforcement Schedules.)

Partially Hierarchical Design An experimental design in which at least one independent variable is nested and at least one is crossed. (*See also* Hierarchical Design.)

EXAMPLE: Two government-operated and two privately operated hospitals are selected. In each hospital, 15 patients are selected from each of three psychiatric wards. The patients in each ward are assigned to one of three conditions, in which they are given one of two dosages of a drug or a placebo. The patients' behavior is rated by the psychiatric staff. In this experiment, patients are nested in wards, wards are nested in hospitals, and hospitals are nested in type of operation. Drug condition is crossed with wards, hospitals, and operation.

Each of the four: (1) operation, (2) hospitals within operation, (3) wards within hospitals, and (4) patients within wards, is an identifiable source of variability, as are drug condition and its interaction with each of the other four sources. In the summary of this design, D is drug, H is hospital, W is ward, and P is patient.

Government Operated

		H₁			H₂	
	W₁	W₂	W₃	W₄	W₅	W₆
D₁	P₁	P₁₆	P₃₁	P₄₆	P	P
	⋮	⋮	⋮	⋮	⋮	⋮
	P₅	P₂₀	P₃₅	P	P	P
D₂	P₆	P₂₁	P₃₆	P	P	P
	⋮	⋮	⋮	⋮	⋮	⋮
	P₁₀	P₂₅	P₄₀	P	P	P
D₃	P₁₁	P₂₆	P₄₁	P	P	P
	⋮	⋮	⋮	⋮	⋮	⋮
	P₁₅	P₃₀	P₄₅	P	P	P

Privately Operated

		H₃			H₄	
	W₇	W₈	W₉	W₁₀	W₁₁	W₁₂
D₁	P	P	P	P	P	P₁₆₆
	⋮	⋮	⋮	⋮	⋮	⋮
	P	P	P	P	P	P₁₇₀
D₂	P	P	P	P	P	P₁₇₁
	⋮	⋮	⋮	⋮	⋮	⋮
	P	P	P	P	P	P₁₇₅
D₃	P	P	P	P	P	P₁₇₆
	⋮	⋮	⋮	⋮	⋮	⋮
	P	P	P	P	P	P₁₈₀

Partition   (1) Division of a set of objects into mutually exclusive and exhaustive subsets. For example, the suits (clubs, diamonds, hearts, and spades) form a partition of the cards in a deck, since every card belongs to one and only one suit. (2) **(contr. Pooling)** Division of a sum of squares into independent and exhaustive components. That is, each component of the partition is a sum of squares that reflects a different source of variability, and the total of all the component sums of squares equals the sum of squares that has been partitioned.

Part–Whole Illusion *See under* Illusions.

Passive Avoidance Training *See* Punishment Training.

Path Analysis A procedure that uses a series of multiple regression analyses to describe the relationships among a set of variables that are logically ordered. Most commonly, this is an ordering in time. It is assumed that this reflects a causal order, so that each variable is determined by one or more of the variables that precede it, and in turn may determine variables that follow it. Latent or unobserved variables that are independent of preceding observed variables may be postulated, to represent the influence of causal variables not included in the set. The model is shown in a path diagram, with arrows representing the direction of influence. Path analysis expresses the same relationships by a set of regression equations, with each variable expressed as a linear function of the preceding variables plus a unique latent variable. The paths are described by the regression coefficients. If the weights for the latent variables are zero, the set of variables is said to show causal closure, that is, causal relationships are completely specified within the set, with little or no residual variation due to factors outside the set.

EXAMPLE: Figure P–1 shows the results of a three-variable path analysis, with E_2 and E_3 representing unobserved variables. The figure shows that occupation influences voting behavior directly as well as

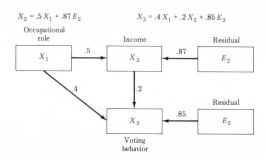

Figure P–1

indirectly through its influence on income, and that neither income nor voting behavior are completely determined by the observed variables. The path weights are the coefficients of the regression equations which correspond to the path diagram.

Pavlovian Conditioning *See* Classical Conditioning.

Payoff Matrix A table showing the rewards and penalties accruing to alternative decisions in a situation. Such matrices commonly are used in game theory, decision theory, and signal detection, that is, situations where decisions must be made in the face of uncertainty. (*For an example see* Zero-Sum/Nonzero-Sum Game.)

PE *See* Probable Error.

Peakedness *See* Kurtosis.

Pearson Product-Moment Correlation *See* Correlation Coefficient.

Pearson *r* *See* Correlation Coefficient.

Penrose Triangle *See under* Illusions.

Percentile (*syn.* Centile) One of the 99 score points that divide a distribution into hundredths. The percentiles are labeled P_1 through P_{99}. The 72nd percentile (P_{72}), for example, is the point below which lie 72% of the scores in a distribution. (*See also* Decile; Quartile.)

Percentile Rank (*syn.* Centile Rank) A measure of relative standing that shows the percentage of scores in a given distribution that fall below a specified score, X. (*See also* Percentile.)

Perceptual-Motor Learning Learning in which the emphasis is on the acquisition of skilled movements, with language processes playing a relatively small role. Perceptual-motor tasks include pursuit tracking, mirror image tracing, and finger maze learning.

Performance Criterion Some specified level of performance used as the basis for defining a dependent variable or as the basis for changing the conditions under which the subject performs. For example, in certain kinds of discrimination learning experiments, the subject may be presented with a set of stimuli in a series of trials that is continued until the subject makes five correct responses in a row. The number of trials needed to reach this criterion could be recorded as a measure of learning speed, and then the series continued with a new set of stimuli. (*See also* Fixed-Trials Criterion.)

Performance Variable *See* Dependent Variable.

Periodic Reinforcement *See* Interval Schedules of Reinforcement.

Permissible Transformation In measurement, changes of every scale value or of every observed value that do not alter the properties of the scale or the relationships among data. The permissible transformations are for nominal measurement: any one-to-one transformation (e.g., changing category names to letters or numbers); for ordinal measurement any increasing monotonic transformation (e.g., changing, 2, 4, and 6 to 3, 7, and 15); for interval measurement any linear transformation with positive slope, and for ratio measurement multiplication by any positive constant.

Permutation   An arrangement or sequence of a set of n different objects so that a given object can appear only once in each arrangement. The number of possible sequences or permutations is $n!$ (n factorial), defined as $n(n-1)(n-2) \ldots 1$. For example, given a set of five colored blocks, red, green, yellow, blue, and orange, there are $5! = 5 \cdot 4 \cdot 3 \cdot 2 \cdot 1 = 120$ permutations of colors, such as YBROG, BYROG, etc. (*See also* Combination.)

Phenomenal Report   *See* Subjective Report.

Phi (*symb.* ϕ)   *See* Appendix B.

Phi Coefficient (*symb.* ϕ; *syn.* Fourfold Point Correlation, *symb.* r_p)
An index of the degree of correlation between two variables that are both true dichotomies, (e.g., male versus female, U.S. citizen versus not U.S. citizen, right versus wrong). Under certain conditions, the statistic may range in value from -1 to $+1$; under most conditions, however, the maximum absolute value, for complete association, is less than 1. When used in conjunction with a chi-square test of independence, it can be computed as

$$\phi = \sqrt{\frac{\chi^2}{N}}$$

where χ^2 is the computed chi-square statistic for the test and N is the total number of observations. Alternatively, the statistic can be computed directly by the formula:

$$\phi = \frac{ad - bc}{\sqrt{(a + b)(c + d)(a + c)(b + d)}}$$

where a and d are the obtained frequencies in the upper left and lower right cells, respectively, of the contingency table, and b and c are the obtained frequencies in the other two cells. (The sums in the denominator are the marginal totals.)

Phi Phenomenon   *See under* Illusions.

Pillai's Criterion   *See* Multivariate Tests of Significance.

Pilot Study   A small-scale investigation that precedes a more complete research project. Its primary purpose is to determine whether certain techniques and procedures will be effective and feasible. It also is conducted to permit control of the power of the research by determining whether selected levels of an independent variable are too similar or dissimilar, and by estimating variability in order to determine a sample size.

Placebo Control   In drug research with humans, a procedure in which subjects in a control condition are given a substance that does not contain the active ingredient(s) under investigation. By extension, the term sometimes is used in the context of drug research with lower animals.

EXAMPLE: To assess the effect of a new anti-insomnia drug, a group of human subjects is given the test drug in capsule form. Since it is possible that at least some of the subjects may form hypotheses or expectations about the effects of the drug, which in turn may alter sleep, a comparable group of subjects is given capsules identical in appearance to those given to the experimental group, and under identical conditions. These capsules, however, contain only ingredients that are largely inert (e.g., milk sugar). Thus, the true effect of the drug will be shown in differences between the two groups.

Plaid Square Design   *See* Confounded Designs.

Planned Comparison   *See* A Priori Test.

Planned Test   *See* A Priori Test.

Plateau   A segment in a curve that shows little or no slope. (*See also* Asymptote.)

Platykurtosis   *See* Kurtosis.

POE (Point of Objective Equality)   *See* Point of Physical Equality.

Poggendorf Illusion   *See under* Illusions.

Point Biserial Correlation Coefficient (*symb.* r_{pb}, r_{pbi}, $r_{p.bis}$)   A measure of the degree of correlation between two variables, one of which is a true dichotomy and the other of which is continuous. Examples of true dichotomies include male versus female, living in California versus not living in California, and being right or wrong in responding to a test item. The measure is used, for example, to determine the degree of correlation between sex and performance on some measure of motor skill, or between being right or wrong in answering a particular item of general knowledge and performance on some longer test. It is computed by the formula $r_{pb} = [(\overline{X}_p - \overline{X}_q)/S] \sqrt{pq}$, where p and q are the proportion of observations in each of the categories of the dichotomous variable, $\overline{X}_p$ and $\overline{X}_q$ are the means on the continuous variable for the observations in each of the two categories, and S is the standard deviation of all the scores on the continuous variable.

Point Estimation   The use of a sample value to estimate the exact value of a population parameter such as a mean, a standard deviation, a proportion, etc. (*See also* Confidence Interval; Confidence Limits; Interval Estimation.)

EXAMPLE: One population can be defined as all children enrolled in a particular elementary school during a particular school year. If the IQ of each of these students were measured, and the mean IQ obtained, the value would be the population mean, μ. This parameter μ would have a numerical value that would fall at some specific point on the number continuum. If a random sample of $n = 100$ students at the school yielded a mean IQ of 102.1, this sample mean is a point estimate of the value of μ.

Point of Objective Equality   *See* Point of Physical Equality.

Point of Physical Equality (*abbr.* PPE; *syn.* Point of Objective Equality (POE); *contr.* Point of Subjective Equality)   In psychophysics, that value of a comparison stimulus which is physically equal to a standard stimulus.

Point of Subjective Equality (*abbr.* PSE; *contr.* Point of Physical Equality)   In psychophysics, that value of the comparison stimulus that is judged by the subject to be equal to the standard stimulus.

Poisson Distribution   A probability distribution with one parameter, λ (lambda), which is the value of both the mean and variance of the distribution. The distribution is used as the model for the temporal or spatial distribution of events that have a low probability of occurring at any particular time or place (e.g., the number of errors per hour or per page for a very simple or highly practiced task). It also is used as an approximation to the binomial distribution when N, the number of observations, is very large, and p, the probability of the event being observed, is very small.

Ponzo Illusion   *See under* Illusions.

Pooled Error Term   *See* Pooling.

Pooled Mean Square   *See* Pooling.

Pooled Variance   *See* Pooling.

Pooling (*contr.* Partition)   Adding together of independent terms, usually with reference to sums of squares and the associated degrees of freedom. The **pooled variance** is the pooled, or summed, sums of squares from two or more independent samples, divided by the pooled (summed) degrees of freedom for the samples. The pooled variance is computed as an estimate of σ^2 when it is assumed that the samples come from populations having the same variance. A **pooled error term,** or **pooled mean square,** in the analysis of variance is formed by pooling the sums of squares for nonsignificant higher order interactions with the sum of squares for their error term, and dividing by the pooled degrees of freedom for these sums of squares.

176

Population The entire collection or set of objects, people, events, etc., of interest in a particular context, or the set of measurements on the members of the population. For example, we may speak of the population of people who reside in the United States, or the population of IQ scores for these people; or we may speak of the population of all possible responses of an individual to a particular stimulus, or the population of response times to this stimulus.

Positive _____ In most cases terms with the modifiers *positive* or *negative* are entered in the unmodified form; for example, *positive correlation* and *negative correlation* are defined in the entry Correlation.

Positive/Negative Relationship Terms that describe the direction of association between two variables, X and Y. A positive relationship exists when values of Y increase as X increases. A negative (or **inverse**) relationship exists when Y decreases as X increases. (*For illustrations of these relationships see* Linear Regression; Monotonic Function; Nonmonotonic Function.)

Positive Stimulus (*contr.* Negative Stimulus) A general term for any stimulus associated with reinforcement. (1) In differential instrumental conditioning, it is the stimulus a response to which is reinforced (*symb.* S+). (2) In differential classical conditioning, it is that conditioned stimulus which is followed by an unconditioned stimulus (*symb.* CS+). (*For examples, see* Differential Classical Conditioning; Differential Instrumental Conditioning.)

Positively Accelerated Function (*contr.* Negatively Accelerated Function) A relationship between two variables such that the rate of change of the dependent variable *(Y)* increases with an increase in the value of the independent variable *(X)*. The curve connecting the values of Y becomes more nearly perpendicular to the x-axis. Y may be either an increasing or a decreasing function of X. Figure P–2 illustrates two positively accelerated functions.

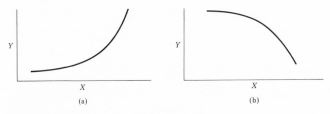

Figure P–2 Positively accelerated increasing (a) and positively accelerated decreasing (b) functions.

Positively Correlated Reinforcement   *See* Correlated Reinforcement.

Posterior Probability   The probability of an event, determined after an experiment is completed, using data from the experiment to adjust the prior probability of that same event. (*See also* Bayesian Statistics.)

Post Hoc Comparison   *See* A Posteriori Test.

Post Hoc Test   *See* A Posteriori Test.

Posterior Distribution   In Bayesian statistics, a probability distribution for possible values of a parameter, such as the population mean, correlation, etc., which takes into consideration both the prior distribution and research data. (*See also* Prior Distribution.)

Posttest Design (*syn.* After-Test Design)   Any research design in which one or more groups of subjects are observed or measured after an experimental treatment is given, or an event has occurred. A control group may be measured also and posttest scores compared.

Power   The probability that the null hypothesis will be correctly rejected by a particular statistical test, if a particular alternative hypothesis is true; the probability that a particular statistical test will detect a treatment effect of a specified magnitude. The power of a test is equal to $1 - \beta$ (beta), where β is the probability of a Type II error. Power is directly related to sample size and to α (level of significance), and to the magnitude of the treatment effect. It is inversely related to the standard deviation. Thus, the power of a test can be increased by increasing the sample size, increasing the value of alpha, increasing the difference between treatments, or decreasing the standard deviation.

Power Curve   *See* Power Function.

Power Function (*syn.* Power Curve; *contr.* Operating Characteristic Curve)   A graph showing the power of a test as a function of alternative values for the hypothesis being tested, that is, with

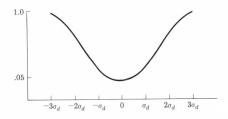

Figure P–3

$1 - \beta$ on the ordinate and alternatives to the null hypothesis on the abscissa.

EXAMPLE: Figure P–3 shows the power function for a two-tail test at the .05 level of significance, of H_0: $\mu_1 - \mu_2 = 0$, using a z test and independent groups, so that

$$\sigma_d = \sigma_{\bar{x}_1 - \bar{x}_2} = \sqrt{\frac{\sigma_1^2}{n_1} + \frac{\sigma_2^2}{n_2}}$$

Power Test (contr. Speed Test)   Any test in which test takers' scores are based solely on the difficulty of the items solved, without regard to the amount of time needed to solve them.

Practice Trial (syn. Pretraining Trial)   Trials given prior to the start of an experimental session, usually to "warm up" or familiarize the subject with the task.

Precision   In measurement, having small measurement error, as indexed by the standard deviation. The more precise a measuring instrument is, the smaller the standard deviation of the values obtained from repeated measurements of an object. (See also Accuracy; Reliability.)

Preconditioning   See Sensory Preconditioning.

Predicted Variance   The proportion of the variance in a dependent variable that is attributed to the differences in one or more independent variables. (See also Determination, Coefficient of; Magnitude of Effect.)

Prediction Equation   A regression equation used for predicting future performance (the criterion variable, Y) from one or more predictor variables (X). Usually a prediction equation is derived from correlational research, in which subjects are randomly sampled and measured on each of the variables. (See also Multiple Regression.)

EXAMPLE: High school counselors were rated on their effectiveness as counselors and on a number of personality variables. The best predictor of effectiveness was found to be self-confidence. For this variable, the prediction equation was $Y' = 50.3 + 2.6X$. Using this equation, the predicted effectiveness rating for a person who scores 14 on the self-confidence scale would be $50.3 + 2.6(14) = 86.7$. The three best predictors were the measures of self-confidence (X_1), openness or willingness to talk about oneself (X_2), and dependability (X_3). The multiple prediction equation using these three variables was $Y' = 28.2 + 3.1X_1 + .7X_2 + 1.6X_3$. For a person who scores 8 on the self-confidence scale, 13 on the openness scale, and 11 on the dependability scale, the predicted effectiveness rating would be $28.2 + 3.1(8) + .7(13) + 1.6(11) = 79.7$.

Predictive Validity   The degree to which test performance predicts future performance. For example, academic aptitude test scores by students are correlated with their grades the following year. The correlation serves as a measure of validity for predicting performance a year later.

Predictor Variable   Any variable used to predict the value of some criterion variable by means of a prediction equation.

Preliminary Test   In statistics, any test done prior to performing a statistical analysis, to determine if one or more assumptions, such as normality, independence of groups, or equal means, variances, or covariances, is met. For example, before carrying out an analysis of variance, a test of the assumption that the groups of data come from populations having equal variance may be done. (*See also* Pretest.)

Preparation   The laboratory arrangement of subjects, apparatus, or materials. For example, the placement of two subjects in a competitive game situation such as the Prisoner's Dilemma is a preparation which allows the experimenter to study cooperation and conflict.

Pre/Post Design   See Pretest/Posttest Design.

Pretest   (1) A performance measure taken prior to administration of a treatment which provides a baseline to which posttreatment performance is compared. (2) In randomized-blocks (matched-subjects) designs, a test administered to all subjects to provide a basis for matching or blocking subjects for assignment to treatment groups. (*See also* Preliminary Test.)

Pretest/Posttest Design (*syn.* Before/After Design)   Any research design in which one or more groups of randomly assigned subjects is observed or measured before and again after an experimental treatment is given or an event has occurred. A control group may be measured the same way, and scores are then compared. These comparisons may be among posttest scores only, or they may be among difference scores obtained by subtracting a subject's pretest score from the posttest score for the subject.

Pretraining Trial   *See* Baseline Trial; Practice Trial.

Primary Reinforcement (*contr.* Conditioned Reinforcement)   A stimulus event whose reinforcing capability is unlearned. Food or water for a hungry or thirsty organism are examples of primary reinforcers.

Primary Stimulus   *See* Unconditioned Stimulus.

Principal Component Analysis   A multivariate analysis procedure aimed at extracting principal components to condense as much of the total variation in the data as possible with a minimum number of such components. The first principal component is that weighted linear combination of the variables which accounts for maximum shared variance. The second principal component is that weighted linear combination of the variables that is uncorrelated with the first principal component and which accounts for the maximum variation in the data not as yet accounted for, and so on. (*See also* Factor Analysis; Factor Rotation.)

Principal Components Rotation *See* Factor Rotation.

Prior Distribution In Bayesian statistics, a probability distribution reflecting the experimenter's subjective belief concerning possible values of a parameter, such as the population mean, correlation, etc. (*See also* Posterior Distribution.)

Prior Odds Odds, subjectively determined prior to gathering experimental data. (*See also* Bayesian Statistics; Subjective Probability.)

Prior Probability The probability of an event determined prior to gathering experimental data. It is usually subjective, but the prior probability for one experiment may be the posterior probability obtained from a previous experiment. (*See also* Bayesian Statistics; Subjective Probability.)

Prisoner's Dilemma *See* Zero-Sum/Nonzero-Sum Game.

Proaction Paradigm *See* Transfer Paradigm.

Probability A quantitative statement of the likelihood of occurrence of an event. A probability of 0 refers to an event that is certain not to occur; a probability of 1 refers to an event that is certain to occur; values in between refer to the likelihood of one event out of several that could occur. Classical statistical inference usually is based on the objective, or relative frequency, definition: the probability of an event is its relative frequency in a population. Bayesian statistical inference uses a subjective definition: the probability of an event is a personal statement of likelihood; based on the individual's accumulated knowledge of the event and circumstances.

Probability Learning Task A type of discrimination learning task in which the subject, on each of a series of trials, must select one stimulus from among two or more stimuli each of which may have different probabilities of being correct.

EXAMPLE: A person faces a panel containing two buttons with lights above them. The left button is programmed to be correct on 70 percent of the trials, and the right button on 30 percent of the trials, on a random basis. If the left button happens to be correct on a given trial, pressing it will illuminate the light above it. If not, the

181

other light will be illuminated. The subject's choice behavior over a lengthy series of trials is recorded.

Probability Sampling Drawing a sample in such a way that the probability of each member of the population being selected can be specified. When these probabilities are all equal, the process is called (simple) random sampling. (*For an example in which the probabilities are not all equal see* Stratified Random Sampling.)

Probable Error (*abbr.* PE) A measure of variability for a sampling distribution, or of accuracy of a parameter estimate. It is equal to 0.6745 times the standard error, and as a measure of accuracy is comparable to a 50% confidence interval. It is seldom used anymore, having been supplanted by the standard error.

Probe Stimulus *See* Interpolated Event.

Probe Technique In memory research, a procedure in which a subject is given a set of items to memorize. One of the items, a test item, is then presented, and the subject's task is to report the item that followed the test item in the original list. (*See also* Interpolated Event.)

EXAMPLE: A subject is given a series of trials on each of which a set of 10 digits is presented in random order. On various test trials the subject is given one of the digits as a test item and is to report which digit followed the test digit. On different trials the test item is the second, third, fourth, fifth, sixth, seventh, or eighth digit in the list. Thus, the number of digits intervening between the test item and the attempt to recall varies from eight to two.

Probit Analysis A statistical procedure for fitting a normal ogive to data. It is used in certain types of research, such as drug or psychophysical research, where it may be assumed that observed frequencies are based on the cumulative probability of some underlying normally distributed response.

Product-Moment Correlation Coefficient *See* Correlation Coefficient.

Production Method Any procedure in which a subject must produce a stimulus having specified characteristics. For example, a subject may be asked to draw a line that is 5 cm long or to manipulate a tone generator to produce a tone that is subjectively half as loud as a standard tone.

Profile A set of test scores or other measurements for an individual, or a set of mean scores for a group of individuals, especially when these are shown graphically. For example, an individual may complete an interest inventory, which will result in a profile of the person's interest in various types of activities. This profile can

182

be compared with average profiles for people in various types of occupations to determine to which group the individual is most similar. (*For an example see* Semantic Differential.)

Profile Analysis (1) A systematic comparison of individual personality trait patterns to a set of norms or standards. (2) In multivariate statistics, the analysis of differences in the curve level and shape among vectors.

Projective Technique Procedures in which subjects are asked to interpret relatively unstructured, ambiguous, or vague stimuli, such as inkblots or pictures, or to respond to incomplete statements.

Projective Test Any test using projective techniques.

Protection Level In statistics, the minimum probability of not making any Type I errors in a set of related significance tests. (*See also* Error Rate.)

PSE *See* Point of Subjective Equality.

Pseudoconditioning Control *See* Unpaired Control.

Pseudo-Effect *See* Artifact.

Pseudo-Experiment A nonscientific research endeavor characterized by poor or no controls. A pseudo-experiment in sleep loss and memory may be performed by an individual who stays awake for 24 hours, then tries to recall the previous day's events. Without an objective specification of recall, adequate testing by an external experimenter, control groups or control sessions, etc., little usable information is obtained. (*See also* Quasi-experiment.)

Psychological Scaling *See* Scaling Methods.

Psychophysical Function An expression of the relationship between a psychological attribute and a physical attribute, for example, the relationship between the perceived brightness of a light and its physical intensity. The relationship may be expressed as a logarithmic function, a power function, or some other function.

Psychophysical Methods Procedures designed to study basic sensory processes. These include fractionation, production, and reproduction methods. Many of these techniques have been adapted for use in other areas of psychology and are listed under Scaling Methods. (*See also* Adjustment, Method of; Constant Stimuli, Method of; Limits, Method of.)

Pulfrich Illusion *See under* Illusions.

Punishment (*contr.* Reinforcement) A set of operations designed to decrease the measured strength of a behavior. **Positive punishment** is the delivery of an aversive stimulus such as electric shock, extreme heat or cold, when the behavior occurs. **Negative punishment** is the removal of the availability of a positive reinforcer, such as food, a toy, etc., when the behavior occurs.

Punishment Training (*syn.* Passive Avoidance Training; *contr.* Reward Training)   An instrumental (operant) conditioning technique in which a response is reduced in strength or eliminated by delivering an aversive stimulus when the response occurs and withholding that stimulus when the response does not occur.

EXAMPLE: A rat placed on a narrow pedestal several centimeters high tends to step down almost immediately. To train the animal to remain on the pedestal, a wire grid is placed on the floor of the apparatus. When the rat steps down it is shocked immediately and removed. Step-down latencies that increase over a series of trials indicate improved performance. If the animal's latency on a given trial exceeds some criterion, it may avoid shock entirely.

Pure Research   *See* Basic Research.

Pursuit Rotor Task   *See* Rotary Pursuit Task.

Pursuit Tracking Task (*contr.* Compensatory Tracking Task)   A psychomotor task in which the subject attempts to keep a movable cursor on a moving target. For example, using a pursuit rotor, the subject attempts to keep a metal stylus in contact with a metal disc that is moving in a circle; or the target may be a randomly moving blip on a display screen, and the subject uses a control knob to attempt to keep another blip superimposed on the target.

***p* Value**   (1) In reporting the results of significance testing, the probability of obtaining a difference as large as or larger than the observed difference. Equivalently, it is the probability of obtaining a value of the test statistic that differs from the expected value by as much as or more than does the observed value, if the null hypothesis is true. If the obtained p value is less than the chosen level of significance (α), the null hypothesis can be rejected. For example, if a t value of 3.62 is obtained, with 14 degrees of freedom, the p value is less than .01 ($p < .01$), since the probability of obtaining a t this large in absolute value is less than .01. If the usual .05 level of significance is being used, the null hypothesis would be rejected. (2) The proportion of people correctly answering a particular question, used as an index of item difficulty (or item easiness).

Q-Sort A set of operations for personality assessment. A subject (or someone making judgments about a subject) is asked individually to sort a considerable number of statements into piles that represent the degrees to which the statements apply to the subject.

EXAMPLE: A group of clinicians and/or their clients are presented with cards, each of which lists a personality trait commonly associated with clinicians (e.g., *helpful, empathic,* etc.). They are asked individually to provide their viewpoint on how these traits apply to them (or their therapist, in the case of the clients) by sorting the cards along a continuum ranging from -4 (least applicable) to 0 (no position) to $+4$ (most applicable). The sets of ranking are then intercorrelated and the data are analyzed, usually by factor analysis.

Quadratic Component *See* Trend Analysis.

Qualitative Variable (*contr.* Quantitative Variable) Any variable measured on a nominal scale. Psychiatric classification (e.g., paranoid, depressive, or schizophrenic) and shape of the visual stimulus (e.g., circle, square, triangle) are such variables.

Quantile A general term for a percentile, decile, or quartile.

Quantitative Variable (*contr.* Qualitative Variable) Any variable measured on an ordinal, interval, or ratio scale, that is, variables with levels differing in magnitude. Examples include amount of food deprivation, brightness of light, or rated popularity of a food product. (*See also* Continuous Variable; Discrete Variable.)

Quartile One of the three score points that divide a distribution into fourths. The first quartile, Q_1, is the point below which 25% of the scores in a distribution lie; it is therefore equal to the 25th percentile, P_{25}. Similarly, Q_2 is equal to the median, P_{50}, and Q_3 is equal to P_{75}.

Quartile Deviation   *See* Semi-interquartile Range.

Quartile Range   *See* Semi-interquartile Range.

Quartimax Rotation   *See* Factor Rotation.

Quasi-Experiment   A refinement of the naturalistic observation study in which changes in the independent variable occur in nature and not by the experimenter's manipulation, but which incorporates as many principles of scientific control as possible under the circumstances. Often there is enough forewarning of the event of interest to allow for pre–post comparisons, definition of control groups and conditions, multiple independent variables, etc. (*See also* Ex Post Facto Study Pseudoexperiment; Quasi-experimental Design.)

Quasi-Experimental Design   A research design in which subjects are not assigned randomly to conditions, although the independent variable(s) may be manipulated. The reason for not assigning randomly is usually because it is impossible or not feasible to do so. For example, the assessment of a new teaching method in a high school that calls for random assignment of students to classes taught by either the old or the new method may be opposed by school authorities as a matter of principle, or because of the logistics involved. Instead, a quasi-experimental method may be used in which intact classes, matched as closely as possible on student composition and meeting time, will be compared on the two methods. (*See also* Intact-Groups Design; Time Series Design.)

Quasi-*F* Ratio   A test procedure for certain experiments involving a random-effects or mixed-effects model, when an appropriate error term is not given by the usual analysis of variance. A quasi-*F* ratio uses an error term that is derived from appropriate linear combination of two or more mean squares, depending on the particular design and model.

Quasi-Latin Square   *See* Confounded Design.

Questionnaire   A set of questions on a given topic that do not test the respondents' ability, but rather measure their opinions, interests, and personality problems, as well as provide biographical information.

Quota Sampling   *See* Stratified Sampling.

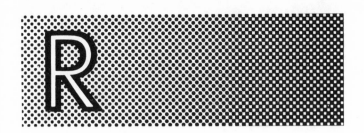

Random A term that describes a process or event in which occurrences are determined strictly by chance, so that the probability of occurrence is the same as the probability of the event in the population. In many cases, *random* means "equally likely." For example, random sampling means each possible sample has an equal chance of being selected; in a random-number table, each of the digits 0 through 9 has an equal chance of occurring in any position. However, in other cases, this may not be so. For example, if a population consists of 40% males and 60% females, then male and female are not equally likely to occur in the random selection of an individual.

Random Assignment A procedure for determining the assignment of subjects to experimental conditions in such a way that the probability of being assigned to a particular condition is the same for all subjects serving in the experiment. Random assignment helps to ensure, but cannot guarantee, that the effects of such subject variables as age, sex, intelligence, socioeconomic background, etc., are distributed equally over the different experimental conditions, and thus are not confounded with the effects of the independent variable(s).

Random-Effects Factor *See* Fixed/Random-Effects Factor.

Random-Effects Model *See* Fixed/Random-Effects Model.

Random Error (*syn.* Accidental Error; Chance Error; Experimental Error; Variable Error; *contr.* Constant Error) An error of measurement or observation that cannot be attributed to any specific cause. Random errors vary in direction and magnitude from observation to observation with respect to both magnitude and sign (i.e., as positive or negative), and thus, tend to average to zero over the long run. Random errors generally are considered to be normally distributed. (*See also* Error Variance; Measurement Error.)

Random Factor   *See* Fixed/Random-Effects Factor.

Random Normal Numbers   A set of numbers that represent random selections from a normal distribution. Tables of random normal numbers most frequently are used in research for generating stimuli for certain types of psychophysical and signal detection experiments. (*See also* Random Numbers.)

Random Numbers   An array of numbers constructed in such a way that each of the digits 0 through 9 has an equal chance of being in any position and that successive digits are independent. In such a set the probability is .1 that a particular digit is any of the values 0 through 9, .01 that any pair of digits take the value 00 through 99, etc. Tables of random numbers may be found in most statistics textbooks and in many experimental methodology books. (*See also* Random Normal Numbers; Random Permutation.)

Random Permutation   An arrangement or sequence of N objects chosen so that each of the possible permutations has an equal chance of being chosen. Tables of random permutations, with each permutation having an equal chance of being in each position in the table, are available in many experimental design and methods texts and are useful for block randomization of stimuli and for assigning subjects in a randomized-block design.

Random Reinforcement   *See* Noncontingent Reinforcement.

Random Sample   *See* Random Sampling.

Random Sampling   Drawing a sample in such a way that each element in the population has an equal probability of being included in the sample. The probability that a given element will or will not be included in the sample is not influenced by whether any other particular element or elements were or were not selected. A random sample may be defined also as one selected so that all possible samples like it are equally likely to be chosen. A random sample is considered to be representative of the population from which it is selected regardless of sample size. However, the precision with which measurements made on the sample will reflect the true values in the population will improve with increase in the size of the sample.

Random Variable (*syn.* Stochastic Variable)   A variable whose different values occur with probabilities that are, at least theoretically, specifiable. For example, the diameter of a circle is a variable. If the stimuli in an experiment are circles with 10 different diameters, arranged in random order, the diameter of the circle appearing on any particular trial is a random variable, used as a stimulus variable, with each possible value having a probability of .1. If the subject manipulates an aperture to try to match the size of the stimulus, the diameter of the circle produced by the subject also is a random variable, used as a dependent variable. The purpose of such an experiment usually is to estimate the probability distribution of responses, or some aspect of it.

Randomized-Blocks Design (*contr.* Randomized-Groups Design)
An experimental design using several homogeneous blocks of subjects, each block being a group of subjects who are matched as closely as possible on whatever subject characteristics the experimenter chooses. There are as many subjects in each block as there are treatment conditions in the experiment, and within each block one subject is randomly assigned to each condition. The blocks may be formed by selecting subjects matched on the basis of age, sex, socioeconomic class, etc., from some larger pool or by randomly selecting the required number of subjects, ranking them on the basis of some pretest or other variable, and then calling the top k subjects the first block, the next k subjects the second block, etc. (*See also* Block; Blocking Variable.)

EXAMPLE: An experimenter plans to test the running speed of rats for three different amounts (50, 100, or 150 mg) of two different rewards (casein or dextrose). Three levels of each of the two rewards makes six conditions, so for a randomized-block design, each block must have six rats. To control for genetic differences in running speed, each block would contain six rats from the same litter. Another procedure could be to train a group of rats to run for a liquid reward and to call the six fastest rats the first block, the next six the second block, etc. When the blocks are formed, the six rats in each block would be randomly assigned to the six conditions.

Randomized-Groups Design (*syn.* Between-Groups Design; Between-Subjects Design; Completely Randomized Design; Independent-Groups Design; Randomized-Subjects Design; *contr.* Randomized-Blocks Design) One category of experimental designs classified in terms of the way subjects are selected and assigned to conditions. Specifically, a design which subjects are randomly selected and randomly assigned to treatment conditions. Each subject is tested under a single condition, and there is only one score for each subject, so the number of observations is the same as the number of subjects. Normally, the random assignment is made with the restriction that the same number of subjects is tested under each condition. (*See also* Mixed Design.)

Randomized-Subjects Design *See* Randomized-Groups Design.

Range A measure of spread or variability in a set of scores, defined as the largest score *(L)* minus the smallest score *(S)*. (Sometimes it is defined as $L - S + 1$, but this is correct only if the scores are integer measures of a continuous variable.) For example, the range of numbers 9, 5, 3, 8, and 6 is $9 - 3$ or 6. For functions the range is the possible values the function may take. The range of the function $Y = X^2$ is 0 to $+\infty$, since X^2 cannot be negative. The range of the normal distribution is $-\infty$ to $+\infty$.

Rank Correlation Coefficient (*symb.* r_s or ρ_s; *syn.* Rank-Difference Correlation; Spearman's Rho) The correlation coefficient for data which are pairs of ranks. It usually is computed by the formula

$$r_s = 1 - \frac{6\Sigma d^2}{N(N^2 - 1)}$$

where d is the difference between paired ranks and N is the number of pairs.

EXAMPLE: Scores are given for a mid-term and the final exam for five students. These are converted to ranks and the rank correlation coefficient computed:

	Scores	$\longrightarrow$	Ranks			
Student	Mid-term	Final	Mid-term	Final	d	d^2
KC	45	57	2	2	0	0
QH	46	55	1	4	-3	9
TI	34	56	3	3	0	0
SJ	32	50	4	5	-1	1
EK	30	58	5	1	4	16
					0	26

$$r_s = 1 - \frac{6(26)}{5(25 - 1)} = -.30$$

Rank-Difference Correlation *See* Rank-Correlation Coefficient.

Rank Order *See* Ranking.

Rank-Order Correlation Any statistical method for measuring the degree of relationship or agreement between two paired sets of ranked data, such as the rank correlation or Kendall's tau.

Rank-Order Scale *See* Ordinal Scale.

Rank-Sum Test (*syn.* Wilcoxon Rank-Sum Test) A distribution-free nonparametric test for two independent groups. It is equivalent to the U test, except that the test statistic (T') is the sum of the ranks for the smaller sample. (With equal sample sizes, the sum of the ranks for either sample can be used.) The data from the combined samples are arranged in order of magnitude and ranked, with the lowest score given rank 1. The ranks assigned to each sample are then summed separately. (*See also* Kruskall-Wallis H Test)

EXAMPLE: Six rhesus monkeys and five squirrel monkeys are tested on a problem solving task. The subject's error scores are shown in order of magnitude, and ranked and identified by specie, as R or S.

Species:	R	R	R	S	R	R	S	S	R	S	S
Score	38	40	44	45	48	51	57	61	62	64	75
Rank	1	2	3	4	5	6	7	8	9	10	11

Here the smaller of the two samples consists of five squirrel monkeys, and the sum of the ranks for these subjects is:

$$T' = 4 + 7 + 8 + 10 + 11 = 40$$

For small samples, the critical values for T' are obtained from special tables. If both samples are larger than 10, then T' has a sampling distribution which is approximately normal with

$$\mu_{T'} = \frac{n_1(n_1 + n_2 + 1)}{2} \quad \text{and} \quad \sigma_{T'} = \sqrt{\frac{n_1 n_2 (n_1 + n_2 + 1)}{12}}$$

and an obtained value of T' can be evaluated in the normal curve table using the test statistic

$$z = \frac{T' - \mu_{T'}}{\sigma_{T'}}$$

Ranking   The arrangement of objects or persons in order of magnitude of some property yielding values from 1 to N (the number of objects or persons being ranked). Tied ranks yield a value that is the mean of the ranks involved.

EXAMPLE:

Score	Rank	
91	1	
82	2.5 }	$\frac{2+3}{2} = 2.5$
82	2.5 }	
71	4	
53	5	

Rao's *V*-Test   *See* Multivariate Tests of Significance.

Rate of Response   A measure of behavior in which the average number of responses made per unit time is calculated. Examples include the number of eyeblinks per minute, grams of food consumed per hour, or movies attended per month.

Rating   The process of subjectively estimating the values of specified characteristics of objects or behaviors. Estimates may be numerical or verbal. It is distinguished from ranking in that ratings are assigned independently of other objects in the set.

Rating Scale Procedure   *See* Signal Detection Task.

Ratio Data   Data obtained from using a ratio scale of measurement.

Ratio Method   *See* Fractionation Method.

Ratio Scale   A numbering system for properties of objects and events that assumes same-size units throughout, in addition to a nonarbitrary zero point. It allows meaningful statements of proportion such as *A* is one-half the size of *B*. Ratio scales are more likely to involve physical than psychological measurements. For example, height or weight can be measured by a ratio scale, whereas intelligence (IQ) cannot: A person who weighs 140 lb is twice as heavy as one who weighs 70 lb, but a person with an IQ of 140 is not "twice as smart" as a person with an IQ of 70, since there is no meaningful zero point of intelligence.

Ratio Schedule of Reinforcement   Any intermittent reinforcement procedure in which delivery of reinforcement depends solely on the number of responses made. For example, a subject required to make four lever presses to obtain one reinforcement is operating on a *fixed-ratio*-4 (FR-4) schedule of reinforcement. (*See also* Fixed-Ratio Schedule of Reinforcement; Variable-Ratio Schedule of Reinforcement.)

Raw Data   Data as they exist when first recorded during the experiment and prior to performing operations that reduce, consolidate, or transform them.

EXAMPLE: Subjects report whether or not tones of different intensity are audible. The raw data are the "Yes" and "No" reports of the subjects. The researcher first reduces these to the total number of "Yes" responses for each tone intensity, then transforms each total into a percentage measure, or some other dependent measure. (*See also* Dependent Variable; Raw Score.)

Raw Score (*symb. X* or *Y*)   An individual datum used as a dependent measure in a statistical analysis. Raw scores may be the same as the raw data, but more frequently are reduced or transformed data. (*See also* Raw Data.)

Reaction   *See* Response.

Reaction Time   The time between the onset of a stimulus that serves as a signal and the beginning of a response that is made as quickly as possible to the signal. Travel time or movement time is not included in reaction time. Different classes of reaction time are identified depending on the number of stimuli and/or responses involved: "a," "b," and "c" reaction times are historical designations of different classes of reaction time measures. The distinctions are based on the differences in the number of stimuli from which the stimulus to be responded to is selected on each trial, and in the number of different responses from which the correct response must be selected. The **"a" reaction time** is the **simple reaction time,** that is, a single stimulus with a single response. The **"b" reaction time** has two or more stimuli, each having a different response—now referred to as **choice** or **disjunctive reaction time.** The **"c" reaction time** involves several stimuli, only one of which requires a response, and other stimuli are to be ignored—now referred to as **discriminative reaction** time. If stimuli are designated with capital letters, and correct responses are designated with the corresponding small letters, the distinction can be summarized as:

Stimuli	Responses	Historical Designation	Contemporary Designation
A	a	a reaction time	simple reaction time
A	a		
B	b		
C	c	b reaction time	choice (disjunctive) reaction time
.	.		
.	.		
A	a		
B	none		
C	none	c reaction time	discriminative reaction time
.	none		
.	none		

(*See also* Associative Reaction Time; Latency of Response.)

Reactive Measure   *See* Instrumentation Effects; Nonreactive Measure.

Ready Signal   Any signal that serves to warn that a trial is about to begin and that the subject should get ready to respond.

Real Limits   *See* Class Interval.

Recall Method   A procedure for measuring the retention of verbal material such as prose or word lists. The subject is required to reproduce as much as possible of the material learned originally without the aid of external cues. The method usually requires that the subject reproduce the original material in the same order as it was learned. If the subject is permitted to reproduce the items without regard to order, the procedure is referred to as free recall. (*See also* Retention Methods.)

Reciprocal Transformation   *See under* Data Transformation.

Recitation Method   A procedure in verbal learning in which a specified proportion of the learning is time spent actively reciting the material from memory, either aloud or silently, as opposed to studying or reading it.

Recognition Method   A procedure for measuring retention that requires a subject to identify previously learned items from a mixture that contains the old items mixed in with a number of new items. The method is applicable to the use of both verbal and nonverbal (e.g., pictorial) stimulus materials. A multiple-choice test where each question has two or more alternatives, one of which is the correct answer, is a common recognition measure. (*See also* Retention Methods.)

Recognition Threshold   The minimum time that a stimulus must be exposed in order for it to be correctly identified by an observer. For example, a word may first be exposed at a duration that is too short to permit any detection at all. As the duration of exposure is gradually increased, the observer will typically first detect a smudge, then some of the letters, and finally the word. (*See also* Absolute Threshold.)

Reconstruction Method   A procedure for testing memory for the order or arrangement of stimuli. The subject is given all the stimulus materials that had been presented originally, but now in random or haphazard arrangement, and is asked to put them back in their original arrangement. The method can be used with verbal stimuli (e.g., presenting the subject with cards, each bearing a word, then shuffling the cards and requiring the subject to put them back in their original order). The method is used also with stimuli such as colors and shapes that may be arranged in two-dimensional patterns or with pieces of wire that can be assembled into three-dimensional figures.

Recovery Rate   A behavioral or physiological measure of response strength. It is the proportion of return to a basal or other criterion level of activity during a time period following a treatment. For example, basal skin resistance may be obtained before exposure to a startling stimulus. The proportion of return to basal level after 10 and 60 sec would index the recovery rate. (*See also* Recovery Time.)

Recovery Time A behavioral or physiological measure of response strength. It is the time needed to return to a basal or other criterion level of activity following some treatment. For example, basal skin resistance values may be obtained before exposure to a startling stimulus. Recovery time would be how long it takes the subject to return to the pretreatment resistance value. (*See also* Recovery Rate.)

Recruitment Time A measure of response strength. It is the time needed for a response to reach its maximum intensity or amplitude. For example, the electrodermal response (EDR) consists of a rapid drop in skin resistance followed by a slower return to a basal level. The interval from onset of the response to its maximum resistance drop is the recruitment time.

Rectangular Distribution (*syn.* Uniform Distribution) Any distribution in which all values have equal or nearly equal frequencies of occurrence.

Redundancy The degree to which prediction of one characteristic or component of the stimulus is improved by knowledge of one or more of its other characteristics. The predicted characteristic is called redundant. In information theory, redundancy is measured by the reduction in uncertainty about the characteristic, expressed as a percentage of the maximum possible uncertainty.

EXAMPLE 1: In the pair of letters $q\_\_$, the maximum possible uncertainty in bits of the second letter is $\log_2 26$, or 4.70, if each letter had an equal chance of occurring. In the English language the actual uncertainty is zero, since q is always followed by u, so the u is 100% redundant.

EXAMPLE 2: In a word that starts expe____, the maximum possible uncertainty for the next letter again is $\log_2 26$, or 4.70 bits. According to *Webster's Third New International Dictionary of the English Language* (1966), however, there are only five letters that could follow these four in a word in the English language. The actual uncertainty of the letter would depend on the probabilities of the five possibilities—if they were equally likely, the uncertainty would be $\log_2 5$, or 2.32 bits. This would be a reduction in uncertainty of 2.38 bits (4.70 − 2.32). Since 2.38 is 50.6% of 4.70, this would represent 50.6% redundancy in the fifth letter.

Reflexivity A property of a relation between two objects or variables for which any object bears that relation to itself. For example, the relation "is the same brightness as" is reflexive, since any object, organism, or person is the same brightness as itself; the relation "is brighter than" is not reflexive, since an object is not brighter than itself. The relation of equality is reflexive, but human judgments frequently fail to meet this criterion, since two presentations of the same stimulus may not be judged as equal.

Regression Analysis   A general term for the statistical procedures concerned with fitting a regression or prediction equation to data, estimating parameters, and testing hypotheses about the true relationship between the dependent or criterion variable and the independent or predictor variable(s). (*See also* Discriminant Analysis; Linear Regression; Multiple Regression; Nonlinear Regression; Trend Analysis.)

Regression Coefficient   In linear regression with one predictor variable, the weight for, or multiplier of, a predictor variable. (*See also b* Coefficient; Beta Coefficient.)

Regression Equation   The equation that expresses the functional relationship between the means of a dependent or criterion variable and one or more independent or predictor variables. (*See also* Linear Regression; Prediction Equation.)

Regression Line   *See* Linear Regression.

Rehearsal   Practice, usually covert, on learned material between the time of learning and the time of testing.

Reinforcement (*contr.* Punishment)   A set of operations designed to increase the measured strength of a behavior. In classical conditioning, it is the presentation of the unconditioned stimulus following the conditioned stimulus. In instrumental conditioning, it is the presentation of a positive stimulus, or the reduction or removal of a negative stimulus, after a response of interest has occurred. Removal of a negative stimulus (e.g., electric shock, heat, or cold) constitutes **negative reinforcement.** Delivery of a positive stimulus (e.g., sweet liquid, pleasurable brain stimulation) constitutes **positive reinforcement (reward).** (*See also* Conditioned Reinforcement.)

Reinforcement Schedule   An arrangement of intermittent reinforcements based on the quantitative or temporal characteristics of the response output, or some combination of these variables. (*See the following individual listings:* Adjusting, Alternative, Chained, Concurrent, Conjoined, Conjunctive, Fixed Interval, Fixed Ratio, Higher Order, Interlocking, Interpolated, Mixed, Multiple, Tandem, Variable Interval, Variable Ratio.)

Reinforcer   (1) In instrumental conditioning, any event that strengthens the behavior(s) that precede it. The event is either positive to the organism or consists of the reduction or termination of stimulus that is aversive to the organism. (2) In classical conditioning, the unconditioned stimulus (US). (*See also* Reinforcement.)

Reitz Limen (*abbr.* RL)   A former designation for **absolute threshold**.

Rejection/Nonrejection Region (*syn.* Critical Region/Acceptance Region)   In hypothesis testing, the intervals for a statistic that determine whether or not the null hypothesis can be rejected. If the obtained value of the statistic lies in the rejection region, the null hypothesis can be rejected; if the obtained value lies in the nonrejection region, the null hypothesis cannot be rejected. The points that divide the rejection region from the nonrejection region are called the **critical values** of the statistic.

EXAMPLE: To test the null hypothesis H_o: $\mu = 50$ against the alternative H_a: $\mu \neq 50$ when the population standard deviation σ is known, a nondirectional (two-tail) z test would be used. For the .05 level of significance, the critical zs are -1.96 and $+1.96$; the rejection regions are $-\infty \leq z \leq -1.96$ and $+1.96 \leq z \leq \infty$, and the nonrejection region is $-1.96 < z < +1.96$. The critical means are 1.96 standard errors above and below the hypothesized value of μ ($\mu_0 \pm 1.96\ \sigma_{\bar{x}}$). If the standard error is 2.4, the critical means (critical values of $\bar{X}$) would be $50 \pm 1.96(2.4)$ or 45.3 and 54.7. Thus, for this test, if the absolute value of z is greater than 1.96, or if $\bar{X}$ is less than 45.3 or greater than 54.7, the null hypothesis, that $\mu = 50$, can be rejected; otherwise, it cannot. This is illustrated in Fig. R-1.

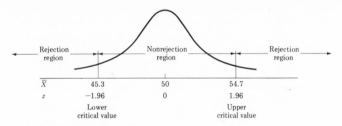

Figure R–1   Sampling Distribution if H_o is True.

Related-Samples Design   *See* Randomized-Blocks Design.

Relation   A property that may be said to hold, or not hold, for a pair of objects in a specified order (an ordered pair), or the ordered pairs for which the property holds. For example, the relation "less than" holds for the pair (1, 3), since 1 is less than 3, but it does not hold for the pairs (3, 3) or (5, 3), since neither 3 nor 5 is less than 3. This relation consists of all ordered pairs (x, y) for which it is true that x is less than y.

Relative Probability   In a free responding situation, the likelihood of occurrence of one behavior from a group of two or more behaviors of interest. It is calculated as the ratio of that behavior's rate of occurrence to the combined rates of occurrence of all behaviors in the group.

EXAMPLE: Given the following rates of occurrence for three mutually exclusive behaviors during sleep: snoring, 10 per hr; changing position, 7 per hr; talking, 10 words per hr. The relative probability of uttering a word is

$$\frac{10}{10 + 10 + 7} = .37$$

Relearning Method A procedure for measuring retention that compares the learning of some material or task at one time with the learning of the same material or task again at a later time. If there is any retention of the original learning, there will be some savings of time and/or trials during relearning. (*See also* Retention Methods; Savings Score.)

Releaser A stimulus used to elicit a species-specific reaction. For example, a model of a female fish displayed in a particular posture, with a particular gill configuration, given the appropriate conditions, will evoke a mating dance in the male of that species.

Relevant Dimension In concept identification, discrimination tasks, etc., the stimulus dimension or attribute the subject must attend to in order to make a correct response. For example, a monkey may be shown, on different trials, either a red circle and a green triangle or a green circle and a red triangle, with the red stimulus on either the left or right side. If shape is the relevant dimension and color and position are irrelevant, then in order to get a reward the monkey must attend to the shape of the stimulus and choose the shape the experimenter has designated as correct.

Reliability A general term denoting consistency of measurements derived from repeated observations on the same subject under the same circumstances. High reliability increases the dependability of a test, since the scores are less subject to chance variability. The degree of reliability of a measurement or test is expressed by a reliability coefficient. (*Procedures for measuring reliability are described under* Alternate-Form Method; Split-Half Procedure; Test–Retest Procedure; *see also* Interreliability; Kuder–Richardson Formula; Spearman–Brown Formula)

Reliability Coefficient A general term for any reliability measure expressed as a correlation coefficient or other measure of association.

Reliability, Index of The correlation between the obtained scores on a given test and the theoretical true scores. It is estimated by the square root of the reliability coefficient. (*See also* Reliability; Reliability Coefficient.)

Repeated-Measures Design (*syn.* Treatment-by-Subjects (T × S) Design; Within-Subjects Design; *contr.* Randomized-Groups Design) Any experimental design in which each subject serves in every treatment condition, so that all subjects receive all levels of the independent variable(s). The design essentially is a randomized-blocks design, with each block consisting of a single subject instead of a group of matched subjects. (*See also* Mixed Design.)

EXAMPLE: In an experiment on the effect of color on rated sweetness of a sugar solution, each subject tasted and rated brown, red, green, and blue solutions presented in different random orders. Thus, every subject provided a score for each of the four colors.

Repeated-Measures Variable *See* Within-Subjects Variable.

Replication (1) Repetition of an experiment with different subjects, and frequently with a different experimenter and different location. If any other aspect of the experiment is changed, or if anything is added or omitted, the new experiment is called a partial replication. (2) In experimental design, obtaining one observation in every cell of the design, so if an independent-groups design has five subjects in each condition there are five replications of the experiment. Similarly, in a within-subjects design, when five subjects are tested under all conditions there are five replications.

Representative Design A research strategy in which the experimenter attempts to ensure that the conditions of the experiment, and the range of variables investigated, are representative of the conditions under which the behavior occurs naturally. For example, since people make distance judgments of objects varying from a few meters to several kilometers away, a representative design for an experiment in judged distance would require judgments to be made over a wide range of distances. An experiment in which the maximum distance was five meters would be generalizable to only a small portion of the judgments people actually make. (*See also* External Validity.)

Representative Sample A nontechnical term connoting a sample that in some respect is similar to the population from which it was drawn. Statistically, any random sample is representative of the population from which it was drawn, even if it appears to be unrepresentative with respect to some particular characteristic, such as containing a disproportionate number of males or females, fast or slow learners, etc. (*See also* Stratified Random Sampling.)

Reproducibility Coefficient A measure of internal consistency for any test constructed by the method of cumulative ratings. The formula for the reproducibility coefficient is

$$1 - \frac{\text{Number of inconsistent responses}}{\text{Total number of responses}}$$

(*See also* Cumulative Ratings, Method of.)

Reproduction Methods A variety of procedures that share in common the requirement that a subject reproduce a stimulus. In some cases, the reproduction is made with the original stimulus still present, and in some cases the reproduction must be made from memory. As a test for visual memory, for example, a subject may be shown a figure or design and later be asked to draw the stimulus from memory following a retention interval that may range from a few minutes to several months. (*See also* Adjustment, Method of; Retention Methods.)

Research Hypothesis (*syn.* Working Hypothesis) A statement that describes a predicted relationship between various levels of an independent variable and a dependent variable. The statement is often directional (e.g., "A will increase the amount of B," rather than "A will have an effect on B"). The research hypothesis corresponds to the statistical alternate hypothesis (H_a or H_1). [*See also* Null/Alternate (Alternative) Hypothesis.]

Residual Effect *See* Carryover Effect.

Residual Variance (1) (*symb.* $s^2_{y|x}$ or $s^2_{y \cdot x}$; *syn.* Variance of Estimate) In correlation and regression analysis, the variance of one variable *(Y)* that is not explained or accounted for by the variability of a correlated variable *(X)*; the variance of the scores around the regression line, as opposed to the original variance of the scores around their mean. The square root of the residual variance is called the standard error of estimate, or standard error of prediction. (*For an example see* Linear Regression.) (2) The error term(s) in certain analyses of variance.

Resistance to Extinction A measure of response persistence after the reinforcing events have been removed. For example, in classical conditioning, resistance to extinction might be measured by the number of trials needed to reach a criterion of five consecutive trials without a measurable conditioned response when the CS no longer is followed by the US. In instrumental conditioning, resistance to extinction might be measured by the amount of time needed for the subject to drop below five responses per minute. (*See also* Response Strength, Measures of.)

Respondent Behavior In the most general meaning, any behavior that is elicited by a specifically identifiable stimulus, as opposed to an emitted response. The term also may refer exclusively to involuntary or reflexive responses such as flexion of a limb to a pain stimulus, pupil constriction to a bright light, adrenalin secretion to a fear stimulus, etc. (*See also* Elicited/Emitted Response; Instrumental/Operant Response.)

Respondent Conditioning   *See* Classical Conditioning.

Response   Any activity or process of an organism that is directly or indirectly observable.

Response Bias   Any tendency of an organism to make one response from a set of possible responses more often than would be expected. Common response biases include position preference, a tendency to respond to either the left or the right one of two stimuli presented side by side; time error, the tendency to overestimate or underestimate the second of two stimuli presented successively; a tendency to make mostly favorable or mostly unfavorable responses to a series of test items; and a tendency to make groups of equal size in a sorting task. Controls for possible response bias must be considered in nearly every experiment. (*See also* ROC Curve; Social Desirability.)

Response Differentiation (*contr.* Response Generalization)   A conditioning procedure in which somewhat similar responses receive differential reinforcement. For example, a dog is trained to raise its left foreleg to a signal. When the left leg is raised, a reward is given. Right-leg- or hind-leg-lifting responses are not rewarded and may incur punishment. (*See also* Stimulus Generalization.)

Response Generalization (*syn.* Response Induction; *contr.* Response Differentiation)   The procedure by which the original response to a stimulus is prevented and a different but similar response is allowed to occur, or allowed to occur and then reinforced. For example, a dog is trained to lift its left foreleg to a signal. The left leg is then secured and the right leg is left free to respond to the command. If this occurs, it is labeled a generalized response. (*See also* Stimulus Generalization.)

Response Induction   *See* Response Generalization.

Response–Reinforcement Interval   *See* Delay of Reinforcement Interval.

Response–Response Interval (*abbr.* R-R)   The time interval occurring between any two consecutive responses of interest, in a free responding situation.

Response–Stimulus Interval (*abbr.* R-S)   In operant conditioning, the time between a response and the next scheduled occurrence of a stimulus.

Response Strength, Measures of   Any feature of a response that, when quantified, may serve as an index of the intensity or vigor of a response. (*See the following individual listings:* Amplitude, Frequency, Intensity, Latency, Magnitude, Probability, Rate, Recovery Time, Recruitment Time; *see also* Dependent Variable.)

Response Time   In research on simple psychomotor responses, the time between onset of a stimulus that serves as a signal and the completion of a response that is made as quickly as possible to the signal, consisting of reaction time plus **movement time (travel time)**. For example, a subject is to press the middle button on a panel as quickly as possible when a red light is turned on. Reaction time is the time from light onset to starting to move the hand from its resting position in front of the panel; movement time is the time required for moving the hand and pressing the button; response time is the time from light onset to pressing the button.

Response Topography   The pattern or form of a response. For example, a rat may learn to depress a lever in a number of ways, which may include slapping, shaking, or biting it.

Response Variable   The particular measure of behavior selected in any investigation of the relationship between events in the subject's environment and responses by the subject that may be correlated with those events. For example, in a study of the relationship between time of day and water consumption by gorillas, the response variable might be the number of gorillas gathered at a water hole at a given time of day.

Restricted Randomization   A technique for eliminating certain systematic sequences that may occur by chance. The desired restrictions are determined by the experimenter, and then the random sequence is formed subject to these restrictions. Restrictions are commonly placed on the number of repetitions of the same condition (e.g., no more than three in a row), the number of successive alternations of two conditions, the number of times the same vowel can occur in a list of CVCs, natural sequences of digits in number stimuli, etc. (*See also* Block Randomization, Gellerman Series.)

Results   A verbal, numerical, and/or graphic summary of the descriptive statistics obtained from research.

Retention Methods   Procedures used to measure memory for previously learned responses. (*See the following individual listings:* Recall, Recognition, Reconstruction, Relearning, Reproduction, Savings.)

Retroactive Paradigm   A type of ABA design used to assess the effect on task performance of being exposed to a set of stimulus conditions. Subjects in one condition receive Task A followed by Task B. They are then retested on Task A. Subjects in a control condition receive Task A followed by an interval that may be unfilled or filled with a control task. They are also retested on Task A. Differences between the two groups during retesting reflect the facilitory or inhibitory effects of Task B.

EXAMPLE: The possible interfering effects of item similarity in information processing are studied. Two groups of subjects are given a list of 20 vegetable names to memorize (e.g., endive, chard, leek). The number of items recalled after a brief study period is recorded. The experimental group then is given a list of 20 different vegetables to learn while the control group is given names of 20 American cities to learn. Both groups are finally retested on the 20 original vegetable names, and their performance is compared.

Reversal Design (*syn.* Steady-State Design)   A single-subject design in which a behavior is first sampled over a number of consecutive sessions (baseline series) to collect baseline performance data. This is followed by introduction of a treatment series for some number of sessions. Often the baseline series is resumed after the treatment series. Sometimes, however, the treatment series is followed by another treatment series with a different value of the independent variable and then a return to baseline. (*See also* Multielement Baseline Design; Multiple-Baseline Design.)

EXAMPLE: A researcher wishes to determine the extent to which two different concentrations of sucrose solution will enhance a rat's bar pressing relative to dry food pellets. Since the subject currently is being reinforced with pellets, this condition is designated as the baseline condition (A), and the two sucrose concentrations as B_1 and B_2. A sequence of baseline sessions and treatment sessions extending over many days might then be arranged as follows:

$$AAAAA / B_1B_1B_1B_1B_1 / AAAAAA / B_2B_2B_2B_2B_2 / AAAAA / B_1B_1B_1. \quad . \quad . \quad \text{etc.}$$

Reversal/Nonreversal Shift (*syn.* Intradimensional/Extradimensional Shift)   Discrimination learning procedures that use visual stimuli that differ on two dimensions, each dimension having two levels. After training a discrimination on one dimension, a reversal shift may be introduced by exchanging the positive and negative stimulus values on the same relevant dimension. A nonreversal shift may be introduced by making the other stimulus dimension relevant.

EXAMPLE: Figure R-2 shows a set of black and white squares and circles. In the original discrimination (left plate), shape is the relevant dimension, and circles are the positive stimuli (i.e., reinforcement is given for a response to either the black or white circle). Following training to some criterion, a reversal shift may be introduced (upper right plate) in which the squares, regardless of color, become the posi-

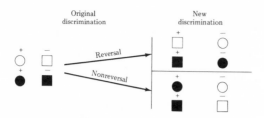

Figure R-2

tive stimuli. If a nonreversal shift is introduced (lower right plate), shape is no longer a relevant dimension, and the subject must respond on the basis of color, in this case to either the black square or circle.

Reversal Training In discrimination learning, a procedure in which the positive and negative stimuli are reversed without signal when some performance criterion is reached. Several reversals may occur within a single test session.

EXAMPLE: A child is given a marble reward for pulling the lever under a red square (positive stimulus) but receives nothing for pulling the lever under a green square (negative stimulus). After the child makes the correct response 10 consecutive times (criterion), the red square becomes the negative stimulus (no reward), and the green square becomes the positive stimulus (reward is given). When the same criterion has been reached, the red square again becomes positive.

Reversible Figures *See under* Illusions.

Reward *See* Reinforcement.

Reward Training (*contr.* Punishment Training) An instrumental/operant conditioning procedure for establishing or increasing the occurrence of some response through the use of contingent positive reinforcement.

EXAMPLE: In order to train a rat to run down the stem of a T-maze and turn into the left arm, the animal is first placed in a mild or moderate deprivation state by restricting its daily water intake. Water placed in the left arm then will serve as a positive reinforcer. The animal is placed in the stem and allowed to explore the maze. If it arrives in the left arm, it is given some time to consume the water, then is removed and rested or restarted. Arrivals in the right arm are not rewarded, and the animal is removed. Effectiveness of the reward may be measured by the proportion of left turns for consecutive series trials, or the time taken to arrive at the rewarded location for each trial.

Rho   *See* Rank-Correlation Coefficient; also see Appendix B, Greek Alphabet.

RL   *See* Reitz Limen.

ROC Curve (*syn.* Isosensitivity Curve)   The receiver-operating-characteristic curve that describes performance in a signal detection task as a function of changes in the observer's criterion for indicating the presence of a weak signal. The graph of an ROC curve shows the proportion or probability of a **hit** (the subject correctly reports the presence of the signal) on the y-axis against the proportion or probability of a **false alarm** (the subject incorrectly reports the presence of the signal when it did not occur) on the x-axis. Changes in the subject's criterion for indicating that a signal was presented can be induced by varying the probability of occurrence of the signal, or the rewards and penalties associated with correct and incorrect decisions. For example, on trials where the subject experiences considerable uncertainty as to whether or not the signal was presented, a liberal response bias to say "Yes it was" will be induced if the reward for a hit is great and the penalty for a false alarm is small. A liberal response bias will be induced also if the proportion of trials on which the signal is presented is greater than the proportion of trials on which it is not presented. A strict response bias to avoid saying "Yes" under conditions of uncertainty will be induced by making the penalty for a false alarm great and the reward for a hit small, or by having the signal present only a small proportion of the trials. (*See also* Signal Detection Task.)

EXAMPLE: A subject serves in five sessions performing an auditory signal detection task using the Yes–No procedure. In each session the subject is given a combined total of 600 signal and noise trials, but the probability that the signal will be presented on any given trial (i.e., the proportion of signal trials) varies in the different sessions as .10, .30, .50, .70, or .90. The subject's hit rates and false alarm rates for the five sessions are

Signal Probability	Proportion of Hits	Proportion of False Alarms
.10	$20/60 = .333$	$49/540 = .091$
.30	$92/180 = .511$	$86/420 = .205$
.50	$214/300 = .713$	$120/300 = .400$
.70	$330/420 = .786$	$91/180 = .506$
.90	$500/540 = .926$	$47/60 = .783$

The graph of the subject's ROC curve is shown in Fig. R–3. The plotted data points are the paired values of the proportion of false alarms

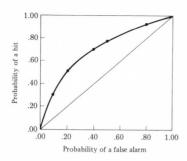

Figure R-3

and the proportion of hits for each value of signal probability: (.091, .333), (.205, .511), etc. The smooth curve fitted through these five points is the ROC curve. Points on this line are interpreted as probabilities.

Root Mean Square Deviation   *See* Standard Deviation.

Rotary Pursuit Task   A perceptual-motor task in which the subject is to keep a stylus in contact with a target that is rotating in a circular path. The standard apparatus, called a pursuit rotor, resembles a phonograph turntable, permitting varying speeds of rotation. Contact with the target establishes an electrical circuit that permits recording the number of seconds of contact during a trial.

Roy's GCR Test   *See* Multivariate Tests of Significance.

Running Average   A procedure for obtaining a smoothed curve of sequential data, such as performance over trials, by computing means for overlapping blocks of observations. (*See also* Learning Curve.)

EXAMPLE: Subjects are tested on a serial verbal learning task. The mean number of correct words for 10 subjects is shown for each of eight trials, and the running average for blocks of four trials is shown:

Trial	Mean No. Correct	Block	Trials	Mean
1	3.2	1	1–4	6.2
2	4.3	2	2–5	7.9
3	7.4	3	3–6	9.6
4	9.9	4	4–7	10.7
5	9.9	5	5–8	11.1
6	11.1			
7	11.8			
8	11.7			

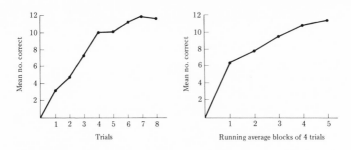

Figure R–4

Runs Test (*syn.* Wald–Wolfowitz Runs Test)   A distribution-free nonparametric test, usually used with independent samples to test for differences in central tendency. The data from the combined samples are arranged in order of magnitude, and the number of runs (clusters of scores from the same sample) is counted. For small samples the critical value for this statistic is obtained from a special table; for large samples there is an approximate z test.

EXAMPLE: Two groups of subjects were tested. For the control group (C), the scores were 19, 39, 35, 27, 24, and 35. For the experimental group (E), the scores were 14, 21, 13, 23, 38, 15, and 11. The data are shown arranged in order of magnitude and identified by which group each came from. There are six runs, which are underlined:

11	13	14	15	19	21	23	24	27	35	35	38	39
E	E	E	E	C	E	E	C	C	C	C	E	C

Since this is a small sample, the value 6 would be compared to the tabled value to test for significance.

207

Sample   A subset of objects, people, observations, etc., selected from a population. (*For procedures used in selecting samples from populations see* Accidental Sampling; Area Sampling; Incidental Sampling; Random Sampling; Stratified Sampling.)

Sampling Bias   Nonrepresentativeness of data that results when the data are based on a nonrandom sample from the target population. For example, selecting subjects from students entering the library or from students in the lounge at the student union both might introduce sampling bias if the intent were to study college students in general. (*See also* Sampling Error.)

Sampling Distribution   The theoretical probability distribution of values that could be obtained for some statistic in random samples of a particular size taken from a particular population. For example, for samples of 25 observations from a population, the sampling distribution of the mean is the theoretical distribution of all the possible sample means that could occur in such samples.

Sampling Error   The discrepancy, due to random sampling, between the true value of a parameter and the sample estimate of that parameter. The expected magnitude of the sampling error is shown by the standard error of the sampling distribution of the statistic used to estimate the parameter value. For example, the mean of a sample is commonly used to estimate the population mean. The larger the sample, the smaller the standard error of the mean, so the larger the sample, the smaller the expected sampling error involved in estimating the population mean. (*See also* Sampling Bias.)

Sander's Illusion   *See under* Illusions.

Sandler's A Test   *See* A Test.

Savings Method   *See* Savings Score.

Savings Score (*syn.* Savings Method) A measure of retention that is the difference between the scores for original learning and relearning, expressed as a proportion or percentage of the original score. For example, if a person took 25 trials to learn a list of nonsense syllables, and six months later took only 15, this would reflect a savings equal to 10 trials, which is 40% of the original number required.

Scaled Test A test in which items are arranged in increased order of difficulty.

Scaled Vector *See* Normalized Vector.

Scaling Methods Techniques for the measurement of subjective attributes such as the perceived loudness or pitch of a tone, the judged brightness of a light, attitudes toward the church, or preference for various paintings or works of music. (*For descriptions of specific methods of psychological scaling, see* Equisection; Magnitude Estimation; Magnitude Production; Paired Comparisons.) (*See also* Psychophysical Methods.)

Scalogram Analysis *See* Cumulative Scaling, Method of.

Scattergram (*syn.* Scatter Diagram; Scatterplot) In correlational research, a graph in which paired values of X and Y are plotted. If the relationship between X and Y is linear, the pattern of the points will tend to be elliptical; the ellipse will be nearly circular if the degree of correlation between X and Y is near zero and will be relatively thin if the correlation is high; in the limiting case, the points will all lie on a straight line if X and Y are perfectly correlated. If X and Y are positively correlated, the pattern of points will show an upward slope from lower left to upper right, and the pattern will slope downward from upper left to lower right if the correlation is negative. If X and Y are nonlinearly related, the pattern formed by the plotted points may reveal a departure from linearity.

EXAMPLE: Figure S–1 shows three scattergrams for linearly related variables. To the left of each scattergram is shown the values of X and Y that are plotted. Scattergrams a, b, and c illustrate positive, near zero, and negative correlations, respectively, with the numerical value of the correlation coefficient, r, being shown for each case.

Scedasticity *See* Homoscedasticity/Heteroscedasticity.

Schedule of Reinforcement *See* Reinforcement Schedule.

Scheffé Test A multiple comparison procedure based on the F distribution, which permits the testing of all possible contrasts among treatment means while holding the probability of one or more Type I errors at α, the level of significance. If there are k treat-

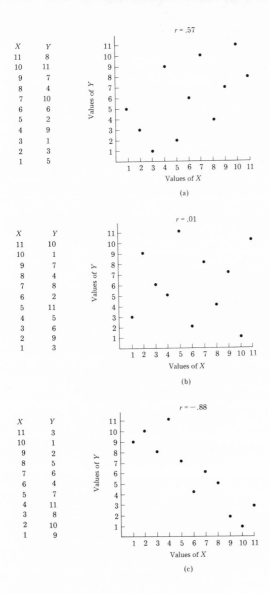

(a)

(b)

(c)

Figure S–1

ment means, the F ratio for each contrast is tested against a critical value that is $(k - 1)$ times the critical F for the main effect of the treatment.

Schröder's Staircase   *See under* Illusions.

Scientific Method   A means of obtaining knowledge that is characterized by (1) observation of a phenomenon, (2) formation of tentative explanations, or statements of cause and effect, (3) further observation and/or experimentation to rule out alternative explanations, (4) revision and refinement of the explanations.

Score Limit   *See* Class Interval.

S^D/S$^\Delta$ *See* Discriminative Stimulus.

SD   *See* Standard Deviation.

SE   *See* Standard Error.

Search Task   Any task in which the subject is required to scan or otherwise examine a stimulus display to detect the presence of particular items. (*For an example see* Embedded-Figures Test.) (*See also* Discrete Search Task; Serial Search Task.)

Second-Order Conditioning   *See* Higher Order Conditioning.

Second-Order Interaction   *See* Higher Order Interaction.

Secondary Correlation   A correlation between two variables that is due primarily to the contribution of a third variable. For example, personal wealth and level of education may be correlated mainly because of a third variable, parental wealth.

Secondary Reinforcement   *See* Conditioned Reinforcement.

Self-Selection   An error in recruitment, selection, and/or assignment of subjects such that the subjects are allowed to assign themselves to the experiment or treatment conditions. This may result in (1) a nonrepresentative sample, which will restrict the generalizability (external validity) of the results, and/or (2) biased treatment groups, which will confound the results, that is, destroy the internal validity of the study.

EXAMPLE: A request for subject volunteers is placed on a central recruiting board that contains a number of other requests for subjects. The experiment is entitled "Study of math computational skills," and it solicits subjects for 9 A.M. and 9 P.M. on a given day. The unannounced purpose of the research is to study time of day as a variable influencing computational performance. This arrangement allows for self-selection in two ways: (1) If subjects have the opportunity to select from among the posted studies, one would expect very few or no "math-shy" volunteers to sign up. Thus, the experiment is sampling from the population of "math competent," or at least "math fearless" students, and the results may not generalize beyond this group. (2) If the subjects are allowed to select their own times, they may select on the basis of work–study–sleep patterns, personality characteristics, or other subject variables, such that one group may differ in many ways from the other. Thus, the experiment also may confound type of subject with type of treatment.

Semantic Conditioning A classical conditioning procedure in which verbal stimuli, such as words, phrases, etc., serve as the conditioned stimuli (CSs). Typically, the verbal CS is presented to the subject and followed quickly by a conventional unconditioned stimulus, such as an electric shock or loud noise, and these trials are continued to some criterion. Normally, a generalization test phase then is begun, in which at least some subjects are given test stimuli that differ semantically from the original CS (e.g., antonyms, synonyms, homonyms, etc.). Infrequently, pictorial representations of objects may be used in the first or second phase, with verbal stimuli related to them used in the other phase. (*For an example see* Semantic Generalization Test.)

Semantic Differential A technique for measuring the connotative meanings of words and objects on a series of seven-point scales. The items sometimes are grouped into factors known as evaluative (e.g., good–bad), potency (e.g., strong–weak), and activity (e.g., active–passive).

EXAMPLE: Figure S–2 shows ratings by two individuals on the stimulus word *abortion*, with the greatest differentiations occurring between the kind–cruel and the fair–unfair meanings.

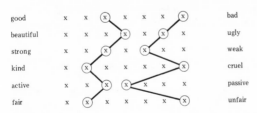

Figure S–2

Semantic Generalization Test In learning research, a procedure for assessing a subject's tendency to make generalized responses to objects, words, or other verbal stimuli, which are semantically related (e.g., antonyms, homonyms, synonyms, etc.) to another object or word that has served as a conditioned stimulus (CS) in a semantic conditioning experiment.

EXAMPLE: A subject receives a series of classical conditioning trials in each of which the word *auto* (the CS) is presented visually and followed immediately by a burst of very loud noise. Growth of the conditioned electrodermal response to *auto* on successive trials is measured. In the generalization test phase, the subject is given one or more test words of varying similarity to *auto,* such as *car, bus, train, boat,* etc. Comparisons of response strength to the original training word and the test words are an index of degree of generalization.

Semi-Interquartile Range (*symb. Q; abbr.* SIQR; *syn.* Quartile Deviation) A measure of variability, defined as one-half the **quartile (interquartile) range,** that is, the distance between the first and third quartiles:

$$Q = \frac{Q_3 - Q_1}{2}$$

Semipartial Correlation *See* Part Correlation.

Sensation Unit The just-noticeable difference (jnd) as a unit for measuring the magnitude of a sensation above the absolute threshold as a point of origin. For example, a 500-Hz tone of a loudness that is just at the absolute threshold produces a sensation that has magnitude zero. If the physical intensity of the tone is increased until the subject is just able to detect the increase in loudness, the resultant sensation is one jnd (sensation unit) above threshold. A further increase in physical intensity until the subject again can detect an increase in loudness yields a sensation that is two jnd above threshold, etc.

Sense Ratio Method *See* Fractionation Method.

Sensitivity The capacity of an experimental apparatus, design, procedure, or subject, to detect differences produced by different levels of an independent variable. (*See also* Power; Signal Detection Task)

Sensory Preconditioning A variation of classical conditioning in which two stimuli to be used as conditioned stimuli (CSs) are first presented to the subject in close temporal order. This is repeated a number of times. One of the CSs is then paired with an unconditioned stimulus (US) for a number of acquisition trials as in the basic classical conditioning procedure. Then the other CS is presented, usually alone, to examine its ability to evoke a conditioned response without having been associated directly with the US.

Sequence Effect *See* Carryover Effect.

Sequential Sampling A research method, and inference procedure, that can be used for some types of research in place of using a fixed sample size. Observations are taken one at a time, either on different subjects or on the same subject. A statistical test is carried out after each observation, which results in one of three decisions. For example, the alternative decisions might be to retain the null hypothesis, reject the null hypothesis, or make an additional observation; or they might be of the following form: μ is less than a specified value, μ is greater than this specified value, or an additional observation, should be made.

EXAMPLE: A researcher is interested in the effect on eating behavior of stimulating a certain part of the brain. Because the technique is difficult and expensive, it is desirable to test no more animals than necessary. Monkeys are treated sequentially: an inplant is made, mild electrical stimulation is applied periodically, and changes in eating behavior are noted. After each monkey is tested, special tables are consulted or the appropriate probability computations are made, and the researcher makes one of the three decisions: the accumulated data are sufficient to show a significant increase in eating, the accumulated data are sufficient to show a significant decrease in eating, or the data are insufficient for making a decision about the effect of brain stimulation, and another observation is necessary.

Serial Anticipation   *See* Anticipation Method.

Serial Learning   A task in which the subject must reproduce a series of stimuli in the same order in which they were presented. Typically, the stimuli are verbal units—words, nonsense syllables, numbers, etc.—and either the anticipation or recall method is used to measure learning. (*See also* Paired-Associate Learning; Verbal Learning.)

EXAMPLE: Subjects are given a 12-item list of nonsense syllables that they are to learn in serial order. On each trial the stimuli are presented in the same sequence on a memory drum, one item at a time, with a star (*) indicating the beginning of the list. After the first trial (i.e., presentation of the entire set of 12 syllables), the subject attempts to anticipate the successive items. Thus, on the second trial when the star appears, the subject attempts to produce the first nonsense syllable; when the first syllable appears, it serves as a cue for the second syllable; etc. The entire sequence of nonsense syllables is presented in this fashion a sufficient number of times for the subject to reach a specified criterion of learning.

Serial Search Task (*contr.* Discrete Search Task)   Tasks in which the subject must attempt to locate each of a set of stimuli, where the stimulus being searched for at a given time is determined by the previously located stimulus. Examples include searching for the successive letters of the alphabet in a random array of letters or for successive numerical values in a random array.

Shadowing   A procedure used in dichotic listening tasks whereby a subject must report, by writing or saying, the messages being delivered to one ear while other messages are being simultaneously presented to the other ear.

Shaping (*syn.* Successive Approximations Method)   An instrumental conditioning technique for training an organism to perform an act that was not originally a part of the organism's behavioral repertoire. Simple components of the behavior and/or crude approximations to it initially are reinforced. As the behavior more closely resembles the desired product, earlier approximations no longer are reinforced, that is, the behavioral requirements for earning reinforcement gradually become more stringent. (*See also* Differential Reinforcement.)

EXAMPLE: A chicken may be taught to play a simple tune ("My Dog Has Fleas") on an avian "piano" consisting of an array of differently colored buttons that when pecked, sound different musical notes. The initial step in training is for the chicken to learn that a reward (a few bits of grain) has just been delivered to a particular location (a bin near the array of buttons). This would be done by sounding a note and delivering grain to the bin whenever the chicken moved toward it. Next, the trainer would either entice the animal to approach the buttons (perhaps by illuminating them) or simply wait until it approached the buttons and would follow this response with a reward. When exploratory pecking of the button array finally occurs, reinforcement of any of the earlier behaviors is discontinued. The chicken must peck at or near the buttons to receive grain. Next, the requirements for reinforcement are altered so that the animal must peck at two particular keys in sequence—say blue, then yellow. The sequence then is lengthened by the addition of keys corresponding to the remaining notes of the tune.

Shared Variance   *See* Communality; Predicted Variance.

Sheppard's Correction   A procedure formerly used to compensate for grouping error when computing a standard deviation from grouped data.

SI   *See* International System of Units.

Sidman Avoidance Conditioning   *See* Nondiscriminated Avoidance Conditioning.

Sigma (*symb.* Σ, σ)   *See* Appendix B, Greek Alphabet.

Sigmoidal Curve   *See* Ogive.

Sign Stimulus   *See* Releaser.

Sign Test   A nonparametric (distribution-free) test for the significance of the difference between two correlated sets of scores. Most commonly the test involves repeated measures where for each subject there is a pair of scores, one under each of two experimental conditions. The procedure involves finding the difference between the two scores, $X_1 - X_2$, for each subject, and noting whether the difference is positive, negative, or zero. The test uses only the differences that are not zero, and if there is no difference between the two populations, it would be expected that half the differences would be positive and half negative. If the proportion of, say, positive differences is significantly different from .50, the conclusion would be that the two sets of scores differ significantly, and inspection of the data will reveal which experimental condition yielded the higher scores.

EXAMPLE: A dominance–submission scale is administered to 16 pairs of twins. In 14 of these pairs the first-born twin scored higher than the second-born twin on dominance, and in two pairs the first-born twin scored lower. Use of the binomial distribution shows that this outcome differs significantly from the expected value of eight higher and eight lower, showing that the first-born twins are significantly higher on dominance than the second-born twins.

Signal Detection Task A task in which a subject must attempt to detect a weak stimulus (signal) against a background of interfering stimuli (noise). For example, in an auditory signal detection task, the subject attempts to detect the presence of a pure tone signal that is imposed on a background of white noise. The data may be displayed in the form of an ROC curve. The signal detection model is applied to other tasks, for example recognition memory, where the old stimuli correspond to signal, and the new distractor stimuli with which the old stimuli are mixed correspond to noise. Three basic experimental procedures are used:

1. **Yes–No Procedure** The subject is given many trials, on some of which the signal is presented (signal trials) and on others of which noise alone is presented (noise trials), with the sequence of signal and noise trials being randomly determined. On each trial the subject must respond either "Yes" or "No," indicating a decision that the signal was or was not present.
2. **Forced-Choice Procedure** On each trial the subject is presented two or more intervals, during one of which the signal is presented, while the other intervals contain only noise. The subject must decide on each trial which interval contained the signal, that is, whether it occurred in the first interval, the second interval, . . . , the kth interval. In practice, the number of intervals used generally is from two to five.
3. **Rating Scale Procedure** Usually used in conjunction with the Yes–No procedure; in addition to responding "Yes" or "No" on each trial, the subject also gives a confidence rating for the decision (e.g., using a five-point scale, where 5 means "Very sure it is signal," 4 means "Fairly sure it is signal," 3 means

"Unsure whether it is signal or noise," 2 means "Fairly sure it is noise," and 1 means "Very sure it is noise"

EXAMPLE: Using the Yes–No procedure, a subject is given 200 trials, on a random half of which the signal is presented (signal trials) and on the other half of which noise alone is presented (noise trials). The subject correctly responds "Yes" on 81 of the 100 signal trials, so there are 81 **hits** (correct detections of the signal), and 19 **misses** (failures to detect the signal); the subject's **hit rate** (proportion of hits) is $81/100 = .81$. The subject incorrectly responds "Yes" on 17 of the 100 noise trials, so there are 17 **false alarms** (indications that the signal was present when it was not) and 83 **correct rejections** (correct indications that the signal was not present). The subject's **false alarm rate** (the proportion of false alarms) is $17/100 = .17$. Hit rate and false alarm rate provide the data for computing the two basic measures of performance in a signal detection task: (1) d', which provides a measure of the subject's sensitivity or skill at the detection task, and (2) β, which provides a measure of the subject's response bias (i.e., the subject's tendency to give an overly high proportion of either "Yes" or "No" responses).

Signal Probability   In a signal detection task, or in an application of signal detection theory to another task such as recognition memory, the probability on any given trial that the signal, or its equivalent, will be presented.

Signed-Ranks Test (syn. Wilcoxon Matched-Pairs Signed-Ranks Test)   A distribution-free nonparametric test for differences between paired observations, which takes into consideration not only the direction (sign) of the differences but also the magnitude of the differences. The absolute values of the differences are ranked, and then the ranks are assigned the sign of the corresponding differences. The test statistic is T, the sum of the ranks with one sign, usually the ranks with the less frequent sign. For small samples the critical value is obtained from a special table; for large samples there is an approximate z test.

Table S–1

Student	Mid-term	Final	Difference	Sign	Rank*
KC	62	57	−5	−	2.5
QH	63	55	−8	−	4
TI	51	56	+5	+	2.5
SJ	49	50	+1	+	1
EK	47	58	+11	+	5

For the ranks with the negative sign, $T = 2.5 + 4 = 6.5$.
* The absolute values of the differences are, in order of magnitude, 1, 5, 5, 8, and 11. The two values of 5 are tied for ranks 2 and 3 and are assigned the average value 2.5.

EXAMPLE: Scores are given for a mid-term and the final exam for five students. Computation of T is shown in Table S-1, testing whether the distributions are different for the two exams.

Significance In hypothesis testing, obtaining an outcome that permits rejection of the null hypothesis. A significant value of a test statistic is one that exceeds the critical values. A **significant difference** between sample statistics is one that is large enough to reject the hypothesis that the corresponding population parameters are equal. A **significant treatment effect** exists when the sample means for different levels of the treatment or independent variable differ significantly. For example, using a t test for the difference between means of two independent groups, a significant t is a computed value of t that exceeds the critical value. If the t is significant, the two sample means are said to differ significantly, or there is a significant difference between the sample means; that is, the difference between the sample means is large enough to reject the hypothesis that the population means do not differ. In the analysis of variance, a significant F value shows the presence of a significant treatment effect, meaning that the sample means for the different levels of the independent variable differ enough from one another to reject the hypothesis that the population means are equal.

Significance Level (*syn.* Alpha Level) (1) The value of alpha (α) (i.e., probability of a Type I error) selected for a significance test, sometimes expressed as a percentage. The accepted value of α under most circumstances is .05; thus, most significance tests are carried out using the .05, or 5%, level of significance. (2) The smallest value of α at which the observed value of a test statistic would be significant. For example, even though α is set at .05, a computed t of 3.24, with 14 degrees of freedom, might be reported as significant at the .01 level of significance, since it exceeds the critical value for a test at that level. (*See also p* Value.)

Significance Testing *See* Hypothesis Testing.

Significant Difference *See* Significance.

Significant Treatment Effect *See* Significance.

Simple Effect (*contr.* Main Effect) In analysis of variance, the effect of one independent variable or the interaction of two or more independent variables at selected levels, or combinations of levels, of the other variables.

EXAMPLE 1: Figure S-3 shows the results of a study of recognition memory for pictures of women's faces and pictures of men's faces. The table shows the probability of a correct response for male subjects and female subjects. As the figure indicates, female subjects scored

219

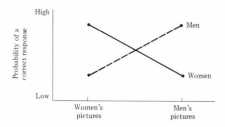

Figure S–3

higher in recognizing women's faces than men's faces, whereas male subjects scored higher in recognizing men's faces than women's faces. A simple main effect could compare mean recognition scores for pictures of women's faces and pictures of men's faces separately for male and female subjects, or it could compare recognition scores for male subjects and female subjects separately for women's pictures and men's pictures.

EXAMPLE 2: An extension of the study included recognition scores for women's names and men's names by male and female subjects. Figure S–4 shows the simple interaction between sex of subject (male and female) and type of stimulus separately for men's names and women's names and for men's faces and women's faces. The figure shows a lack of interaction when the stimuli were names (left panel) but the presence of an interaction when the stimuli were pictures (right panel).

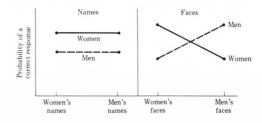

Figure S–4

Simple Experiment Any replicable procedure for obtaining a single datum; usually identical to a single trial. Examples include presenting a multiple-choice question and noting which of the five alternatives is selected, measuring the time a subject takes to solve the anagram NEDM, etc. A **Bernoulli experiment** is a simple experiment in which the observation is dichotomous (e.g., correct or incorrect, true or false).

Simple Interaction *See* Simple Effect.

Simple Main Effect *See* Simple Effect.

Simple Random Sampling *See* Random Sampling.

Simple Reaction Time *See* Reaction Time.

Simulation Research Any research procedure designed to model certain essential features of a real-life circumstance. Simulation procedures can be used when it is impossible to reproduce such conditions (e.g., war games in lieu of wars) or when it is not economical to do so (e.g., a space flight training simulator in lieu of actual space flight training). (*See also* Zero-Sum/Nonzero-Sum Games.)

Simultaneous Conditioning A classical conditioning procedure in which onset of the conditioned stimulus (CS) and unconditioned stimulus (US) occur virtually at the same time. The term sometimes is used to refer to arrangements in which CS onset precedes US onset from 0.5 sec to 5.0 sec. (*See also* Delayed Conditioning; Trace Conditioning.)

Simultaneous Discrimination *See under* Differential Instrumental Conditioning.

Single Blind *See* Blind Procedures.

Single-Factor Design (*syn.* One-Way Design) Any experimental design with only one independent variable.

Single-Group Design As a general term, any design involving no more than one group of subjects. More specifically, a quasi-experimental procedure in which an intact or naturally formed, nonrandomly assigned group of subjects undergoes repeated measurements before and after the experimental treatment. (*See also* Quasi-experimental Designs.)

Single Stimuli, Method of *See* Absolute Judgment, Method of.

Single-subject Design Any experimental design for single-subject research characterized by controls for many of the carryover effects that are present in this research. (*See the following individual listings;* Multielement Baseline Design; Multiple Baseline Design; Reversal Design.)

Single-subject Research A research strategy used chiefly in operant conditioning and behavior modification. It consists of conducting many data collection sessions with the same subject in which treatments are repeatedly administered, sometimes in alternation with control or baseline sessions. (*See also* Single-Subject Designs.)

SIQR *See* Semi-interquartile Range.

Situational Variable *See* Independent Variable.

Size-Weight Illusion *See under* Illusions.

Skewness The extent to which a distribution of scores deviates from symmetry. Skewed distributions are described as being positively skewed if the "tail" points to the right, in the direction of increasing scores, and as negatively skewed if the "tail" points to the left, in the direction of decreasing scores. The two types of skewed distributions are illustrated in Fig. S–5

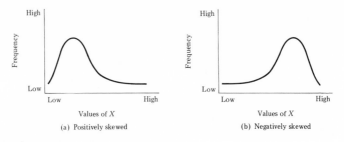

(a) Positively skewed

(b) Negatively skewed

Figure S–5

Skinner Box *See* Operant Chamber.

Slope Constant *See* Linear Regression.

Small-Sample Research A research strategy in psychophysics and operant conditioning that employs very few subjects, or sometimes only one subject. The reliability of experimental treatments is established by demonstrating the stability of performance over many replications within the subject and over many experimental sessions. Traditional significance testing techniques seldom are used. (*See also* Single-Subject Research.)

Smoothing Any procedure for preparing data for graphic presentation that is designed to remove the irregularities of raw data in order to show the underlying shape or process. Common procedures for smoothing data include construction of grouped frequency distributions, computing means for successive blocks of trials, and computing running averages. (*See also* Trial Block.)

Social Acquiescence *See* Social Desirability.

Social Desirability An item characteristic that produces a response set (bias) based on the subject's perception of what response is socially desirable. For example, knowing that it is not socially desirable to express any form of racial prejudice, the respondent may unconditionally endorse test items that refer to racial minorities in a positive way. Similarly, a subject may manifest the socially desirable characteristic of acquiescing, and thus tend to agree unconditionally to most of the positively worded test items. (*See also* Response Bias.)

Social Distance Scale (*syn.* Bogardus Scale)   A rating scale constructed by the method of cumulative rating in which respondents are asked to indicate their willingness to admit members of a particular group (e.g., Jews, Orientals, etc.) to each of seven levels of social distance, ranging from very near (e.g., "to close kinship by marriage") to very remote (e.g., "to exclusion from my country"). (*See also* Cumulative Rating, Method of.)

Sociogram   The graphic presentation of data derived from sociometry. In the conventional sociogram (Fig. S–5), individuals are represented by small circles from which arrows are drawn to designate each individual's expressed sociometric choice(s) or rejection(s).

EXAMPLE: Figure S–6 shows a conventional sociogram depicting interpersonal attractions based on a sociometric assessment of a group of 11 children. Child A, who received a large number of choices, is called a "star." One who receives no choice at all, despite being nominally a member of the group, such as Children F, G, H, I, J, and K, is known as an "isolate." There also is a clear-cut separation between the two subgroups.

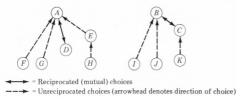

◆——▶ = Reciprocated (mutual) choices
– – –▶ = Unreciprocated choices (arrowhead denotes direction of choice)

Figure S–6

Sociometric Index   Any measure of relationships among members of a group derived from sociometry. (*See also* sociometry.)

Sociometry   Generally, any measurement of social relationships. More specifically, the systematic assessment of group members' liking (or respect or admiration) for each other. In standard sociometric procedure, a verbal statement (e.g., "the person you like best in the group") serves as the sociometric criterion and subjects are asked to list, or rank-order, which person(s) in their group fit the criterion. These data can be described by sociograms or quantitatively by sociometric indices.

Solomon Four-Group Design   An experimental design that combines the posttest-only design and the pretest–posttest design. It is used primarily in situations that require pre- and posttreatment measures of behavior, but where carryover effects from a pretest may contaminate the outcome. The four groups are arranged as follows:

Group	Pretest	Treatment	Posttest
A	Yes	Yes	Yes
B	Yes	No	Yes
C	No	Yes	Yes
D	No	No	Yes

The design may be analyzed as a 2×2 factorial arrangement of (1) presence or absence of a pretest (Groups A and B versus C and D), and (2) presence or absence of the experimental treatment (Groups A and C versus B and D).

Sorting Task   A task in which a subject is presented a set of stimuli differing along two or more dimensions and is asked to sort them into groups that belong together. It generally is left to the subject to discover what basis for classification is appropriate.

Spaced Practice   *See* Distribution of Practice.

Spatial Discrimination   Any discrimination learning procedure in which the subject must learn the correct location (e.g., left or right) of a stimulus. (*For an example see* Differential Instrumental Conditioning.)

Spearman–Brown Formula   A procedure for estimating the reliability (r_{nn}) of a test n times as long as the test whose reliability (r_{11}) has been computed. The general formula is

$$r_{nn} = \frac{n r_{11}}{1 + (n-1) r_{11}}$$

The Spearman–Brown formula is most commonly used to estimate the total test reliability (r_{tt}) from the split-half reliability (r_{11}). For this purpose the formula becomes

$$r_{tt} = \frac{2 r_{11}}{1 + r_{11}}$$

Specific Comparison   *See* Multiple-Comparison Test.

Specific Variance   In factor analysis, the variance in the scores on one of the variables (e.g., a test) that is due to a factor that is not measured by any other variable (e.g., another test). (*See also* Common-Factor Variance; Uniqueness.)

Speed Test (*contr.* Power Test)   Any test in which the score is based on the number of problems solved within a given time period.

Spiral Omnibus Test   *See* Omnibus Test.

Split-Half Reliability   An internal consistency measure of test reliability, obtained by dividing the items into halves and correlating the scores on these halves. The most common procedure is to obtain the **odd–even reliability** by correlating the scores on odd-numbered and even-numbered test items.

Split-Plot Design   *See* Mixed Design.

Spurious Correlation   A correlation between two variables whose magnitude is inflated because each variable is related to a third variable that is not a part of the process relating the two. For example, the correlation between height and the number of hours per week spent in intramural athletic activities would be spuriously high if the data were obtained at a college with no intramural program for women. In this case both variables, height and participation in intramural athletics, are related to sex, but for different reasons. (*See also* Artifact.)

Square Root Transformation   *See under* Data Transformation.

Stability, Coefficient of   An index of the stability over time of the trait measured by a test. It is the reliability coefficient obtained by the test–retest procedure.

Staircase Method (*syn.* Titration Method; Up-and-Down Method; Von Békésey Method)   In psychophysics, a modification of the method of limits for determining absolute and difference thresholds. In this procedure the direction of minimal change in the value of a stimulus presented on a given trial depends on how the subject responded on the previous trial. For the determination of absolute thresholds, if the stimulus is detected, its value on the next trial is reduced one step; if it is not detected, its value on the next trial is increased one step. For the determination of difference thresholds, if the comparison stimulus is responded to as different from the standard, the difference between the values of the comparison and standard stimuli on the next trial is reduced one step; otherwise the difference in the values is increased one step. Thus, the stimulus value presented varies back and forth across the subject's absolute or difference threshold over the course of a laboratory session.

EXAMPLE: In determining an absolute visual threshold for a pigeon, the bird is trained to peck one key (Key A) while a circular patch of light is visible and to peck another key (Key B) when the patch is dark. The intensity of the light is controlled by the pigeon's pecks. Pecks on Key A gradually reduce the intensity of the light until it passes below threshold value, at which point the pigeon shifts to pecking Key B. Pecks on Key B gradually increase the intensity of the light until it becomes visible, at which point the pigeon shifts to pecking Key A again. The mean of the intensity values at which the pigeon shifts from one key to the other during the course of an experimental session is taken as a measure of the absolute threshold.

Standard Deviation (*symb. σ, s; abbr. SD; syn.* Root Mean Square Deviation, *abbr.* RMS) A measure of the variability or dispersion in a set of scores that provides an indication of the average amount by which the scores deviate from the mean of the distribution. It is the square root of the variance, so the symbols (σ for a population, s for a sample) and the general definitional formulas for the standard deviation are readily derived from those for the variance. (*For illustrations of the interpretation of the standard deviation for several distributions see* Normal Distribution.) (*See also* Average Deviation; Data Transformation; Z Transformation.)

EXAMPLE: The distribution in Table S–2 shows height in centimeters for a sample of seven male university students. The raw scores (X) have a mean of 175 cm, and the deviation scores (x) show the number of centimeters that each score deviates from the mean. The sum of the squared deviation scores is called the sum of squares, abbreviated Σx^2, or SS. If interest is only in the students in the sample,

Table S–2

Raw scores (in cm) X	Deviation scores (in cm) $x = X - \bar{X}$	Squared deviation scores $x^2 = (X - \bar{X})^2$
188	13	169
179	4	16
177	2	4
176	1	1
174	−1	1
168	−7	49
163	−12	144
$\Sigma X = 1225$	$\Sigma x = \Sigma (X - \bar{X}) = \quad 0$	$\Sigma x^2 = \Sigma (X - \bar{X})^2 = 384$
$\bar{X} = \quad 175$		

Sample standard deviation: $SD = \sqrt{\dfrac{\Sigma (X - \bar{X})^2}{n}} = \sqrt{\dfrac{384}{7}} = 7.41$ cm

Estimate of population standard deviation σ: $SD = \sqrt{\dfrac{\Sigma (X - \bar{X})^2}{n - 1}} = \sqrt{\dfrac{384}{6}} = 8.00$ cm the sum of squares, here 384, is divided by the number of scores, here $n = 7$, and the square root of the resulting value yields a standard deviation of 7.41 cm. If interest is in estimating the standard deviation of the population from which the sample was randomly drawn, then the estimate is computed by dividing the sum of squares by $n - 1$ (its degrees of freedom) and taking the square root with a resulting value of 8 cm.

Standard Error *(abbr. SE)*   The standard deviation of a sampling distribution. Standard errors can be computed for a variety of sample statistics (e.g., sample means or proportions). A standard error is commonly symbolized using the small Greek sigma, a common symbol for a standard deviation, with a subscript to indicate the particular sample statistic concerned. For example, the standard error of a sample mean and a sample proportion, respectively, with their computational formulae, are

$$\sigma_{\bar{x}} = \frac{\sigma}{\sqrt{n}} \quad \text{and} \quad \sigma_p = \sqrt{\frac{pq}{n}}$$

Standard Error of Estimate *(symb. $\sigma_{y \cdot x}$ or $s_{y \cdot x}$)*   In correlational analysis, the standard deviation of the values of Y around the regression line of Y on X, or the standard deviation of the obtained values of X around the regression line of X on Y. The standard error of estimate is the standard deviation of the values of Y for any value of X, or the standard deviation of the values of X for any value of Y. For example, if X is the distribution of heights of fathers and Y is the distribution of heights of sons, then $s_{y \cdot x}$ is the standard deviation of the height scores among sons all of whose fathers are the same height. Similarly, $s_{x \cdot y}$ is the standard deviation of height scores among the fathers of sons who all are the same height. One pair of formulas for the standard error of estimate is $s_{y \cdot x} = s_y \sqrt{1 - r^2}$ and $s_{x \cdot y} = s_x \sqrt{1 - r^2}$, where s_y and s_x are the standard deviations of the sample values of Y and X, respectively, and r is the product-moment correlation coefficient between X and Y.

Standard Normal Distribution *(syn. Unit-Normal Distribution; z Distribution)*   The normal distribution with a mean of zero and a standard deviation of 1.0. It is the distribution referred to as the Table of the Normal Curve, or the Table of z.

Standard Score   *See* Data Transformation (2).

Standard Stimulus   In psychophysics, the stimulus to which another stimulus (the comparison or variable stimulus) is compared.

Stanine   *See under* Data Transformation.

Stated Limits   *See* Class Interval.

Statistic (*contr.* Parameter, Def. 1)   Any numerical index computed from a sample that (1) describes the sample (e.g., the mean, correlation, proportion correct, etc.) or (2) is used for inference about the population (e.g., the variance estimate, obtained value of t).

Statistical Control (*contr.* Experimental Control)   Any statistical procedure for estimating what the effect of an independent variable would be if one or more extraneous variables had been experimentally controlled. The most common procedures are analysis of covariance and multivariate analysis of covariance.

Statistical Significance   *See* p Value; Significance; Significance Level.

Status Variable   *See* Subject Variable.

Steady-State Design   *See* Reversal Design.

Stepdown *F* Procedure   See Multivariate Analysis of Variance.

Stepdown MANOVA   *See* Multivariate Analysis of Variance.

Stepwise Discriminant Analysis   *See* Discriminant Analysis.

Stepwise Regression   An iterative (multistep) procedure for obtaining coefficients for a multiple regression equation that includes two or more of a set of independent variables. At each step in the analysis, one of the variables is either added or deleted, new multiple regression coefficients are computed, and the resulting changes are evaluated. Any of several criteria may be used to determine which variable is to be added or deleted on any step. The process is continued until some optimum criterion (e.g., F tests) shows that none of the remaining variables would markedly increase the variance accounted for in the dependent variable, or until all the independent variables have been included in the regression equation.

Stimulus   (1) Any physical energy change. (2) An energy change of sufficient magnitude to excite an appropriate receptor. An **exteroceptive stimulus** originates from outside the organism (e.g., onset of a room light). An **interoceptive stimulus** originates from within the organism (e.g., a stomach contraction).

Stimulus Generalization   In learning research, any procedure that examines the extent to which a subject who has been trained to respond to one stimulus will respond to new stimuli varying in different degrees from the original stimulus, that is, the degree to which the subject fails to discriminate among stimuli. For example, a pigeon is first trained to peck at a red key. Subsequently, the animal is placed in test situations in which the color of the key is orange, yellow, or white. The strength of responding to any of the test keys relative to the original red key serves as an index of generalization. (*See also* Discrimination Learning; Response Generalization.)

Stimulus Threshold   *See* Absolute Threshold.

Stimulus Variable   *See* Independent Variable.

Stochastic Model (*contr.* Deterministic Model)   A mathematical model or theory that predicts the probability distribution of responses. For example, a stochastic choice model might predict the probability that each of several objects will be chosen on a particular occasion.

Stochastic Process   A series of experiments or observations in which each outcome is at least in part determined by chance factors.

Stochastic Variable   *See* Random Variable.

Stratified Random Sampling   A sampling procedure in which the population is divided into two or more strata (levels) on the basis of one or more variables. For example, college students might be stratified on the basis of age into strata of under 20, 20–24, 25–29, and over 29, or they might be stratified on both age and sex, giving strata such as females under 20, males under 20, etc. A random sample is then drawn from each stratum. The sample sizes may be equal, proportional to the number of elements in the strata, or determined on the basis of special considerations.

Stratified Sampling (*syn.* Quota Sampling)   Any sampling procedure that draws elements in proportion to their frequency in the subgroups that make up the population to be sampled. For example, if the population is the American public, the sample should include the same proportion of males, females, blacks, whites, etc., as listed in the U.S. government census information.

Strength of Association   *See* Magnitude of Effect.

Studentized Range Statistic (*symb. q*)   A statistic used as the critical value for several multiple-comparison tests, obtained from special tables.

Student's *t*   *See* *t*-Test.

Subject Variable (*syn.* Organismic Variable; Status Variable)   Any feature or characteristic of an experimental subject that cannot be manipulated by the experimenter. Examples include weight, intelligence, socioeconomic status, etc. (*See also* Nonmanipulated Variable.)

Subjective Probability   A measure between 0 and 1 that reflects an individual's degree of belief in some uncertain event, hypothesis, etc. It may be based in part on experience and may be modified on the basis of objective data, but it is not confined to replicable events. For example, the probability that a particular team will win the league championship is typically based on a variety of considerations that realistically, are only partly quantifiable, and the estimate of this probability varies from person to person. (*See also* Bayesian Statistics.)

Subjective Report (*syn.* Phenomenal Report; Verbal Report) A verbal account by a subject of the sensations, cognitions, emotions, etc., experienced during a specified time or in response to specified events.

Subtraction Method A procedure, using reaction time (RT) data, for identifying and measuring components of information processing. It is computed by subtracting RT for a given task from RT for a more complex task.

EXAMPLE: A subject is presented a letter in the left aperture of a memory drum, and after a brief period the cover of the right aperture is raised, revealing a second letter. The subject's task is to respond as quickly as possible by pressing either of two buttons, pressing one if the two letters are the same and the other if they are different. There are two classes of "Same" stimuli, physically identical, as AA, or same in name but different in that one is in upper case and the other is in lower case, as Aa. It is found that mean RT for identical matches is 420 msec, whereas mean RT for name matches is 502 msec. The difference in mean RT is $502 - 420 = 82$ msec. This difference may be interpreted as the processing time for naming stimuli and comparing names.

Successive Approximations Method *See* Shaping.

Successive Discrimination *See* Differential Instrumental Conditioning.

Sum of Products (*abbr. SP, SS_{xy}*) The sum of products of deviations of paired scores from their respective means, $\Sigma(X - \bar{X})(Y - \bar{Y})$, or using deviation scores, Σxy.

Sum of Squares (*abbr. SS*) A sum of squared deviations. For a set of scores, it is the sum of squared deviations of the scores from their mean, $\Sigma(X - \bar{X})^2$; or, using deviation scores, Σx^2. In other contexts it may refer to deviations of scores from predicted values, or sample means from their mean value or from some other estimate of their expected value. (*See also* Mean Square; Variance.)

Summary Table *See* Analysis of Variance Summary Table.

Summated Ratings, Method of A scaling procedure in which respondents express degrees of agreement or disagreement, usually in five or six categories ranging from complete and unqualified agreement to complete and unqualified disagreement (or vice versa) to a number of items. Customary scoring procedures involve the assignment of successive values, such as 1, 2, 3, etc., to each response category in a consistent direction so that scores can be estimated by the summation of the agreement rating assigned by the respondent to each item. Attitude scales derived from this method are known as Likert or Likert-type scales.

EXAMPLE: The three-item scale below represents a hypothetical Likert scale for the assessment of prejudice against women.

	Strongly agree	Agree	No opinion	Disagree	Strongly disagree
1. Women can attain the same technical skills as men.	(√)	( )	( )	( )	( )
2. Because of their physiological make-up, women are not as emotionally stable as men.	( )	( )	( )	(√)	( )
3. Female sport reporters should be allowed into male athletes' locker rooms for interviews.	( )	( )	(√)	( )	( )

The scale is a five-point (odd item category) scale, thus allowing for a neutral (no opinion) response. The maximum summated score for prejudice against women is 15 $(5 + 5 + 5)$, and the minimum summated score is 3 $(1 + 1 + 1)$. Since the second item is negatively worded, score assignments for that item must be reversed. In the preceding example the respondent's score is $(1 + 2 + 3) = 6$.

Supplemental Test   see A Posteriori Test.

Suppressor Variable   A predictor variable used to improve prediction of a criterion by suppressing potentially undesirable or irrelevant portions of other predictors.

EXAMPLE: College grade point average (GPA) is designated as one predictor of the criterion success in pilot training. GPA scores correlate with pilot training because they include such components as motivation, innovation, aptitude in math, etc., all of which are important in pilot training. GPA scores, however, also reflect to a large extent verbal ability, which is relatively unimportant in pilot training, since it is weakly correlated with pilot performance. A college history test that correlates with GPA because it reflects not only knowledge of history but verbal ability as well is introduced as a second predictor. It also serves as the suppressor variable, since it does not correlate with the criterion. Thus, an applicant with a high GPA and a low history test score would be preferred for pilot training to an applicant with a high GPA and a high history score.

Survey Research   The assessment of public opinion using oral or written questionnaires.

Systematic Variance (*contr.* Error Variance)   Variance in the dependent variable due to the influence of the independent variable (treatment variance), and/or variance due to the presence of an extraneous (confounding) variable. (*See also* Communality; Predicted Variance.)

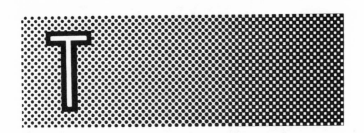

Tailored Testing An interviewing technique in which the content of the subject's answer to one question determines which one of two or more subsequent questions will be asked, producing a branching sequence of questions.

Tailored Yoking *See* Yoked Control.

Tandem Schedule of Reinforcement (*abbr.* Tand) An operant conditioning procedure identical to a chained schedule of reinforcement but in which no discriminative stimuli accompany the component schedules.

Target Person In social psychology experiments, the person about whom judgments are made by subjects.

Target Stimulus A stimulus object to be tracked, monitored, or identified by a subject.

Task Variable A characteristic of the task assigned to the subject. It may be an independent variable or a control variable. Examples include complexity level of problems to be solved, amount of physical effort to operate an apparatus, etc. (*See also* Instructional Variable.)

Tau Coefficient *See* Kendall's Rank Correlation Coefficient.

***t* Distribution (*syn.* Student's *t* Distribution)** A probability distribution similar to the unit normal (z) distribution. Like the z distribution, the t distribution has a mean of zero, but the t distribution is more peaked with higher tails. (*See also* t Test.)

Temporal Conditioning A classical conditioning procedure in which the unconditioned stimulus occurs at regular temporal intervals (e.g., once every 30 sec) and no external conditioned stimulus is used. (*See also* Nondiscriminated Avoidance Learning.)

Temporal Discrimination   Any discrimination training procedure in which the subject must learn the specific temporal location (e.g., first versus second) of a stimulus. (*For an example see* Differential Instrumental conditioning.)

Terminal Threshold   *See under* Absolute Threshold.

Test for Significance of Changes   *See* Correlated Proportions Test.

Test–Retest Procedure   Any procedure for measuring the reliability of a test by correlating the test scores from the same group of people on two different occasions.

Test Trial   A trial on which data are collected to assess the effect of a prior treatment.

Tetrachoric Correlation *(symb. r_t)*   An index of the degree of correlation between two variables that either are continuous variables which have been reduced to a dichotomy or are dichotomous variables that are assumed to reflect an underlying continuous variable. Examples include performance test scores classified as above or below the median, or responses of agree or disagree that are assumed to reflect an underlying continuum of degree of agreement. The formula for the tetrachoric correlation is complex, and various procedures have been developed for estimating its value.

Theoretical Construct   *See* Hypothetical Construct.

Theoretical Frequency   *See* Expected Frequency.

Theory   Any systematic set of propositions designed to explain a collection of empirical relationships.

Three-Factor Design   Any experimental design that uses three independent variables (factors).

Three-Factor Mixed Design   An experimental design in which one factor (independent variable) is administered in a between-subjects fashion and the remaining factors in a within-subjects (repeated measures) fashion. Conversely, two factors may be administered in a between-subjects fashion, and the remaining factor in a within-subjects fashion. The former arrangement sometimes is referred to as a **one-between/two-within design** (syn. Lindquist Type III Design). The latter sometimes is referred to as a **two-between–one-within design** (syn. Lindquist Type VI Design).

Three-Way Interaction (*syn.* Second-Order Interaction)   An interaction of three independent variables. (*See also* Higher Order Interactions.)

234

Threshold (*syn.* Limen)   The minimum value of a stimulus that will produce a specified response. (*See also* Absolute Threshold; Difference Threshold; Recognition Threshold.)

Thurstone Scale   A scale constructed by the method of equal-appearing intervals. (*For an example see* Equal-Appearing Intervals, Method of.)

Time Error   In psychophysics, a constant error produced when making comparisons of stimuli that are presented successively, that is, separated in time. For example, a comparison stimulus must be judged as greater, lesser, or equal in magnitude to a standard stimulus. If the standard stimulus is always given first, followed by the comparison stimulus, any bias in judgment of the comparison stimulus constitutes a time error.

Time on Target (*abbr.* TOT)   In a tracking task, the time that a subject maintains contact with a moving stimulus (target). For example, in a rotary pursuit task, the subject is to keep the tip of a metal stylus in contact with a rotating metal disc. The number of seconds of contact time during a trial of, say, 60 sec constitutes the time on target.

Time Out (*abbr.* TO)   In operant conditioning, a negative punishment procedure in which a response temporarily suspends the availability of reinforcement; that is, it renders a schedule of reinforcement inoperative. (*See also* Omission Training; Punishment.)

EXAMPLE: An operant chamber is programmed so that a rat is reinforced every fifth time it presses the left bar (fixed-ratio-5 schedule of reinforcement), during periods when a cue light above that bar is lighted. If the animal presses the right bar, however, the light above the left bar is extinguished and the left bar is withdrawn from the chamber for 3 min.

Time Sampling   A procedure for obtaining the frequency with which one or more behaviors occur during predetermined time intervals. The intervals may be chosen systematically, such as observations for 5 min every hour, or they may be chosen randomly.

Time Schedule   *See* Deprivation Schedule; Interval Schedules of Reinforcement.

Time Series Design   A quasi-experimental procedure in which one or more intact or naturally formed groups is subjected to repeated measurements or observations, usually before and after the experimental treatment. (*For an example see* Multiple-Group Design.)

Titration Method   *See* Staircase Method.

Titration Schedule of Reinforcement An operant conditioning procedure in which the delivery of reinforcements is programmed according to the staircase method, a psychophysical technique for obtaining thresholds. (*For an example see* Staircase Method.)

Trace Conditioning A classical conditioning procedure in which there is a measurable time interval between offset of the conditioned stimulus (CS) and onset of the unconditioned stimulus (US). Sometimes the term is used to refer to only those arrangements in which this interval is 1 min or longer. (*See also* Delayed Conditioning; Simultaneous Conditioning.)

Tracking *See* Compensatory Tracking Task; Pursuit Tracking Task.

Training Trial (*syn.* Acquisition Trial) A trial on which conditions are arranged so that the subject may learn a response. (*See also* Practice Trial.)

Transfer Paradigm (*syn.* Proaction Paradigm) A procedure for determining the effect of a previous experience on the subsequent performance of some task. In the basic design, a comparison is made between the performance of an experimental group and a control group on Task Y; prior to being given Task Y, the experimental group, but not the control group, has been given experience in performing Task X, so that the design is

Group	Task X	Task Y
Experimental	Yes	Yes
Control	No	Yes

If the experimental group is superior to the control group in performance on Task Y, the result is referred to as positive transfer; if the performance of the experimental group is inferior to that of the control group, the result is referred to as negative transfer.

Transformation *See* Data Transformation.

Trapezoidal Window *See under* Illusions.

Travel Time *See* Response Time.

Treatment (*syn.* Experimental Treatment) A term that generally refers to one level or value of a manipulated variable in an experiment. For example, in a study of problem solving in which the number of alternatives to choose from (2, 4, 6, or 8) is varied, a treatment would be any one of the four levels of this variable. (*See also* Condition.)

Treatment-by-Levels Design A factorial design with two or more independent variables, of which at least one is experimentally manipulated (treatment variable) and at least one is nonmanipulated. For example, groups may be formed by age or intelligence levels, or by high, medium, or low scores on a pretest. A levels variable may be defined also by intact groups, such as second-, third-, and fourth-grade classes from a particular school. (*See also* Randomized-Blocks Design; Treatment-by-Blocks Design.)

Treatment-by-Subjects Design *See* Repeated-Measures Design.

Treatment Effect (*syn.* Experimental Effect) Differences among group means or between the mean of one group and the grand mean, which are attributable to the independent variable. (*See also* Magnitude of Effect.)

Treatment Variable *See* Manipulated Variable.

Trend Analysis An analysis of variance procedure for an experiment with one or more quantitative independent variables. The procedure gives separate orthogonal (independent) tests for linear trend and degrees of curvature (quadratic, cubic, etc.) of the means, and for the interaction of these trends with other independent variables.

EXAMPLE: Rats were tested after 2, 4, 6, 8, or 10 hours of food deprivation, and their respective rates of bar pressing for food pellets showed a positively accelerated increasing trend. In a trend analysis, the general increase would appear as linear and quadratic trend. If two different food rewards were used factorially with hours of deprivation, a reward by linear trend interaction might be found if the increase in rate of responding is greater with one reward than with the other.

Trial A single instance or event from which a datum is collected.

Trial Block (1) A sequence of trials that contains a specified number (usually all) of the different treatment conditions in the experiment. (2) A sequence of trials under a single condition, the scores from which are averaged, reducing the amount of data to be analyzed or inspected. For example, a series of 12 trials may be divided into six blocks of two trials each, four blocks of three trials, or two blocks of six trials.

Trials to Criterion A measure of behavior in which the number of trials needed to reach some specified level of performance is computed. (*For an example see* Performance Criterion.)

Trigram A combination of three letters. Usually, trigrams are either consonant–vowel–consonant (CVC) or three consonants (CCC). **Nonsense syllables** are CVCs that are not words in the English language.

True Experiment *See* Experiment.

True Negative *See* Decision.

True Positive *See* Decision.

True Score A theoretical score free from bias or random error. A subject's mean score on a large number of observations usually is considered to be the best estimate of the true score.

True Yoking *See* Yoked Control.

T × S (T by S) Design *See* Repeated-Measures Design.

T Score *See under* Data Transformation.

T² (T Square) *See* Hotelling's T^2.

t Statistic The test statistic used for testing various hypotheses when the population variance is unknown.

t Test Any of several significance tests for hypotheses about the means of normal distributions that are used when the population variance is unknown. For one sample, the test statistic t (also called Student's t) is computed by the formula:

$$t = \frac{\overline{X} - \mu_0}{s_{\overline{x}}}$$

where $\overline{X}$ is the sample mean, μ_0 is the hypothesized mean, and $s_{\overline{x}}$ is the estimated standard error of the mean. Similar formulas are used with independent samples and with paired samples for testing hypotheses about differences between means, for testing hypotheses about the slope of a regression line, etc. The degrees of freedom for a t test are the degrees of freedom for the variance estimate used in the denominator of the statistic.

Tukey's Test (*syn.* Honestly Significant Difference procedure; *abbr.* HSD Procedure) A multiple-comparison procedure that uses the same critical value of the Studentized range statistic q for all comparisons. This procedure sometimes is called Tukey's (a) Test to Distinguish it from Tukey's (b) Test. The latter is an infrequently used procedure that employs critical values that are intermediate between those for the Tukey (a) Test and the corresponding critical values for the Newman–Keuls procedure. (*See also* Multiple-Comparison Test.)

Twisted-Cord Illusion *See under* Illusions.

Two-Factor Design Any experimental design that uses two independent variables (factors).

Two-Factor Mixed Design (*syn.* Lindquist Type I Design; One-Between/One-Within Design) An experimental design in which one independent variable is administered in a between-groups fashion and a second independent variable is administered in a within-subjects (repeated-measures) fashion. (*See also* Mixed Design.)

Two-Sided Test   *See* One-Tail/Two-Tail Test.

Two-Tail Test   *See* One-Tail/Two-Tail Test.

Two-Way Interaction   *See* First-Order Interaction.

Two-Within/One-Between Design   *See* Three-Factor Mixed Design

Type I Error (*syn.* Alpha Error)   In hypothesis testing, the rejection of a true null hypothesis when it should not have been rejected. This may lead to the claim that the independent variable(s) in a study produced an experimental effect, when in fact there was none.

Type II Error (*syn.* Beta Error)   In hypothesis testing, the failure to reject a false null hypothesis when it should have been rejected. This may lead to the claim that the independent variable(s) in the study did not produce an experimental effect, when in fact there was one.

Type R Conditioning   *See* Instrumental Conditioning.

Type S Conditioning   *See* Classical Conditioning.

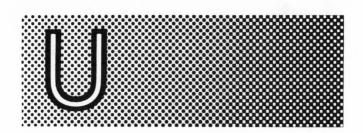

UCS See Unconditioned Stimulus.

Umweg Problem *See* Detour Task.

Unbiased Estimate A sample statistic whose expected value (i.e., long-run average) is equal to the population parameter being estimated (i.e., whose sampling distribution has a mean equal to the parameter). For example, the mean, median, and mode are unbiased estimators of the mean of a normal distribution. The variance estimate, $\Sigma(X-\bar{X})^2/(N-1)$, is an unbiased estimator of the population variance.

Uncertainty *(symb. H)* A measure of the amount of information, in bits, associated with a message source. A distinction is made between stimulus uncertainty (H_s), which refers to the uncertainty in predicting which of a set of alternative stimuli will be presented, and response uncertainty (H_r), which refers to the uncertainty involved in selecting from among a set of alternative responses to stimuli.

Unconditioned Response (*abbr.* UCR; UR) In classical conditioning, an unlearned response elicited by the unconditioned stimulus. Examples include salivation to meat powder, leg flexion to electric shock delivered to the paw, eyeblink to a puff of air delivered to the cornea, etc.

Unconditioned Stimulus (*abbr.* UCS; US) In classical conditioning, the stimulus used to elicit the unconditioned response (i.e., a stimulus that will elicit the response without requiring previous conditioning).

Uncorrelated Reinforcement *See* Noncontingent Reinforcement.

Unidimensional Scaling In testing, the establishment of a single underlying response pattern to multiple stimulus items by eliminating irrelevant or ambiguous items. For example, in attitude testing it involves the analysis of the correlation of each item with the total score. Items that do not show a high correlation with the total score are discarded, since they are likely to tap an attitude different from what is tapped by the total. (*See also* Multidimensional Scaling.)

Uniform Distribution   *See* Rectangular Distribution.

Unimodal Distribution   *See* Mode.

Uniqueness   In factor analysis, the proportion of variance in the scores on one of the variables (e.g., a test) that is not common-factor variance, that is, the proportion of variance not due to factors that the variable has in common with other variables (e.g., other tests). It is the specific variance plus error variance, expressed as a proportion; alternatively, it is 1.0 minus the communality.

Unit Normal Distribution   *See* Standard Normal Distribution.

Univariate Statistics   Descriptive and inferential statistical procedures designed for use when the analysis involves a single dependent variable. (*See also* Bivariate Statistics; Multivariate Statistics.)

Unobtrusive Measure   *See* Nonreactive Measure.

Unpaired Control   (1) In classical conditioning, a procedure in which only the conditioned stimulus (CS) or the unconditioned stimulus (US) is presented on a given trial, so that the temporal contiguity of the two is removed. For example, if subjects in an experimental group each received 20 conventional conditioning trials of the CS followed by the US, subjects in an unpaired control group would receive a 40-trial sequence in which 20 CSs and 20 USs were given in random order. Such a procedure often is referred to as **explicit unpairing.** In a variation of this procedure, CSs and USs are programmed to occur in random order and at randomly different times, so that the amount of temporal contiguity between the CS and US varies randomly. (2) In instrumental (operant) conditioning, the term most often refers to procedures in which the contingencies between certain behaviors and certain reinforcing, punishing, or other stimulus events is removed. (*For an example see* Yoked Control.)

Unweighted   Not differentially weighted. An unweighted sum is a simple total, with each term given a weight of 1. The arithmetic mean of a set of scores is an unweighted mean in which each score receives the same weight. [*See* also Weight(ed).]

Unweighted Means Analysis   An analysis of variance procedure used when treatment cells contain unequal numbers of observations for reasons not related to the nature of the treatment. The analysis gives equal weights to all cell means, even though some are based on more data than others. An unweighted means analysis would be appropriate if, for example, some subjects forgot to come or were called out of town or if data were lost due to equipment failure. The analysis is not appropriate if the loss of data is or may be related to the treatment condition, for example, if only animals in the stress condition become ill, or if only subjects in the difficult condition fail to complete the experiment. [*See* also Weight(ed).]

Up-and-Down Method   *See* Staircase Method.

UR   *See* Unconditioned Response.

US   *See* Unconditioned Stimulus.

U **Statistic (*syn.* Wilk's Lambda)**   *See* Multivariate Tests of Significance.

U **Test (*syn.* Mann–Whitney *U* Test)**   A distribution-free nonparametric test for independent samples usually used to test for a difference in central tendency. The data from the combined samples are arranged in order of magnitude and ranked, with the lowest score given rank 1. The test statistic is the smaller of two values U and U' based on the sum of the ranks for one of the samples (T_1):

$$U = N_1 N_2 + \frac{N_1(N_1 + 1)}{2} - T_1; \qquad U' = N_1 N_2 - U$$

For small samples the critical value for this statistic is obtained from a special table; for large samples there is an approximate z test.

EXAMPLE: Two groups of subjects were tested. For the control group (C) the scores were 19, 24, 27, 35, and 35. For the experimental group (E) the scores were 14, 21, 13, 23, 15, and 11. The data are shown arranged in order of magnitude and ranked, and identified by the group from which each score came:

Group	E	E	E	E	C	E	E	C	C	C	C
Score	11	13	14	15	19	21	23	24	27	35	35
Rank	1	2	3	4	5	6	7	8	9	10	11

The sum of the ranks for the experimental group (T_1) is $1 + 2 + 3 + 4 + 6 + 7 = 23$. The number of scores in the experimental group (N_1) is 6 and the number in the control group (N_2) is 5, so $U = 6 \times 5 + (6 \times 7)/2 - 23 = 28$, and $U' = 6 \times 5 - 28 = 2$. The smaller of these two values, $U' = 2$, would be compared to the tabled value to test for significance.

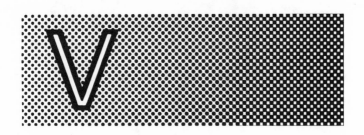

Validity A general term denoting correctness of a measure (i.e., that it does in fact measure what it purports to measure). (*For specific types of validity see the appropriate entry, such as* Content Validity; External Validity; Predictive Validity, etc.)

Validity Coefficient A general term for any validity measure expressed as a correlation coefficient.

Variable (*contr.* Constant) Any event or characteristic with values that can change from time to time or object to object. In psychological research, specific types of variables include independent variables, dependent variables, subject variables, etc.

Variable Error *See* Random Error.

Variable-Interval Schedule of Reinforcement (*abbr.* VI) An operant conditioning procedure in which a variable period of time must elapse before the response being conditioned is reinforced. The first response made after this interval expires is reinforced, beginning a new (and different) period of time. For example, in a variable-interval 30-sec schedule (VI-30), the first response to occur after a mean interval of 30 sec is reinforced, with the actual intervals perhaps varying between 10 and 50 sec. (*See also* Fixed-Interval Schedule of Reinforcement.)

Variable-Ratio Schedule of Reinforcement (*abbr.* VR) An operant conditioning procedure in which a specified number of responses must be made to earn reinforcement, but the exact number needed for each reinforcement varies. For example, in a variable-ratio-5 (VR-5) schedule, the subject receives reinforcement after every 5th response on the average, but the exact number may vary between 3 and 7 responses.

Variable Stimulus *See* Comparison Stimulus.

Variability   The extent to which the scores in a distribution differ from one another. Commonly used measures of variability include the range, variance, and standard deviation.

Variance *(symb. σ^2, s^2)* A measure of the variability of scores defined as the mean (for a sample) or expected value (for a population) of the squared deviations from the mean. The variance of a population is expressed as $\sigma^2 = \mathrm{E}(X - \mu)^2$, and the variance of a sample as $s^2 = \Sigma(X - \bar{X})^2/n$, where μ and $\bar{X}$ are the means of the population and sample, respectively, and n is the number of observations in the sample. Variations of these symbols are used to distinguish between the sample variance and sample estimate of the population variance, $\Sigma(X - \bar{X})^2/(n-1)$, which also is called a mean square. A commonly used descriptive statistic, the standard deviation, is the square root of the variance.

Variance Estimate   *See* Mean Square.

Variance Ratio   In general, any ratio of two variances, but most commonly used as synonymous with the F ratio.

Variate   *see* Random Variable.

Variation, Coefficient of *(symb. V)*   An infrequently used measure of the dispersion of a set of scores, defined either as the standard deviation divided by the mean or as 100 times this ratio.

Varimax Rotation   *See* Factor Rotation.

Vector   A row or column of values, such as means, factor loadings, etc., or a line drawn from the origin of a set of axes to the point represented by these values. (*See also* Mean Vector; Normalized Vector.)

Verbal Conditioning   The application of operant conditioning procedures to the modification of emitted verbal responses. The subject may be asked to recite single words aloud or to comment at length on a topic, or the subject may be asked a series of questions. Certain words or classes of verbalization are targeted, and when they occur, reinforcement or punishment in the form of smiles or frowns or utterances such as "good," "uh-huh," or "hmmm" is given.

EXAMPLE: A subject is given a series of interview questions that purport to sample attitudes toward various political and social issues. Of interest to the experimenter is the frequency with which the subject uses singular pronouns (I, me) or plural pronouns (we, us), and not the attitude itself. The experimenter may collect data to establish a base rate of use of each term. Then an acquisition phase is initiated in which, for example, the experimenter immediately follows each singular pronoun with any one of a variety of negative facial expressions or utterances (e.g., frowning, looking away, or grunting). When the subject uses a plural pronoun, however, the experimenter emits positive expressions or utterances (e.g., a smile, a look of interest, "oh, yes?" etc.). This phase may be followed by an extinction phase, during which no reinforcement or punishment is given.

Verbal Learning   Learning in which the stimulus materials are verbal units, numbers, or other symbols, which are to be committed to memory in some manner. The units may be poetry or prose passages, random sequences of words, nonsense syllables, digits, etc. (*For examples see* Free Learning; Paired-Associate Learning; Serial Learning.)

Verbal Reinforcement   The presentation of oral expressions, facial expressions, gestures, etc., that are generally considered to be positive in an interpersonal situation. They are assumed to strengthen verbal or social behaviors that precede them. (*For examples see* Verbal Conditioning.)

VI   *See* Variable-Interval Schedule of Reinforcement.

Vigilance Task   A task in which the subject monitors a stimulus display for long periods of time and is required to report the occurrence of occasional, often weak, signals. Radar monitoring is an example of such a task.

Vincent(ized) Learning Curve   One of a class of learning curves that permit direct comparison and averaging of data when subjects require different numbers of trials to reach a fixed performance criterion. For each subject, the entire learning period is divided into fifths, usually, or, less frequently, tenths. The total number of correct responses or errors is computed for each fifth of the learning period, using interpolation in fractions of trials. The resulting scores are averaged across subjects. (*See also* Backward Learning Curve; Melton Curve.)

EXAMPLE: Subjects are given a list of 12 items in serial order to a criterion of two perfect trials. The number of correct responses on each trial is shown for one of the subjects.

Trial:	1	2	3	4	5	6	7	8	9	10	11	12	13	14	15	16	17
No. Correct:	0	2	3	4	6	6	8	8	9	10	9	9	12	11	11	12	12

Including the criterion trials, this subject took 17 trials to learn the list, so each fifth of the learning took 3.4 trials. The number of correct responses during the first 3.4 trials is found by taking all the correct responses on Trials 1, 2, and 3, plus .4 of the correct responses on Trial 4: $0 + 2 + 3 + .4(4) = 6.6$. The next 3.4 trials include the remaining

.6 of the correct responses on Trial 4, all of those on Trials 5 and 6, and .8 of those on Trial 7: $.6(4) + 6 + 6 + .8(8) = 20.8$. Correct responses for the remaining fifths of learning would be computed in the same way. For a subject who took 12 trials to criterion, each Vincentized fifth would be 2.4 trials. The learning curve would show the mean number correct for each Vincentized fifth.

Visual Discrimination   Any discrimination training procedure in which differential reinforcement is associated with specific visual stimuli (e.g., circle versus square), and where such factors as temporal or spatial location of the stimuli are controlled. (*For an example see* Differential Instrumental Conditioning.)

Visual Search   *See* Search Task.

Von Békésey Method   *See* Staircase Method.

VR   *See* Variable-Ratio Schedule of Reinforcement.

Wald-Wolfowitz Runs Test   *See* Runs Test.

Weight(ed)   In statistics and measurement, weights are coefficients or multipliers of terms in a sum. A **weighted score** on a test is obtained by using different weights for different items or subtests. For example, in a test composed of multiple-choice and true–false items, multiple-choice items might be weighted by 2, so the weighted score would be two times the number of correct multiple-choice items plus the number of correct true–false items. A **weighted mean** is a weighted sum divided by the sum of the weights. For example, a grade point average is a weighted sum. Letter grades are converted to numbers, weighted (multiplied) by the number of credit hours for which each was obtained, summed, and divided by the total number of credit hours. (*See also* Unweighted.)

Weight Schedule   *See* Deprivation Schedule.

Wherry–Doolittle Method   A method for solving a set of simultaneous equations, designed for use with a calculator. The method can be used for computing multiple regression coefficients and for factor analysis.

Wilcoxon Matched-Pairs Signed-Ranks Test   *See* Signed-Ranks Test

Wilcoxon Rank-Sum Test   *See* Rank-Sum Test.

Wilcoxon Signed-Ranks Test   *See* Signed-Ranks Test.

Wilks' Lambda Test   *See* Multivariate Tests of significance.

Within-Subjects Design   *See* Repeated-Measures Design.

Within-Subjects Variable (*syn.* Repeated Measures Variable; *contr.* Between Subjects Variable)   Any independent variable administered so that each subject receives all of its levels. (*For an example see* Repeated-Measures Design; *see also* Mixed Design.)

Word Association Test   *See* Free Association.

Working Hypothesis   *See* Research Hypothesis.

x *See* Deviation Score.

x′ A symbol for the number of points by which a raw score, *X*, differs from an arbitrary value other than the mean of the distribution of scores of which *X* is a part. (*See also* Deviation Score.)

X A commonly used symbol to designate a single raw score in a distribution of scores.

X̄ A commonly used symbol to designate a sample mean.

***x*-Axis** *See* Abscissa.

***x*-Value** The numerical value of *x* along the *x*-axis or abscissa when specifying the coordinates of a point in a set of *x* and *y* axes.

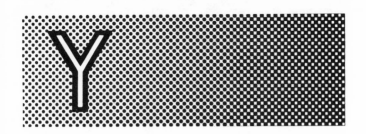

y *See* Deviation Score.

Yates' Correction for Continuity   *See* Correction for Continuity.

***y*-Axis**   *See* Ordinate.

Yes–No Method   *See* Signal Detection Task.

Yoked Control   A noncontingent control procedure in which a control
   subject is paired with a particular experimental subject, such that
   it receives exactly the same treatment as its pair mate, save for
   one critical aspect (the experimental treatment). The control subject may receive its treatment events at the same time as its
   pairmate (**true yoking**), or a protocol may be derived from the
   behavior of the experimental subject and given to the control
   subject later (**tailored yoking**).

   EXAMPLE: To study the reinforcing effects of direct stimulation
   of "pleasure centers" in the brain, one monkey receives stimulation
   each time it correctly solves a shape-matching problem. A control monkey is placed in an exact replica of the apparatus housing its pairmate.
   Whenever the experimental monkey is stimulated, the control animal
   also receives brain stimulation, regardless of its behavior at the time.

Youden Square Design   *See* Confounded Designs.

Yule's *Q*   *See* Association, Coefficient of.

***y*-Value**   The numerical value of y along the y-axis or ordinate when
   specifying the coordinates of a point in a set of x and y axes.

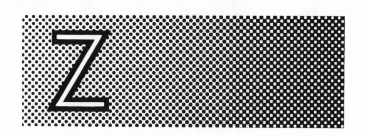

z Distribution   *See* Standard Normal Distribution.

Zero-Order Correlation   In multivariate statistics, the correlation between any two variables, without regard to the remaining variables. (*See also* Multiple Correlation; Part Correlation; Partial Correlation.)

Zero-Sum/Nonzero-Sum Game   In experimental social psychology, a research procedure involving different arrangements of players in a game. In the zero-sum game, the winnings of one player are intentionally arranged to equal the losses of the other. In the nonzero-sum game, winnings of one player are not equal to the losses of the other.

EXAMPLE 1:   A zero-sum game in matrix form:

		Player B	
	Choice	Red	Black
	Red	A wins 6	A wins 5
		B loses 6	B loses 5
Player A			
	Black	A wins 5	A wins 4
		B loses 5	B loses 4

This matrix shows, for example, that if A chooses red and B chooses black, A wins 5. Each player's winnings equal the other's losses, but there is a strategy by which A can maximize his winnings and B can minimize his losses. Rationally, Player A should select the "red" strategy, since A will win at least 5 regardless of what the other player does. Likewise, Player B should select the "black" strategy, since B will lose at most 5, regardless of what the other player does. The game is, overall, quite unfair to Player B, who can never win.

EXAMPLE 2: A nonzero-sum game in matrix form:

		Player B	
		Red	Black
Player A	Red	A wins 15(C) B wins 15(C)	A wins 1(S) B wins 20(T)
	Black	A wins 20(T) B wins 1(S)	A wins 10(P) B wins 10(P)

This game, known as the **Prisoner's Dilemma** (PD) game, also is referred to as a **mixed-motive** game. A "red" strategy of cooperation (C) would be rational, since it maximizes both players' winnings. However, since this nonzero-sum matrix deliberately does not equate wins and losses, other strategies may be chosen: Temptation (T), where each player tries to maximize his winnings at the expense of the other; Sucker (S), where each player loses for trusting the other; and Punishment (P), where both players win less for yielding to temptation.

Zöllner Illusion *See under* Illusions.

z Score *See under* Data Transformation: *z* Transformation.

Z Score *See under* Data Transformation.

z Statistic A test statistic used for testing various hypotheses when the population variance is known. The general form is $z = (\overline{X} - \mu)/\sigma_{\overline{x}}$, where $\overline{X}$ is the sample mean, μ is the population mean, and $\sigma_{\overline{x}}$ is the standard error of the mean.

z Transformation A linear transformation that converts a set of scores, X, into a set of standard scores with a mean of zero and a standard deviation of 1. The *z* transformation is $z = (X - \overline{X})/S$, where $\overline{X}$ and S are the mean and standard deviation of the raw scores. (*See also under* Data Transformation.)

z' Transformation (*syn.* Fisher's z' Transformation) A log transformation of the sample values of the Pearson product moment correlation coefficient *r*. The *z'* transformation is used for such purposes as testing the hypothesis that a sample is randomly selected from a population with a specified value of ρ other than zero, establishing a confidence interval for ρ, or testing the significance of the difference between two sample values of *r*. Conversion tables showing the values of *z'* for various values of *r*, and vice versa, are available in most standard statistical texts.

Appendix A
Guide to
Major Statistical
Procedures

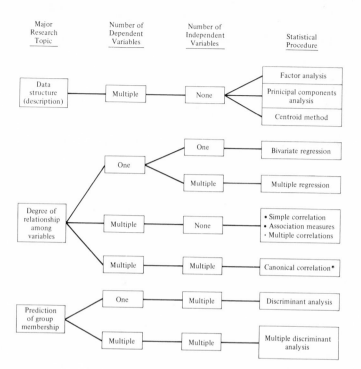

Major Research Topic	Number of Dependent Variables	Number of Independent Variables	Statistical Procedure
Data structure (description)	Multiple	None	Factor analysis
			Prinicipal components analysis
			Centroid method
Degree of relationship among variables	One	One	Bivariate regression
	One	Multiple	Multiple regression
	Multiple	None	• Simple correlation • Association measures · Multiple correlations
	Multiple	Multiple	Canonical correlation*
Prediction of group membership	One	Multiple	Discriminant analysis
	Multiple	Multiple	Multiple discriminant analysis

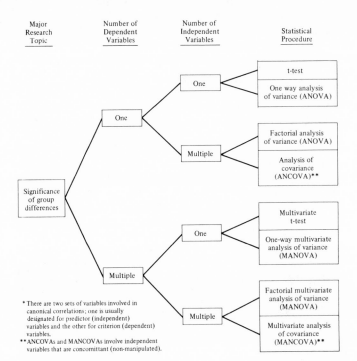

| Major Research Topic | Number of Dependent Variables | Number of Independent Variables | Statistical Procedure |

- Significance of group differences
  - One
    - One
      - t-test
      - One way analysis of variance (ANOVA)
    - Multiple
      - Factorial analysis of variance (ANOVA)
      - Analysis of covariance (ANCOVA)**
  - Multiple
    - One
      - Multivariate t-test
      - One-way multivariate analysis of variance (MANOVA)
    - Multiple
      - Factorial multivariate analysis of variance (MANOVA)
      - Multivariate analysis of covariance (MANCOVA)**

* There are two sets of variables involved in canonical correlations; one is usually designated for predictor (independent) variables and the other for criterion (dependent) variables.

**ANCOVAs and MANCOVAs involve independent variables that are concomittant (non-manipulated).

259

Appendix B
Greek Letter Symbols and Their Common Usages

	Upper Case	Lower Case
Alpha	A	α
Beta	B	β
Gamma	Γ	γ
Delta	Δ	δ
Epsilon	E	ϵ
Zeta	Z	ζ
Eta	H	η
Theta	Θ	θ
Iota	I	i
Kappa	K	κ
Lambda	Λ	λ
Mu	M	μ
Nu	N	ν
Xi	Ξ	ξ
Omicron	O	o
Pi	Π	π
Rho	P	ρ
Sigma	Σ	σ
Tau	T	τ
Upsilon	Υ	υ
Phi	Φ	ϕ
Chi	X	χ
Psi	Ψ	ψ
Omega	Ω	ω

Common Symbolic Uses
of the Greek Alphabet

α	Significance level; probability of a Type I error; intercept constant of a true linear regression equation
β	Probability of a Type II error; slope constant of a true linear regression equation; a standardized coefficient in a multiple regression equation; the Beta probability distribution
$1-\beta$	Power of a statistical test
γ	The Gamma probability distribution
δ or Δ	Difference between variables or parameters; increment or change
ϵ	Random error; difference of an observed score from true score
η	Correlation ratio
η^2	A measure of strength of association
θ or Θ	Any parameter
λ	Likelihood; the parameter of a Poisson distribution
μ	Population mean; a moment of a probability distribution
ν	Degrees of freedom
ξ	Coefficients of orthogonal polynomials
π	Probability; parameter of the Bernoulli and binomial distributions
Π	The product of
ρ	True correlation coefficient
ρ_s	Rank-order correlation coefficient
σ	Population standard deviation
σ^2	Population variance
σ_{xy}	Population covariance
$\sigma_{y \cdot x}$	True standard error of estimate
Σ	The sum of
τ	Kendall's rank correlation coefficient; treatment effect
ϕ	Phi coefficient; the physiological variable in a psychophysical relationship
ϕ^2	Mean square contingency index
ϕ'	Cramer's statistic
χ^2	The chi-square variable or test statistic
ψ	A contrast among treatment means or totals; the psychological variable in a psychophysical relationship
Ψ	Psychology
ω	The set of possible parameter values specified by the null hypothesis;
ω^2	A measure of strength of association
Ω	The set of possible parameter values

Appendix C
Metric Symbols
and Conversion Values

Symbols

G	10^9	Times (a unit);	Giga-	m 10^{-3}	Times (a unit);	Milli—
M	10	Times (a unit);	Mega-	μ 10^{-6}	Times (a unit);	Micro-
K	10^9	Times (a unit);	Kilo-	n 10^{-9}	Times (a unit);	Nano-
H	10^2	Times (a unit);	Hecto-	$\mu\mu$ 10^{-12}	Times (a unit);	Micromicro-
DK	10	Times (a unit);	Deka-	A. Angstrom		
D	10^{-1}	Times (a unit);	Deci-	$\mu\mu$ Micromicron		
C	10^{-2}	Times (a unit);	Centi-	μ Micron		

Area

Unit		Metric Equivalent		U.S. Equivalent	
Square Millimeter	(mm²)	0.000001	Centare	0.00155	Square Inch
Square Centimeter	(cm²)	0.0001	Centare	0.155	Square Inch
Square Decimeter	(dm²)	0.01	Centare	15.5	Square Inches
Centare, also	(ca)	1.0	Centare	10.76	Square Feet
Square Meter	(m²)				
Are, also	(a)	100.0	Centares	0.0247	Acre
Square Dekameter	(dkm²)				
Hectare	(ha)	10,000.0	Centares	2.47	Acres
Square Kilometer	(km²)	1,000,000.0	Centares	0.386	Square Mile

Volume

Unit		Metric Equivalent		U.S. Equivalent	
Cubic Millimeter	(mm³)	0.001	Cubic Centimeter	0.016	Minim
Cubic Centimeter	(cc,cm³)	0.001	Cubic Decimeter	0.016	Cubic Inch
Cubic Decimeter	(dm³)	0.001	Cubic Meter	61.023	Cubic Inches
Stere, also	(s)	1.0	Cubic Meter	1.308	Cubic Yards
Cubic Meter	(m³)				
Cubic Dekameter	(dkm³)	1000.0	Cubic Meters	1307.943	Cubic Yards
Cubic Hectometer	(hm³)	1,000,000.0	Cubic Meters	1,307,942.8	Cubic Yards
Cubic Kilometer	(km³)	1,000,000,000.0	Cubic Meters	0.25	Cubic Mile

Length

Unit		Metric Equivalent		U.S. Equivalent	
Millimeter	(mm)	0.001	Meter	0.03937	Inch
Centimeter	(cm)	0.01	Meter	0.3937	Inch
Decimeter	(dm)	0.1	Meter	3.937	Inches
Meter	(m)	1.0	Meter	39.37	Inches
Dekameter	(dkm)	10.0	Meters	10.93	Yards
Hectometer	(hm)	100.0	Meters	328.08	Feet
Kilometer	(km)	1000.0	Meters	0.6214	Mile

Capacity

Unit		Metric Equivalent		U.S. Equivalent	
Milliliter	(ml)	0.001	Liter	0.034	Fluid Ounce
Centiliter	(cl)	0.01	Liter	0.338	Fluid Ounce
Deciliter	(dl)	0.1	Liter	3.38	Fluid Ounces
Liter	(l)	1.0	Liter	1.05	Liquid Quarts
Dekaliter	(dkl)	10.0	Liters	0.284	Bushel
Hectoliter	(hl)	100.0	Liters	2.837	Bushels
Kiloliter	(kl)	1000.0	Liters	264.18	Gallons

Weight or Mass

Unit		Metric Equivalent		U.S. Equivalent	
Milligram	(mg)	0.001	Gram	0.0154	Grain
Centigram	(cg)	0.01	Gram	0.1543	Grain
Decigram	(dg)	0.1	Gram	1.543	Grains
Gram	(g)	1.0	Gram	15.43	Grains
Dekagram	(dkg)	10.0	Grams	0.3527	Ounces Avoirdupois
Hectogram	(hg)	100.0	Grams	3.527	Ounces Avoirdupois
Kilogram	(kg)	1000.0	Grams	2.2	Pounds Avoirdupois

Appendix D
Table of Random Numbers and Random Permutations of the Digits 0 to 9

This table contains 500 random permutations of the digits 0 to 9 arranged in rows numbered 1 to 500. The permutations have been selected without regard for duplication, so the same permutation may occur more than once. With this sampling procedure, each column provides an effective table of random numbers for the same digits.

Table of Random Numbers

1.	7	6	0	2	8	9	4	1	5	3
2.	4	5	7	6	2	9	0	1	3	8
3.	5	8	4	7	0	6	9	3	2	1
4.	8	5	2	3	1	6	7	0	9	4
5.	1	2	0	7	9	8	6	4	3	5
6.	4	0	5	3	7	8	2	9	1	6
7.	3	4	2	1	7	8	0	5	6	9
8.	8	5	6	7	1	4	3	0	2	9
9.	6	8	7	2	4	1	3	5	9	0
10.	2	3	7	6	9	4	5	0	1	8
11.	0	6	5	3	8	4	1	9	7	2
12.	3	9	7	4	1	8	0	2	6	5
13.	6	3	7	1	5	8	4	2	0	9
14.	9	4	6	7	3	1	0	5	8	2
15.	2	0	8	5	4	7	1	6	3	9
16.	5	6	4	8	3	2	9	0	7	1
17.	8	3	7	0	6	2	5	1	9	4
18.	4	8	1	7	9	6	2	3	5	0
19.	0	2	9	6	8	4	7	5	3	1
20.	9	7	6	4	0	3	5	8	2	1
21.	9	8	7	4	3	1	0	6	2	5
22.	2	4	8	7	9	6	5	1	3	0
23.	9	0	7	8	4	5	1	3	2	6
24.	7	2	5	8	3	0	1	9	4	6
25.	4	9	8	5	1	7	0	2	6	3
26.	3	1	7	2	4	9	0	8	5	6
27.	5	0	7	8	4	3	6	2	9	1

Continued

28.	3	8	5	9	0	1	4	6	2	7
29.	3	5	1	9	2	8	4	7	0	6
30.	3	6	4	2	9	0	5	8	7	1
31.	2	9	0	3	1	5	8	7	4	6
32.	7	6	8	0	5	2	9	4	1	3
33.	7	0	2	6	8	5	4	1	9	3
34.	2	1	8	4	5	3	6	9	7	0
35.	0	1	3	4	2	8	6	5	7	9
36.	5	7	0	8	6	9	1	3	4	2
37.	7	2	4	9	1	5	8	0	6	3
38.	0	6	3	9	5	7	2	8	4	1
39.	1	8	4	2	3	6	9	0	5	7
40.	7	9	6	4	2	0	5	3	8	1
41.	3	7	8	4	0	9	6	1	2	5
42.	3	1	8	7	2	5	6	4	0	9
43.	5	1	3	7	9	6	2	8	4	0
44.	9	8	5	7	3	4	6	2	0	1
45.	9	3	2	5	7	8	1	6	0	4
46.	1	2	0	3	7	6	8	9	4	5
47.	0	4	3	8	7	5	6	1	2	9
48.	9	3	4	5	6	0	8	2	7	1
49.	1	2	4	8	9	5	0	6	7	3
50.	6	5	2	7	3	1	4	9	0	8
51.	4	1	3	9	0	5	7	6	8	2
52.	5	2	8	6	9	3	1	0	4	7
53.	2	9	3	6	7	1	8	4	5	0
54.	4	3	1	8	2	0	9	6	5	7
55.	9	0	4	3	8	6	5	2	7	1
56.	9	1	8	2	5	6	4	3	7	0
57.	5	7	3	6	9	1	0	2	8	4
58.	2	7	4	9	6	5	1	8	0	3
59.	1	6	5	0	4	2	3	7	9	8
60.	1	6	5	8	3	2	0	7	4	9
61.	1	4	2	7	3	6	5	8	0	9
62.	8	0	6	3	1	7	5	9	4	2
63.	0	6	1	4	9	7	8	2	5	3
64.	4	6	1	3	2	5	0	8	9	7
65.	3	4	7	8	1	5	0	2	9	6
66.	6	0	7	8	9	2	3	4	1	5
67.	1	6	2	7	8	5	4	9	3	0
68.	9	8	4	5	0	3	7	6	2	1
69.	1	8	5	7	3	4	0	6	2	9
70.	7	9	4	6	3	5	1	8	2	0
71.	2	6	3	5	9	4	0	8	1	7
72.	6	7	4	9	2	3	0	5	1	8
73.	3	9	6	0	1	8	7	4	2	5
74.	3	7	5	4	1	9	8	0	1	6
75.	2	5	1	6	8	3	4	7	0	9
76.	0	6	9	2	1	8	7	3	4	5
77.	2	9	7	1	0	8	3	4	6	5
78.	0	3	4	7	6	2	1	5	9	8
79.	4	1	7	3	8	0	5	9	6	2
80.	8	9	3	2	6	1	0	7	5	4

Continued

266

81.	6	7	9	0	4	1	2	5	3	8
82.	6	4	5	7	1	8	0	9	3	2
83.	1	4	6	8	3	9	5	2	0	7
84.	7	8	0	5	2	3	4	1	6	9
85.	0	5	1	8	7	4	3	9	6	2
86.	3	5	6	0	4	2	9	7	1	8
87.	3	4	6	9	2	7	8	5	1	0
88.	6	4	9	7	5	0	3	2	1	8
89.	5	2	9	6	0	7	4	3	8	1
90.	3	1	2	6	5	8	4	7	0	9
91.	5	0	3	8	1	4	2	6	9	7
92.	7	6	9	1	3	2	0	5	8	4
93.	2	0	3	6	9	5	4	8	1	7
94.	8	3	9	7	4	5	0	2	6	1
95.	4	3	1	7	9	6	2	0	8	5
96.	1	2	4	7	0	5	6	3	8	9
97.	7	9	5	2	6	1	8	3	4	0
98.	3	7	4	0	5	8	9	6	1	2
99.	5	4	2	9	1	3	7	8	6	0
100.	7	9	4	8	6	2	5	0	1	3
101.	5	0	7	4	1	2	3	6	8	9
102.	7	3	2	6	8	5	9	0	4	1
103.	6	1	4	8	9	7	3	0	5	2
104.	0	6	9	5	3	1	2	7	8	4
105.	1	9	4	5	2	7	6	8	0	3
106.	8	0	7	5	1	2	3	6	9	4
107.	1	0	2	7	5	3	6	9	8	4
108.	0	4	8	5	9	7	2	6	1	3
109.	3	4	7	1	8	9	5	2	0	6
110.	2	3	7	1	8	4	5	6	0	9
111.	8	7	6	5	3	4	2	1	0	9
112.	0	7	9	3	1	2	4	8	5	6
113.	2	5	3	0	6	1	9	8	7	4
114.	4	9	8	6	1	2	0	5	7	3
115.	4	3	7	6	9	2	5	8	0	1
116.	0	2	5	8	6	1	7	3	9	4
117.	4	9	2	6	3	7	8	1	0	5
118.	7	8	2	6	5	0	1	4	3	9
119.	5	8	4	7	6	3	0	1	2	9
120.	2	5	9	3	8	6	7	0	4	1
121.	9	7	6	1	2	3	4	0	5	8
122.	2	1	0	6	4	7	3	8	5	9
123.	1	5	6	0	3	2	8	9	7	4
124.	3	1	5	2	9	0	6	7	4	8
125.	4	9	2	7	0	3	5	6	8	1
126.	4	8	3	7	2	0	9	5	6	1
127.	7	8	2	0	6	4	3	5	9	1
128.	9	1	3	4	0	7	6	8	5	2
129.	9	3	1	8	2	4	0	7	5	6
130.	4	1	9	3	5	8	6	0	2	7
131.	5	9	8	0	3	1	4	2	6	7
132.	5	0	7	3	1	2	8	9	6	4
133.	5	4	8	0	1	9	2	7	3	6

Continued

267

134.	8	3	4	5	1	9	0	2	6	7
135.	7	6	3	9	4	5	0	2	8	1
136.	3	5	8	1	6	2	4	7	9	0
137.	8	3	6	4	7	1	2	5	9	0
138.	5	2	4	3	8	1	9	7	6	0
139.	8	5	6	1	9	4	0	2	7	3
140.	5	0	6	8	4	3	2	7	9	1
141.	8	5	0	3	6	4	1	9	7	2
142.	7	0	5	2	3	1	8	9	4	6
143.	1	9	0	4	7	5	2	8	3	6
144.	3	7	9	2	5	0	6	4	1	8
145.	1	6	7	4	9	5	2	3	8	0
146.	5	0	3	7	6	1	2	9	4	8
147.	7	8	5	4	2	0	1	3	9	6
148.	3	9	4	8	2	0	7	5	1	6
149.	4	7	0	1	8	9	3	5	2	6
150.	5	8	4	1	3	9	6	7	0	2
151.	1	5	0	3	2	8	4	6	9	7
152.	2	8	3	4	9	7	6	1	5	0
153.	2	3	1	4	7	6	9	8	0	5
154.	2	3	9	6	7	0	5	8	1	4
155.	2	9	3	6	4	8	0	7	1	5
156.	6	9	0	3	1	2	8	7	4	5
157.	1	3	4	6	5	0	7	8	2	9
158.	4	3	1	8	0	6	5	2	9	7
159.	3	9	8	7	6	2	5	0	4	1
160.	3	6	9	1	8	2	0	7	5	4
161.	0	3	9	4	8	5	6	2	1	7
162.	7	6	1	8	3	4	5	2	0	9
163.	5	2	7	3	1	8	9	4	6	0
164.	7	1	8	0	9	2	3	6	4	5
165.	7	6	1	9	0	2	8	4	3	5
166.	9	7	6	1	2	5	0	8	3	4
167.	5	4	2	6	0	7	9	8	1	3
168.	2	0	9	4	8	7	3	1	5	6
169.	5	8	0	3	2	9	7	1	4	6
170.	8	1	4	6	7	2	3	5	9	0
171.	4	1	8	6	2	9	3	7	5	0
172.	1	4	5	7	9	2	3	6	8	0
173.	7	9	2	0	3	4	6	1	5	8
174.	0	7	8	3	1	2	9	4	6	5
175.	9	3	4	0	1	6	7	8	5	2
176.	2	0	5	9	3	6	7	8	4	1
177.	4	9	7	3	5	6	0	8	1	2
178.	6	9	1	3	2	8	7	5	0	4
179.	5	4	0	7	1	9	8	3	6	2
180.	3	7	2	5	1	6	0	8	9	4
181.	5	6	7	1	9	8	4	3	2	0
182.	1	6	5	2	9	7	0	4	3	8
183.	8	3	9	6	7	5	1	4	2	0
184.	4	6	7	5	2	9	8	1	0	3
185.	1	5	2	8	3	9	0	4	7	6
186.	8	4	3	2	5	7	9	1	0	6

Continued

187.	9	0	6	8	1	7	3	4	5	2
188.	9	6	4	3	7	0	1	2	5	8
189.	2	3	5	1	7	0	4	8	6	9
190.	0	8	3	6	2	5	7	4	1	9
191.	3	6	4	1	0	8	9	7	2	5
192.	0	9	2	1	3	8	7	6	4	5
193.	7	0	1	9	8	4	5	2	6	3
194.	7	6	1	8	5	0	2	9	3	4
195.	2	3	9	7	6	8	4	5	0	1
196.	5	4	3	2	6	1	9	7	8	0
197.	0	2	3	8	5	6	1	9	7	4
198.	2	1	8	9	6	0	3	5	4	7
199.	0	4	3	9	5	6	7	2	1	8
200.	8	3	1	6	2	7	4	9	5	0
201.	7	9	3	6	1	0	8	4	2	5
202.	3	8	2	6	7	4	9	1	5	0
203.	7	9	4	6	5	2	8	1	3	0
204.	8	3	9	4	5	7	0	1	2	6
205.	1	4	2	3	6	5	9	8	0	7
206.	3	5	9	1	8	0	6	2	7	4
207.	6	9	5	8	0	3	7	4	2	1
208.	0	6	4	9	3	2	7	5	8	1
209.	5	8	7	6	3	2	1	4	9	0
210.	2	1	3	7	6	0	5	4	9	8
211.	7	1	0	3	9	6	2	4	8	5
212.	5	8	2	0	1	7	6	3	4	9
213.	7	0	2	6	4	3	1	9	5	8
214.	2	0	1	5	8	4	3	6	9	7
215.	9	0	5	1	2	7	8	4	6	3
216.	9	5	1	7	0	8	2	6	4	3
217.	0	2	8	5	1	3	4	6	7	9
218.	3	4	2	7	8	6	0	5	1	9
219.	0	2	6	1	7	9	8	4	5	3
220.	8	2	6	4	5	1	7	3	9	0
221.	3	9	4	0	5	1	2	7	8	6
222.	8	4	0	7	9	6	1	5	2	3
223.	7	8	2	5	9	6	3	4	0	1
224.	1	8	5	3	6	0	7	9	2	4
225.	6	4	0	7	5	8	9	3	2	1
226.	7	1	6	4	8	0	5	2	3	9
227.	4	3	9	8	5	2	6	7	1	0
228.	7	0	9	6	3	2	5	4	8	1
229.	2	1	3	4	8	0	7	9	6	5
230.	2	3	9	8	1	7	5	6	0	4
231.	9	0	2	5	4	1	3	6	7	8
232.	6	8	7	0	5	1	3	2	4	9
233.	8	1	6	3	2	7	9	4	5	0
234.	1	8	5	4	6	3	0	2	7	9
235.	3	8	5	6	7	1	4	9	0	2
236.	9	7	5	0	1	4	8	6	2	3
237.	4	8	3	1	9	2	7	6	5	0
238.	6	1	9	0	3	4	7	8	5	2
239.	5	6	4	8	7	9	2	3	1	0

Continued

269

240.	5	0	7	9	8	4	2	6	1	3
241.	9	4	7	6	0	5	3	2	8	1
242.	7	5	3	8	9	4	0	2	1	6
243.	3	2	5	1	6	7	0	9	8	4
244.	3	9	8	4	1	5	6	7	2	0
245.	1	6	4	8	5	9	2	3	7	0
246.	5	7	0	8	2	1	3	9	4	6
247.	8	2	7	4	6	9	1	5	0	3
248.	8	3	5	7	6	1	2	9	0	4
249.	5	0	8	9	3	1	7	2	4	6
250.	1	3	5	2	9	7	8	0	4	6
251.	4	1	8	2	9	6	5	0	3	7
252.	4	7	9	2	3	0	1	8	6	5
253.	8	1	0	3	5	2	9	6	4	7
254.	9	6	2	8	0	7	1	5	3	4
255.	2	5	9	3	0	1	8	7	4	6
256.	9	3	1	4	2	0	8	6	7	5
257.	9	0	5	8	6	2	1	3	4	7
258.	0	1	6	7	3	2	9	5	4	8
259.	2	1	0	7	6	5	4	9	8	3
260.	3	8	1	6	2	7	0	4	5	9
261.	8	6	7	0	2	9	3	5	4	1
262.	8	6	9	0	4	2	1	5	7	3
263.	8	1	4	2	0	6	5	7	9	3
264.	6	5	8	2	7	4	0	1	3	9
265.	1	4	2	6	8	7	3	5	9	0
266.	3	2	1	4	8	0	7	5	9	6
267.	6	0	5	9	4	3	7	1	8	2
268.	0	3	2	1	4	7	6	5	9	8
269.	5	3	6	4	7	2	8	0	9	1
270.	0	4	1	2	8	6	9	7	5	3
271.	3	8	2	4	7	1	6	9	5	0
272.	2	9	8	6	3	5	7	1	4	0
273.	2	4	0	9	6	7	3	1	8	5
274.	6	1	8	4	0	3	2	9	7	5
275.	2	6	8	0	7	4	1	5	9	3
276.	4	5	0	7	3	1	6	9	8	2
277.	3	7	2	9	8	5	6	4	1	0
278.	9	2	8	6	1	5	7	0	4	3
279.	3	2	1	6	5	9	7	0	8	4
280.	6	1	9	8	5	0	4	3	2	7
281.	1	2	0	3	8	4	5	9	6	7
282.	8	0	7	2	9	1	3	4	5	6
283.	0	1	6	2	5	7	3	8	9	4
284.	9	2	0	5	4	1	8	7	6	3
285.	4	5	8	3	6	2	1	0	9	7
286.	0	2	4	7	6	9	5	1	3	8
287.	1	6	0	5	4	7	8	3	2	9
288.	8	7	1	3	4	2	0	5	6	9
289.	0	2	8	4	3	9	5	7	1	6
290.	8	5	7	4	9	6	0	1	3	2
291.	2	8	0	4	9	7	5	3	6	1
292.	2	3	9	7	8	4	6	0	1	5

Continued

293.	9	7	6	2	4	1	5	8	3	0
294.	0	5	8	3	1	6	9	4	2	7
295.	4	7	9	2	3	1	6	5	0	8
296.	5	7	3	0	6	1	8	9	2	4
297.	6	4	1	8	0	9	7	3	2	5
298.	2	0	3	7	1	5	9	4	8	6
299.	6	1	8	5	7	3	9	0	4	2
300.	3	8	0	4	1	9	2	5	6	7
301.	7	8	4	6	2	5	9	3	0	1
302.	1	4	0	7	2	9	6	8	5	3
303.	0	8	1	6	5	4	7	3	9	2
304.	3	9	8	2	4	1	5	0	6	7
305.	5	7	4	1	8	0	3	2	9	6
306.	6	5	4	1	3	9	8	2	7	0
307.	7	3	9	5	1	4	0	8	6	2
308.	1	7	8	9	6	3	2	5	0	4
309.	4	2	7	0	3	6	9	5	8	1
310.	8	1	3	2	7	0	9	5	6	4
311.	1	6	0	2	4	9	5	8	7	3
312.	4	1	5	8	6	9	2	0	7	3
313.	3	5	6	2	4	7	0	1	8	9
314.	1	0	9	7	6	2	5	4	8	3
315.	8	0	2	7	4	3	1	6	5	9
316.	0	1	4	2	5	9	3	8	7	6
317.	7	5	9	4	2	6	3	1	8	0
318.	1	3	7	2	9	0	8	6	4	5
319.	9	7	6	2	0	1	3	5	8	4
320.	7	1	3	5	8	6	9	2	0	4
321.	7	1	0	9	6	5	4	8	2	3
322.	7	4	0	5	1	3	9	6	2	8
323.	0	1	9	2	8	4	7	6	3	5
324.	1	3	7	5	4	2	0	9	8	6
325.	8	6	3	1	4	5	2	7	9	0
326.	3	5	1	7	0	9	4	6	2	8
327.	3	9	2	0	5	8	4	6	7	1
328.	0	8	3	1	2	7	6	5	4	9
329.	5	3	2	0	6	7	9	4	8	1
330.	4	9	6	2	5	3	1	7	0	8
331.	9	3	1	2	4	7	6	8	0	5
332.	2	5	0	6	9	7	8	1	3	4
333.	5	9	7	4	6	8	0	2	1	3
334.	3	2	6	4	5	1	8	0	7	9
335.	5	8	9	1	4	0	7	6	2	3
336.	1	2	6	9	5	8	0	4	7	3
337.	5	8	2	0	1	3	4	6	7	9
338.	1	5	8	2	0	9	6	4	7	3
339.	2	4	7	3	6	9	8	1	5	0
340.	3	5	0	2	1	9	4	6	7	8
341.	4	9	1	3	2	8	0	6	7	5
342.	3	8	7	9	0	5	1	4	6	2
343.	9	5	8	3	6	0	1	4	7	2
344.	3	6	2	9	7	4	8	0	1	5
345.	0	8	2	9	3	4	6	5	1	7

Continued

271

346.	9	2	8	6	7	1	4	3	0	5
347.	4	7	6	3	5	2	0	1	9	8
348.	1	0	3	8	6	2	9	5	7	4
349.	0	7	6	4	1	3	2	8	5	9
350.	8	2	0	7	9	4	6	5	1	3
351.	8	7	5	3	0	1	6	9	4	2
352.	0	4	8	9	1	5	7	3	2	6
353.	9	0	6	2	1	4	5	7	3	8
354.	8	2	7	6	3	9	5	0	1	4
355.	6	2	5	7	9	3	1	8	4	0
356.	6	2	4	5	0	8	1	7	3	9
357.	7	4	9	8	0	3	6	2	5	1
358.	3	9	8	4	0	5	7	2	6	1
359.	2	8	6	4	7	1	9	3	0	5
360.	0	3	4	2	6	9	7	5	8	1
361.	5	8	2	9	1	4	6	7	0	3
362.	5	2	9	1	7	0	4	3	8	6
363.	9	1	0	8	5	3	6	4	2	7
364.	3	8	7	6	9	0	2	1	5	4
365.	3	2	5	8	0	4	7	6	1	9
366.	8	2	7	1	3	6	5	4	9	0
367.	7	1	3	4	8	6	5	9	0	2
368.	0	4	9	1	6	7	5	2	8	3
369.	1	5	8	9	2	7	3	4	6	0
370.	9	7	5	6	8	4	2	3	0	1
371.	1	6	9	4	3	2	5	7	8	0
372.	6	0	8	9	1	3	5	7	2	4
373.	0	2	5	9	1	4	8	7	3	6
374.	5	2	7	6	8	0	4	3	9	1
375.	7	2	9	3	5	8	0	1	6	4
376.	4	6	3	5	0	2	1	7	9	8
377.	2	7	6	1	4	5	3	0	9	8
378.	6	2	5	9	4	0	1	3	7	8
379.	0	9	3	4	6	5	1	8	2	7
380.	1	8	7	5	0	4	9	6	3	2
381.	3	5	7	4	6	0	9	1	2	8
382.	4	9	0	3	6	2	7	5	1	8
383.	3	0	7	8	4	5	1	6	2	9
384.	9	1	8	7	6	0	4	3	5	2
385.	4	7	3	6	8	9	0	2	1	5
386.	4	5	1	0	3	2	6	8	7	9
387.	2	3	5	4	6	9	8	1	7	0
388.	6	5	7	4	8	9	3	1	2	0
389.	2	1	0	7	3	9	5	8	4	6
390.	6	4	9	7	0	5	8	3	1	2
391.	5	8	7	4	1	6	0	2	9	3
392.	1	8	9	7	2	5	4	0	3	6
393.	2	8	6	0	4	1	5	3	9	7
394.	9	5	2	0	7	1	6	4	8	3
395.	6	8	9	1	5	2	7	0	3	4
396.	5	4	1	3	2	0	7	6	8	9
397.	5	4	0	8	1	9	2	3	7	6
398.	9	2	6	0	7	5	8	1	3	4

Continued

399.	8	2	1	5	6	7	9	0	3	4
400.	7	3	5	2	4	1	9	0	6	8
401.	6	8	9	2	4	0	3	1	5	7
402.	4	0	3	8	1	9	7	5	6	2
403.	4	7	9	3	5	0	6	8	2	1
404.	3	8	9	4	0	2	7	1	6	5
405.	6	0	1	9	3	2	5	4	7	8
406.	4	5	7	8	1	2	9	0	3	6
407.	5	0	6	8	9	4	1	2	3	7
408.	2	0	1	3	8	6	9	4	5	7
409.	6	2	4	5	1	0	3	7	9	8
410.	0	4	6	1	3	5	7	9	2	8
411.	0	2	8	9	5	3	7	6	1	4
412.	7	9	6	0	3	1	4	2	5	8
413.	1	0	6	4	5	9	2	3	8	7
414.	9	0	8	6	1	4	3	7	5	2
415.	6	0	7	3	4	8	2	9	1	5
416.	1	0	9	7	8	2	3	6	4	5
417.	7	3	0	6	2	1	8	9	4	5
418.	8	7	0	6	4	9	2	5	1	3
419.	3	0	6	7	4	2	1	8	9	5
420.	1	9	4	8	3	0	7	6	2	5
421.	0	3	8	5	9	4	1	6	2	7
422.	1	5	0	7	3	4	9	2	6	8
423.	8	0	2	7	4	1	3	9	5	6
424.	6	7	0	9	1	2	8	4	5	3
425.	1	5	6	2	0	9	8	3	4	7
426.	1	6	9	5	7	8	3	0	2	4
427.	0	4	9	5	8	2	6	1	7	3
428.	9	7	6	5	3	4	8	0	2	1
429.	5	0	6	7	1	8	2	9	4	3
430.	8	3	7	6	5	0	9	4	2	1
431.	4	8	9	5	6	3	7	2	0	1
432.	8	4	9	3	0	2	7	5	6	1
433.	6	4	8	1	9	2	0	7	5	3
434.	8	9	0	2	3	7	4	6	1	5
435.	6	4	1	7	2	3	9	0	8	5
436.	4	5	6	9	7	0	2	8	1	3
437.	1	0	3	7	4	6	9	2	8	5
438.	7	0	1	4	3	9	2	6	5	8
439.	0	7	9	2	6	5	4	8	1	3
440.	0	9	8	1	7	2	5	3	4	6
441.	9	2	6	4	3	8	1	5	0	7
442.	2	6	7	3	5	4	0	9	8	1
443.	0	9	2	8	1	4	3	7	5	6
444.	9	7	0	6	4	3	2	8	5	1
445.	6	9	7	0	8	2	3	1	4	5
446.	0	2	8	4	3	9	7	6	5	1
447.	8	5	6	3	4	1	0	7	2	9
448.	4	8	9	5	0	1	2	6	3	7
449.	2	6	5	9	8	7	4	0	3	1
450.	8	3	6	4	2	5	1	0	9	7
451.	9	7	2	6	0	8	3	4	5	1

Continued

273

452.	3	4	0	7	2	6	5	8	9	1
453.	1	8	7	6	5	0	9	2	4	3
454.	9	5	0	1	4	7	8	3	2	6
455.	5	2	4	7	8	9	1	0	3	6
456.	5	2	8	9	7	4	6	3	1	0
457.	9	0	4	1	8	3	6	5	7	2
458.	2	4	0	7	5	9	3	8	1	6
459.	5	9	3	1	2	0	6	8	4	7
460.	5	0	2	4	3	6	8	1	9	7
461.	1	7	5	4	2	0	3	6	9	8
462.	4	8	0	1	6	3	9	2	5	7
463.	2	8	5	1	7	4	0	9	6	3
464.	4	0	6	5	9	1	3	2	8	7
465.	7	9	0	1	4	6	5	2	3	8
466.	6	2	3	4	5	8	9	0	7	1
467.	0	5	7	4	3	1	9	2	6	8
468.	8	1	9	0	2	5	4	7	6	3
469.	0	5	7	6	9	3	1	4	8	2
470.	1	5	3	6	8	9	7	2	4	0
471.	5	6	2	3	8	7	0	9	4	1
472.	9	4	0	2	5	8	6	7	1	3
473.	5	8	6	3	1	9	2	7	4	0
474.	0	5	9	3	6	4	2	7	1	8
475.	0	7	1	6	2	4	3	5	8	9
476.	2	3	6	7	1	8	9	0	5	4
477.	3	1	6	5	9	8	2	7	0	4
478.	4	9	6	3	1	2	0	5	7	8
479.	2	9	8	6	5	3	7	4	0	1
480.	5	7	0	6	9	4	3	1	8	2
481.	9	6	5	2	1	7	8	3	0	4
482.	8	1	2	0	4	5	3	7	9	6
483.	9	7	3	8	1	4	6	5	2	0
484.	6	8	3	2	1	7	9	0	5	4
485.	5	9	6	2	8	0	7	3	1	4
486.	4	3	0	2	6	8	9	1	5	7
487.	3	6	0	2	7	4	5	8	9	1
488.	2	5	0	4	1	7	8	6	9	3
489.	1	6	2	5	7	4	3	8	0	9
490.	8	9	5	0	1	6	2	7	4	3
491.	9	5	3	8	0	7	4	6	1	2
492.	3	9	1	2	6	4	8	5	7	0
493.	4	0	5	1	9	8	6	3	7	2
494.	6	3	2	1	9	8	0	5	4	7
495.	6	5	7	4	3	0	2	1	9	8
496.	6	1	7	5	3	8	2	4	9	0
497.	7	8	5	1	4	6	9	0	3	2
498.	6	5	8	0	3	1	7	9	4	2
499.	4	9	5	7	8	1	0	6	3	2
500.	4	5	8	6	2	1	0	7	3	9

Appendix E
Statistical Tables

Table 1 The Standard Normal Curve

(1)	(2)	(3)	(4)	(1)	(2)	(3)	(4)
z	A AREA FROM MEAN TO z	B AREA IN LARGER PORTION	C AREA IN SMALLER PORTION	z	A AREA FROM MEAN TO z	B AREA IN LARGER PORTION	C AREA IN SMALLER PORTION
0.00	.0000	.5000	.5000	0.30	.1179	.6179	.3821
0.01	.0040	.5040	.4960	0.31	.1217	.6217	.3783
0.02	.0080	.5080	.4920	0.32	.1255	.6255	.3745
0.03	.0120	.5120	.4880	0.33	.1293	.6293	.3707
0.04	.0160	.5160	.4840	0.34	.1331	.6331	.3669
0.05	.0199	.5199	.4801	0.35	.1368	.6368	.3632
0.06	.0239	.5239	.4761	0.36	.1406	.6406	.3594
0.07	.0279	.5279	.4721	0.37	.1443	.6443	.3557
0.08	.0319	.5319	.4681	0.38	.1480	.6480	.3520
0.09	.0359	.5359	.4641	0.39	.1517	.6517	.3483
0.10	.0398	.5398	.4602	0.40	.1554	.6554	.3446
0.11	.0438	.5438	.4562	0.41	.1591	.6591	.3409
0.12	.0478	.5478	.4522	0.42	.1628	.6628	.3372
0.13	.0517	.5517	.4483	0.43	.1664	.6664	.3336
0.14	.0557	.5557	.4443	0.44	.1700	.6700	.3300
0.15	.0596	.5596	.4404	0.45	.1736	.6736	.3264
0.16	.0636	.5636	.4364	0.46	.1772	.6772	.3228
0.17	.0675	.5675	.4325	0.47	.1808	.6808	.3192
0.18	.0714	.5714	.4286	0.48	.1844	.6844	.3156
0.19	.0753	.5753	.4247	0.49	.1879	.6879	.3121
0.20	.0793	.5793	.4207	0.50	.1915	.6915	.3085
0.21	.0832	.5832	.4168	0.51	.1950	.6950	.3050
0.22	.0871	.5871	.4129	0.52	.1985	.6985	.3015
0.23	.0910	.5910	.4090	0.53	.2019	.7019	.2981
0.24	.0948	.5948	.4052	0.54	.2054	.7054	.2946
0.25	.0987	.5987	.4013	0.55	.2088	.7088	.2912
0.26	.1026	.6026	.3974	0.56	.2123	.7123	.2877
0.27	.1064	.6064	.3936	0.57	.2157	.7157	.2843
0.28	.1103	.6103	.3897	0.58	.2190	.7190	.2810
0.29	.1141	.6141	.3859	0.59	.2224	.7224	.2776

Continued

275

Table 1 (Continued)

(1)	(2)	(3)	(4)	(1)	(2)	(3)	(4)
	A AREA FROM MEAN TO	B AREA IN LARGER PORTION	C AREA IN SMALLER PORTION		A AREA FROM MEAN TO	B AREA IN LARGER PORTION	C AREA IN SMALLER PORTION
z	z			z	z		
0.60	.2257	.7257	.2743	0.95	.3289	.8289	.1711
0.61	.2291	.7291	.2709	0.96	.3315	.8315	.1685
0.62	.2324	.7324	.2676	0.97	.3340	.8340	.1660
0.63	.2357	.7357	.2643	0.98	.3365	.8365	.1635
0.64	.2389	.7389	.2611	0.99	.3389	.8389	.1611
0.65	.2422	.7422	.2578	1.00	.3413	.8413	.1587
0.66	.2454	.7454	.2546	1.01	.3438	.8438	.1562
0.67	.2486	.7486	.2514	1.02	.3461	.8461	.1539
0.68	.2517	.7517	.2483	1.03	.3485	.8485	.1515
0.69	.2549	.7549	.2451	1.04	.3508	.8508	.1492
0.70	.2580	.7580	.2420	1.05	.3531	.8531	.1469
0.71	.2611	.7611	.2389	1.06	.3554	.8554	.1446
0.72	.2642	.7642	.2358	1.07	.3577	.8577	.1423
0.73	.2673	.7673	.2327	1.08	.3599	.8599	.1401
0.74	.2704	.7704	.2296	1.09	.3621	.8621	.1379
0.75	.2734	.7734	.2266	1.10	.3643	.8643	.1357
0.76	.2764	.7764	.2236	1.11	.3665	.8665	.1335
0.77	.2794	.7794	.2206	1.12	.3686	.8686	.1314
0.78	.2823	.7823	.2177	1.13	.3708	.8708	.1292
0.79	.2852	.7852	.2148	1.14	.3729	.8729	.1271
0.80	.2881	.7881	.2119	1.15	.3749	.8749	.1251
0.81	.2910	.7910	.2090	1.16	.3770	.8770	.1230
0.82	.2939	.7939	.2061	1.17	.3790	.8790	.1210
0.83	.2967	.7967	.2033	1.18	.3810	.8810	.1190
0.84	.2995	.7995	.2005	1.19	.3830	.8830	.1170
0.85	.3023	.8023	.1977	1.20	.3849	.8849	.1151
0.86	.3051	.8051	.1949	1.21	.3869	.8869	.1131
0.87	.3078	.8078	.1922	1.22	.3888	.8888	.1112
0.88	.3106	.8106	.1894	1.23	.3907	.8907	.1093
0.89	.3133	.8133	.1867	1.24	.3925	.8925	.1075
0.90	.3159	.8159	.1841	1.25	.3944	.8944	.1056
0.91	.3186	.8186	.1814	1.26	.3962	.8962	.1038
0.92	.3212	.8212	.1788	1.27	.3980	.8980	.1020
0.93	.3238	.8238	.1762	1.28	.3997	.8997	.1003
0.94	.3264	.8264	.1736	1.29	.4015	.9015	.0985

Continued

Table 1 *(Continued)*

(1)	(2)	(3)	(4)	(1)	(2)	(3)	(4)
	A	B	C		A	B	C
	AREA FROM	AREA IN	AREA IN		AREA FROM	AREA IN	AREA IN
	MEAN TO	LARGER	SMALLER		MEAN TO	LARGER	SMALLER
z	z	PORTION	PORTION	z	z	PORTION	PORTION
1.30	.4032	.9032	.0968	1.65	.4505	.9505	.0495
1.31	.4049	.9049	.0951	1.66	.4515	.9515	.0485
1.32	.4066	.9066	.0934	1.67	.4525	.9525	.0475
1.33	.4082	.9082	.0918	1.68	.4535	.9535	.0465
1.34	.4099	.9099	.0901	1.69	.4545	.9545	.0455
1.35	.4115	.9115	.0885	1.70	.4554	.9554	.0446
1.36	.4131	.9131	.0869	1.71	.4564	.9564	.0436
1.37	.4147	.9147	.0853	1.72	.4573	.9573	.0427
1.38	.4162	.9162	.0838	1.73	.4582	.9582	.0418
1.39	.4177	.9177	.0823	1.74	.4591	.9591	.0409
1.40	.4192	.9192	.0808	1.75	.4599	.9599	.0401
1.41	.4207	.9207	.0793	1.76	.4608	.9608	.0392
1.42	.4222	.9222	.0778	1.77	.4616	.9616	.0384
1.43	.4236	.9236	.0764	1.78	.4625	.9625	.0375
1.44	.4251	.9251	.0749	1.79	.4633	.9633	.0367
1.45	.4265	.9265	.0735	1.80	.4641	.9641	.0359
1.46	.4279	.9279	.0721	1.81	.4649	.9649	.0351
1.47	.4292	.9292	.0708	1.82	.4656	.9656	.0344
1.48	.4306	.9306	.0694	1.83	.4664	.9664	.0336
1.49	.4319	.9319	.0681	1.84	.4671	.9671	.0329
1.50	.4332	.9332	.0668	1.85	.4678	.9678	.0322
1.51	.4345	.9345	.0655	1.86	.4686	.9686	.0314
1.52	.4357	.9357	.0643	1.87	.4693	.9693	.0307
1.53	.4370	.9370	.0630	1.88	.4699	.9699	.0301
1.54	.4382	.9382	.0618	1.89	.4706	.9706	.0294
1.55	.4394	.9394	.0606	1.90	.4713	.9713	.0287
1.56	.4406	.9406	.0594	1.91	.4719	.9719	.0281
1.57	.4418	.9418	.0582	1.92	.4726	.9726	.0274
1.58	.4429	.9429	.0571	1.93	.4732	.9732	.0268
1.59	.4441	.9441	.0559	1.94	.4738	.9738	.0262
1.60	.4452	.9452	.0548	1.95	.4744	.9744	.0256
1.61	.4463	.9463	.0537	1.96	.4750	.9750	.0250
1.62	.4474	.9474	.0526	1.97	.4756	.9756	.0244
1.63	.4484	.9484	.0516	1.98	.4761	.9761	.0239
1.64	.4495	.9495	.0505	1.99	.4767	.9767	.0233

Continued

Table 1 *(Continued)*

(1)	(2)	(3)	(4)	(1)	(2)	(3)	(4)
z	A AREA FROM MEAN TO z	B AREA IN LARGER PORTION	C AREA IN SMALLER PORTION	z	A AREA FROM MEAN TO z	B AREA IN LARGER PORTION	C AREA IN SMALLER PORTION
2.00	.4772	.9772	.0228	2.35	.4906	.9906	.0094
2.01	.4778	.9778	.0222	2.36	.4909	.9909	.0091
2.02	.4783	.9783	.0217	2.37	.4911	.9911	.0089
2.03	.4788	.9788	.0212	2.38	.4913	.9913	.0087
2.04	.4793	.9793	.0207	2.39	.4916	.9916	.0084
2.05	.4798	.9798	.0202	2.40	.4918	.9918	.0082
2.06	.4803	.9803	.0197	2.41	.4920	.9920	.0080
2.07	.4808	.9808	.0192	2.42	.4922	.9922	.0078
2.08	.4812	.9812	.0188	2.43	.4925	.9925	.0075
2.09	.4817	.9817	.0183	2.44	.4927	.9927	.0073
2.10	.4821	.9821	.0179	2.45	.4929	.9929	.0071
2.11	.4826	.9826	.0174	2.46	.4931	.9931	.0069
2.12	.4830	.9830	.0170	2.47	.4932	.9932	.0068
2.13	.4834	.9834	.0166	2.48	.4934	.9934	.0066
2.14	.4838	.9838	.0162	2.49	.4936	.9936	.0064
2.15	.4842	.9842	.0158	2.50	.4938	.9938	.0062
2.16	.4846	.9846	.0154	2.51	.4940	.9940	.0060
2.17	.4850	.9850	.0150	2.52	.4941	.9941	.0059
2.18	.4854	.9854	.0146	2.53	.4943	.9943	.0057
2.19	.4857	.9857	.0143	2.54	.4945	.9945	.0055
2.20	.4861	.9861	.0139	2.55	.4946	.9946	.0054
2.21	.4864	.9864	.0136	2.56	.4948	.9948	.0052
2.22	.4868	.9868	.0132	2.57	.4949	.9949	.0051
2.23	.4871	.9871	.0129	2.58	.4951	.9951	.0049
2.24	.4875	.9875	.0125	2.59	.4952	.9952	.0048
2.25	.4878	.9878	.0122	2.60	.4953	.9953	.0047
2.26	.4881	.9881	.0119	2.61	.4955	.9955	.0045
2.27	.4884	.9884	.0116	2.62	.4956	.9956	.0044
2.28	.4887	.9887	.0113	2.63	.4957	.9957	.0043
2.29	.4890	.9890	.0110	2.64	.4959	.9959	.0041
2.30	.4893	.9893	.0107	2.65	.4960	.9960	.0040
2.31	.4896	.9896	.0104	2.66	.4961	.9961	.0039
2.32	.4898	.9898	.0102	2.67	.4962	.9962	.0038
2.33	.4901	.9901	.0099	2.68	.4963	.9963	.0037
2.34	.4904	.9904	.0096	2.69	.4964	.9964	.0036

Continued

Table 1 *(Continued)*

(1)	(2)	(3)	(4)	(1)	(2)	(3)	(4)
z	A AREA FROM MEAN TO z	B AREA IN LARGER PORTION	C AREA IN SMALLER PORTION	z	A AREA FROM MEAN TO z	B AREA IN LARGER PORTION	C AREA IN SMALLER PORTION
2.70	.4965	.9965	.0035	3.00	.4987	.9987	.0013
2.71	.4966	.9966	.0034	3.01	.4987	.9987	.0013
2.72	.4967	.9967	.0033	3.02	.4987	.9987	.0013
2.73	.4968	.9968	.0032	3.03	.4988	.9988	.0012
2.74	.4969	.9969	.0031	3.04	.4988	.9988	.0012
2.75	.4970	.9970	.0030	3.05	.4989	.9989	.0011
2.76	.4971	.9971	.0029	3.06	.4989	.9989	.0011
2.77	.4972	.9972	.0028	3.07	.4989	.9989	.0011
2.78	.4973	.9973	.0027	3.08	.4990	.9990	.0010
2.79	.4974	.9974	.0026	3.09	.4990	.9990	.0010
2.80	.4974	.9974	.0026	3.10	.4990	.9990	.0010
2.81	.4975	.9975	.0025	3.11	.4991	.9991	.0009
2.82	.4976	.9976	.0024	3.12	.4991	.9991	.0009
2.83	.4977	.9977	.0023	3.13	.4991	.9991	.0009
2.84	.4977	.9977	.0023	3.14	.4992	.9992	.0008
2.85	.4978	.9978	.0022	3.15	.4992	.9992	.0008
2.86	.4979	.9979	.0021	3.16	.4992	.9992	.0008
2.87	.4979	.9979	.0021	3.17	.4992	.9992	.0008
2.88	.4980	.9980	.0020	3.18	.4993	.9993	.0007
2.89	.4981	.9981	.0019	3.19	.4993	.9993	.0007
2.90	.4981	.9981	.0019	3.20	.4993	.9993	.0007
2.91	.4982	.9982	.0018	3.21	.4993	.9993	.0007
2.92	.4982	.9982	.0018	3.22	.4994	.9994	.0006
2.93	.4983	.9983	.0017	3.23	.4994	.9994	.0006
2.94	.4984	.9984	.0016	3.24	.4994	.9994	.0006
2.95	.4984	.9984	.0016	3.30	.4995	.9995	.0005
2.96	.4985	.9985	.0015	3.40	.4997	.9997	.0003
2.97	.4985	.9985	.0015	3.50	.4998	.9998	.0002
2.98	.4986	.9986	.0014	3.60	.4998	.9998	.0002
2.99	.4986	.9986	.0014	3.70	.4999	.9999	.0001

SOURCE: Reprinted from Appendix C of N. M. Downie and A. R. Starry, *Descriptive and Inferential Statistics* (New York: Harper & Row, 1977), pp. 301–305. Reprinted with permission.

Table 2 Critical Values of the *t* Distribution

	Levels of Significance (α)			
		DIRECTIONAL TEST		
	.05	.025	.005	.0005
		NONDIRECTIONAL TEST		
df	.1	.05	.01	.001
1	6.314	12.706	63.657	636.619
2	2.920	4.303	9.925	31.598
3	2.353	3.182	5.841	12.941
4	2.132	2.776	4.604	8.610
5	2.015	2.571	4.032	6.859
6	1.943	2.447	3.707	5.959
7	1.895	2.365	3.499	5.405
8	1.860	2.306	3.355	5.041
9	1.833	2.262	3.250	4.781
10	1.812	2.228	3.169	4.587
11	1.796	2.201	3.106	4.437
12	1.782	2.179	3.055	4.318
13	1.771	2.160	3.012	4.221
14	1.761	2.145	2.977	4.140
15	1.753	2.131	2.947	4.073
16	1.746	2.120	2.921	4.015
17	1.740	2.110	2.898	3.965
18	1.734	2.101	2.878	3.922
19	1.729	2.093	2.861	3.883
20	1.725	2.086	2.845	3.850
21	1.721	2.080	2.831	3.819
22	1.717	2.074	2.819	3.792
23	1.714	2.069	2.807	3.767
24	1.711	2.064	2.797	3.745
25	1.708	2.060	2.787	3.725
26	1.706	2.056	2.779	3.707
27	1.703	2.052	2.771	3.690
28	1.701	2.048	2.763	3.674
29	1.699	2.045	2.756	3.659
30	1.697	2.042	2.750	3.646
40	1.684	2.021	2.704	3.551
60	1.671	2.000	2.660	3.460
120	1.658	1.980	2.617	3.373
∞	1.645	1.960	2.576	3.291

SOURCE: Abridged from Table III of R. A. Fisher and F. Yates, *Statistical Tables for Biological, Agricultural, and Medical Research,* published by Longman Group Ltd., London (previously published by Oliver and Boyd Ltd., Edinburgh). Reprinted with permission of the authors and publishers.

Table 3 Critical Values of the X² Distribution

		Levels of Significance			
df	.10	.05	.02	.01	.001
1	2.706	3.841	5.412	6.635	10.827
2	4.605	5.991	7.824	9.210	13.815
3	6.251	7.815	9.837	11.345	16.268
4	7.779	9.488	11.668	13.277	18.465
5	9.236	11.070	13.388	15.086	20.517
6	10.645	12.592	15.033	16.812	22.457
7	12.017	14.067	16.622	18.475	24.322
8	13.362	15.507	18.168	20.090	26.125
9	14.684	16.919	19.679	21.666	27.877
10	15.987	18.307	21.161	23.209	29.588
11	17.275	19.675	22.618	24.725	31.264
12	18.549	21.026	24.054	26.217	32.909
13	19.812	22.362	25.472	27.688	34.528
14	21.064	23.685	26.873	29.141	36.123
15	22.307	24.996	28.259	30.578	37.697
16	23.542	26.296	29.633	32.000	39.252
17	24.769	27.587	30.995	33.409	40.790
18	25.989	28.869	32.346	34.805	42.312
19	27.204	30.144	33.687	36.191	43.820
20	28.412	31.410	35.020	37.566	45.315
21	29.615	32.671	36.343	38.932	46.797
22	30.813	33.924	37.659	40.289	48.268
23	32.007	35.172	38.968	41.638	49.728
24	33.196	36.415	40.270	42.980	51.179
25	34.382	37.652	41.566	44.314	52.620
26	35.563	38.885	42.856	45.642	54.052
27	36.741	40.113	44.140	46.963	55.476
28	37.916	41.337	45.419	48.278	56.893
29	39.087	42.557	46.693	49.588	58.302
30	40.256	43.773	47.962	50.892	59.703

SOURCE: From Table IV of R. A. Fisher and F. Yates, *Statistical Tables for Biological, Agricultural, and Medical Research*, published by Longman Group Ltd., London (previously published by Oliver and Boyd Ltd., Edinburgh). Reprinted with permission of the authors and publishers.

Table 4a Critical Values of the F Distribution

Degrees of Freedom for the Denominator

		1	2	3	4	5	6	7	8	9	10	11	12
	1	161	200	216	225	230	234	237	239	241	242	243	244
		4,052	**4,999**	**5,403**	**5,625**	**5,764**	**5,859**	**5,928**	**5,981**	**6,022**	**6,056**	**6,082**	**6,106**
	2	18.51	19.00	19.16	19.25	19.30	19.33	19.36	19.37	19.38	19.39	19.40	19.41
		98.49	**99.00**	**99.17**	**99.25**	**99.30**	**99.33**	**99.34**	**99.36**	**99.38**	**99.40**	**99.41**	**99.42**
	3	10.13	9.55	9.28	9.12	9.01	8.94	8.88	8.84	8.81	8.78	8.76	8.74
		34.12	**30.82**	**29.46**	**28.71**	**28.24**	**27.91**	**27.67**	**27.49**	**27.34**	**27.23**	**27.13**	**27.05**
	4	7.71	6.94	6.59	6.39	6.26	6.16	6.09	6.04	6.00	5.96	5.93	5.91
		21.20	**18.00**	**16.69**	**15.98**	**15.52**	**15.21**	**14.98**	**14.80**	**14.66**	**14.54**	**14.45**	**14.37**
	5	6.61	5.79	5.41	5.19	5.05	4.95	4.88	4.82	4.78	4.74	4.70	4.68
		16.26	**13.27**	**12.06**	**11.39**	**10.97**	**10.67**	**10.45**	**10.27**	**10.15**	**10.05**	**9.96**	**9.89**
	6	5.99	5.14	4.76	4.53	4.39	4.28	4.21	4.15	4.10	4.06	4.03	4.00
		13.74	**10.92**	**9.78**	**9.15**	**8.75**	**8.47**	**8.26**	**8.10**	**7.98**	**7.87**	**7.79**	**7.72**
	7	5.59	4.74	4.35	4.12	3.97	3.87	3.79	3.73	3.68	3.63	3.60	3.57
		12.25	**9.55**	**8.45**	**7.85**	**7.46**	**7.19**	**7.00**	**6.84**	**6.71**	**6.62**	**6.54**	**6.47**
	8	5.32	4.46	4.07	3.84	3.69	3.58	3.50	3.44	3.39	3.34	3.31	3.28
		11.26	**8.65**	**7.59**	**7.01**	**6.63**	**6.37**	**6.19**	**6.03**	**5.91**	**5.82**	**5.74**	**5.67**
	9	5.12	4.26	3.86	3.63	3.48	3.37	3.29	3.23	3.18	3.13	3.10	3.07
		10.56	**8.02**	**6.99**	**6.42**	**6.06**	**5.80**	**5.62**	**5.47**	**5.35**	**5.26**	**5.18**	**5.11**
	10	4.96	4.10	3.71	3.48	3.33	3.22	3.14	3.07	3.02	2.97	2.94	2.91
		10.04	**7.56**	**6.55**	**5.99**	**5.64**	**5.39**	**5.21**	**5.06**	**4.95**	**4.85**	**4.78**	**4.71**
	11	4.84	3.98	3.59	3.36	3.20	3.09	3.01	2.95	2.90	2.86	2.82	2.79
		9.65	**7.20**	**6.22**	**5.67**	**5.32**	**5.07**	**4.88**	**4.74**	**4.63**	**4.54**	**4.46**	**4.40**
	12	4.75	3.88	3.49	3.26	3.11	3.00	2.92	2.85	2.80	2.76	2.72	2.69
		9.33	**6.93**	**5.95**	**5.41**	**5.06**	**4.82**	**4.65**	**4.50**	**4.39**	**4.30**	**4.22**	**4.16**
	13	4.67	3.80	3.41	3.18	3.02	2.92	2.84	2.77	2.72	2.67	2.63	2.60
		9.07	**6.70**	**5.74**	**5.20**	**4.86**	**4.62**	**4.44**	**4.30**	**4.19**	**4.10**	**4.02**	**3.96**
	14	4.60	3.74	3.34	3.11	2.96	2.85	2.77	2.70	2.65	2.60	2.56	2.53
		8.86	**6.51**	**5.56**	**5.03**	**4.69**	**4.46**	**4.28**	**4.14**	**4.03**	**3.94**	**3.86**	**3.80**
	15	4.54	3.68	3.29	3.06	2.90	2.79	2.70	2.64	2.59	2.55	2.51	2.48
		8.68	**6.36**	**5.42**	**4.89**	**4.56**	**4.32**	**4.14**	**4.00**	**3.89**	**3.80**	**3.73**	**3.67**

14	16	20	24	30	40	50	75	100	200	500	∞	
245	246	248	249	250	251	252	253	253	254	254	254	1
6,142	6,169	6,208	6,234	6,258	6,286	6,302	6,323	6,344	6,352	6,361	6,366	
19.42	19.43	19.44	1.945	19.46	19.47	19.47	19.48	19.49	19.49	19.50	19.50	2
99.43	99.44	99.45	99.46	99.47	99.48	99.48	99.49	99.49	99.49	99.50	99.50	
8.71	8.69	8.66	8.64	8.62	8.60	8.58	8.57	8.56	8.54	8.54	8.53	3
26.92	26.83	26.69	26.60	26.50	26.41	26.35	26.27	26.23	26.18	26.14	26.12	
5.87	5.84	5.80	5.77	5.74	5.71	5.70	5.68	5.66	5.65	5.64	5.63	4
14.24	14.15	14.02	13.93	13.83	13.74	13.69	13.61	13.57	13.52	13.48	13.46	
4.64	4.60	4.56	4.53	4.50	4.46	4.44	4.42	4.40	4.38	4.37	4.36	5
9.77	9.68	9.55	9.47	9.38	9.29	9.24	9.17	9.13	9.07	9.04	9.02	
3.96	3.92	3.87	3.84	3.81	3.77	3.75	3.72	3.71	3.69	3.68	3.67	6
7.60	7.52	7.39	7.31	7.23	7.14	7.09	7.02	6.99	6.94	6.90	6.88	
3.52	3.49	3.44	3.41	3.38	3.34	3.32	3.29	3.28	3.25	3.24	3.23	7
6.35	6.27	6.15	6.07	5.98	5.90	5.85	5.78	5.75	5.70	5.67	5.65	
3.23	3.20	3.15	3.12	3.08	3.05	3.03	3.00	2.98	2.96	2.94	2.93	8
5.56	5.48	5.36	5.28	5.20	5.11	5.06	5.00	4.96	4.91	4.88	4.86	
3.02	2.98	2.93	2.90	2.86	2.82	2.80	2.77	2.76	2.73	2.72	2.71	9
5.00	4.92	4.80	4.73	4.64	4.56	4.51	4.45	4.41	4.36	4.33	4.31	
2.86	2.82	2.77	2.74	2.70	2.67	2.64	2.61	2.59	2.56	2.55	2.54	10
4.60	4.52	4.41	4.33	4.25	4.17	4.12	4.05	4.01	3.96	3.93	3.91	
2.74	2.70	2.65	2.61	2.57	2.53	2.50	2.47	2.45	2.42	2.41	2.40	11
4.29	4.21	4.10	4.02	3.94	3.86	3.80	3.74	3.70	3.66	3.62	3.60	
2.64	2.60	2.54	2.50	2.46	2.42	2.40	2.36	2.35	2.32	2.31	2.30	12
4.05	3.98	3.86	3.78	3.70	3.61	3.56	3.49	3.46	3.41	3.38	3.36	
2.55	2.51	2.46	2.42	2.38	2.34	2.32	2.28	2.26	2.24	2.22	2.21	13
3.85	3.78	3.67	3.59	3.51	3.42	3.37	3.30	3.27	3.21	3.18	3.16	
2.48	2.44	2.39	2.35	2.31	2.27	2.24	2.21	2.19	2.16	2.14	2.13	14
3.70	3.62	3.51	3.43	3.34	3.26	3.21	3.14	3.11	3.06	3.02	3.00	
2.43	2.39	2.33	2.29	2.25	2.21	2.18	2.15	2.12	2.10	2.08	2.07	15
3.56	3.48	3.36	3.29	3.20	3.12	3.07	3.00	2.97	2.92	2.89	2.87	

Continued

												Degrees of Freedom for
		1	2	3	4	5	6	7	8	9	10	11	12
	16	4.49	3.63	3.24	3.01	2.85	2.74	2.66	2.59	2.54	2.49	2.45	2.42
		8.53	**6.23**	**5.29**	**4.77**	**4.44**	**4.20**	**4.03**	**3.89**	**3.78**	**3.69**	**3.61**	**3.55**
	17	4.45	3.59	3.20	2.96	2.81	2.70	2.62	2.55	2.50	2.45	2.41	2.38
		8.40	**6.11**	**5.18**	**4.67**	**4.34**	**4.10**	**3.93**	**3.79**	**3.68**	**3.59**	**3.52**	**3.45**
	18	4.41	3.55	3.16	2.93	2.77	2.66	2.58	2.51	2.46	2.41	2.37	2.34
		8.28	**6.01**	**5.09**	**4.58**	**4.25**	**4.01**	**3.85**	**3.71**	**3.60**	**3.51**	**3.44**	**3.37**
	19	4.38	3.52	3.13	2.90	2.74	2.63	2.55	2.48	2.43	2.38	2.34	2.31
		8.18	**5.93**	**5.01**	**4.50**	**4.17**	**3.94**	**3.77**	**3.63**	**3.52**	**3.43**	**3.36**	**3.30**
	20	4.35	3.49	3.10	2.87	2.71	2.60	2.52	2.45	2.40	2.35	2.31	2.28
		8.10	**5.85**	**4.94**	**4.43**	**4.10**	**3.87**	**3.71**	**3.56**	**3.45**	**3.37**	**3.30**	**3.23**
	21	4.32	3.47	3.07	2.84	2.68	2.57	2.49	2.42	2.37	2.32	2.28	2.25
		8.02	**5.78**	**4.87**	**4.37**	**4.04**	**3.81**	**3.65**	**3.51**	**3.40**	**3.31**	**3.24**	**3.17**
	22	4.30	3.44	3.05	2.82	2.66	2.55	2.47	2.40	2.35	2.30	2.26	2.23
		7.94	**5.72**	**4.82**	**4.31**	**3.99**	**3.76**	**3.59**	**3.45**	**3.35**	**3.26**	**3.18**	**3.12**
	23	4.28	3.42	3.03	2.80	2.64	2.53	2.45	2.38	2.32	2.28	2.24	2.20
		7.88	**5.66**	**4.76**	**4.26**	**3.94**	**3.71**	**3.54**	**3.41**	**3.30**	**3.21**	**3.14**	**3.07**
	24	4.26	3.40	3.01	2.78	2.62	2.51	2.43	2.36	2.30	2.26	2.22	2.18
		7.82	**5.61**	**4.72**	**4.22**	**3.90**	**3.67**	**3.50**	**3.36**	**3.25**	**3.17**	**3.09**	**3.03**
	25	4.24	3.38	2.99	2.76	2.60	2.49	2.41	2.34	2.28	2.24	2.20	2.16
		7.77	**5.57**	**4.68**	**4.18**	**3.86**	**3.63**	**3.46**	**3.32**	**3.21**	**3.13**	**3.05**	**2.99**
	26	4.22	3.37	2.98	2.74	2.59	2.47	2.39	2.32	2.27	2.22	2.18	2.15
		7.72	**5.53**	**4.64**	**4.14**	**3.82**	**3.59**	**3.42**	**3.29**	**3.17**	**3.09**	**3.02**	**2.96**
	27	4.21	3.35	2.96	2.73	2.57	2.46	2.37	2.30	2.25	2.20	2.16	2.13
		7.68	**5.49**	**4.60**	**4.11**	**3.79**	**3.56**	**3.39**	**3.26**	**3.14**	**3.06**	**2.98**	**2.93**
	28	4.20	3.34	2.95	2.71	2.56	2.44	2.36	2.29	2.24	2.19	2.15	2.12
		7.64	**5.45**	**4.57**	**4.07**	**3.76**	**3.53**	**3.36**	**3.23**	**3.11**	**3.03**	**2.95**	**2.90**
	29	4.18	3.33	2.93	2.70	2.54	2.43	2.35	2.28	2.22	2.18	2.14	2.10
		7.60	**5.42**	**4.54**	**4.04**	**3.73**	**3.50**	**3.33**	**3.20**	**3.08**	**3.00**	**2.92**	**2.87**
	30	4.17	3.32	2.92	2.69	2.53	2.42	2.34	2.27	2.21	2.16	2.12	2.09
		7.56	**5.39**	**4.51**	**4.02**	**3.70**	**3.47**	**3.30**	**3.17**	**3.06**	**2.98**	**2.90**	**2.84**

Degrees of Freedom for the Denominator

14	16	20	24	30	40	50	75	100	200	500	∞	
2.37	2.33	2.28	2.24	2.20	2.16	2.13	2.09	2.07	2.04	2.02	2.01	16
3.45	**3.37**	**3.25**	**3.18**	**3.10**	**3.01**	**2.96**	**2.89**	**2.86**	**2.80**	**2.77**	**2.75**	
2.33	2.29	2.23	2.19	2.15	2.11	2.08	2.04	2.02	1.99	1.97	1.96	17
3.35	**3.27**	**3.16**	**3.08**	**3.00**	**2.92**	**2.86**	**2.79**	**2.76**	**2.70**	**2.67**	**2.65**	
2.29	2.25	2.19	2.15	2.11	2.07	2.04	2.00	1.98	1.95	1.93	1.92	18
3.27	**3.19**	**3.07**	**3.00**	**2.91**	**2.83**	**2.78**	**2.71**	**2.68**	**2.62**	**2.59**	**2.57**	
2.26	2.21	2.15	2.11	2.07	2.02	2.00	1.96	1.94	1.91	1.90	1.88	19
3.19	**3.12**	**3.00**	**2.92**	**2.84**	**2.76**	**2.70**	**2.63**	**2.60**	**2.54**	**2.51**	**2.49**	
2.23	2.18	2.12	2.08	2.04	1.99	1.96	1.92	1.90	1.87	1.85	1.84	20
3.13	**3.05**	**2.94**	**2.86**	**2.77**	**2.69**	**2.63**	**2.56**	**2.53**	**2.47**	**2.44**	**2.42**	
2.20	2.15	2.09	2.05	2.00	1.96	1.93	1.89	1.87	1.84	1.82	1.81	21
3.07	**2.99**	**2.88**	**2.80**	**2.72**	**2.63**	**2.58**	**2.51**	**2.47**	**2.42**	**2.38**	**2.36**	
2.18	2.13	2.07	2.03	1.98	1.93	1.91	1.87	1.84	1.81	1.80	1.78	22
3.02	**2.94**	**2.83**	**2.75**	**2.67**	**2.58**	**2.53**	**2.46**	**2.42**	**2.37**	**2.33**	**2.31**	
2.14	2.10	2.04	2.00	1.96	1.91	1.88	1.84	1.82	1.79	1.77	1.76	23
2.97	**2.89**	**2.78**	**2.70**	**2.62**	**2.53**	**2.48**	**2.41**	**2.37**	**2.32**	**2.28**	**2.26**	
2.13	2.09	2.02	1.98	1.94	1.89	1.86	1.82	1.80	1.76	1.74	1.73	24
2.93	**2.85**	**2.74**	**2.66**	**2.58**	**2.49**	**2.44**	**2.36**	**2.33**	**2.27**	**2.23**	**2.21**	
2.11	2.06	2.00	1.96	1.92	1.87	1.84	1.80	1.77	1.74	1.72	1.71	25
2.89	**2.81**	**2.70**	**2.62**	**2.54**	**2.45**	**2.40**	**2.32**	**2.29**	**2.23**	**2.19**	**2.17**	
2.10	2.05	1.99	1.95	1.90	1.85	1.82	1.78	1.76	1.72	1.70	1.69	26
2.86	**2.77**	**2.66**	**2.58**	**2.50**	**2.41**	**2.36**	**2.28**	**2.25**	**2.19**	**2.15**	**2.13**	
2.08	2.03	1.97	1.93	1.88	1.84	1.80	1.76	1.74	1.71	1.68	1.67	27
2.83	**2.74**	**2.63**	**2.55**	**2.47**	**2.38**	**2.33**	**2.25**	**2.21**	**2.16**	**2.12**	**2.10**	
2.06	2.02	1.96	1.91	1.87	1.81	1.78	1.75	1.72	1.69	1.67	1.65	28
2.80	**2.71**	**2.60**	**2.52**	**2.44**	**2.35**	**2.30**	**2.22**	**2.18**	**2.13**	**2.09**	**2.06**	
2.05	2.00	1.94	1.90	1.85	1.80	1.77	1.73	1.71	1.68	1.65	1.64	29
2.77	**2.68**	**2.57**	**2.49**	**2.41**	**2.32**	**2.27**	**2.19**	**2.15**	**2.10**	**2.06**	**2.03**	
2.04	1.99	1.93	1.89	1.84	1.79	1.76	1.72	1.69	1.66	1.64	1.62	30
2.74	**2.66**	**2.55**	**2.47**	**2.38**	**2.29**	**2.24**	**2.16**	**2.13**	**2.07**	**2.03**	**2.01**	

Continued

Table 4a *(Continued)*

		1	2	3	4	5	6	7	8	9	10	11	12
32		4.15	3.30	2.90	2.67	2.51	2.40	2.32	2.25	2.19	2.14	2.10	2.07
		7.50	**5.34**	**4.46**	**3.97**	**3.66**	**3.42**	**3.25**	**3.12**	**3.01**	**2.94**	**2.86**	**2.80**
34		4.13	3.28	2.88	2.65	2.49	2.38	2.30	2.23	2.17	2.12	2.08	2.05
		7.44	**5.29**	**4.42**	**3.93**	**3.61**	**3.38**	**3.21**	**3.08**	**2.97**	**2.89**	**2.82**	**2.76**
36		4.11	3.26	2.86	2.63	2.48	2.36	2.28	2.21	2.15	2.10	2.06	2.03
		7.39	**5.25**	**4.38**	**3.89**	**3.58**	**3.35**	**3.18**	**3.04**	**2.94**	**2.86**	**2.78**	**2.72**
38		4.10	3.25	2.85	2.62	2.46	2.35	2.26	2.19	2.14	2.09	2.05	2.02
		7.35	**5.21**	**4.34**	**3.86**	**3.54**	**3.32**	**3.15**	**3.02**	**2.91**	**2.82**	**2.75**	**2.69**
40		4.08	3.23	2.84	2.61	2.45	2.34	2.25	2.18	2.12	2.07	2.04	2.00
		7.31	**5.18**	**4.31**	**3.83**	**3.51**	**3.29**	**3.12**	**2.99**	**2.88**	**2.80**	**2.73**	**2.66**
42		4.07	3.22	2.83	2.59	2.44	2.32	2.24	2.17	2.11	2.06	2.02	1.99
		7.27	**5.15**	**4.29**	**3.80**	**3.49**	**3.26**	**3.10**	**2.96**	**2.86**	**2.77**	**2.70**	**2.64**
44		4.06	3.21	2.82	2.58	2.43	2.31	2.23	2.16	2.10	2.05	2.01	1.98
		7.24	**5.12**	**4.26**	**3.78**	**3.46**	**3.24**	**3.07**	**2.94**	**2.84**	**2.75**	**2.68**	**2.62**
46		4.05	3.20	2.81	2.57	2.42	2.30	2.22	2.14	2.09	2.04	2.00	1.97
		7.21	**5.10**	**4.24**	**3.76**	**3.44**	**3.22**	**3.05**	**2.92**	**2.82**	**2.73**	**2.66**	**2.60**
48		4.04	3.19	2.80	2.56	2.41	2.30	2.21	2.14	2.08	2.03	1.99	1.96
		7.19	**5.08**	**4.22**	**3.74**	**3.42**	**3.20**	**3.04**	**2.90**	**2.80**	**2.71**	**2.64**	**2.58**
50		4.03	3.18	2.79	2.56	2.40	2.29	2.20	2.13	2.07	2.02	1.98	1.95
		7.17	**5.06**	**4.20**	**3.72**	**3.41**	**3.18**	**3.02**	**2.88**	**2.78**	**2.70**	**2.62**	**2.56**
55		4.02	3.17	2.78	2.54	2.38	2.27	2.18	2.11	2.05	2.00	1.97	1.93
		7.12	**5.01**	**4.16**	**3.68**	**3.37**	**3.15**	**2.98**	**2.85**	**2.75**	**2.66**	**2.59**	**2.53**
60		4.00	3.15	2.76	2.52	2.37	2.25	2.17	2.10	2.04	1.99	1.95	1.92
		7.08	**4.98**	**4.13**	**3.65**	**3.34**	**3.12**	**2.95**	**2.82**	**2.72**	**2.63**	**2.56**	**2.50**
65		3.99	3.14	2.75	2.51	2.36	2.24	2.15	2.08	2.02	1.98	1.94	1.90
		7.04	**4.95**	**4.10**	**3.62**	**3.31**	**3.09**	**2.93**	**2.79**	**2.70**	**2.61**	**2.54**	**2.47**
70		3.98	3.13	2.74	2.50	2.35	2.23	2.14	2.07	2.01	1.97	1.93	1.89
		7.01	**4.92**	**4.08**	**3.60**	**3.29**	**3.07**	**2.91**	**2.77**	**2.67**	**2.59**	**2.51**	**2.45**
80		3.96	3.11	2.72	2.48	2.33	2.21	2.12	2.05	1.99	1.95	1.91	1.88
		6.96	**4.88**	**4.04**	**3.56**	**3.25**	**3.04**	**2.87**	**2.74**	**2.64**	**2.55**	**2.48**	**2.41**

Degrees of Freedom for

Degrees of Freedom for the Denominator

14	16	20	24	30	40	50	75	100	200	500	∞	
2.02	1.97	1.91	1.86	1.82	1.76	1.74	1.69	1.67	1.64	1.61	1.59	32
2.70	**2.62**	**2.51**	**2.42**	**2.34**	**2.25**	**2.20**	**2.12**	**2.08**	**2.02**	**1.98**	**1.96**	
2.00	1.95	1.89	1.84	1.80	1.74	1.71	1.67	1.64	1.61	1.59	1.57	34
2.66	**2.58**	**2.47**	**2.38**	**2.30**	**2.21**	**2.15**	**2.08**	**2.04**	**1.98**	**1.94**	**1.91**	
1.98	1.93	1.87	1.82	1.78	1.72	1.69	1.65	1.62	1.59	1.56	1.55	36
2.62	**2.54**	**2.43**	**2.35**	**2.26**	**2.17**	**2.12**	**2.04**	**2.00**	**1.94**	**1.90**	**1.87**	
1.96	1.92	1.85	1.80	1.76	1.71	1.67	1.63	1.60	1.57	1.54	1.53	38
2.59	**2.51**	**2.40**	**2.32**	**2.22**	**2.14**	**2.08**	**2.00**	**1.97**	**1.90**	**1.86**	**1.84**	
1.95	1.90	1.84	1.79	1.74	1.69	1.66	1.61	1.59	1.55	1.53	1.51	40
2.56	**2.49**	**2.37**	**2.29**	**2.20**	**2.11**	**2.05**	**1.97**	**1.94**	**1.88**	**1.84**	**1.81**	
1.94	1.89	1.82	1.78	1.73	1.68	1.64	1.60	1.57	1.54	1.51	1.49	42
2.54	**2.46**	**2.35**	**2.26**	**2.17**	**2.08**	**2.02**	**1.94**	**1.91**	**1.85**	**1.80**	**1.78**	
1.92	1.88	1.81	1.76	1.72	1.66	1.63	1.58	1.56	1.52	1.50	1.48	44
2.52	**2.44**	**2.32**	**2.24**	**2.15**	**2.06**	**2.00**	**1.92**	**1.88**	**1.82**	**1.78**	**1.75**	
1.91	1.87	1.80	1.75	1.71	1.65	1.62	1.57	1.54	1.51	1.48	1.46	46
2.50	**2.42**	**2.30**	**2.22**	**2.13**	**2.04**	**1.98**	**1.90**	**1.86**	**1.80**	**1.76**	**1.72**	
1.90	1.86	1.79	1.74	1.70	1.64	1.61	1.56	1.53	1.50	1.47	1.45	48
2.48	**2.40**	**2.28**	**2.20**	**2.11**	**2.02**	**1.96**	**1.88**	**1.84**	**1.78**	**1.73**	**1.70**	
1.90	1.85	1.78	1.74	1.69	1.63	1.60	1.55	1.52	1.48	1.46	1.44	50
2.46	**2.39**	**2.26**	**2.18**	**2.10**	**2.00**	**1.94**	**1.86**	**1.82**	**1.76**	**1.71**	**1.68**	
1.88	1.83	1.76	1.72	1.67	1.61	1.58	1.52	1.50	1.46	1.43	1.41	55
2.43	**2.35**	**2.23**	**2.15**	**2.06**	**1.96**	**1.90**	**1.82**	**1.78**	**1.71**	**1.66**	**1.64**	
1.86	1.81	1.75	1.70	1.65	1.59	1.56	1.50	1.48	1.44	1.41	1.39	60
2.40	**2.32**	**2.20**	**2.12**	**2.03**	**1.93**	**1.87**	**1.79**	**1.74**	**1.68**	**1.63**	**1.60**	
1.85	1.80	1.73	1.68	1.63	1.57	1.54	1.49	1.46	1.42	1.39	1.37	65
2.37	**2.30**	**2.18**	**2.09**	**2.00**	**1.90**	**1.84**	**1.76**	**1.71**	**1.64**	**1.60**	**1.56**	
1.84	1.79	1.72	1.67	1.62	1.56	1.53	1.47	1.45	1.40	1.37	1.35	70
2.35	**2.28**	**2.15**	**2.07**	**1.98**	**1.88**	**1.82**	**1.74**	**1.69**	**1.62**	**1.56**	**1.53**	
1.82	1.77	1.70	1.65	1.60	1.54	1.51	1.45	1.42	1.38	1.35	1.32	80
2.32	**2.24**	**2.11**	**2.03**	**1.94**	**1.84**	**1.78**	**1.70**	**1.65**	**1.57**	**1.52**	**1.49**	

Continued

Table 4a *(Continued)*

		1	2	3	4	5	6	7	8	9	10	11	12
											Degrees of Freedom for		
	100	3.94	3.09	2.70	2.46	2.30	2.19	2.10	2.03	1.97	1.92	1.88	1.85
		6.90	**4.82**	**3.98**	**3.51**	**3.20**	**2.99**	**2.82**	**2.69**	**2.59**	**2.51**	**2.43**	**2.36**
	125	3.92	3.07	2.68	2.44	2.29	2.17	2.08	2.01	1.95	1.90	1.86	1.83
		6.84	**4.78**	**3.94**	**3.47**	**3.17**	**2.95**	**2.79**	**2.65**	**2.56**	**2.47**	**2.40**	**2.33**
	150	3.91	3.06	2.67	2.43	2.27	2.16	2.07	2.00	1.94	1.89	1.85	1.82
		6.81	**4.75**	**3.91**	**3.44**	**3.14**	**2.92**	**2.76**	**2.62**	**2.53**	**2.44**	**2.37**	**2.30**
	200	3.89	3.04	2.65	2.41	2.26	2.14	2.05	1.98	1.92	1.87	1.83	1.80
		6.76	**4.71**	**3.88**	**3.41**	**3.11**	**2.90**	**2.73**	**2.60**	**2.50**	**2.41**	**2.34**	**2.28**
	400	3.86	3.02	2.62	2.39	2.23	2.12	2.03	1.96	1.90	1.85	1.81	1.78
		6.70	**4.66**	**3.83**	**3.36**	**3.06**	**2.85**	**2.69**	**2.55**	**2.46**	**2.37**	**2.29**	**2.23**
	1000	3.85	3.00	2.61	2.38	2.22	2.10	2.02	1.95	1.89	1.84	1.80	1.76
		6.66	**4.62**	**3.80**	**3.34**	**3.04**	**2.82**	**2.66**	**2.53**	**2.43**	**2.34**	**2.26**	**2.20**
	∞	3.84	2.99	2.60	2.37	2.21	2.09	2.01	1.94	1.88	1.83	1.79	1.75
		6.64	**4.60**	**3.78**	**3.32**	**3.02**	**2.80**	**2.64**	**2.51**	**2.41**	**2.32**	**2.24**	**2.18**

(Row label, left vertical: Degrees of Freedom for the Denominator*)*

SOURCE: Reprinted by permission from George W. Snedecor and William G. Cochran, *Statistical Methods*, 6th ed., © 1967 by Iowa State University Press, Ames, Iowa.

14	16	20	24	30	40	50	75	100	200	500	∞	
1.79	1.75	1.68	1.63	1.57	1.51	1.48	1.42	1.39	1.34	1.30	1.28	100
2.26	**2.19**	**2.06**	**1.98**	**1.89**	**1.79**	**1.73**	**1.64**	**1.59**	**1.51**	**1.46**	**1.43**	
1.77	1.72	1.65	1.60	1.55	1.49	1.45	1.39	1.36	1.31	1.27	1.25	125
2.23	**2.15**	**2.03**	**1.94**	**1.85**	**1.75**	**1.68**	**1.59**	**1.54**	**1.46**	**1.40**	**1.37**	
1.76	1.71	1.64	1.59	1.54	1.47	1.44	1.37	1.34	1.29	1.25	1.22	150
2.20	**2.12**	**2.00**	**1.91**	**1.83**	**1.72**	**1.66**	**1.56**	**1.51**	**1.43**	**1.37**	**1.33**	
1.74	1.69	1.62	1.57	1.52	1.45	1.42	1.35	1.32	1.26	1.22	1.19	200
2.17	**2.09**	**1.97**	**1.88**	**1.79**	**1.69**	**1.62**	**1.53**	**1.48**	**1.39**	**1.33**	**1.28**	
1.72	1.67	1.60	1.54	1.49	1.42	1.38	1.32	1.28	1.22	1.16	1.13	400
2.12	**2.04**	**1.92**	**1.84**	**1.74**	**1.64**	**1.57**	**1.47**	**1.42**	**1.32**	**1.24**	**1.19**	
1.70	1.65	1.58	1.53	1.47	1.41	1.36	1.30	1.26	1.19	1.13	1.08	1000
2.09	**2.01**	**1.89**	**1.81**	**1.71**	**1.61**	**1.54**	**1.44**	**1.38**	**1.28**	**1.19**	**1.11**	
1.69	1.64	1.57	1.52	1.46	1.40	1.35	1.28	1.24	1.17	1.11	1.00	∞
2.07	**1.99**	**1.87**	**1.79**	**1.69**	**1.59**	**1.52**	**1.41**	**1.36**	**1.25**	**1.15**	**1.00**	

Table 4b $\alpha = .001$

df for the Denominator	1	2	3	4	5	*df* for the 6
4	74.14	61.25	56.18	53.44	51.71	50.53
5	47.18	37.12	33.20	31.09	29.75	28.84
6	35.51	27.00	23.70	21.92	20.81	20.03
7	29.25	21.69	18.77	17.19	16.21	15.52
8	25.42	18.49	15.83	14.39	13.49	12.86
9	22.86	16.39	13.90	12.56	11.71	11.13
10	21.04	14.91	12.55	11.28	10.48	9.92
11	19.69	13.81	11.56	10.35	9.58	9.05
12	18.64	12.97	10.80	9.63	8.89	8.38
13	17.81	12.31	10.21	9.07	8.35	7.86
14	17.14	11.78	9.73	8.62	7.92	7.43
15	16.59	11.34	9.34	8.25	7.57	7.09
16	16.11	10.97	9.00	7.95	7.27	6.81
17	15.72	10.66	8.73	7.68	7.02	6.56
18	15.38	10.39	8.49	7.46	6.81	6.35
19	15.08	10.16	8.28	7.26	6.62	6.18
20	14.82	9.95	8.10	7.10	6.46	6.02
21	14.59	9.77	7.94	6.95	6.32	5.88
22	14.38	9.61	7.80	6.81	6.19	5.76
23	14.19	9.47	7.67	6.69	6.08	5.65
24	14.03	9.34	7.55	6.59	5.98	5.55
25	13.88	9.22	7.45	6.49	5.88	5.46
26	13.74	9.12	7.36	6.41	5.80	5.38
27	13.61	9.02	7.27	6.33	5.73	5.31
28	13.50	8.93	7.19	6.25	5.66	5.24
29	13.39	8.85	7.12	6.19	5.59	5.18
30	13.29	8.77	7.05	6.12	5.53	5.12
40	12.61	8.25	6.60	5.70	5.13	4.73
60	11.97	7.76	6.17	5.31	4.76	4.37
120	11.38	7.32	5.79	4.95	4.42	4.04
∞	10.83	6.91	5.42	4.62	4.10	3.74

SOURCE: Adapted from "Percentage Points, *F*-Distribution," *Handbook of Tables for Mathematicians,* © CRC Press, Cleveland, Ohio, 1970, p. 626. Used by permission.

Numerator							
7	8	9	10	20	40	∞	
49.66	49.00	48.47	48.05	46.10	45.00	44.05	4
28.16	27.64	27.24	26.92	25.39	24.60	23.79	5
19.46	19.03	18.69	18.41	17.12	16.44	15.75	6
15.02	14.63	14.33	14.08	12.93	12.33	11.70	7
12.40	12.04	11.77	11.54	10.48	9.92	9.33	8
10.70	10.37	10.11	9.89	8.90	8.37	7.81	9
9.52	9.20	8.96	8.75	7.80	7.30	6.76	10
8.66	8.35	8.12	7.92	7.01	6.52	6.00	11
8.00	7.71	7.48	7.29	6.40	5.93	5.42	12
7.49	7.21	6.98	6.80	5.93	5.47	4.97	13
7.08	6.80	6.58	6.40	5.56	5.10	4.60	14
6.75	6.47	6.26	6.08	5.25	4.80	4.31	15
6.46	6.19	5.98	5.81	4.99	4.54	4.06	16
6.22	5.96	5.75	5.58	4.78	4.33	3.85	17
6.02	5.76	5.56	5.39	4.59	4.15	3.67	18
5.85	5.59	5.39	5.22	4.43	3.99	3.51	19
5.69	5.44	5.24	5.08	4.29	3.86	3.38	20
5.56	5.31	5.11	4.95	4.17	3.74	3.26	21
5.44	5.19	4.99	4.83	4.06	3.63	3.15	22
5.33	5.09	4.89	4.73	3.96	3.53	3.05	23
5.23	4.99	4.80	4.64	3.87	3.45	2.97	24
5.15	4.91	4.71	4.56	3.79	3.37	2.89	25
5.07	4.83	4.64	4.48	3.72	3.30	2.82	26
5.00	4.76	4.57	4.41	3.66	3.23	2.75	27
4.93	4.69	4.50	4.35	3.60	3.18	2.69	28
4.87	4.64	4.45	4.29	3.54	3.12	2.64	29
4.82	4.58	4.39	4.24	3.49	3.07	2.59	30
4.44	4.21	4.02	3.87	3.15	2.73	2.23	40
4.09	3.87	3.69	3.54	2.83	2.41	1.89	60
3.77	3.55	3.38	3.24	2.53	2.11	1.54	120
3.47	3.27	3.10	2.96	2.27	1.84	1.00	∞

Table 5 The F_{max} Statistic

Alpha = .05 and .01 (in italics)

df \ k	2	3	4	5	6	7	8	9	10	11	12
2	39.0	87.5	142.	202.	266.	333.	403.	475.	550.	626.	704.
	199.	*448.*	*729.*	*1036.*	*1362.*	*1705.*	*2063.*	*2432.*	*2813.*	*3204.*	*3605.*
3	15.4	27.8	39.2	50.7	62.0	72.9	83.5	93.9	104.	114.	124.
	47.5	*85.*	*120.*	*151.*	*184.*	*216.**	*249.**	*281.**	*310.**	*337.**	*361.**
4	9.60	15.5	20.6	25.2	29.5	33.6	37.5	41.1	44.6	48.0	51.4
	23.2	*37.*	*49.*	*59.*	*69.*	*79.*	*89.*	*97.*	*106.*	*113.*	*120.*
5	7.15	10.8	13.7	16.3	18.7	20.8	22.9	24.7	26.5	28.2	29.9
	14.9	*22.*	*28.*	*33.*	*38.*	*42.*	*46.*	*50.*	*54.*	*57.*	*60.*
6	5.82	8.38	10.4	12.1	13.7	15.0	16.3	17.5	18.6	19.7	20.7
	11.1	*15.5*	*19.1*	*22.*	*25.*	*27.*	*30.*	*32.*	*34.*	*36.*	*37.*
7	4.99	6.94	8.44	9.70	10.8	11.8	12.7	13.5	14.3	15.1	15.8
	8.89	*12.1*	*14.5*	*16.5*	*18.4*	*20.*	*22.*	*23.*	*24.*	*26.*	*27.*
8	4.43	6.00	7.18	8.12	9.03	9.78	10.5	11.1	11.7	12.2	12.7
	7.50	*9.9*	*11.7*	*13.2*	*14.5*	*15.8*	*16.9*	*17.9*	*18.9*	*19.8*	*21.*
9	4.03	5.34	6.31	7.11	7.80	8.41	8.95	9.45	9.91	10.3	10.7
	6.54	*8.5*	*9.9*	*11.1*	*12.1*	*13.1*	*13.9*	*14.7*	*15.3*	*16.0*	*16.6*
10	3.72	4.85	5.67	6.34	6.92	7.42	7.87	8.28	8.66	9.01	9.34
	5.85	*7.4*	*8.6*	*9.6*	*10.4*	*11.1*	*11.8*	*12.4*	*12.9*	*13.4*	*13.9*
12	3.28	4.16	4.79	5.30	5.72	6.09	6.42	6.72	7.00	7.25	7.48
	4.91	*6.1*	*6.9*	*7.6*	*8.2*	*8.7*	*9.1*	*9.5*	*9.9*	*10.2*	*10.6*
15	2.86	3.54	4.01	4.37	4.68	4.95	5.19	5.40	5.59	5.77	5.93
	4.07	*4.9*	*5.5*	*6.0*	*6.4*	*6.7*	*7.1*	*7.3*	*7.5*	*7.8*	*8.0*
20	2.46	2.95	3.29	3.54	3.76	3.94	4.10	4.24	4.37	4.49	4.59
	3.32	*3.8*	*4.3*	*4.6*	*4.9*	*5.1*	*5.3*	*5.5*	*5.6*	*5.8*	*5.9*
30	2.07	2.40	2.61	2.78	2.91	3.02	3.12	3.21	3.29	3.36	3.39
	2.63	*3.0*	*3.3*	*3.4*	*3.6*	*3.7*	*3.8*	*3.9*	*4.0*	*4.1*	*4.2*
60	1.67	1.85	1.96	2.04	2.11	2.17	2.22	2.26	2.30	2.33	2.36
	1.96	*2.2*	*2.3*	*2.4*	*2.4*	*2.5*	*2.5*	*2.6*	*2.6*	*2.7*	*2.7*
∞	1.00	1.00	1.00	1.00	1.00	1.00	1.00	1.00	1.00	1.00	1.00
	1.00	*1.00*	*1.00*	*1.00*	*1.00*	*1.00*	*1.00*	*1.00*	*1.00*	*1.00*	*1.00*

* Values in the column $k = 2$ and in the rows $df = 2$ and ∞ are exact. Elsewhere the third digit may be in error by a few units for $F_{.95}$ and several units for $F_{.99}$. The third digit figures of the values marked by an asterisk are the most uncertain. k = number of groups (variances), each with degrees of freedom = df.

SOURCE: Reproduced from Table 31 of E. S. Pearson and H. O. Hartley, *Biometrika for Statisticians*, Vol. 1, 2nd ed., 1958, published by the Syndics of the Cambridge University Press, London. Used with permission.

Table 6 Critical Values of Cochran's Test for Homogeneity of Variance

Values given are for the statistic (Largest s^2)/(Σs_i^2), where each of the k values of s^2 has v degrees of freedom

Percentile 95

v \ k	1	2	3	4	5	6	7	8	9	10	16	36	144	∞
2	0.9985	0.9750	0.9392	0.9057	0.8772	0.8534	0.8332	0.8159	0.8010	0.7880	0.7341	0.6602	0.5813	0.5000
3	0.9669	0.8709	0.7977	0.7457	0.7071	0.6771	0.6530	0.6333	0.6167	0.6025	0.5466	0.4748	0.4031	0.3333
4	0.9065	0.7679	0.6841	0.6287	0.5895	0.5598	0.5365	0.5175	0.5017	0.4884	0.4366	0.3720	0.3093	0.2500
5	0.8412	0.6838	0.5981	0.5441	0.5065	0.4783	0.4564	0.4387	0.4241	0.4118	0.3645	0.3066	0.2513	0.2000
6	0.7808	0.6161	0.5321	0.4803	0.4447	0.4184	0.3980	0.3817	0.3682	0.3568	0.3135	0.2612	0.2119	0.1667
7	0.7271	0.5612	0.4800	0.4307	0.3974	0.3726	0.3535	0.3384	0.3259	0.3154	0.2756	0.2278	0.1833	0.1429
8	0.6798	0.5157	0.4377	0.3910	0.3595	0.3362	0.3185	0.3043	0.2926	0.2829	0.2462	0.2022	0.1616	0.1250
9	0.6385	0.4775	0.4027	0.3584	0.3286	0.3067	0.2901	0.2768	0.2659	0.2568	0.2226	0.1820	0.1446	0.1111
10	0.6020	0.4450	0.3733	0.3311	0.3029	0.2823	0.2666	0.2541	0.2439	0.2353	0.2032	0.1655	0.1308	0.1000
12	0.5410	0.3924	0.3264	0.2880	0.2624	0.2439	0.2299	0.2187	0.2098	0.2020	0.1737	0.1403	0.1100	0.0833
15	0.4709	0.3346	0.2758	0.2419	0.2195	0.2034	0.1911	0.1815	0.1736	0.1671	0.1429	0.1144	0.0889	0.0667
20	0.3894	0.2705	0.2205	0.1921	0.1735	0.1602	0.1501	0.1422	0.1357	0.1303	0.1108	0.0879	0.0675	0.0500
24	0.3434	0.2354	0.1907	0.1656	0.1493	0.1374	0.1286	0.1216	0.1160	0.1113	0.0942	0.0743	0.0567	0.0417
30	0.2929	0.1980	0.1593	0.1377	0.1237	0.1137	0.1061	0.1002	0.0958	0.0921	0.0771	0.0604	0.0457	0.0333
40	0.2370	0.1576	0.1259	0.1082	0.0968	0.0887	0.0827	0.0780	0.0745	0.0713	0.0595	0.0462	0.0347	0.0250
60	0.1737	0.1131	0.0895	0.0765	0.0682	0.0623	0.0583	0.0552	0.0520	0.0497	0.0411	0.0316	0.0234	0.0167
120	0.0998	0.0632	0.0495	0.0419	0.0371	0.0337	0.0312	0.0292	0.0279	0.0266	0.0218	0.0165	0.0120	0.0083
∞	0	0	0	0	0	0	0	0	0	0	0	0	0	0

SOURCE: Reproduced from C. Eisenhart, M. W. Hastay, and W. A. Wallis, *Techniques of Statistical Analysis* (New York: McGraw-Hill, 1947), chapter 15.

Table 7 Critical Values of the Studentized Range q

df* FOR DENOMI-NATOR	α	J (NUMBER OF MEANS IN SET)																
		2	3	4	5	6	7	8	9	10	11	12	13	14	15	16	17	18
1	.10	8.93	13.4	16.4	18.5	20.2	21.5	22.6	23.6	24.5	25.2	25.9	26.5	27.1	27.6	28.1	28.5	29.0
	.05	18.0	27.0	32.8	37.1	40.4	43.1	45.4	47.4	49.1	50.6	52.0	53.2	54.3	55.4	56.3	57.2	58.0
	.01	90.0	135	164	186	202	216	227	237	246	253	260	266	272	277	282	286	290
2	.10	4.13	5.73	6.78	7.54	8.14	8.63	9.05	9.41	9.73	10.0	10.3	10.5	10.7	10.9	11.1	11.2	11.4
	.05	6.09	8.3	9.8	10.9	11.7	12.4	13.0	13.5	14.0	14.4	14.7	15.1	15.4	15.7	15.9	16.1	16.4
	.01	14.0	19.0	23.3	24.7	26.6	28.2	29.5	30.7	31.7	32.6	33.4	34.1	34.8	35.4	36.0	36.5	37.0
3	.10	3.33	4.47	5.20	5.74	6.16	6.51	6.81	7.06	7.29	7.49	7.67	7.83	7.98	8.12	8.25	8.37	8.78
	.05	4.50	5.91	6.82	7.50	8.04	8.48	8.85	9.18	9.46	9.72	9.95	10.2	10.4	10.5	10.7	10.8	11.0
	.01	8.26	10.6	12.2	13.3	14.2	15.0	15.6	16.2	16.7	17.1	17.5	17.9	18.2	18.5	18.8	19.1	19.3
4	.10	3.01	3.98	4.59	5.04	5.39	5.69	5.93	6.14	6.33	6.50	6.65	6.78	6.91	7.03	7.13	7.23	7.33
	.05	3.93	5.04	5.76	6.29	6.71	7.05	7.35	7.60	7.83	8.03	8.21	8.37	8.52	8.66	8.79	8.91	9.03
	.01	6.51	8.12	9.17	9.96	10.6	11.1	11.5	11.9	12.3	12.6	12.8	13.1	13.3	13.5	13.7	13.9	14.1
5	.10	2.85	3.72	4.26	4.66	4.98	5.24	5.44	5.65	5.82	5.97	6.10	6.22	6.34	6.44	6.54	6.63	6.71
	.05	3.64	4.60	5.22	5.67	6.03	6.33	6.58	6.80	6.99	7.17	7.32	7.47	7.60	7.72	7.83	7.93	8.03
	.01	5.70	6.97	7.80	8.42	8.91	9.32	9.67	9.97	10.2	10.5	10.7	10.9	11.1	11.2	11.4	11.6	11.7
6	.10	2.75	3.56	4.07	4.44	4.73	4.97	5.17	5.34	5.50	5.64	5.76	5.88	5.98	6.08	6.16	6.25	6.33
	.05	3.46	4.34	4.90	5.31	5.63	5.89	6.12	6.32	6.49	6.65	6.79	6.92	7.03	7.14	7.24	7.34	7.43
	.01	5.24	6.33	7.03	7.56	7.97	8.32	8.61	8.87	9.10	9.30	9.49	9.65	9.81	9.95	10.1	10.2	10.3
7	.10	2.68	3.45	3.93	4.28	4.56	4.78	4.97	5.14	5.28	5.41	5.53	5.64	5.74	5.83	5.91	5.99	6.06
	.05	3.34	4.16	4.69	5.06	5.36	5.61	5.82	6.00	6.16	6.30	6.43	6.55	6.66	6.76	6.85	6.94	7.02
	.01	4.95	5.92	6.54	7.01	7.37	7.68	7.94	8.17	8.37	8.55	8.71	8.86	9.00	9.12	9.24	9.35	9.46
8	.10	2.63	3.37	3.83	4.17	4.43	4.65	4.83	4.99	5.13	5.25	5.36	5.46	5.56	5.64	5.74	5.83	5.87
	.05	3.26	4.04	4.53	4.89	5.17	5.40	5.60	5.77	5.92	6.05	6.18	6.29	6.39	6.48	6.57	6.65	6.73
	.01	4.74	5.63	6.20	6.63	6.96	7.24	7.47	7.68	7.78	8.03	8.18	8.31	8.44	8.55	8.66	8.76	8.85
9	.10	2.59	3.32	3.76	4.08	4.34	4.55	4.72	4.87	5.01	5.13	5.23	5.33	5.42	5.51	5.58	5.66	5.72
	.05	3.20	3.95	4.42	4.76	5.02	5.24	5.43	5.60	5.74	5.87	5.98	6.09	6.19	6.28	6.36	6.44	6.51
	.01	4.60	5.43	5.96	6.35	6.66	6.91	7.13	7.32	7.49	7.65	7.78	7.91	8.03	8.13	8.23	8.33	8.41
10	.10	2.56	3.28	3.70	4.02	4.26	4.47	4.64	4.78	4.91	5.03	5.13	5.23	5.32	5.40	5.47	5.54	5.61
	.05	3.15	3.88	4.33	4.65	4.91	5.12	5.30	5.46	5.60	5.72	5.83	5.93	6.03	6.11	6.19	6.27	6.34
	.01	4.48	5.27	5.77	6.14	6.43	6.67	6.87	7.05	7.21	7.36	7.48	7.60	7.71	7.81	7.91	8.00	8.08
11	.10	2.54	3.23	3.66	3.97	4.21	4.40	4.57	4.71	4.84	4.95	5.05	5.15	5.23	5.31	5.38	5.45	5.51
	.05	3.11	3.82	4.26	4.57	4.82	5.03	5.20	5.35	5.49	5.61	5.71	5.81	5.90	5.99	6.06	6.18	6.20
	.01	4.39	5.14	5.62	5.97	6.25	6.48	6.67	6.84	6.99	7.13	7.26	7.36	7.46	7.56	7.65	7.73	7.81

df	α																	
12	.10	2.52	3.20	3.62	3.92	4.16	4.35	4.51	4.65	4.78	4.89	4.99	5.08	5.16	5.24	5.31	5.37	5.44
	.05	3.08	3.77	4.20	4.51	4.75	4.95	5.12	5.27	5.40	5.51	5.62	5.71	5.80	5.88	5.95	6.02	6.09
	.01	4.32	5.04	5.50	5.84	6.10	6.32	6.51	6.67	6.81	6.94	7.06	7.17	7.26	7.36	7.44	7.52	7.50
13	.10	2.51	3.18	3.59	3.89	4.12	4.31	4.46	4.60	4.72	4.83	4.93	5.02	5.10	5.18	5.25	5.31	5.37
	.05	3.06	3.73	4.15	4.45	4.69	4.88	5.05	5.19	5.32	5.43	5.53	5.63	5.71	5.79	5.86	5.93	6.00
	.01	4.26	4.96	5.40	5.73	5.98	6.19	6.37	6.53	6.67	6.79	6.90	7.01	7.10	7.19	7.27	7.37	7.42
14	.10	2.49	3.16	3.56	3.83	4.08	4.27	4.42	4.56	4.68	4.79	4.88	4.97	5.05	5.12	5.19	5.26	5.32
	.05	3.03	3.70	4.11	4.41	4.64	4.83	4.99	5.13	5.25	5.36	5.46	5.55	5.64	5.72	5.79	5.85	5.92
	.01	4.21	4.89	5.32	5.63	5.88	6.08	6.26	6.41	6.54	6.66	6.77	6.87	6.96	7.05	7.13	7.20	7.27
16	.10	2.47	3.12	3.52	3.80	4.03	4.21	4.36	4.49	4.61	4.71	4.81	4.89	4.97	5.04	5.11	5.17	5.23
	.05	3.00	3.65	4.05	4.33	4.56	4.74	4.90	5.03	5.15	5.26	5.35	5.44	5.52	5.59	5.66	5.73	5.79
	.01	4.13	4.78	5.19	5.49	5.72	5.92	6.08	6.22	6.35	6.46	6.56	6.66	6.74	6.82	6.90	6.97	7.03
18	.10	2.45	3.10	3.49	3.77	3.98	4.16	4.31	4.44	4.55	4.66	4.75	4.83	4.91	4.98	5.04	5.10	5.16
	.05	2.97	3.61	4.00	4.28	4.49	4.67	4.82	4.96	5.07	5.17	5.27	5.35	5.43	5.50	5.57	5.63	5.69
	.01	4.07	4.70	5.09	5.38	5.60	5.79	5.94	6.08	6.20	6.31	6.41	6.50	6.58	6.65	6.73	6.79	6.85
20	.10	2.44	3.08	3.46	3.74	3.95	4.12	4.27	4.40	4.51	4.61	4.70	4.78	4.86	4.92	4.99	5.05	5.10
	.05	2.95	3.58	3.96	4.23	4.45	4.62	4.77	4.90	5.01	5.11	5.20	5.28	5.36	5.43	5.49	5.55	5.61
	.01	4.02	4.64	5.02	5.29	5.51	5.69	5.84	5.97	6.09	6.19	6.29	6.37	6.45	6.52	6.59	6.65	6.71
24	.10	2.42	3.05	3.42	3.69	3.90	4.07	4.21	4.34	4.45	4.54	4.63	4.71	4.78	4.85	4.91	4.97	5.02
	.05	2.92	3.53	3.90	4.17	4.37	4.54	4.68	4.81	4.92	5.01	5.10	5.18	5.25	5.32	5.38	5.44	5.49
	.01	3.96	4.54	4.91	5.17	5.37	5.54	5.69	5.81	5.92	6.02	6.11	6.19	6.26	6.33	6.39	6.45	6.51
30	.10	2.40	3.02	3.39	3.65	3.85	4.02	4.16	4.28	4.38	4.47	4.56	4.64	4.71	4.77	4.83	4.89	4.94
	.05	2.89	3.49	3.84	4.10	4.30	4.46	4.60	4.72	4.83	4.92	5.00	5.08	5.15	5.21	5.27	5.33	5.38
	.01	3.89	4.45	4.80	5.05	5.24	5.40	5.54	5.65	5.76	5.85	5.93	6.01	6.08	6.14	6.20	6.26	6.31
40	.10	2.38	2.99	3.35	3.61	3.80	3.96	4.10	4.22	4.32	4.41	4.49	4.56	4.63	4.70	4.75	4.81	4.86
	.05	2.86	3.44	3.79	4.04	4.23	4.39	4.52	4.63	4.74	4.82	4.91	4.98	5.05	5.11	5.16	5.22	5.27
	.01	3.82	4.37	4.70	4.93	5.11	5.27	5.39	5.50	5.60	5.69	5.77	5.84	5.90	5.96	6.02	6.07	6.11
60	.10	2.36	2.96	3.31	3.56	3.76	3.91	4.04	4.16	4.26	4.34	4.42	4.49	4.56	4.62	4.68	4.73	4.78
	.05	2.83	3.40	3.74	3.98	4.16	4.31	4.44	4.55	4.65	4.73	4.81	4.88	4.94	5.00	5.06	5.11	5.15
	.01	3.76	4.28	4.60	4.82	4.99	5.13	5.25	5.36	5.45	5.53	5.60	5.67	5.73	5.79	5.84	5.89	5.93
120	.10	2.34	2.93	3.28	3.52	3.71	3.86	3.99	4.10	4.19	4.28	4.35	4.42	4.49	4.56	4.60	4.65	4.69
	.05	2.80	3.36	3.69	3.92	4.10	4.24	4.36	4.48	4.56	4.64	4.72	4.78	4.84	4.90	4.95	5.00	5.04
	.01	3.70	4.20	4.50	4.71	4.87	5.01	5.12	5.21	5.30	5.38	5.44	5.51	5.56	5.61	5.66	5.71	5.75
∞	.10	2.33	2.90	3.24	3.48	3.66	3.81	3.93	4.04	4.13	4.21	4.29	4.35	4.41	4.47	4.52	4.57	4.61
	.05	2.77	3.31	3.63	3.86	4.03	4.17	4.29	4.39	4.47	4.55	4.62	4.68	4.74	4.80	4.85	4.89	4.93
	.01	3.64	4.12	4.40	4.60	4.76	4.88	4.99	5.08	5.16	5.23	5.29	5.35	5.40	5.45	5.49	5.54	5.57

SOURCE: Abridged from Table 29 in E. S. Pearson and H. O. Hartley (Eds.), *Biometrika Tables for Statisticians*, vol. 1, 2nd ed. (1962). Used by permission.
* In the one-factor ANOVA with n observations in each of J groups, $df = n - J$. In general, df is the number of degrees of freedom for the means square within (MS_w) in an analysis of variance.

Table 8 Critical Values of the Bonferroni t Statistic*

K	EW	5	7	10	12	15	20	24	30	40	60	120
							df_{error}					
2	0.01	4.7742	4.0265	3.5815	3.4284	3.2864	3.1531	3.0920	3.0297	2.9701	2.9134	2.8618
	0.05	3.1614	2.8438	2.6349	2.5615	2.4898	2.4238	2.3921	2.3600	2.3274	2.2986	2.2735
	0.10	2.5689	2.3640	2.2269	2.1793	2.1306	2.0854	2.0624	2.0438	2.0203	2.0014	1.9822
3	0.01	5.2476	4.3537	3.8292	3.6474	3.4819	3.3296	3.2591	3.1869	3.1218	3.0581	2.9961
	0.05	3.5319	3.1281	2.8705	2.7793	2.6957	2.6122	2.5736	2.5372	2.4974	2.4628	2.4306
	0.10	2.9101	2.6421	2.4686	2.4040	2.3438	2.2850	2.2567	2.2312	2.2054	2.1793	2.1562
4	0.01	5.6099	4.5909	4.0027	3.8073	3.6245	3.4561	3.3759	3.3009	3.2278	3.1569	3.0901
	0.05	3.8073	3.3375	3.0383	2.9362	2.8371	2.7448	2.6993	2.6565	2.6168	2.5763	2.5391
	0.10	3.1614	2.8438	2.6349	2.5615	2.4898	2.4238	2.3921	2.3600	2.3274	2.2986	2.2735
5	0.01	5.8999	4.7842	4.1432	3.9291	3.7346	3.5505	3.4656	3.3851	3.3072	3.2320	3.1597
	0.05	4.0324	3.5007	3.1719	3.0571	2.9459	2.8471	2.7964	2.7492	2.7054	2.6610	2.6204
	0.10	3.3688	2.9981	2.7621	2.6833	2.6021	2.5278	2.4921	2.4560	2.4218	2.3921	2.3620
6	0.01	6.1337	4.9459	4.2581	4.0294	3.8198	3.6302	3.5405	3.4561	3.3723	3.2918	3.2177
	0.05	4.2185	3.6356	3.2755	3.1554	3.0352	2.9272	2.8755	2.8253	2.7742	2.7274	2.6851
	0.10	3.5319	3.1281	2.8705	2.7793	2.6957	2.6122	2.5736	2.5371	2.4974	2.4628	2.4306
7	0.01	6.3552	5.0779	4.3571	4.1158	3.8971	3.6965	3.6022	3.5143	3.4271	3.3439	3.2650
	0.05	4.3848	3.7531	3.3688	3.2374	3.1112	2.9965	2.9402	2.8887	2.8362	2.7858	2.7405
	0.10	3.6813	3.2374	2.9572	2.8626	2.7708	2.6851	2.6412	2.6030	2.5610	2.5249	2.4883
8	0.01	6.5364	5.2043	4.4431	4.1918	3.9608	3.7537	3.6572	3.5614	3.4733	3.3864	3.3081
	0.05	4.5218	3.8571	3.4499	3.3088	3.1795	3.0571	2.9973	2.9427	2.8871	2.8337	2.7862
	0.10	3.8073	3.3375	3.0383	2.9362	2.8371	2.7448	2.6993	2.6565	2.6168	2.5763	2.5391
9	0.01	6.7128	5.3120	4.5209	4.2581	4.0217	3.8058	3.7022	3.6068	3.5145	3.4275	3.3444
	0.05	4.6507	3.9469	3.5156	3.3723	3.2359	3.1074	3.0446	2.9877	2.9297	2.8780	2.8253
	0.10	3.9306	3.4228	3.1074	2.9985	2.8928	2.7986	2.7522	2.7050	2.6610	2.6204	2.5833
10	0.01	6.8707	5.4043	4.5870	4.3193	4.0706	3.8486	3.7466	3.6458	3.5505	3.4613	3.3741
	0.05	4.7742	4.0265	3.5815	3.4284	3.2864	3.1531	3.0920	3.0297	2.9701	2.9134	2.8618
	0.10	4.0324	3.5007	3.1719	3.0571	2.9459	2.8471	2.7964	2.7491	2.7054	2.6610	2.6204
15	0.01	7.4932	5.7980	4.8537	4.5495	4.2733	4.0228	3.9072	3.7970	3.6895	3.5912	3.4966
	0.05	5.2476	4.3537	3.8292	3.6474	3.4819	3.3296	3.2591	3.1869	3.1218	3.0581	2.9961
	0.10	4.4592	3.8058	3.4092	3.2755	3.1474	3.0258	2.9691	2.9144	2.8618	2.8113	2.7632
20	0.01	7.9786	6.0791	5.0508	4.7151	4.4148	4.1468	4.0191	3.9024	3.7901	3.6804	3.5798
	0.05	5.6099	4.5909	4.0027	3.8073	3.6245	3.4561	3.3759	3.3009	3.2278	3.1569	3.0901
	0.10	4.7742	4.0265	3.5815	3.4284	3.2864	3.1531	3.0920	3.0297	2.9701	2.9134	2.8618
25	0.01	8.3687	6.3076	5.2005	4.8445	4.5265	4.2418	4.1080	3.9837	3.8650	3.7501	3.6443
	0.05	5.8999	4.7842	4.1432	3.9291	3.7346	3.5505	3.4656	3.3851	3.3072	3.2320	3.1597
	0.10	5.0272	4.2074	3.7186	3.5505	3.3961	3.2527	3.1832	3.1170	3.0542	2.9951	2.9373
30	0.01	8.6867	6.5030	5.3321	4.9540	4.6266	4.3176	4.1808	4.0505	3.9243	3.8058	3.6955
	0.05	6.1337	4.9459	4.2581	4.0294	3.8198	3.6302	3.5405	3.4561	3.3723	3.2918	3.2177
	0.10	5.2476	4.3537	3.8292	3.6474	3.4819	3.3296	3.2591	3.1869	3.1218	3.0581	2.9961

* K = number of contrasts to be made. EW = desired error rate (experimentwise).

SOURCE: Table A-12 of J. Myers, *Fundamentals of Experimental Design*, 2nd ed. (Boston: Allyn and Bacon, 1972), pp. 457–458.

Table 8 *(Continued)*

K	EW	5	7	10	12	15	df_{error} 20	24	30	40	60	120
35	0.01	8.9736	6.6660	5.4380	5.0449	4.6969	4.3869	4.2418	4.1044	3.9753	3.8554	3.7386
	0.05	6.3552	5.0779	4.3571	4.1158	3.8971	3.6965	3.6022	3.5143	3.4271	3.3439	3.2650
	0.10	5.4351	4.4845	3.9238	3.7330	3.5585	3.3996	3.3220	3.2490	3.1776	3.1112	3.0469
40	0.01	9.2387	6.8185	5.5351	5.1270	4.7654	4.4417	4.2951	4.1540	4.0191	3.8948	3.7763
	0.05	6.5364	5.2043	4.4431	4.1918	3.9608	3.7537	3.6572	3.5614	3.4733	3.3864	3.3081
	0.10	5.6099	4.5909	4.0027	3.8073	3.6245	3.4561	3.3759	3.3009	3.2278	3.1569	3.0901
45	0.01	9.4650	6.9484	5.6199	5.1984	4.8237	4.4926	4.3408	4.1955	4.0594	3.9314	3.8102
	0.05	6.7128	5.3120	4.5209	4.2581	4.0217	3.8058	3.7022	3.6068	3.5145	3.4275	3.3444
	0.10	5.7578	4.6955	4.0780	3.8687	3.6804	3.5049	3.4236	3.3444	3.2693	3.1968	3.1289
50	0.01	9.6736	7.0653	5.6930	5.2646	4.8780	4.5388	4.3801	4.2330	4.0944	3.9626	3.8384
	0.05	6.8707	5.4043	4.5870	4.3193	4.0706	3.8486	3.7466	3.6458	3.5505	3.4613	3.3741
	0.10	5.8999	4.7842	4.1432	3.9291	3.7346	3.5505	3.4656	3.3851	3.3072	3.2320	3.1597
100	0.01	11.1879	7.8828	6.2124	5.6930	5.2398	4.8368	4.6563	4.4810	4.3202	4.1688	4.0255
	0.05	7.9786	6.0791	5.0508	4.7151	4.4148	4.1468	4.0191	3.9024	3.7901	3.6804	3.5798
	0.10	6.8707	5.4043	4.5870	4.3193	4.0706	3.8486	3.7466	3.6458	3.5505	3.4613	3.3741
250	0.01	8.3687	6.3076	5.2005	4.8445	4.5265	4.2418	4.1080	3.9837	3.8650	3.7501	3.6443
	0.05	5.8999	4.7842	4.1432	3.9291	3.7346	3.5505	3.4656	3.3851	3.3072	3.2320	3.1597
	0.10	5.0272	4.2074	3.7186	3.5505	3.3961	3.2527	3.1832	3.1170	3.0542	2.9951	2.9373
500	0.01	15.5370	10.1031	7.5249	6.7622	6.1111	5.5438	5.2902	5.0539	4.8349	4.6307	4.4434
	0.05	11.1879	7.8828	6.2124	5.6930	5.2398	4.8368	4.6563	4.4810	4.3202	4.1688	4.0255
	0.10	9.6736	7.0653	5.6930	5.2646	4.8790	4.5388	4.2801	4.2330	4.0944	3.9626	3.8384
1000	0.01	17.8990	11.2212	8.1545	7.2604	6.5025	5.8543	5.5648	5.2990	5.0516	4.8253	4.6131
	0.05	12.8956	8.7857	6.7581	6.1400	5.6073	5.1393	4.9284	4.7278	4.5429	4.3716	4.2088
	0.10	11.1879	7.8828	6.2124	5.6930	5.2398	4.8368	4.6563	4.4810	4.3202	4.1688	4.0255
2000	0.01	20.5717	12.4338	8.8132	7.7805	6.9053	6.1718	5.8463	5.5438	5.2682	5.0145	4.7816
	0.05	14.8505	9.7656	7.3344	6.6076	5.9864	5.4455	5.2005	4.9735	4.7631	4.5675	4.3865
	0.10	12.8956	8.7857	6.7581	6.1400	5.6073	5.1393	4.9284	4.7278	4.5429	4.3716	4.2088
3000	0.01	22.3259	13.2039	9.2161	8.0944	7.1505	6.3595	6.0093	5.6899	5.3970	5.1248	4.8786
	0.05	16.1299	10.3796	7.6890	6.8918	6.2094	5.6239	5.3619	5.1193	4.8933	4.6832	4.4883
	0.10	14.0089	9.3485	7.0916	6.4130	5.8288	5.3174	5.0865	4.8733	4.6743	4.4867	4.3137
4000	0.01	23.6703	13.7837	9.5144	8.3241	7.3242	6.4917	6.1264	5.7903	5.4847	5.2037	4.9468
	0.05	17.0898	10.8498	7.9486	7.0969	6.3723	5.7516	5.4762	5.2220	4.9829	4.7631	4.5593
	0.10	14.8505	9.7656	7.3344	6.6076	5.9864	5.4455	5.2005	4.9735	4.7631	4.5675	4.3865
5000	0.01	24.7926	14.2488	9.7525	8.5026	7.4675	6.5984	6.2169	5.8702	5.5543	5.2637	4.9986
	0.05	17.8990	11.2212	8.1545	7.2604	6.5025	5.8543	5.5648	5.2990	5.0516	4.8253	4.6131
	0.10	15.5370	10.1031	7.5249	6.7622	6.1111	5.5438	5.2902	5.0539	4.8349	4.6307	4.4434

Table 9 Critical Values of the Duncan Multiple Range Test*

(a) Alpha = .10

df \ k	2	3	4	5	6	7	8	9	10	11	12	13	14	15	16	17	18	19
2	4.130																	
3	3.328	3.330																
4	3.015	3.074	3.081															
5	2.850	2.934	2.964	2.970														
6	2.748	2.846	2.890	2.908	2.911													
7	2.680	2.785	2.838	2.864	2.876	2.878												
8	2.630	2.742	2.800	2.832	2.849	2.857	2.858											
9	2.592	2.708	2.771	2.808	2.829	2.840	2.845	2.847										
10	2.563	2.682	2.748	2.788	2.813	2.827	2.835	2.839	2.839									
11	2.540	2.660	2.730	2.772	2.799	2.817	2.827	2.833	2.835	2.835								
12	2.521	2.643	2.714	2.759	2.789	2.808	2.821	2.828	2.832	2.833	2.833							
13	2.505	2.628	2.701	2.748	2.779	2.800	2.815	2.824	2.829	2.832	2.832	2.832						
14	2.491	2.616	2.690	2.739	2.771	2.794	2.810	2.820	2.827	2.831	2.832	2.833	2.833					
15	2.479	2.605	2.681	2.731	2.765	2.789	2.805	2.817	2.825	2.830	2.832	2.833	2.834	2.834				
16	2.469	2.596	2.673	2.723	2.759	2.784	2.802	2.815	2.824	2.829	2.833	2.834	2.836	2.836	2.836			
17	2.460	2.588	2.665	2.717	2.753	2.780	2.798	2.812	2.822	2.829	2.833	2.835	2.836	2.838	2.838	2.838		
18	2.452	2.580	2.659	2.712	2.749	2.776	2.796	2.810	2.821	2.828	2.834	2.836	2.838	2.838	2.840	2.840	2.840	
19	2.445	2.574	2.653	2.707	2.745	2.773	2.793	2.808	2.820	2.828	2.834	2.838	2.840	2.840	2.843	2.843	2.843	2.843
20	2.439	2.568	2.648	2.702	2.741	2.770	2.791	2.807	2.819	2.828	2.834	2.839	2.841	2.842	2.845	2.845	2.845	2.845
24	2.420	2.550	2.632	2.688	2.729	2.760	2.783	2.801	2.816	2.827	2.835	2.842	2.848	2.851	2.854	2.856	2.857	2.857
30	2.400	2.532	2.615	2.674	2.717	2.750	2.776	2.796	2.813	2.826	2.837	2.846	2.853	2.859	2.863	2.867	2.869	2.871
40	2.381	2.514	2.600	2.660	2.705	2.741	2.769	2.791	2.810	2.825	2.838	2.849	2.858	2.866	2.873	2.878	2.883	2.887
60	2.363	2.497	2.584	2.646	2.694	2.731	2.761	2.786	2.807	2.825	2.839	2.853	2.864	2.874	2.883	2.890	2.897	2.903
120	2.344	2.479	2.568	2.632	2.682	2.722	2.754	2.781	2.804	2.824	2.842	2.857	2.871	2.883	2.893	2.903	2.912	2.920
∞	2.326	2.462	2.552	2.619	2.670	2.712	2.746	2.776	2.801	2.824	2.844	2.861	2.877	2.892	2.905	2.918	2.929	2.939

* K = number of ranked means in the comparison. df = degrees of freedom for error mean square.

SOURCE: Appendix I of J. L. Bruning and B. L. Kintz, *Computational Handbook of Statistics*, 2nd ed. (Glenview, Ill.: Scott, Foresman, 1977), pp. 237–241.

Table 9 *(Continued)*

(b) Alpha = .05

$\frac{k}{df}$	2	3	4	5	6	7	8	9	10	11	12	13	14	15	16	17	18	19
2	6.085																	
3	4.501	4.516																
4	3.927	4.013	4.033															
5	3.635	3.749	3.797	3.814														
6	3.461	3.587	3.649	3.680	3.694													
7	3.344	3.477	3.548	3.588	3.611	3.622												
8	3.261	3.399	3.475	3.521	3.549	3.566	3.575											
9	3.199	3.339	3.420	3.470	3.502	3.523	3.536	3.544										
10	3.151	3.293	3.376	3.430	3.465	3.489	3.505	3.516	3.522									
11	3.113	3.256	3.342	3.397	3.435	3.462	3.480	3.493	3.501	3.506								
12	3.082	3.225	3.313	3.370	3.410	3.439	3.459	3.474	3.484	3.491	3.496							
13	3.055	3.200	3.289	3.348	3.389	3.419	3.442	3.458	3.470	3.478	3.484	3.488						
14	3.033	3.178	3.268	3.329	3.372	3.403	3.426	3.444	3.457	3.467	3.474	3.479	3.482					
15	3.014	3.160	3.250	3.312	3.356	3.389	3.413	3.432	3.446	3.457	3.465	3.471	3.476	3.478				
16	2.998	3.144	3.235	3.298	3.343	3.376	3.402	3.422	3.437	3.449	3.458	3.465	3.470	3.473	3.477			
17	2.984	3.130	3.222	3.285	3.331	3.366	3.392	3.412	3.429	3.441	3.451	3.459	3.465	3.469	3.473	3.475		
18	2.971	3.118	3.210	3.274	3.321	3.356	3.383	3.405	3.421	3.435	3.445	3.454	3.460	3.465	3.470	3.473	3.474	
19	2.960	3.107	3.199	3.264	3.311	3.347	3.375	3.397	3.415	3.429	3.440	3.449	3.456	3.462	3.467	3.472	3.472	3.473
20	2.950	3.097	3.190	3.255	3.303	3.339	3.368	3.391	3.409	3.424	3.436	3.445	3.453	3.459	3.464	3.467	3.470	3.472
24	2.919	3.066	3.160	3.226	3.276	3.315	3.345	3.370	3.390	3.406	3.420	3.432	3.441	3.449	3.456	3.461	3.465	3.469
30	2.888	3.035	3.131	3.199	3.250	3.290	3.322	3.349	3.371	3.389	3.405	3.418	3.430	3.439	3.447	3.454	3.460	3.466
40	2.858	3.006	3.102	3.171	3.224	3.266	3.300	3.328	3.352	3.373	3.390	3.405	3.418	3.429[a]	3.439	3.448	3.456	3.463
60	2.829	2.976	3.073	3.143	3.198	3.241	3.277	3.307	3.333	3.355	3.374	3.391	3.406	3.419	3.431	3.442	3.451	3.460
120	2.800	2.947	3.045	3.116	3.172	3.217	3.254	3.287	3.314	3.337	3.359	3.377	3.394	3.409	3.423	3.435	3.446	3.457
∞	2.772	2.918	3.017	3.089	3.146	3.193	3.232	3.265	3.294	3.320	3.343	3.363	3.382	3.399	3.414	3.428	3.442	3.454

Table 9 (Continued)

(c) Alpha = .01

k \ df	2	3	4	5	6	7	8	9	10	11	12	13	14	15	16	17	18	19
2	14.04																	
3	8.261	8.321																
4	6.512	6.677	6.740															
5	5.702	5.893	5.989	6.040														
6	5.243	5.439	5.549	5.614	5.655													
7	4.949	5.145	5.260	5.334	5.383	5.416												
8	4.746	4.939	5.057	5.135	5.189	5.227	5.256											
9	4.596	4.787	4.906	4.986	5.043	5.086	5.118	5.142										
10	4.482	4.671	4.790	4.871	4.931	4.975	5.010	5.037	5.058									
11	4.392	4.579	4.697	4.780	4.841	4.887	4.924	4.952	4.975	4.994								
12	4.320	4.504	4.622	4.706	4.767	4.815	4.852	4.883	4.907	4.927	4.944							
13	4.260	4.442	4.560	4.644	4.706	4.755	4.793	4.824	4.850	4.872	4.889	4.904						
14	4.210	4.391	4.508	4.591	4.654	4.704	4.743	4.775	4.802	4.824	4.843	4.859	4.872					
15	4.168	4.347	4.463	4.547	4.610	4.660	4.700	4.733	4.760	4.783	4.803	4.820	4.834	4.846				
16	4.131	4.309	4.425	4.509	4.572	4.622	4.663	4.696	4.724	4.748	4.768	4.786	4.800	4.813	4.825			
17	4.099	4.275	4.391	4.475	4.539	4.589	4.630	4.664	4.693	4.717	4.738	4.756	4.771	4.785	4.797	4.807		
18	4.071	4.246	4.362	4.445	4.509	4.560	4.601	4.635	4.664	4.689	4.711	4.729	4.745	4.759	4.772	4.783	4.792	
19	4.046	4.220	4.335	4.419	4.483	4.534	4.575	4.610	4.639	4.665	4.686	4.705	4.722	4.736	4.749	4.761	4.771	4.780
20	4.024	4.197	4.312	4.395	4.459	4.510	4.552	4.587	4.617	4.642	4.664	4.684	4.701	4.716	4.729	4.741	4.751	4.761
24	3.956	4.126	4.239	4.322	4.386	4.437	4.480	4.516	4.546	4.573	4.596	4.616	4.634	4.651	4.665	4.678	4.690	4.700
30	3.889	4.056	4.168	4.250	4.314	4.366	4.409	4.445	4.477	4.504	4.528	4.550	4.569	4.586	4.601	4.615	4.628	4.640
40	3.825	3.988	4.098	4.180	4.244	4.296	4.339	4.376	4.408	4.436	4.461	4.483	4.503	4.521	4.537	4.553	4.566	4.579
60	3.762	3.922	4.031	4.111	4.174	4.226	4.270	4.307	4.340	4.368	4.394	4.417	4.438	4.456	4.474	4.490	4.504	4.518
120	3.702	3.858	3.965	4.044	4.107	4.158	4.202	4.239	4.272	4.301	4.327	4.351	4.372	4.392	4.410	4.426	4.442	4.456
∞	3.643	3.796	3.900	3.978	4.040	4.091	4.135	4.172	4.205	4.235	4.261	4.285	4.307	4.327	4.345	4.363	4.379	4.394

Table 9 (Continued)

(d) Alpha = .005

df \ k	2	3	4	5	6	7	8	9	10	11	12	13	14	15	16	17	18	19
2	19.93																	
3	10.55	10.63																
4	7.916	8.126	8.210															
5	6.751	6.980	7.100	7.167														
6	6.105	6.334	6.466	6.547	6.600													
7	5.699	5.922	6.057	6.145	6.207	6.250												
8	5.420	5.638	5.773	5.864	5.930	5.978	6.014											
9	5.218	5.430	5.565	5.657	5.725	5.776	5.815	5.846										
10	5.065	5.273	5.405	5.498	5.567	5.620	5.662	5.695	5.722									
11	4.945	5.149	5.280	5.372	5.442	5.496	5.539	5.574	5.603	5.626								
12	4.849	5.048	5.178	5.270	5.341	5.396	5.439	5.475	5.505	5.531	5.552							
13	4.770	4.966	5.094	5.186	5.256	5.312	5.356	5.393	5.424	5.450	5.472	5.492						
14	4.704	4.897	5.023	5.116	5.185	5.241	5.286	5.324	5.355	5.382	5.405	5.425	5.442					
15	4.647	4.838	4.964	5.055	5.125	5.181	5.226	5.264	5.297	5.324	5.348	5.368	5.386	5.402				
16	4.599	4.787	4.912	5.003	5.073	5.129	5.175	5.213	5.245	5.273	5.298	5.319	5.338	5.354	5.368			
17	4.557	4.744	4.867	4.958	5.027	5.084	5.130	5.168	5.201	5.229	5.254	5.275	5.295	5.311	5.327	5.340		
18	4.521	4.705	4.828	4.918	4.987	5.043	5.090	5.129	5.162	5.190	5.215	5.237	5.256	5.274	5.289	5.303	5.316	
19	4.488	4.671	4.793	4.883	4.952	5.008	5.054	5.093	5.127	5.156	5.181	5.203	5.222	5.240	5.256	5.270	5.283	5.295
20	4.460	4.641	4.762	4.851	4.920	4.976	5.022	5.061	5.095	5.124	5.150	5.172	5.193	5.210	5.226	5.241	5.254	5.266
24	4.371	4.547	4.666	4.753	4.822	4.877	4.924	4.963	4.997	5.027	5.053	5.076	5.097	5.116	5.133	5.148	5.162	5.175
30	4.285	4.456	4.572	4.658	4.726	4.781	4.827	4.867	4.901	4.931	4.958	4.981	5.003	5.022	5.040	5.056	5.071	5.085
40	4.202	4.369	4.482	4.566	4.632	4.687	4.733	4.772	4.806	4.837	4.864	4.888	4.910	4.930	4.948	4.965	4.980	4.995
60	4.122	4.284	4.394	4.476	4.541	4.595	4.640	4.679	4.713	4.744	4.771	4.796	4.818	4.838	4.857	4.874	4.890	4.905
120	4.045	4.201	4.308	4.388	4.452	4.505	4.550	4.588	4.622	4.652	4.679	4.704	4.726	4.747	4.766	4.784	4.800	4.815
∞	3.970	4.121	4.225	4.303	4.365	4.417	4.461	4.499	4.532	4.562	4.589	4.614	4.636	4.657	4.676	4.694	4.710	4.726

Table 9 *(Continued)*

(e) Alpha = .001

df \ k	2	3	4	5	6	7	8	9	10	11	12	13	14	15	16	17	18	19
2	44.69																	
3	18.28	18.45																
4	12.18	12.52	12.67															
5	9.714	10.05	10.24	10.35														
6	8.427	8.743	8.932	9.055	9.139													
7	7.648	7.943	8.127	8.252	8.342	8.409												
8	7.130	7.407	7.584	7.708	7.799	7.869	7.924											
9	6.762	7.024	7.195	7.316	7.407	7.478	7.535	7.582										
10	6.487	6.738	6.902	7.021	7.111	7.182	7.240	7.287	7.327									
11	6.275	6.516	6.676	6.791	6.880	6.950	7.008	7.056	7.097	7.132								
12	6.106	6.340	6.494	6.607	6.695	6.765	6.822	6.870	6.911	6.947	6.978							
13	5.970	6.195	6.346	6.457	6.543	6.612	6.670	6.718	6.759	6.795	6.826	6.854						
14	5.856	6.075	6.223	6.332	6.416	6.485	6.542	6.590	6.631	6.667	6.699	6.727	6.752					
15	5.760	5.974	6.119	6.225	6.309	6.377	6.433	6.481	6.522	6.558	6.590	6.619	6.644	6.666				
16	5.678	5.888	6.030	6.135	6.217	6.284	6.340	6.388	6.429	6.465	6.497	6.525	6.551	6.574	6.595			
17	5.608	5.813	5.953	6.056	6.138	6.204	6.260	6.307	6.348	6.384	6.416	6.444	6.470	6.493	6.514	6.533		
18	5.546	5.748	5.886	5.988	6.068	6.134	6.189	6.236	6.277	6.313	6.345	6.373	6.399	6.422	6.443	6.462	6.480	
19	5.492	5.691	5.826	5.927	6.007	6.072	6.127	6.174	6.214	6.250	6.281	6.310	6.336	6.359	6.380	6.400	6.418	6.434
20	5.444	5.640	5.774	5.873	5.952	6.017	6.071	6.117	6.158	6.193	6.225	6.254	6.279	6.303	6.324	6.344	6.362	6.379
24	5.297	5.484	5.612	5.708	5.784	5.846	5.899	5.945	5.984	6.020	6.051	6.079	6.105	6.129	6.150	6.170	6.188	6.205
30	5.156	5.335	5.457	5.549	5.622	5.682	5.734	5.778	5.817	5.851	5.882	5.910	5.935	5.958	5.980	6.000	6.018	6.036
40	5.022	5.191	5.308	5.396	5.466	5.524	5.574	5.617	5.654	5.688	5.718	5.745	5.770	5.793	5.814	5.834	5.852	5.869
60	4.894	5.055	5.166	5.249	5.317	5.372	5.420	5.461	5.498	5.530	5.559	5.586	5.610	5.632	5.653	5.672	5.690	5.707
120	4.771	4.924	5.029	5.109	5.173	5.226	5.271	5.311	5.346	5.377	5.405	5.431	5.454	5.476	5.496	5.515	5.532	5.549
∞	4.654	4.798	4.898	4.974	5.034	5.085	5.128	5.166	5.199	5.229	5.256	5.280	5.303	5.324	5.343	5.361	5.378	5.394

Table 10   Critical Values of the Dunnett *d* Statistic

(a) Table of *t* for one-sided comparisons between *k* treatment means and a control for a joint confidence coefficient of $P = 95$ percent.

	k, Number Of Treatment Means (Excluding The Control)								
df	1	2	3	4	5	6	7	8	9
5	2.02	2.44	2.68	2.85	2.98	3.08	3.16	3.24	3.30
6	1.94	2.34	2.56	2.71	2.83	2.92	3.00	3.07	3.12
7	1.89	2.27	2.48	2.62	2.73	2.82	2.89	2.95	3.01
8	1.86	2.22	2.42	2.55	2.66	2.74	2.81	2.87	2.92
9	1.83	2.18	2.37	2.50	2.60	2.68	2.75	2.81	2.86
10	1.81	2.15	2.34	2.47	2.56	2.64	2.70	2.76	2.81
11	1.80	2.13	2.31	2.44	2.53	2.60	2.67	2.72	2.77
12	1.78	2.11	2.29	2.41	2.50	2.58	2.64	2.69	2.74
13	1.77	2.09	2.27	2.39	2.48	2.55	2.61	2.66	2.71
14	1.76	2.08	2.25	2.37	2.46	2.53	2.59	2.64	2.69
15	1.75	2.07	2.24	2.36	2.44	2.51	2.57	2.62	2.67
16	1.75	2.06	2.23	2.34	2.43	2.50	2.56	2.61	2.65
17	1.74	2.05	2.22	2.33	2.42	2.49	2.54	2.59	2.64
18	1.73	2.04	2.21	2.32	2.41	2.48	2.53	2.58	2.62
19	1.73	2.03	2.20	2.31	2.40	2.47	2.52	2.57	2.61
20	1.72	2.03	2.19	2.30	2.39	2.46	2.51	2.56	2.60
24	1.71	2.01	2.17	2.28	2.36	2.43	2.48	2.53	2.57
30	1.70	1.99	2.15	2.25	2.33	2.40	2.45	2.50	2.54
40	1.68	1.97	2.13	2.23	2.31	2.37	2.42	2.47	2.51
60	1.67	1.95	2.10	2.21	2.28	2.35	2.39	2.44	2.48
120	1.66	1.93	2.08	2.18	2.26	2.32	2.37	2.41	2.45
inf.	1.64	1.92	2.06	2.16	2.23	2.29	2.34	2.38	2.42

source: Tables 10a-d are reprinted from C. W. Dunnett, "A multiple comparison procedure for comparing several treatments with a control." *Journal of the American Statistical Association*, 1955, *50*, 1096–1121. Used with permission.

Table 10 *(Continued)*

(b) Table of t for one-sided comparisons between k treatment means and a control for a joint confidence coefficient of $P = 99$ percent.

df	k, NUMBER OF TREATMENT MEANS (EXCLUDING THE CONTROL)								
	1	2	3	4	5	6	7	8	9
5	3.37	3.90	4.21	4.43	4.60	4.73	4.85	4.94	5.03
6	3.14	3.61	3.88	4.07	4.21	4.33	4.43	4.51	4.59
7	3.00	3.42	3.66	3.83	3.96	4.07	4.15	4.23	4.30
8	2.90	3.29	3.51	3.67	3.79	3.88	3.96	4.03	4.09
9	2.82	3.19	3.40	3.55	3.66	3.75	3.82	3.89	3.94
10	2.76	3.11	3.31	3.45	3.56	3.64	3.71	3.78	3.83
11	2.72	3.06	3.25	3.38	3.48	3.56	3.63	3.69	3.74
12	2.68	3.01	3.19	3.32	3.42	3.50	3.56	3.62	3.67
13	2.65	2.97	3.15	3.27	3.37	3.44	3.51	3.56	3.61
14	2.62	2.94	3.11	3.23	3.32	3.40	3.46	3.51	3.56
15	2.60	2.91	3.08	3.20	3.29	3.36	3.42	3.47	3.52
16	2.58	2.88	3.05	3.17	3.26	3.33	3.39	3.44	3.48
17	2.57	2.86	3.03	3.14	3.23	3.30	3.36	3.41	3.45
18	2.55	2.84	3.01	3.12	3.21	3.27	3.33	3.38	3.42
19	2.54	2.83	2.99	3.10	3.18	3.25	3.31	3.36	3.40
20	2.53	2.81	2.97	3.08	3.17	3.23	3.29	3.34	3.38
24	2.49	2.77	2.92	3.03	3.11	3.17	3.22	3.27	3.31
30	2.46	2.72	2.87	2.97	3.05	3.11	3.16	3.21	3.24
40	2.42	2.68	2.82	2.92	2.99	3.05	3.10	3.14	3.18
60	2.39	2.64	2.78	2.87	2.94	3.00	3.04	3.08	3.12
120	2.36	2.60	2.73	2.82	2.89	2.94	2.99	3.03	3.06
inf.	2.33	2.56	2.68	2.77	2.84	2.89	2.93	2.97	3.00

Table 10 *(Continued)*

(c) Table of t for two-sided comparisons between k treatment means and a control for a joint confidence coefficient of $P = 95$ percent.

	k, Number Of Treatment Means (Excluding The Control)								
df	1	2	3	4	5	6	7	8	9
5	2.57	3.03	3.39	3.66	3.88	4.06	4.22	4.36	4.49
6	2.45	2.86	3.18	3.41	3.60	3.75	3.88	4.00	4.11
7	2.36	2.75	3.04	3.24	3.41	3.54	3.66	3.76	3.86
8	2.31	2.67	2.94	3.13	3.28	3.40	3.51	3.60	3.68
9	2.26	2.61	2.86	3.04	3.18	3.29	3.39	3.48	3.55
10	2.23	2.57	2.81	2.97	3.11	3.21	3.31	3.39	3.46
11	2.20	2.53	2.76	2.92	3.05	3.15	3.24	3.31	3.38
12	2.18	2.50	2.72	2.88	3.00	3.10	3.18	3.25	3.32
13	2.16	2.48	2.69	2.84	2.96	3.06	3.14	3.21	3.27
14	2.14	2.46	2.67	2.81	2.93	3.02	3.10	3.17	3.23
15	2.13	2.44	2.64	2.79	2.90	2.99	3.07	3.13	3.19
16	2.12	2.42	2.63	2.77	2.88	2.96	3.04	3.10	3.16
17	2.11	2.41	2.61	2.75	2.85	2.94	3.01	3.08	3.13
17	2.10	2.40	2.59	2.73	2.84	2.92	2.99	3.05	3.11
19	2.09	2.39	2.58	2.72	2.82	2.90	2.97	3.04	3.09
20	2.09	2.38	2.57	2.70	2.81	2.89	2.96	3.02	3.07
24	2.06	2.35	2.53	2.66	2.76	2.84	2.91	2.96	3.01
30	2.04	2.32	2.50	2.62	2.72	2.79	2.86	2.91	2.96
40	2.02	2.29	2.47	2.58	2.67	2.75	2.81	2.86	2.90
60	2.00	2.27	2.43	2.55	2.63	2.70	2.76	2.81	2.85
120	1.98	2.24	2.40	2.51	2.59	2.66	2.71	2.76	2.80
inf.	1.96	2.21	2.37	2.47	2.55	2.62	2.67	2.71	2.75

Table 10 *(Continued)*

(d) Table of t for two-sided comparisons between k treatment means and a control for joint confidence coefficient of $P = 99$ percent.

	k, Number Of Treatment Means (Excluding The Control)								
df	1	2	3	4	5	6	7	8	9
5	4.03	4.63	5.09	5.44	5.73	5.97	6.18	6.36	6.53
6	3.71	4.22	4.60	4.88	5.11	5.30	5.47	5.61	5.74
7	3.50	3.95	4.28	4.52	4.71	4.87	5.01	5.13	5.24
8	3.36	3.77	4.06	4.27	4.44	4.58	4.70	4.81	4.90
9	3.25	3.63	3.90	4.09	4.24	4.37	4.48	4.57	4.65
10	3.17	3.53	3.78	3.95	4.10	4.21	4.31	4.40	4.47
11	3.11	3.45	3.68	3.85	3.98	4.09	4.18	4.26	4.33
12	3.05	3.39	3.61	3.76	3.89	3.99	4.08	4.15	4.22
13	3.01	3.33	3.54	3.69	3.81	3.91	3.99	4.06	4.13
14	2.98	3.29	3.49	3.64	3.75	3.84	3.92	3.99	4.05
15	2.95	3.25	3.45	3.59	3.70	3.79	3.86	3.93	3.99
16	2.92	3.22	3.41	3.55	3.65	3.74	3.82	3.88	3.93
17	2.90	3.19	3.38	3.51	3.62	3.70	3.77	3.83	3.89
18	2.88	3.17	3.35	3.48	3.58	3.67	3.74	3.80	3.85
19	2.86	3.15	3.33	3.46	3.55	3.64	3.70	3.76	3.81
20	2.85	3.13	3.31	3.43	3.53	3.61	3.67	3.73	3.78
24	2.80	3.07	3.24	3.36	3.45	3.52	3.58	3.64	3.69
30	2.75	3.01	3.17	3.28	3.37	3.44	3.50	3.55	3.59
40	2.70	2.95	3.10	3.21	3.29	3.36	3.41	3.46	3.50
60	2.66	2.90	3.04	3.14	3.22	3.28	3.33	3.38	3.42
120	2.62	2.84	2.98	3.08	3.15	3.21	3.25	3.30	3.33
inf.	2.58	2.79	2.92	3.01	3.08	3.14	3.18	3.22	3.25

Table 11 Critical Values of the Correlation Coefficient

df	.1	.05	.02	.01	.001
1	.98769	.99692	.999507	.999877	.9999988
2	.90000	.95000	.98000	.990000	.99900
3	.8054	.8783	.93433	.95873	.99116
4	.7293	.8114	.8822	.91720	.97406
5	.6694	.7545	.8329	.8745	.95074
6	.6215	.7067	.7887	.8343	.92493
7	.5822	.6664	.7498	.7977	.8982
8	.5494	.6319	.7155	.7646	.8721
9	.5214	.6021	.6851	.7348	.8471
10	.4973	.5760	.6581	.7079	.8233
11	.4762	.5529	.6339	.6835	.8010
12	.4575	.5324	.6120	.6614	.7800
13	.4409	.5139	.5923	.6411	.7603
14	.4259	.4973	.5742	.6226	.7420
15	.4124	.4821	.5577	.6055	.7246
16	.4000	.4683	.5425	.5897	.7084
17	.3887	.4555	.5285	.5751	.6932
18	.3783	.4438	.5155	.5614	.6787
19	.3687	.4329	.5034	.5487	.6652
20	.3598	.4227	.4921	.5368	.6524
25	.3233	.3809	.4451	.4869	.5974
30	.2960	.3494	.4093	.4487	.5541
35	.2746	.3246	.3810	.4182	.5189
40	.2573	.3044	.3578	.3932	.4896
45	.2428	.2875	.3384	.3721	.4648
50	.2306	.2732	.3218	.3541	.4433
60	.2108	.2500	.2948	.3248	.4078
70	.1954	.2319	.2737	.3017	.3799
80	.1829	.2172	.2565	.2830	.3568
90	.1726	.2050	.2422	.2673	.3375
100	.1638	.1946	.2301	.2540	.3211

SOURCE: Reprinted from Table VI of R. A. Fisher and F. Yates, *Statistical Tables for Biological, Agricultural, and Medical Research,* published by Longman Group Ltd., London (previously published by Oliver and Boyd Ltd., Edinburgh). Reprinted with permission of the authors and publishers.

Table 12 *r* to *z'* Transformation*

r	*Z*	*r*	*Z*	*r*	*Z*	*r*	*Z*
.20†	.203	.40	.424	.60	.693	.80	1.099
.21	.213	.41	.436	.61	.709	.81	1.127
.22	.224	.42	.448	.62	.725	.82	1.157
.23	.234	.43	.460	.63	.741	.83	1.188
.24	.245	.44	.472	.64	.758	.84	1.221
.25	.255	.45	.485	.65	.775	.85	1.256
.26	.266	.46	.497	.66	.793	.86	1.293
.27	.277	.47	.510	.67	.811	.87	1.333
.28	.288	.48	.523	.68	.829	.88	1.376
.29	.299	.49	.536	.69	.848	.89	1.422
.30	.310	.50	.549	.70	.867	.90	1.472
.31	.321	.51	.563	.71	.887	.91	1.528
.32	.332	.52	.577	.72	.908	.92	1.589
.33	.343	.53	.590	.73	.929	.93	1.658
.34	.354	.54	.604	.74	.950	.94	1.738
.35	.365	.55	.618	.75	.973	.95	1.832
.36	.377	.56	.633	.76	.996	.96	1.946
.37	.388	.57	.648	.77	1.020	.97	2.092
.38	.400	.58	.662	.78	1.045	.98	2.298
.39	.412	.59	.678	.79	1.071	.99	2.647

SOURCE: Reprinted from Appendix H of N. M. Downie and A. R. Starry, *Descriptive and Inferential Statistics* (New York: Harper & Row, 1977), p. 322. Used with permission.
* Based on the solution of the formula $z = \frac{1}{2} [\log_e (1 + r) - \log_e (1 - r)]$.
† For values below .20, *r* and *z* are practically identical.

Table 13 Critical Values of the *A* Test.

For any given value of $N - 1$, the table shows the values of *A* corresponding to various levels of probability. *A* is significant at a given level if it is equal to or *less than* the value shown in the table.

	LEVELS OF SIGNIFICANCE FOR A DIRECTIONAL TEST					
	.05	.025	.01	.005	.0005	
	LEVELS OF SIGNIFICANCE FOR A NON-DIRECTIONAL TEST					
$N - 1^*$	.10	.05	.02	.01	.001	$N - 1$
1	0.5125	0.5031	0.50049	0.50012	0.5000012	1
2	0.412	0.369	0.347	0.340	0.334	2
3	0.385	0.324	0.286	0.272	0.254	3
4	0.376	0.304	0.257	0.238	0.211	4
5	0.372	0.293	0.240	0.218	0.184	5
6	0.370	0.286	0.230	0.205	0.167	6
7	0.369	0.281	0.222	0.196	0.155	7
8	0.368	0.278	0.217	0.190	0.146	8
9	0.368	0.276	0.213	0.185	0.139	9
10	0.368	0.274	0.210	0.181	0.134	10
11	0.368	0.273	0.207	0.178	0.130	11
12	0.368	0.271	0.205	0.176	0.126	12
13	0.368	0.270	0.204	0.174	0.124	13
14	0.368	0.270	0.202	0.172	0.121	14
15	0.368	0.269	0.201	0.170	0.119	15
16	0.368	0.268	0.200	0.169	0.117	16
17	0.368	0.268	0.199	0.168	0.116	17
18	0.368	0.267	0.198	0.167	0.114	18
19	0.368	0.267	0.197	0.166	0.113	19
20	0.368	0.266	0.197	0.165	0.112	20
21	0.368	0.266	0.196	0.165	0.111	21
22	0.368	0.266	0.196	0.164	0.110	22
23	0.368	0.266	0.195	0.163	0.109	23
24	0.368	0.265	0.195	0.163	0.108	24
25	0.368	0.265	0.194	0.162	0.108	25
26	0.368	0.265	0.194	0.162	0.107	26
27	0.368	0.265	0.193	0.161	0.107	27
28	0.368	0.265	0.193	0.161	0.106	28
29	0.368	0.264	0.193	0.161	0.106	29
30	0.368	0.264	0.193	0.160	0.105	30
40	0.368	0.263	0.191	0.158	0.102	40
60	0.369	0.262	0.189	0.155	0.099	60
120	0.369	0.261	0.187	0.153	0.095	120
∞	0.370	0.260	0.185	0.151	0.092	∞

* N = the number of pairs.

SOURCE: J. Sandler. "A test of the difference between the means of correlated measures, based upon a simplification of Student's *t*." *British Journal of Psychology*, 1955, *46*, 225–226. Used with permission.

Table 14 Criteria for Testing Outliers

Statistic	Number of obs., k	Critical values						
		$\alpha = .30$	$\alpha = .20$	$\alpha = .10$	$\alpha = .05$	$\alpha = .02$	$\alpha = .01$	$\alpha = .005$
$r_{10} = \dfrac{X_2 - X_1}{X_k - X_1}$	3	.684	.781	.886	.941	.976	.988	.994
	4	.471	.560	.679	.765	.846	.889	.926
	5	.373	.451	.557	.642	.729	.780	.821
	6	.318	.386	.482	.560	.644	.698	.740
	7	.281	.344	.434	.507	.586	.637	.680
$r_{11} = \dfrac{X_2 - X_1}{X_{k-1} - X_1}$	8	.318	.385	.479	.554	.631	.683	.725
	9	.288	.352	.441	.512	.587	.635	.677
	10	.265	.325	.409	.477	.551	.597	.639
$r_{21} = \dfrac{X_3 - X_1}{X_{k-1} - X_1}$	11	.391	.442	.517	.576	.638	.679	.713
	12	.370	.419	.490	.546	.605	.642	.675
	13	.351	.399	.467	.521	.578	.615	.649
$r_{22} = \dfrac{X_3 - X_1}{X_{k-2} - X_1}$	14	.370	.421	.492	.546	.602	.641	.674
	15	.353	.402	.472	.525	.579	.616	.647
	16	.338	.386	.454	.507	.559	.595	.624
	17	.325	.373	.438	.490	.542	.577	.605
	18	.314	.361	.424	.475	.527	.561	.589
	19	.304	.350	.412	.462	.514	.547	.575
	20	.295	.340	.401	.450	.502	.535	.562
	21	287	.331	.391	.440	.491	.524	.551
	22	.280	.323	.382	.430	.481	.514	.541
	23	.274	.316	.374	.421	.472	.505	.532
	24	.268	.310	.367	.413	.464	.497	.524
	25	.262	.304	.360	.406	.457	.489	.516

SOURCE: Reproduced from W. J. Dixon, "Processing data for outliers." *Biometrics*, 1953, *9*, p. 74. Used with permission.

Table 15 Critical Values of D for the Kolmogorov-Smirnov Test (One Sample)

Sample size (N)	Level of significance for $D = \text{maximum } |F_0(X) - S_N(X)|$				
	.20	.15	.10	.05	.01
1	.900	.925	.950	.975	.995
2	.684	.726	.776	.842	.929
3	.565	.597	.642	.708	.828
4	.494	.525	.564	.624	.733
5	.446	.474	.510	.565	.669
6	.410	.436	.470	.521	.618
7	.381	.405	.438	.486	.577
8	.358	.381	.411	.457	.543
9	.339	.360	.388	.432	.514
10	.322	.342	.368	.410	.490
11	.307	.326	.352	.391	.468
12	.295	.313	.338	.375	.450
13	.284	.302	.325	.361	.433
14	.274	.292	.314	.349	.418
15	.266	.283	.304	.338	.404
16	.258	.274	.295	.328	.392
17	.250	.266	.286	.318	.381
18	.244	.259	.278	.309	.371
19	.237	.252	.272	.301	.363
20	.231	.246	.264	.294	.356
25	.21	.22	.24	.27	.32
30	.19	.20	.22	.24	.29
35	.18	.19	.21	.23	.27
Over 35	$\dfrac{1.07}{\sqrt{N}}$	$\dfrac{1.14}{\sqrt{N}}$	$\dfrac{1.22}{\sqrt{N}}$	$\dfrac{1.36}{\sqrt{N}}$	$\dfrac{1.63}{\sqrt{N}}$

SOURCE: Adapted from F. J. Massey, Jr., "The Kolmogorov-Smirnov test for goodness of fit." *Journal of the American Statistics Association*, 1951, *46*, 70. Used with permission.

311

Table 16 Critical Values of D for the Kolmogorov-Smirnov Two-Sample, Two-Sided Test.

N	One-tailed test*		Two-tailed test†	
	$\alpha = .05$	$\alpha = .01$	$\alpha = .05$	$\alpha = .01$
3	3	—	—	—
4	4	—	4	—
5	4	5	5	5
6	5	6	5	6
7	5	6	6	6
8	5	6	6	7
9	6	7	6	7
10	6	7	7	8
11	6	8	7	8
12	6	8	7	8
13	7	8	7	9
14	7	8	8	9
15	7	9	8	9
16	7	9	8	10
17	8	9	8	10
18	8	10	9	10
19	8	10	9	10
20	8	10	9	11
21	8	10	9	11
22	9	11	9	11
23	9	11	10	11
24	9	11	10	12
25	9	11	10	12
26	9	11	10	12
27	9	12	10	12
28	10	12	11	13
29	10	12	11	13
30	10	12	11	13
35	11	13	12	
40	11	14	13	

SOURCE: * Abridged from L. A. Goodman, "Kolmogorov-Smirnov tests for psychological research." *Psychol. Bull.*, 1954, *51*, 167. Used with permission. † Derived from Table 1 of F. J. Massey, Jr., "The distribution of the maximum deviation between two sample cumulative step functions." *Ann. Math. Statist.*, 1951, *22*, 126–127. Used with permission.

Table 17 Critical Values of T for the Signed Rank Test

	LEVEL OF SIGNIFICANCE FOR ONE-TAILED TEST		
	.025	.01	.005
	LEVEL OF SIGNIFICANCE FOR TWO-TAILED TEST		
N	.05	.02	.01
6	0	—	—
7	2	0	—
8	4	2	0
9	6	3	2
10	8	5	3
11	11	7	5
12	14	10	7
13	17	13	10
14	21	16	13
15	25	20	16
16	30	24	20
17	35	28	23
18	40	33	28
19	46	38	32
20	52	43	38
21	59	49	43
22	66	56	49
23	73	62	55
24	81	69	61
25	89	77	68

SOURCE: Adapted from Table I of F. Wilcoxon. *Some Rapid Approximate Statistical Procedures* (New York: American Cyanamid Co., 1949), p. 13. Reproduced with permission.

313

Table 18 Distribution of U in the Mann-Whitney Test

(a) **Critical Values of U for a One-Tailed Test at .001 or for a Two-Tailed Test at .002**

n_1 \ n_2	9	10	11	12	13	14	15	16	17	18	19	20
1												
2												
3										0	0	0	0
4		0	0	0	1	1	1	2	2	3	3	3
5	1	1	2	2	3	3	4	5	5	6	7	7
6	2	3	4	4	5	6	7	8	9	10	11	12
7	3	5	6	7	8	9	10	11	13	14	15	16
8	5	6	8	9	11	12	14	15	17	18	20	21
9	7	8	10	12	14	15	17	19	21	23	25	26
10	8	10	12	14	17	19	21	23	25	27	29	32
11	10	12	15	17	20	22	24	27	29	32	34	37
12	13	14	17	20	23	25	28	31	34	37	40	42
13	14	17	20	23	26	29	32	35	38	42	45	48
14	15	19	22	25	29	32	36	39	43	46	50	54
15	17	21	24	28	32	36	40	43	47	51	55	59
16	19	23	27	31	35	39	43	48	52	56	60	65
17	21	25	29	34	38	43	47	52	57	61	66	70
18	23	27	32	37	42	46	51	56	61	66	71	76
19	25	29	34	40	45	50	55	60	66	71	77	82
20	26	32	37	42	48	54	59	65	70	76	82	88

SOURCE: Adapted from Tables 1, 3, 5, and 7 of D. Auble, "Extended tables for the Mann-Whitney statistic." *Bulletin of the Institute of Educational Research at Indiana University*, 1953, *I*, No. 2. Reprinted with permission.

Table 18 *(Continued)*

n_1 \ n_2	9	10	11	12	13	14	15	16	17	18	19	20
1												
2					0	0	0	0	0	0	1	1
3	1	1	1	2	2	2	3	3	4	4	4	5
4	3	3	4	5	5	6	7	7	8	9	9	10
5	5	6	7	8	9	10	11	12	13	14	15	16
6	7	8	9	11	12	13	15	16	18	19	20	22
7	9	11	12	14	16	17	19	21	23	24	26	28
8	11	13	15	17	20	22	24	26	28	30	32	34
9	14	16	18	21	23	26	28	31	33	36	38	40
10	16	19	22	24	27	30	33	36	38	41	44	47
11	18	22	25	28	31	34	37	41	44	47	50	53
12	21	24	28	31	35	38	42	46	49	53	56	60
13	23	27	31	35	39	43	47	51	55	59	63	67
14	26	30	34	38	43	47	51	56	60	65	69	73
15	28	33	37	42	47	51	56	61	66	70	75	80
16	31	36	41	46	51	56	61	66	71	76	82	87
17	33	38	44	49	55	60	66	71	77	82	88	93
18	36	41	47	53	59	65	70	76	82	88	94	100
19	38	44	50	56	63	69	75	82	88	94	101	107
20	40	47	53	60	67	73	80	87	93	100	107	114

n_1 \ n_2	9	10	11	12	13	14	15	16	17	18	19	20
1												
2	0	0	0	1	1	1	1	1	2	2	2	2
3	2	3	3	4	4	5	5	6	6	7	7	8
4	4	5	6	7	8	9	10	11	11	12	13	13
5	7	8	9	11	12	13	14	15	17	18	19	20
6	10	11	13	14	16	17	19	21	22	24	25	27
7	12	14	16	18	20	22	24	26	28	30	32	34
8	15	17	19	22	24	26	29	31	34	36	38	41
9	17	20	23	26	28	31	34	37	39	42	45	48
10	20	23	26	29	33	36	39	42	45	48	52	55
11	23	26	30	33	37	40	44	47	51	55	58	62
12	26	29	33	37	41	45	49	53	57	61	65	69
13	28	33	37	41	45	50	54	59	63	67	72	76
14	31	36	40	45	50	55	59	64	67	74	78	83
15	34	39	44	49	54	59	64	70	75	80	85	90
16	37	42	47	53	59	64	70	75	81	86	92	98
17	39	45	51	57	63	67	75	81	87	93	99	105
18	42	48	55	61	67	74	80	86	93	99	106	112
19	45	52	58	65	72	78	85	92	99	106	113	119
20	48	55	62	69	76	83	90	98	105	112	119	127

Continued

Table 18 *(Continued)*

(d) Critical Values of U for a One-Tailed Test at .05 or for a
Two-Tailed Test at .10

n_1 \ n_2	9	10	11	12	13	14	15	16	17	18	19	20
1											0	0
2	1	1	1	2	2	2	3	3	3	4	4	4
3	3	4	5	5	6	7	7	8	9	9	10	11
4	6	7	8	9	10	11	12	14	15	16	17	18
5	9	11	12	13	15	16	18	19	20	22	23	25
6	12	14	16	17	19	21	23	25	26	28	30	32
7	15	17	19	21	24	26	28	30	33	35	37	39
8	18	20	23	26	28	31	33	36	39	41	44	47
9	21	24	27	30	33	36	39	42	45	48	51	54
10	24	27	31	34	37	41	44	48	51	55	58	62
11	27	31	34	38	42	46	50	54	57	61	65	69
12	30	34	38	42	47	51	55	60	64	68	72	77
13	33	37	42	47	51	56	61	65	70	75	80	84
14	36	41	46	51	56	61	66	71	77	82	87	92
15	39	44	50	55	61	66	72	77	83	88	94	100
16	42	48	54	60	65	71	77	83	89	95	101	107
17	45	51	57	64	70	77	83	89	96	102	109	115
18	48	55	61	68	75	82	88	95	102	109	116	123
19	51	58	65	72	80	87	94	101	109	116	123	130
20	54	62	69	77	84	92	100	107	115	123	130	138

Table 19 Critical Values of T' for the Wilcoxon Rank Sum Test

		Level of significance for one-tailed test			
		.05	.025	.01	.005
		Level of significance for two-tailed test			
$n_{smaller}$ n_{larger}		.10	.05	.02	.01
2	5	3 or smaller, 13 or larger			
	6	3			
	7	3			
	8	4	3 or smaller, 19 or larger		
	9	4	3		
	10	4	3		
3	3	6			
	4	6			
	5	7	6		
	6	8	7	6 or smaller, 27 or larger	
	7	8	7	6	
	8	9	8	6	6 or smaller, 33 or larger
	9	10	8	7	6
	10	10	9	7	6
4	4	11	10		
	5	12	11	10	
	6	13	12	11	10
	7	14	13	11	10
	8	15	14	12	11
	9	16	15	13	11
	10	17	15	13	12

SOURCE: Adapted from F. Wilcoxon, S. K. Katti, and R. Wilcox, "Critical values and probability levels for the Wilcoxon rank sum test and the Wilcoxon signed rank test." Published by Lederle Laboratories Division, American Cyanamid Co., 1968. Used with permission.

Continued

Table 19 (Continued)

		Level of significance for one-tailed test							
		.05		.025		.01		.005	
		Level of significance for two-tailed test							
		.10		.05		.02		.01	
$n_{smaller}$	n_{larger}								
5	5	19	36	17	38	16	39	15	40
	6	20	40	18	42	17	43	16	44
	7	21	44	20	45	18	47	17	48
	8	23	47	21	49	19	51	18	52
	9	24	51	22	53	20	55	18	57
	10	26	54	23	57	21	59	19	61
6	6	28	50	26	52	24	54	23	55
	7	29	55	27	57	25	59	24	60
	8	31	59	29	61	27	63	25	65
	9	33	63	31	65	28	68	26	70
	10	35	67	32	70	29	73	28	74
7	7	39	66	36	69	34	71	32	73
	8	41	71	38	74	36	76	34	78
	9	43	76	40	79	37	82	35	84
	10	45	81	42	84	39	87	37	89
8	8	51	85	49	87	46	90	44	92
	9	54	90	51	93	48	96	45	99
	10	56	96	53	99	50	102	47	105
9	9	66	105	63	108	59	112	57	114
	10	69	111	65	115	61	119	59	121
10	10	82	128	78	132	74	136	71	139

Table 20 Distribution of Values in the Wald-Wolfowitz Runs Test

Given in the bodies of Table 20a and b are various critical values of r for various values of n_1 and n_2. For the one-sample runs test, any value of r which is equal to or smaller than that shown in Table 20a or equal to or larger than that shown in Table 20b is significant at the .05 level. For the Wald-Wolfowitz two-sample runs test, any value of r which is equal to or smaller than that shown in Table 20a is significant at the .05 level.

(a)

n_1 \ n_2	2	3	4	5	6	7	8	9	10	11	12	13	14	15	16	17	18	19	20
2											2	2	2	2	2	2	2	2	2
3				2	2	2	2	2	2	2	2	2	2	3	3	3	3	3	3
4			2	2	2	3	3	3	3	3	3	3	3	4	4	4	4	4	4
5		2	2	3	3	3	3	3	4	4	4	4	4	4	4	4	5	5	5
6		2	2	3	3	3	4	4	4	4	5	5	5	5	5	5	6	6	6
7		2	2	3	3	4	4	5	5	5	5	5	6	6	6	6	6	6	6
8		2	3	3	3	4	4	5	5	5	6	6	6	6	6	7	7	7	7
9		2	3	3	4	4	5	5	5	6	6	6	7	7	7	7	8	8	8
10		2	3	3	4	5	5	5	6	6	7	7	7	7	8	8	8	8	9
11		2	3	4	4	5	5	6	6	7	7	7	8	8	8	9	9	9	9
12	2	2	3	4	4	5	6	6	7	7	7	8	8	8	9	9	9	10	10
13	2	2	3	4	5	5	6	6	7	7	8	8	9	9	9	10	10	10	10
14	2	2	3	4	5	5	6	7	7	8	8	9	9	9	10	10	10	11	11
15	2	3	3	4	5	6	6	7	7	8	8	9	9	10	10	11	11	11	12
16	2	3	4	4	5	6	6	7	8	8	9	9	10	10	11	11	11	12	12
17	2	3	4	4	5	6	7	7	8	9	9	10	10	11	11	11	12	12	13
18	2	3	4	5	5	6	7	8	8	9	9	10	10	11	11	12	12	13	13
19	2	3	4	5	6	6	7	8	8	9	10	10	11	11	12	12	13	13	13
20	2	3	4	5	6	6	7	8	9	9	10	10	11	12	12	13	13	13	14

SOURCE: Adapted from F. S. Swed and C. Eisenhart, "Tables for testing randomness of grouping in a sequence of alternatives." *Ann. Math. Statist.*, 1943, *14*, 83–86. Used with permission.

Table 20 *(Continued)*

(b)

n_1 \ n_2	2	3	4	5	6	7	8	9	10	11	12	13	14	15	16	17	18	19	20
2																			
3																			
4				9	9														
5			9	10	10	11	11												
6			9	10	11	12	12	13	13	13	13								
7				11	12	13	13	14	14	14	14	15	15	15					
8				11	12	13	14	14	15	15	16	16	16	16	17	17	17	17	17
9					13	14	14	15	16	16	16	17	17	18	18	18	18	18	18
10					13	14	15	16	16	17	17	18	18	18	19	19	19	20	20
11					13	14	15	16	17	17	18	19	19	19	20	20	20	21	21
12					13	14	16	16	17	18	19	19	20	20	21	21	21	22	22
13						15	16	17	18	19	19	20	20	21	21	22	22	23	23
14						15	16	17	18	19	20	20	21	22	22	23	23	23	24
15						15	16	18	18	19	20	21	22	22	23	23	24	24	25
16							17	18	19	20	21	21	22	23	23	24	25	25	25
17							17	18	19	20	21	22	23	23	24	25	25	26	26
18							17	18	19	20	21	22	23	24	25	25	26	26	27
19							17	18	20	21	22	23	23	24	25	26	26	27	27
20							17	18	20	21	22	23	24	25	25	26	27	27	28

Table 21   Arcsin Transformation Values

The numbers in this table are the angles (in degrees) corresponding to given percentages under the transformation arcsin $\sqrt{\text{percentage}}$.

%	0	1	2	3	4	5	6	7	8	9
0.0	0	0.57	0.81	0.99	1.15	1.28	1.40	1.52	1.62	1.72
0.1	1.81	1.90	1.99	2.07	2.14	2.22	2.29	2.36	2.43	2.50
0.2	2.56	2.63	2.69	2.75	2.81	2.87	2.92	2.98	3.03	3.09
0.3	3.14	3.19	3.24	3.29	3.34	3.39	3.44	3.49	3.53	3.58
0.4	3.63	3.67	3.72	3.76	3.80	3.85	3.89	3.93	3.97	4.01
0.5	4.05	4.09	4.13	4.17	4.21	4.25	4.29	4.33	4.37	4.40
0.6	4.44	4.48	4.52	4.55	4.59	4.62	4.66	4.69	4.73	4.76
0.7	4.80	4.83	4.87	4.90	4.93	4.97	5.00	5.03	5.07	5.10
0.8	5.13	5.16	5.20	5.23	5.26	5.29	5.32	5.35	5.38	5.41
0.9	5.44	5.47	5.50	5.53	5.56	5.59	5.62	5.65	5.68	5.71
1	5.74	6.02	6.29	6.55	6.80	7.04	7.27	7.49	7.71	7.92
2	8.13	8.33	8.53	8.72	8.91	9.10	9.28	9.46	9.63	9.81
3	9.98	10.14	10.31	10.47	10.63	10.78	10.94	11.09	11.24	11.39
4	11.54	11.68	11.83	11.97	12.11	12.25	12.39	12.52	12.66	12.79
5	12.92	13.05	13.18	13.31	13.44	13.56	13.69	13.81	13.94	14.06
6	14.18	14.30	14.42	14.54	14.65	14.77	14.89	15.00	15.12	15.23
7	15.34	15.45	15.56	15.68	15.79	15.89	16.00	16.11	16.22	16.32
8	16.43	16.54	16.64	16.74	16.85	16.95	17.05	17.16	17.26	17.36
9	17.46	17.56	17.66	17.76	17.85	17.95	18.05	18.15	18.24	18.34
10	18.44	18.53	18.63	18.72	18.81	18.91	19.00	19.09	19.19	19.28
11	19.37	19.46	19.55	19.64	19.73	19.82	19.91	20.00	20.09	20.18
12	20.27	20.36	20.44	20.53	20.62	20.70	20.79	20.88	20.96	21.05
13	21.13	21.22	21.30	21.39	21.47	21.56	21.64	21.72	21.81	21.89
14	21.97	22.06	22.14	22.22	22.30	22.38	22.46	22.55	22.63	22.71
15	22.79	22.87	22.95	23.03	23.11	23.19	23.26	23.34	23.42	23.50
16	23.58	23.66	23.73	23.81	23.89	23.97	24.04	24.12	24.20	24.27
17	24.35	24.43	24.50	24.58	24.65	24.73	24.80	24.88	24.95	25.03
18	25.10	25.18	25.25	25.33	25.40	25.48	25.55	25.62	25.70	25.77
19	25.84	25.92	25.99	26.06	26.13	26.21	26.28	26.35	26.42	26.49
20	26.56	26.64	26.71	26.78	26.85	26.92	26.99	27.06	27.13	27.20
21	27.28	27.35	27.42	27.49	27.56	27.63	27.69	27.76	27.83	27.90
22	27.97	28.04	28.11	28.18	28.25	28.32	28.38	28.45	28.52	28.59
23	28.66	28.73	28.79	28.86	28.93	29.00	29.06	29.13	29.20	29.27
24	29.33	29.40	29.47	29.53	29.60	29.67	29.73	29.80	29.87	29.93
25	30.00	30.07	30.13	30.20	30.26	30.33	30.40	30.46	30.53	30.59
26	30.66	30.72	30.79	30.85	30.92	30.98	31.05	31.11	31.18	31.24
27	31.31	31.37	31.44	31.50	31.56	31.63	31.69	31.76	31.82	31.88
28	31.95	32.01	32.08	32.14	32.20	32.27	32.33	32.39	32.46	32.52
29	32.58	32.65	32.71	32.77	32.83	32.90	32.96	33.02	33.09	33.15
30	33.21	33.27	33.34	33.40	33.46	33.52	33.58	33.65	33.71	33.77

SOURCE: Reprinted from Table VIII in H. L. Alder and E. B. Roessler, *Introduction to Probability and Statistics* (San Francisco: Freeman, 1960), pp. 291–293. Used with permission.

Continued

Table 21 *(Continued)*

%	0	1	2	3	4	5	6	7	8	9
31	33.83	33.89	33.96	34.02	34.08	34.14	34.20	34.27	34.33	34.39
32	34.45	34.51	34.57	34.63	34.70	34.76	34.82	34.88	34.94	35.00
33	35.06	35.12	35.18	35.24	35.30	35.37	35.43	35.49	35.55	35.61
34	35.67	35.73	35.79	35.85	35.91	35.97	36.03	36.09	36.15	36.21
35	36.27	36.33	36.39	36.45	36.51	36.57	36.63	36.69	36.75	36.81
36	36.87	36.93	36.99	37.05	37.11	37.17	37.23	37.29	37.35	37.41
37	37.47	37.52	37.58	37.64	37.70	37.76	37.82	37.88	37.94	38.00
38	38.06	38.12	38.17	38.23	38.29	38.35	38.41	38.47	38.53	38.59
39	38.65	38.70	38.76	38.82	38.88	38.94	39.00	39.06	39.11	39.17
40	39.23	39.29	39.35	39.41	39.47	39.52	39.58	39.64	39.70	39.76
41	39.82	39.87	39.93	39.99	40.05	40.11	40.16	40.22	40.28	40.34
42	40.40	40.46	40.51	40.57	40.63	40.69	40.74	40.80	40.86	40.92
43	40.98	41.03	41.09	41.15	41.21	41.27	41.32	41.38	41.44	41.50
44	41.55	41.61	41.67	41.73	41.78	41.84	41.90	41.96	42.02	42.07
45	42.13	42.19	42.25	42.30	42.36	42.42	42.48	42.53	42.59	42.65
46	42.71	42.76	42.82	42.88	42.94	42.99	43.05	43.11	43.17	43.22
47	43.28	43.34	43.39	43.45	43.51	43.57	43.62	43.68	43.74	43.80
48	43.85	43.91	43.97	44.03	44.08	44.14	44.20	44.25	44.31	44.37
49	44.43	44.48	44.54	44.60	44.66	44.71	44.77	44.83	44.89	44.94
50	45.00	45.06	45.11	45.17	45.23	45.29	45.34	45.40	45.46	45.52
51	45.57	45.63	45.69	45.75	45.80	45.86	45.92	45.97	46.03	46.09
52	46.15	46.20	46.26	46.32	46.38	46.43	46.49	46.55	46.61	46.66
53	46.72	46.78	46.83	46.89	46.95	47.01	47.06	47.12	47.18	47.24
54	47.29	47.35	47.41	47.47	47.52	47.58	47.64	47.70	47.75	47.81
55	47.87	47.93	47.98	48.04	48.10	48.16	48.22	48.27	48.33	48.39
56	48.45	48.50	48.56	48.62	48.68	48.73	48.79	48.85	48.91	48.97
57	49.02	49.08	49.14	49.20	49.26	49.31	49.37	49.43	49.49	49.54
58	49.60	49.66	49.72	49.78	49.84	49.89	49.95	50.01	50.07	50.13
59	50.18	50.24	50.30	50.36	50.42	50.48	50.53	50.59	50.65	50.71
60	50.77	50.83	50.89	50.94	51.00	51.06	51.12	51.18	51.24	51.30
61	51.35	51.41	51.47	51.53	51.59	51.65	51.71	51.77	51.83	51.88
62	51.94	52.00	52.06	52.12	52.18	52.24	52.30	52.36	52.42	52.48
63	52.53	52.59	52.65	52.71	52.77	52.83	52.89	52.95	53.01	53.07
64	53.13	53.19	53.25	53.31	53.37	53.43	53.49	53.55	53.61	53.67
65	53.73	53.79	53.85	53.91	53.97	54.03	54.09	54.15	54.21	54.27
66	54.33	54.39	54.45	54.51	54.57	54.63	54.70	54.76	54.82	54.88
67	54.94	55.00	55.06	55.12	55.18	55.24	55.30	55.37	55.43	55.49
68	55.55	55.61	55.67	55.73	55.80	55.86	55.92	55.98	56.04	56.11
69	56.17	56.23	56.29	56.35	56.42	56.48	56.54	56.60	56.66	56.73
70	56.79	56.85	56.91	56.98	57.04	57.10	57.17	57.23	57.29	57.35
71	57.42	57.48	57.54	57.61	57.67	57.73	57.80	57.86	57.92	57.99
72	58.05	58.12	58.18	58.24	58.31	58.37	58.44	58.50	58.56	58.63
73	58.69	58.76	58.82	58.89	58.95	59.02	59.08	59.15	59.21	59.28
74	59.34	59.41	59.47	59.54	59.60	59.67	59.74	59.80	59.87	59.93
75	60.00	60.07	60.13	60.20	60.27	60.33	60.40	60.47	60.53	60.60

Continued

Table 21 *(Continued)*

76	60.67	60.73	60.80	60.87	60.94	61.00	61.07	61.14	61.21	61.27
77	61.34	61.41	61.48	61.55	61.62	61.68	61.75	61.82	61.89	61.96
78	62.03	62.10	62.17	62.24	62.31	62.37	62.44	62.51	62.58	62.65
79	62.72	62.80	62.87	62.94	63.01	63.08	63.15	63.22	63.29	63.36
80	63.44	63.51	63.58	63.65	63.72	63.79	63.87	63.94	64.01	64.08
81	64.16	64.23	64.30	64.38	64.45	64.52	64.60	64.67	64.75	64.82
82	64.90	64.97	65.05	65.12	65.20	65.27	65.35	65.42	65.50	65.57
83	65.65	65.73	65.80	65.88	65.96	66.03	66.11	66.19	66.27	66.34
84	66.42	66.50	66.58	66.66	66.74	66.81	66.89	66.97	67.05	67.13
85	67.21	67.29	67.37	67.45	67.54	67.62	67.70	67.78	67.86	67.94
86	68.03	68.11	68.19	68.28	68.36	68.44	68.53	68.61	68.70	68.78
87	68.87	68.95	69.04	69.12	69.21	69.30	69.38	69.47	69.56	69.64
88	69.73	69.82	69.91	70.00	70.09	70.18	70.27	70.36	70.45	70.54
89	70.63	70.72	70.81	70.91	71.00	71.09	71.19	71.28	71.37	71.47
90	71.56	71.66	71.76	71.85	71.95	72.05	72.15	72.24	72.34	72.44
91	72.54	72.64	72.74	72.84	72.95	73.05	73.15	73.26	73.36	73.46
92	73.57	73.68	73.78	73.89	74.00	74.11	74.21	74.32	74.44	74.55
93	74.66	74.77	74.88	75.00	75.11	75.23	75.35	75.46	75.58	75.70
94	75.82	75.94	76.06	76.19	76.31	76.44	76.56	76.69	76.82	76.95
95	77.08	77.21	77.34	77.48	77.61	77.75	77.89	78.03	78.17	78.32
96	78.46	78.61	78.76	78.91	79.06	79.22	79.37	79.53	79.69	79.86
97	80.02	80.19	80.37	80.54	80.72	80.90	81.09	81.28	81.47	81.67
98	81.87	82.08	82.29	82.51	82.73	82.96	83.20	83.45	83.71	83.98
99.0	84.26	84.29	84.32	84.35	84.38	84.41	84.44	84.47	84.50	84.53
99.1	84.56	84.59	84.62	84.65	84.68	84.71	84.74	84.77	84.80	84.84
99.2	84.87	84.90	84.93	84.97	85.00	85.03	85.07	85.10	85.13	85.17
99.3	85.20	85.24	85.27	85.31	85.34	85.38	85.41	85.45	85.48	85.52
99.4	85.56	85.60	85.63	85.67	85.71	85.75	85.79	85.83	85.87	85.91
99.5	85.95	85.99	86.03	86.07	86.11	86.15	86.20	86.24	86.28	86.33
99.6	86.37	86.42	86.47	86.51	86.56	86.61	86.66	86.71	86.76	86.81
99.7	86.86	86.91	86.97	87.02	87.08	87.13	87.19	87.25	87.31	87.37
99.8	87.44	87.50	87.57	87.64	87.71	87.78	87.86	87.93	88.01	88.10
99.9	88.19	88.28	88.38	88.48	88.60	88.72	88.85	89.01	89.19	89.43
100.0	90.00	—	—	—	—	—	—	—	—	—

Table 22 *H*-Values for the Kruskal-Wallis Test

\	Sample Sizes	\	\	Level	\
N_1	N_2	N_3	.10	.05	.01
2	2	2	4.57		
3	2	1	4.29		
3	2	2	4.50	4.71	
3	3	1	4.57	5.14	
3	3	2	4.56	5.36	6.25
3	3	3	4.62	5.60	6.49
4	2	1	4.50		
4	2	2	4.46	5.33	
4	3	1	4.06	5.21	
4	3	2	4.51	5.44	6.30
4	3	3	4.70	5.73	6.75
4	4	1	4.17	4.79	6.67
4	4	2	4.55	5.45	6.87
4	4	3	4.55	5.60	7.14
4	4	4	4.65	5.69	7.54
5	2	1	4.20	5.00	
5	2	2	4.37	5.16	6.53
5	3	1	4.02	4.96	
5	3	2	4.49	5.25	6.82
5	3	3	4.53	5.44	6.98
5	4	1	3.99	4.99	6.84
5	4	2	4.52	5.27	7.12
5	4	3	4.55	5.63	7.40
5	4	4	4.62	5.62	7.74
5	5	1	4.11	5.13	6.84
5	5	2	4.51	5.25	7.27
5	5	3	4.55	5.63	7.54
5	5	4	4.52	5.64	7.79
5	5	5	4.56	5.66	7.98

SOURCE: Abridged from Table 6.1 of W. H. Kruskal and W. A. Wallis. "Use of ranks on one-criterion variance analysis." *Journal of the American Statistical Association*, 1952, *47*, 584–621. Reproduced from Appendix L of N. M. Downie and R. W. Heath, *Basic Statistical Methods*, 4th ed. (New York: Harper & Row, 1974), p. 321.

Table 23 The Binomial Distribution

N = 5

P x	.05	.10	.15	.20	.25	.30	.35	.40	.45	.50
0	.7738	.5905	.4437	.3277	.2373	.1681	.1160	.0778	.0503	.0312
1	.2036	.3280	.3915	.4096	.3955	.3601	.3124	.2592	.2059	.1563
2	.0214	.0729	.1382	.2048	.2637	.3087	.3364	.3456	.3369	.3125
3	.0011	.0081	.0244	.0512	.0879	.1323	.1811	.2304	.2757	.3125
4	.0000	.0004	.0022	.0064	.0146	.0283	.0488	.0768	.1128	.1563
5		.0000	.0001	.0003	.0010	.0024	.0053	.0102	.0185	.0312

N = 6

P x	.05	.10	.15	.20	.25	.30	.35	.40	.45	.50
0	.7351	.5314	.3771	.2621	.1780	.1176	.0754	.0467	.0277	.0156
1	.2321	.3543	.3993	.3932	.3560	.3025	.2437	.1866	.1359	.0938
2	.0305	.0984	.1762	.2458	.2966	.3241	.3280	.3110	.2780	.2344
3	.0021	.0146	.0415	.0819	.1318	.1852	.2355	.2765	.3032	.3125
4	.0001	.0012	.0055	.0154	.0330	.0595	.0951	.1382	.1861	.2344
5	.0000	.0001	.0004	.0015	.0044	.0102	.0205	.0369	.0609	.0938
6		.0000	.0000	.0001	.0002	.0007	.0018	.0041	.0083	.0156

N = 7

P x	.05	.10	.15	.20	.25	.30	.35	.40	.45	.50
0	.6983	.4783	.3206	.2097	.1335	.0824	.0490	.0280	.0152	.0078
1	.2573	.3720	.3960	.3670	.3115	.2471	.1848	.1306	.0872	.0547
2	.0406	.1240	.2097	.2753	.3115	.3177	.2985	.2613	.2140	.1641
3	.0036	.0230	.0617	.1147	.1730	.2269	.2679	.2903	.2918	.2734
4	.0002	.0026	.0109	.0287	.0577	.0972	.1442	.1935	.2388	.2734
5	.0000	.0002	.0012	.0043	.0115	.0250	.0466	.0774	.1172	.1641
6		.0000	.0001	.0004	.0013	.0036	.0084	.0172	.0320	.0547
7			.0000	.0000	.0001	.0002	.0006	.0016	.0037	.0078

N = 8

P x	.05	.10	.15	.20	.25	.30	.35	.40	.45	.50
0	.6634	.4305	.2725	.1678	.1001	.0576	.0319	.0168	.0084	.0039
1	.2793	.3826	.3847	.3355	.2670	.1977	.1373	.0896	.0548	.0312
2	.0515	.1488	.2376	.2936	.3115	.2965	.2587	.2090	.1569	.1094
3	.0054	.0331	.0839	.1468	.2076	.2541	.2786	.2787	.2568	.2188
4	.0004	.0046	.0185	.0459	.0865	.1361	.1875	.2322	.2627	.2734
5	.0000	.0004	.0026	.0092	.0231	.0467	.0808	.1239	.1719	.2188
6		.0000	.0002	.0011	.0038	.0100	.0217	.0413	.0703	.1094
7			.0000	.0001	.0004	.0012	.0033	.0079	.0164	.0312
8				.0000	.0000	.0001	.0002	.0007	.0017	.0039

N = 9

P x	.05	.10	.15	.20	.25	.30	.35	.40	.45	.50
0	.6302	.3874	.2316	.1342	.0751	.0404	.0207	.0101	.0046	.0020
1	.2985	.3874	.3679	.3020	.2253	.1556	.1004	.0605	.0339	.0176
2	.0629	.1722	.2597	.3020	.3003	.2668	.2162	.1612	.1110	.0703
3	.0077	.0446	.1069	.1762	.2336	.2668	.2716	.2508	.2119	.1641
4	.0006	.0074	.0283	.0661	.1168	.1715	.2194	.2508	.2600	.2461
5	.0000	.0008	.0050	.0165	.0389	.0735	.1181	.1672	.2128	.2461
6	.0000	.0001	.0006	.0028	.0087	.0210	.0424	.0743	.1160	.1641
7		.0000	.0000	.0003	.0012	.0039	.0098	.0212	.0407	.0703
8			.0000	.0000	.0001	.0004	.0013	.0035	.0083	.0176
9					.0000	.0000	.0001	.0003	.0008	.0020

SOURCE: Reprinted Table B in R. Carlson, *Statistics* (San Francisco: Holden-Day, 1973), pp. 356–366. Used with permission.

Continued

Table 23 *(Continued)*

N = 10

P / X	.05	.10	.15	.20	.25	.30	.35	.40	.45	.50
0	.5987	.3487	.1969	.1074	.0563	.0282	.0135	.0060	.0025	.0010
1	.3151	.3874	.3474	.2684	.1877	.1211	.0725	.0403	.0207	.0098
2	.0746	.1937	.2759	.3020	.2816	.2335	.1757	.1209	.0763	.0439
3	.0105	.0574	.1298	.2013	.2503	.2668	.2522	.2150	.1665	.1172
4	.0010	.0112	.0401	.0881	.1460	.2001	.2377	.2508	.2384	.2051
5	.0001	.0015	.0085	.0264	.0584	.1029	.1536	.2007	.2340	.2461
6	.0000	.0001	.0012	.0055	.0162	.0368	.0689	.1115	.1596	.2051
7		.0000	.0001	.0008	.0031	.0090	.0212	.0425	.0746	.1172
8			.0000	.0001	.0004	.0014	.0043	.0106	.0229	.0439
9				.0000	.0000	.0001	.0005	.0016	.0042	.0098
10						.0000	.0000	.0001	.0003	.0010

N = 11

P / X	.05	.10	.15	.20	.25	.30	.35	.40	.45	.50
0	.5688	.3138	.1673	.0859	.0422	.0198	.0088	.0036	.0014	.0005
1	.3293	.3835	.3248	.2362	.1549	.0932	.0518	.0266	.0125	.0054
2	.0867	.2131	.2866	.2953	.2581	.1998	.1395	.0887	.0513	.0269
3	.0137	.0710	.1517	.2215	.2581	.2568	.2254	.1774	.1259	.0806
4	.0014	.0158	.0536	.1107	.1721	.2201	.2428	.2365	.2060	.1611
5	.0001	.0025	.0132	.0388	.0803	.1321	.1830	.2207	.2360	.2256
6	.0000	.0003	.0023	.0097	.0268	.0566	.0985	.1471	.1931	.2256
7		.0000	.0003	.0017	.0064	.0173	.0379	.0701	.1128	.1611
8		.0000	.0000	.0002	.0011	.0037	.0102	.0234	.0462	.0806
9			.0000	.0000	.0001	.0005	.0018	.0052	.0126	.0269
10					.0000	.0000	.0002	.0007	.0021	.0054
11						.0000	.0000	.0000	.0002	.0005

N = 12

P / X	.05	.10	.15	.20	.25	.30	.35	.40	.45	.50
0	.5404	.2824	.1422	.0687	.0317	.0138	.0057	.0022	.0008	.0002
1	.3413	.3766	.3012	.2062	.1267	.0712	.0368	.0174	.0075	.0029
2	.0988	.2301	.2924	.2835	.2323	.1678	.1088	.0639	.0339	.0161
3	.0173	.0852	.1720	.2362	.2581	.2397	.1954	.1419	.0923	.0537
4	.0021	.0213	.0683	.1329	.1936	.2311	.2367	.2128	.1700	.1208
5	.0002	.0038	.0193	.0532	.1032	.1585	.2039	.2270	.2225	.1934
6	.0000	.0005	.0040	.0155	.0401	.0792	.1281	.1766	.2124	.2256
7		.0000	.0006	.0033	.0115	.0291	.0591	.1009	.1489	.1934
8		.0000	.0001	.0005	.0024	.0078	.0199	.0420	.0762	.1208
9			.0000	.0001	.0004	.0015	.0048	.0125	.0277	.0537
10				.0000	.0000	.0002	.0008	.0025	.0068	.0161
11					.0000	.0000	.0001	.0003	.0010	.0029
12						.0000	.0000	.0001	.0002	

Continued

Table 23 *(Continued)*

N = 13

p x	.05	.10	.15	.20	.25	.30	.35	.40	.45	.50
0	.5133	.2542	.1209	.0550	.0238	.0097	.0037	.0013	.0004	.0001
1	.3512	.3672	.2774	.1787	.1029	.0540	.0259	.0113	.0045	.0016
2	.1109	.2448	.2937	.2680	.2059	.1388	.0836	.0453	.0220	.0095
3	.0214	.0997	.1900	.2457	.2517	.2181	.1651	.1107	.0660	.0349
4	.0028	.0277	.0838	.1535	.2097	.2337	.2222	.1845	.1350	.0873
5	.0003	.0055	.0266	.0691	.1258	.1803	.2154	.2214	.1989	.1571
6	.0000	.0008	.0063	.0230	.0559	.1030	.1546	.1968	.2169	.2095
7		.0001	.0011	.0058	.0186	.0442	.0833	.1312	.1775	.2095
8		.0000	.0001	.0011	.0047	.0142	.0336	.0656	.1089	.1571
9			.0000	.0001	.0009	.0034	.0101	.0243	.0495	.0873
10				.0000	.0001	.0006	.0022	.0065	.0162	.0349
11				.0000	.0000	.0001	.0003	.0012	.0036	.0095
12						.0000	.0000	.0001	.0005	.0016
13							.0000	.0000	.0000	.0001

N = 14

p x	.05	.10	.15	.20	.25	.30	.35	.40	.45	.50
0	.4877	.2288	.1028	.0440	.0178	.0068	.0024	.0008	.0002	.0001
1	.3593	.3559	.2539	.1539	.0832	.0407	.0181	.0073	.0027	.0009
2	.1229	.2570	.2912	.2501	.1802	.1134	.0634	.0317	.0141	.0056
3	.0259	.1142	.2056	.2501	.2402	.1943	.1366	.0845	.0462	.0222
4	.0037	.0349	.0998	.1720	.2202	.2290	.2022	.1549	.1040	.0611
5	.0004	.0078	.0352	.0860	.1468	.1963	.2178	.2066	.1701	.1222
6	.0000	.0013	.0093	.0322	.0734	.1262	.1759	.2066	.2088	.1833
7	.0000	.0002	.0019	.0092	.0280	.0618	.1082	.1574	.1952	.2095
8		.0000	.0003	.0020	.0082	.0232	.0510	.0918	.1398	.1833
9		.0000	.0000	.0003	.0018	.0066	.0183	.0408	.0762	.1222
10			.0000	.0000	.0003	.0014	.0049	.0136	.0312	.0611
11				.0000	.0000	.0002	.0010	.0033	.0093	.0222
12					.0000	.0000	.0001	.0005	.0019	.0056
13						.0000	.0000	.0001	.0002	.0009
14								.0000	.0000	.0001

N = 15

p x	.05	.10	.15	.20	.25	.30	.35	.40	.45	.50
0	.4633	.2059	.0874	.0352	.0134	.0047	.0016	.0005	.0001	.0000
1	.3658	.3432	.2312	.1319	.0668	.0305	.0126	.0047	.0016	.0005
2	.1348	.2669	.2856	.2309	.1559	.0916	.0476	.0219	.0090	.0032
3	.0307	.1285	.2184	.2501	.2252	.1700	.1110	.0634	.0318	.0139
4	.0049	.0428	.1156	.1876	.2252	.2186	.1792	.1268	.0780	.0417
5	.0006	.0105	.0449	.1032	.1651	.2061	.2123	.1859	.1404	.0916
6	.0000	.0019	.0132	.0430	.0917	.1472	.1906	.2066	.1914	.1527
7	.0000	.0003	.0030	.0138	.0393	.0811	.1319	.1771	.2013	.1964
8		.0000	.0005	.0035	.0131	.0348	.0710	.1181	.1647	.1964
9		.0000	.0001	.0007	.0034	.0116	.0298	.0612	.1048	.1527
10			.0000	.0001	.0007	.0030	.0096	.0245	.0515	.0916
11				.0000	.0001	.0006	.0024	.0074	.0191	.0417
12					.0000	.0001	.0004	.0016	.0052	.0139
13						.0000	.0001	.0003	.0010	.0032
14							.0000	.0000	.0001	.0005
15								.0000	.0000	.0000

Continued

Table 23 *(Continued)*

N = 16

P x	.05	.10	.15	.20	.25	.30	.35	.40	.45	.50
0	.4401	.1853	.0743	.0281	.0100	.0033	.0010	.0003	.0001	.0000
1	.3706	.3294	.2097	.1126	.0535	.0228	.0087	.0030	.0009	.0002
2	.1463	.2745	.2775	.2111	.1336	.0732	.0353	.0150	.0056	.0018
3	.0359	.1423	.2285	.2463	.2079	.1465	.0888	.0468	.0215	.0085
4	.0061	.0514	.1311	.2001	.2252	.2040	.1553	.1014	.0572	.0278
5	.0008	.0137	.0555	.1201	.1802	.2099	.2008	.1623	.1123	.0667
6	.0001	.0028	.0180	.0550	.1101	.1649	.1982	.1983	.1684	.1222
7	.0000	.0004	.0045	.0197	.0524	.1010	.1524	.1889	.1969	.1746
8		.0001	.0009	.0055	.0197	.0487	.0923	.1417	.1812	.1964
9		.0000	.0001	.0012	.0058	.0185	.0442	.0840	.1318	.1746
10			.0000	.0002	.0014	.0056	.0167	.0392	.0755	.1222
11			.0000	.0000	.0002	.0013	.0049	.0142	.0337	.0667
12				.0000	.0000	.0002	.0011	.0040	.0115	.0278
13					.0000	.0000	.0002	.0008	.0029	.0085
14						.0000	.0000	.0001	.0005	.0018
15							.0000	.0000	.0001	.0002
16									.0000	.0000

N = 17

P x	.05	.10	.15	.20	.25	.30	.35	.40	.45	.50
0	.4181	.1668	.0631	.0225	.0075	.0023	.0007	.0002	.0000	.0000
1	.3741	.3150	.1893	.0957	.0426	.0169	.0060	.0019	.0005	.0001
2	.1575	.2800	.2673	.1914	.1136	.0581	.0260	.0102	.0035	.0010
3	.0415	.1556	.2359	.2393	.1893	.1245	.0701	.0341	.0144	.0052
4	.0076	.0605	.1457	.2093	.2209	.1868	.1320	.0796	.0411	.0182
5	.0010	.0175	.0668	.1361	.1914	.2081	.1849	.1379	.0875	.0472
6	.0001	.0039	.0236	.0680	.1276	.1784	.1991	.1839	.1432	.0944
7	.0000	.0007	.0065	.0267	.0668	.1201	.1685	.1927	.1841	.1484
8		.0001	.0014	.0084	.0279	.0644	.1134	.1606	.1883	.1855
9		.0000	.0003	.0021	.0093	.0276	.0611	.1070	.1540	.1855
10			.0000	.0004	.0025	.0095	.0263	.0571	.1008	.1484
11			.0000	.0001	.0005	.0026	.0090	.0242	.0525	.0944
12				.0000	.0001	.0006	.0024	.0081	.0215	.0472
13					.0000	.0001	.0005	.0021	.0068	.0182
14					.0000	.0000	.0001	.0004	.0016	.0052
15							.0000	.0001	.0003	.0010
16								.0000	.0000	.0001
17									.0000	.0000

Continued

Table 23 *(Continued)*

N = 18

p x	.05	.10	.15	.20	.25	.30	.35	.40	.45	.50
0	.3972	.1501	.0536	.0180	.0056	.0016	.0004	.0001	.0000	.0000
1	.3763	.3002	.1704	.0811	.0338	.0126	.0042	.0012	.0003	.0001
2	.1683	.2835	.2556	.1723	.0958	.0458	.0190	.0069	.0022	.0006
3	.0473	.1680	.2406	.2297	.1704	.1046	.0547	.0246	.0095	.0031
4	.0093	.0700	.1592	.2153	.2130	.1681	.1104	.0614	.0291	.0117
5	.0014	.0218	.0787	.1507	.1988	.2017	.1664	.1146	.0666	.0327
6	.0002	.0052	.0301	.0816	.1436	.1873	.1941	.1655	.1181	.0708
7	.0000	.0010	.0091	.0350	.0820	.1376	.1792	.1892	.1657	.1214
8	.0000	.0002	.0022	.0120	.0376	.0811	.1327	.1734	.1864	.1669
9		.0000	.0004	.0033	.0139	.0386	.0794	.1284	.1694	.1855
10		.0000	.0001	.0008	.0042	.0149	.0385	.0771	.1248	.1669
11			.0000	.0001	.0010	.0046	.0151	.0374	.0742	.1214
12				.0000	.0002	.0012	.0047	.0145	.0354	.0708
13				.0000	.0000	.0002	.0012	.0045	.0134	.0327
14					.0000	.0000	.0002	.0011	.0039	.0117
15						.0000	.0000	.0002	.0009	.0031
16							.0000	.0000	.0001	.0006
17								.0000	.0000	.0001
18										.0000

N = 19

p x	.05	.10	.15	.20	.25	.30	.35	.40	.45	.50
0	.3774	.1351	.0456	.0144	.0042	.0011	.0003	.0001	.0000	.0000
1	.3774	.2852	.1529	.0685	.0268	.0093	.0029	.0008	.0002	.0000
2	.1787	.2852	.2428	.1540	.0803	.0358	.0138	.0046	.0013	.0003
3	.0533	.1796	.2428	.2182	.1517	.0869	.0422	.0175	.0062	.0018
4	.0112	.0798	.1714	.2182	.2023	.1491	.0909	.0467	.0203	.0074
5	.0018	.0266	.0907	.1636	.2023	.1916	.1468	.0933	.0497	.0222
6	.0002	.0069	.0374	.0955	.1574	.1916	.1844	.1451	.0949	.0518
7	.0000	.0014	.0122	.0443	.0974	.1525	.1844	.1797	.1443	.0961
8	.0000	.0002	.0032	.0166	.0487	.0981	.1489	.1797	.1771	.1442
9		.0000	.0007	.0051	.0198	.0514	.0980	.1464	.1771	.1762
10		.0000	.0001	.0013	.0066	.0220	.0528	.0976	.1449	.1762
11			.0000	.0003	.0018	.0077	.0233	.0532	.0970	.1442
12			.0000	.0000	.0004	.0022	.0083	.0237	.0529	.0961
13				.0000	.0001	.0005	.0024	.0085	.0233	.0518
14					.0000	.0001	.0006	.0024	.0082	.0222
15					.0000	.0000	.0001	.0005	.0022	.0074
16						.0000	.0000	.0001	.0005	.0018
17							.0000	.0000	.0001	.0003
18								.0000	.0000	
19										.0000

Continued

Table 23 *(Continued)*

N = 20

P x	.05	.10	.15	.20	.25	.30	.35	.40	.45	.50
0	.3585	.1216	.0388	.0115	.0032	.0008	.0002	.0000	.0000	
1	.3774	.2702	.1368	.0576	.0211	.0068	.0020	.0005	.0001	.0000
2	.1887	.2852	.2293	.1369	.0669	.0278	.0100	.0031	.0008	.0002
3	.0596	.1901	.2428	.2054	.1339	.0716	.0323	.0123	.0040	.0011
4	.0133	.0898	.1821	.2182	.1897	.1304	.0738	.0350	.0139	.0046
5	.0022	.0319	.1028	.1746	.2023	.1789	.1272	.0746	.0365	.0148
6	.0003	.0089	.0454	.1091	.1686	.1916	.1712	.1244	.0746	.0370
7	.0000	.0020	.0160	.0545	.1124	.1643	.1844	.1659	.1221	.0739
8	.0000	.0004	.0046	.0222	.0609	.1144	.1614	.1797	.1623	.1201
9		.0001	.0011	.0074	.0271	.0654	.1158	.1597	.1771	.1602
10		.0000	.0002	.0020	.0099	.0308	.0686	.1171	.1593	.1762
11			.0000	.0005	.0030	.0120	.0336	.0710	.1185	.1602
12			.0000	.0001	.0008	.0039	.0136	.0355	.0727	.1201
13				.0000	.0002	.0010	.0045	.0146	.0366	.0739
14				.0000	.0000	.0002	.0012	.0049	.0150	.0370
15					.0000	.0000	.0003	.0013	.0049	.0148
16						.0000	.0000	.0003	.0013	.0046
17							.0000	.0000	.0002	.0011
18								.0000	.0000	.0002
19									.0000	.0000

N = 21

P x	.05	.10	.15	.20	.25	.30	.35	.40	.45	.50
0	.3406	.1094	.0329	.0092	.0024	.0006	.0001	.0000	.0000	
1	.3764	.2553	.1221	.0484	.0166	.0050	.0013	.0003	.0001	.0000
2	.1981	.2837	.2155	.1211	.0555	.0215	.0072	.0020	.0005	.0001
3	.0660	.1996	.2408	.1917	.1172	.0585	.0245	.0086	.0026	.0006
4	.0156	.0998	.1912	.2156	.1757	.1128	.0593	.0259	.0095	.0029
5	.0028	.0377	.1147	.1833	.1992	.1643	.1085	.0588	.0263	.0097
6	.0004	.0112	.0540	.1222	.1770	.1878	.1558	.1045	.0574	.0259
7	.0000	.0027	.0204	.0655	.1265	.1725	.1798	.1493	.1007	.0554
8	.0000	.0005	.0063	.0286	.0738	.1294	.1694	.1742	.1442	.0970
9		.0001	.0016	.0103	.0355	.0801	.1318	.1677	.1704	.1402
10		.0000	.0003	.0031	.0142	.0412	.0851	.1342	.1673	.1682
11		.0000	.0001	.0008	.0047	.0176	.0458	.0895	.1369	.1682
12			.0000	.0002	.0013	.0063	.0206	.0497	.0933	.1402
13			.0000	.0000	.0003	.0019	.0077	.0229	.0529	.0970
14				.0000	.0001	.0005	.0024	.0087	.0247	.0554
15					.0000	.0001	.0006	.0027	.0094	.0259
16					.0000	.0000	.0001	.0007	.0029	.0097
17						.0000	.0000	.0001	.0007	.0029
18							.0000	.0000	.0001	.0006
19								.0000	.0000	.0001
20									.0000	.0000

Continued

Table 23 (Continued)

N = 22

p x	.05	.10	.15	.20	.25	.30	.35	.40	.45	.50
0	.3235	.0985	.0280	.0074	.0018	.0004	.0001	.0000	.0000	
1	.3746	.2407	.1087	.0406	.0131	.0037	.0009	.0002	.0000	.0000
2	.2070	.2808	.2015	.1065	.0458	.0166	.0051	.0014	.0003	.0001
3	.0726	.2080	.2370	.1775	.1017	.0474	.0184	.0060	.0016	.0004
4	.0182	.1098	.1987	.2108	.1611	.0965	.0471	.0190	.0064	.0017
5	.0034	.0439	.1262	.1898	.1933	.1489	.0913	.0456	.0187	.0063
6	.0005	.0138	.0631	.1344	.1826	.1808	.1393	.0862	.0434	.0178
7	.0001	.0035	.0255	.0768	.1391	.1771	.1714	.1314	.0812	.0407
8	.0000	.0007	.0084	.0360	.0869	.1423	.1730	.1642	.1246	.0762
9		.0001	.0023	.0140	.0451	.0949	.1449	.1703	.1586	.1186
10		.0000	.0005	.0046	.0195	.0529	.1015	.1476	.1687	.1542
11		.0000	.0001	.0012	.0071	.0247	.0596	.1073	.1506	.1682
12			.0000	.0003	.0022	.0097	.0294	.0656	.1129	.1542
13			.0000	.0001	.0006	.0032	.0122	.0336	.0711	.1186
14				.0000	.0001	.0009	.0042	.0144	.0374	.0762
15				.0000	.0000	.0002	.0012	.0051	.0163	.0407
16					.0000	.0000	.0003	.0015	.0058	.0178
17						.0000	.0001	.0004	.0017	.0063
18							.0000	.0001	.0004	.0017
19								.0000	.0001	.0004
20									.0000	.0001
21										.0000

N = 23

p x	.05	.10	.15	.20	.25	.30	.35	.40	.45	.50
0	.3074	.0886	.0238	.0059	.0013	.0003	.0000	.0000	.0000	
1	.3721	.2265	.0966	.0339	.0103	.0027	.0006	.0001	.0000	.0000
2	.2154	.2768	.1875	.0933	.0376	.0127	.0037	.0009	.0002	.0000
3	.0794	.2153	.2317	.1633	.0878	.0382	.0138	.0041	.0010	.0002
4	.0209	.1196	.2044	.2042	.1463	.0818	.0371	.0138	.0042	.0011
5	.0042	.0505	.1371	.1940	.1853	.1332	.0758	.0350	.0132	.0040
6	.0007	.0168	.0726	.1455	.1853	.1712	.1225	.0700	.0323	.0120
7	.0001	.0045	.0311	.0883	.1500	.1782	.1602	.1133	.0642	.0292
8	.0000	.0010	.0110	.0442	.1000	.1527	.1725	.1511	.1051	.0584
9		.0002	.0032	.0184	.0555	.1091	.1548	.1679	.1433	.0974
10		.0000	.0008	.0064	.0259	.0655	.1167	.1567	.1642	.1364
11		.0000	.0002	.0019	.0102	.0332	.0743	.1234	.1587	.1612
12			.0000	.0005	.0034	.0142	.0400	.0823	.1299	.1612
13			.0000	.0001	.0010	.0052	.0182	.0464	.0899	.1364
14				.0000	.0002	.0016	.0070	.0221	.0525	.0974
15				.0000	.0000	.0004	.0023	.0088	.0258	.0584
16					.0000	.0001	.0006	.0029	.0106	.0292
17					.0000	.0000	.0001	.0008	.0036	.0120
18						.0000	.0000	.0002	.0010	.0040
19							.0000	.0000	.0002	.0011
20								.0000	.0000	.0002
21									.0000	.0000
22										.0000

Continued

Table 23 *(Continued)*

N = 24

x	.05	.10	.15	.20	.25	.30	.35	.40	.45	.50
0	.2920	.0798	.0202	.0047	.0010	.0002	.0000	.0000		
1	.3688	.2127	.0857	.0283	.0080	.0020	.0004	.0001	.0000	.0000
2	.2232	.2718	.1739	.0815	.0308	.0097	.0026	.0006	.0001	.0000
3	.0862	.2215	.2251	.1493	.0752	.0305	.0102	.0028	.0007	.0001
4	.0238	.1292	.2065	.1960	.1316	.0687	.0289	.0099	.0028	.0006
5	.0050	.0574	.1472	.1960	.1755	.1177	.0622	.0265	.0091	.0025
6	.0008	.0202	.0822	.1552	.1853	.1598	.1061	.0560	.0237	.0080
7	.0001	.0058	.0373	.0998	.1588	.1761	.1470	.0960	.0499	.0206
8	.0000	.0014	.0140	.0530	.1125	.1604	.1682	.1360	.0867	.0438
9	.0000	.0003	.0044	.0236	.0667	.1222	.1610	.1612	.1261	.0779
10		.0000	.0012	.0088	.0333	.0785	.1300	.1612	.1548	.1169
11		.0000	.0003	.0028	.0141	.0428	.0891	.1367	.1612	.1488
12			.0000	.0008	.0051	.0199	.0520	.0988	.1429	.1612
13			.0000	.0002	.0016	.0079	.0258	.0608	.1079	.1488
14			.0000	.0000	.0004	.0026	.0109	.0318	.0694	.1169
15					.0000	.0008	.0039	.0141	.0378	.0779
16					.0000	.0002	.0012	.0053	.0174	.0438
17					.0000	.0000	.0003	.0017	.0067	.0206
18							.0000	.0004	.0021	.0080
19							.0000	.0001	.0006	.0025
20							.0000	.0000	.0001	.0006
21								.0000	.0000	.0001
22									.0000	.0000
23										.0000

N = 25

x	.05	.10	.15	.20	.25	.30	.35	.40	.45	.50
0	.2774	.0718	.0172	.0038	.0008	.0001	.0000	.0000		
1	.3650	.1994	.0759	.0236	.0063	.0014	.0003	.0000	.0000	
2	.2305	.2659	.1607	.0708	.0251	.0074	.0018	.0004	.0001	.0000
3	.0930	.2265	.2174	.1358	.0641	.0243	.0076	.0019	.0004	.0001
4	.0269	.1384	.2110	.1867	.1175	.0572	.0224	.0071	.0018	.0004
5	.0060	.0646	.1564	.1960	.1645	.1030	.0506	.0199	.0063	.0016
6	.0010	.0239	.0920	.1633	.1828	.1472	.0908	.0442	.0172	.0053
7	.0001	.0072	.0441	.1108	.1654	.1712	.1327	.0800	.0381	.0143
8	.0000	.0018	.0175	.0623	.1241	.1651	.1607	.1200	.0701	.0322
9	.0000	.0004	.0058	.0294	.0781	.1336	.1635	.1511	.1084	.0609
10		.0001	.0016	.0118	.0417	.0916	.1409	.1612	.1419	.0974
11		.0000	.0004	.0040	.0189	.0536	.1034	.1465	.1583	.1328
12		.0000	.0001	.0012	.0074	.0268	.0650	.1140	.1511	.1550
13			.0000	.0003	.0025	.0115	.0350	.0760	.1236	.1550
14			.0000	.0001	.0007	.0042	.0161	.0434	.0867	.1328
15				.0000	.0002	.0013	.0064	.0212	.0520	.0974
16				.0000	.0000	.0004	.0021	.0088	.0266	.0609
17					.0000	.0001	.0006	.0031	.0115	.0322
18						.0000	.0001	.0009	.0042	.0143
19						.0000	.0000	.0002	.0013	.0053
20							.0000	.0000	.0003	.0016
21								.0000	.0001	.0004
22									.0000	.0001
23										.0000

Continued

Table 23 *(Continued)*

					N = 26					
P X	.05	.10	.15	.20	.25	.30	.35	.40	.45	.50
0	.2635	.0646	.0146	.0030	.0006	.0001	.0000	.0000		
1	.3606	.1867	.0671	.0196	.0049	.0010	.0002	.0000	.0000	
2	.2372	.2592	.1480	.0614	.0204	.0056	.0013	.0002	.0000	.0000
3	.0999	.2304	.2089	.1228	.0544	.0192	.0055	.0013	.0003	.0000
4	.0302	.1472	.2119	.1765	.1042	.0473	.0172	.0050	.0012	.0002
5	.0070	.0720	.1646	.1941	.1528	.0893	.0407	.0148	.0043	.0010
6	.0013	.0280	.1016	.1699	.1782	.1339	.0767	.0345	.0123	.0034
7	.0002	.0089	.0512	.1213	.1698	.1640	.1180	.0657	.0287	.0098
8	.0000	.0023	.0215	.0720	.1344	.1669	.1509	.1040	.0557	.0233
9	.0000	.0005	.0076	.0360	.0896	.1431	.1625	.1386	.0912	.0466
10		.0001	.0023	.0153	.0508	.1042	.1488	.1571	.1268	.0792
11		.0000	.0006	.0056	.0246	.0650	.1165	.1524	.1509	.1151
12		.0000	.0001	.0017	.0103	.0348	.0784	.1270	.1543	.1439
13			.0000	.0005	.0037	.0161	.0455	.0912	.1360	.1550
14			.0000	.0001	.0011	.0064	.0227	.0564	.1033	.1439
15				.0000	.0003	.0022	.0098	.0301	.0676	.1151
16				.0000	.0001	.0006	.0036	.0138	.0380	.0792
17					.0000	.0002	.0011	.0054	.0183	.0466
18					.0000	.0000	.0003	.0018	.0075	.0233
19						.0000	.0001	.0005	.0026	.0098
20							.0000	.0001	.0007	.0034
21							.0000	.0000	.0002	.0010
22								.0000	.0000	.0002
23									.0000	.0000
24										.0000

					N = 27					
P X	.05	.10	.15	.20	.25	.30	.35	.40	.45	.50
0	.2503	.0581	.0124	.0024	.0004	.0001	.0000	.0000		
1	.3558	.1744	.0592	.0163	.0038	.0008	.0001	.0000	.0000	
2	.2434	.2520	.1358	.0530	.0165	.0042	.0009	.0002	.0000	.0000
3	.1068	.2333	.1997	.1105	.0459	.0151	.0041	.0009	.0002	.0000
4	.0337	.1555	.2115	.1658	.0917	.0389	.0131	.0035	.0008	.0001
5	.0082	.0795	.1717	.1906	.1406	.0767	.0325	.0109	.0029	.0006
6	.0016	.0324	.1111	.1747	.1719	.1205	.0641	.0266	.0087	.0022
7	.0002	.0108	.0588	.1311	.1719	.1550	.1036	.0532	.0213	.0066
8	.0000	.0030	.0259	.0819	.1432	.1660	.1394	.0887	.0435	.0165
9	.0000	.0007	.0097	.0432	.1008	.1502	.1585	.1248	.0752	.0349
10		.0001	.0031	.0195	.0605	.1159	.1536	.1497	.1108	.0629
11		.0000	.0008	.0075	.0312	.0768	.1278	.1543	.1401	.0971
12		.0000	.0002	.0025	.0138	.0439	.0918	.1371	.1528	.1295
13			.0000	.0007	.0053	.0217	.0570	.1055	.1443	.1494
14			.0000	.0002	.0018	.0093	.0307	.0703	.1180	.1494
15			.0000	.0000	.0005	.0035	.0143	.0406	.0837	.1295
16				.0000	.0001	.0011	.0058	.0203	.0514	.0971
17				.0000	.0000	.0003	.0020	.0088	.0272	.0629
18					.0000	.0001	.0006	.0032	.0124	.0349
19						.0000	.0002	.0010	.0048	.0165
20						.0000	.0000	.0003	.0016	.0066
21							.0000	.0001	.0004	.0022
22								.0000	.0001	.0006
23								.0000	.0000	.0001
24									.0000	.0000
25										.0000

Continued

Table 23 *(Continued)*

p / x	.05	.10	.15	.20	.25	.30	.35	.40	.45	.50
0	.2378	.0523	.0106	.0019	.0003	.0000	.0000			
1	.3505	.1628	.0522	.0135	.0030	.0006	.0001	.0000	.0000	
2	.2490	.2442	.1243	.0457	.0133	.0032	.0006	.0001	.0000	.0000
3	.1136	.2352	.1901	.0990	.0385	.0119	.0030	.0006	.0001	.0000
4	.0374	.1633	.2097	.1547	.0803	.0318	.0099	.0025	.0005	.0001
5	.0094	.0871	.1776	.1856	.1284	.0654	.0257	.0079	.0019	.0004
6	.0019	.0371	.1202	.1779	.1641	.1074	.0530	.0203	.0061	.0014
7	.0003	.0130	.0667	.1398	.1719	.1446	.0897	.0426	.0156	.0044
8	.0000	.0038	.0309	.0917	.1504	.1627	.1269	.0745	.0335	.0116
9	.0000	.0009	.0121	.0510	.1114	.1550	.1518	.1103	.0610	.0257
10		.0002	.0041	.0242	.0706	.1262	.1553	.1398	.0948	.0489
11		.0000	.0012	.0099	.0385	.0885	.1368	.1525	.1269	.0800
12		.0000	.0003	.0035	.0182	.0537	.1044	.1440	.1471	.1133
13			.0001	.0011	.0075	.0283	.0692	.1181	.1481	.1395
14			.0000	.0003	.0027	.0130	.0399	.0844	.1298	.1494
15			.0000	.0001	.0008	.0052	.0201	.0525	.0991	.1395
16				.0000	.0002	.0018	.0088	.0284	.0659	.1133
17				.0000	.0001	.0005	.0033	.0134	.0381	.0800
18					.0000	.0001	.0011	.0055	.0190	.0489
19					.0000	.0003	.0019	.0082	.0257	
20						.0000	.0001	.0006	.0030	.0116
21						.0000	.0000	.0001	.0009	.0044
22							.0000	.0000	.0002	.0014
23								.0000	.0001	.0004
24									.0000	.0001
25									.0000	.0000
26										.0000

p / x	.05	.10	.15	.20	.25	.30	.35	.40	.45	.50
0	.2259	.0471	.0090	.0015	.0002	.0000	.0000			
1	.3448	.1518	.0459	.0112	.0023	.0004	.0001	.0000		
2	.2541	.2361	.1135	.0393	.0107	.0024	.0004	.0001	.0000	
3	.1204	.2361	.1803	.0883	.0322	.0093	.0021	.0004	.0001	.0000
4	.0412	.1705	.2068	.1436	.0698	.0258	.0075	.0017	.0003	.0000
5	.0108	.0947	.1825	.1795	.1164	.0553	.0202	.0058	.0013	.0002
6	.0023	.0421	.1288	.1795	.1552	.0948	.0435	.0154	.0042	.0009
7	.0004	.0154	.0747	.1474	.1699	.1335	.0769	.0337	.0113	.0029
8	.0001	.0047	.0362	.1013	.1558	.1573	.1139	.0617	.0255	.0080
9	.0000	.0012	.0149	.0591	.1212	.1573	.1431	.0960	.0486	.0187
10		.0003	.0053	.0296	.0808	.1348	.1541	.1280	.0796	.0373
11		.0001	.0016	.0128	.0465	.0998	.1433	.1474	.1124	.0644
12		.0000	.0004	.0048	.0233	.0642	.1157	.1474	.1380	.0967
13		.0000	.0001	.0016	.0101	.0360	.0815	.1285	.1476	.1264
14			.0000	.0004	.0039	.0176	.0502	.0979	.1381	.1445
15			.0000	.0001	.0013	.0075	.0270	.0653	.1130	.1445
16				.0000	.0004	.0028	.0127	.0381	.0809	.1264
17				.0000	.0001	.0009	.0052	.0194	.0506	.0967
18					.0000	.0003	.0019	.0086	.0276	.0644
19					.0000	.0001	.0006	.0033	.0131	.0373
20						.0000	.0002	.0011	.0053	.0187
21						.0000	.0000	.0003	.0019	.0080
22							.0000	.0001	.0006	.0029
23							.0000	.0000	.0001	.0009
24								.0000	.0000	.0002
25									.0000	.0000
26										.0000

Continued

Table 23 *(Continued)*

N = 30

P x	.05	.10	.15	.20	.25	.30	.35	.40	.45	.50
0	.2146	.0424	.0076	.0012	.0002	.0000	.0000			
1	.3389	.1413	.0404	.0093	.0018	.0003	.0000	.0000		
2	.2586	.2277	.1034	.0337	.0086	.0018	.0003	.0000	.0000	
3	.1270	.2361	.1703	.0785	.0269	.0072	.0015	.0003	.0000	.0000
4	.0451	.1771	.2028	.1325	.0604	.0208	.0056	.0012	.0002	.0000
5	.0124	.1023	.1861	.1723	.1047	.0464	.0157	.0041	.0008	.0001
6	.0027	.0474	.1368	.1795	.1455	.0829	.0353	.0115	.0029	.0006
7	.0005	.0180	.0828	.1538	.1662	.1219	.0652	.0263	.0081	.0019
8	.0001	.0058	.0420	.1106	.1593	.1501	.1009	.0505	.0191	.0055
9	.0000	.0016	.0181	.0676	.1298	.1573	.1328	.0823	.0382	.0133
10	.0000	.0004	.0067	.0355	.0909	.1416	.1502	.1152	.0656	.0280
11		.0001	.0022	.0161	.0551	.1103	.1471	.1396	.0976	.0509
12		.0000	.0006	.0064	.0291	.0749	.1254	.1474	.1265	.0806
13		.0000	.0001	.0022	.0134	.0444	.0935	.1360	.1433	.1115
14			.0000	.0007	.0054	.0231	.0611	.1101	.1424	.1354
15			.0000	.0002	.0019	.0106	.0351	.0783	.1242	.1445
16				.0000	.0006	.0042	.0177	.0489	.0953	.1354
17				.0000	.0002	.0015	.0079	.0269	.0642	.1115
18				.0000	.0000	.0005	.0031	.0129	.0379	.0806
19					.0000	.0001	.0010	.0054	.0196	.0509
20					.0000	.0000	.0003	.0020	.0088	.0280
21						.0000	.0001	.0006	.0034	.0133
22						.0000	.0000	.0002	.0012	.0055
23							.0000	.0000	.0003	.0019
24								.0000	.0001	.0006
25								.0000	.0000	.0001
26									.0000	.0000
27										.0000